341.6
5881s
c.2

JX
1987
A47
568

W9-CNM-791

TO THE YOUNG MEN AND WOMEN OF WORLD
WAR II WHOSE LIVES HAVE BEEN SO CRUELLY
DISARRANGED BY THE FAILURE OF THEIR
ELDERS TO BUILD PEACE AFTER WORLD WAR I

= F 44 SUS al (army...

= 317289

S. O. LEVINSON
AND THE
PACT OF PARIS

THE UNIVERSITY OF CHICAGO PRESS
CHICAGO, ILLINOIS

*

THE BAKER & TAYLOR COMPANY
NEW YORK

THE CAMBRIDGE UNIVERSITY PRESS
LONDON

S. O. LEVINSON
AND THE
PACT OF PARIS

A Study in the Techniques of Influence

JOHN E. STONER

Department of Government, Indiana University

THE UNIVERSITY OF CHICAGO PRESS

CHICAGO · ILLINOIS

COPYRIGHT 1943 BY THE UNIVERSITY OF CHICAGO
ALL RIGHTS RESERVED. PUBLISHED JANUARY 1943

✳

COMPOSED AND PRINTED BY THE UNIVERSITY OF CHICAGO PRESS
CHICAGO, ILLINOIS, U.S.A.

FOREWORD

IT WAS a rare privilege to be associated in any way and in any capacity with Salmon Levinson. The association had a specially significant value when it was connected with the cause of peace among nations—the cause to which Levinson gave his best and constant thought and energy. There was stimulus—indeed, there was a kind of inspiration—in coming in contact with his abounding energy, which surpassed that of any single person I have ever known and which might easily have provided a group or organization with power to carry on extensive activities. It was great physically; but more than that it was moral power. Mr. Levinson was a man who would not and could not be discouraged either by the immensity of the task he set himself or by the obstacles he encountered.

Levinson's vigor and power were given to a cause that was worthy of them. His devotion was selfless. It was so intense it could not help stirring others, if only from a sense of shame, out of their lethargy. His faith was so ardent that indifference changed to warmth in his presence. His faith was wedded to works. He was an outstanding example of the complete union of faith and energy. His faith was in the possibility of the triumph of the cause of peace to which he gave himself. But this faith was rooted in faith in his fellow-beings, in the common people of the earth. He refused to believe that in their heart of hearts they really wanted the wars by which in the end they are so tragically victimized. He strove as a social inventor, as other men have worked at physical and industrial inventions. He wanted to find and to help others to find the social implement and instrumentality by which men could make effective their underlying desire for peaceful relations. His immediate purpose was defeated as the second World War so tragically testifies. But I believe that the conditions in which we live but emphasize our need to recover and strengthen Levinson's faith that the great mass of men and women would welcome an era in which the war system has no standing and his faith in the possibility of social means by which to secure this end.

As I prized association with Levinson as a rare privilege, so I am greatly honored to be asked to contribute a Foreword to this present volume. I respond the more willingly because of the quality of the pages to which these lines are prefixed. Mr. Stoner has done more than accomplish a fine piece of scholarly research. He has seen the dramatic aspect of the work of Levinson in such a way as to communicate it to readers. It is not often that an important example of historic investigation is done in such close connection with the time of the events dealt with and with such full access to all sources of information. Because of the variety and scope of Levinson's contacts, Mr. Stoner in writing about him has also made, it seems to me, a valuable contribution to many aspects of contemporary history. He has done a solid and substantial work which will remain authoritative in the matters with which he deals. Let us hope that it will be a historic document not only with respect to the past but also in stimulating others to renewed faith in the cause to which Levinson was devoted and in the possibility of its triumph.

JOHN DEWEY

INTRODUCTION

THIS volume was initiated and carried on in close connection with the Cooperative Investigation of the Causes of War, supported by the Social Science Research Committee at the University of Chicago from 1927 to 1942. It deals, however, not so much with the causes as with the preventives of war. Dr. Stoner's exhaustive and careful study of the vast correspondence which Salmon O. Levinson left to the University of Chicago discloses the methods by which the outlawry-of-war movement, which began in Levinson's mind, became in a few years a worldwide influence which statesmen could not ignore. This movement was of great importance in bringing about the negotiation and general ratification of the Kellogg-Briand Pact. There were other movements in America which also contributed to these diplomatic events, but it is safe to say that if Levinson had not moved the isolationist Middle West and the isolationist Senator Borah to support the Pact, it would not have been achieved.

It may be asked in the light of conditions in October, 1942, whether anything was achieved. Most of the states which in 1928 solemnly condemned war and renounced it as an instrument of national policy are now at war. Some say that the Pact of Paris permitted Americans and others to believe that they had achieved peace and therefore that they could safely crawl into the hole of complacent isolationism. The Axis powers, it is suggested, were enabled to prepare to use war as an instrument of policy, while their victims, anesthetized by the Pact, remained in a state of somnolence.

There doubtless were many who neglected the warning made by M. Briand when he signed the Pact of Paris: "Peace is proclaimed: that is well, that is much. But it still remains necessary to organize it. For solutions of force, juridical solutions must be substituted. That is to be the work of tomorrow." On the whole, however, the criticism of detractors of the Pact is unjust. The instrument served as a stimulus rather than as a deterrent to more effective international organization, though the actions taken to implement it were too little and too late. Levinson himself never diminished his activity after the Pact was ratified. Up to the day of his death in February, 1941, he labored continuously at projects for realizing its principles in practice.

The Pact has, in fact, had an important practical influence, and this influence may increase after the present war. Levinson approached the problem of peace as a lawyer. He was shocked to discover during World War I that war was legal under international law. His aim was to delegalize it, and he thought this could be done by incorporating in international law the principles that the initiation of war is illegal and that the initiator of war should be determined by a world court, should not acquire legal title to the fruits of his aggression, and should not be treated by third states equally with his victim acting in self-defense.

These principles were implicit in the League of Nations Covenant. In fact, they were implicit in the writings of Grotius and the other founders of international law. In the nineteenth century, however, international jurists generally repudiated all criteria for determining the just side in a war, denied the possibility of compulsory adjudication of all international disputes, and permitted title by conquest and impartial neutrality in all wars. The outlawry-of-war movement and the Pact of Paris could therefore be characterized as a return to Grotius. They stimulated international lawyers and the officials of the League of Nations to re-examine their concepts. As a result the Levinson principles achieved widespread indorsement. The Pact of Paris was ratified by nearly all states of the world. The optional clause of the Statute of the Permanent Court of International Justice was accepted by a large number of states—not, however, by the United States. The Stimson doctrine refusing recognition to fruits of aggression was accepted by the United States and by the members of the League of Nations. Numerous states, particularly the United States and other American states, branded the Axis powers as aggressors and refused to be impartial in the war. It is especially noteworthy that the Pact and the legal ideas it supports

were explicitly referred to by the Senate, by the House of Representatives, and by the administration as the legal foundation for
the Lend-Lease Act of March, 1941, which marked the formal
repudiation of neutrality by the United States. It seems unlikely
that in the future states will feel justified in treating the aggressor
and his victim alike.

The Pact, therefore, had a practical influence in mobilizing the
moral and legal conscience of mankind against present aggressors. It provided the cause of the United Nations with a status of
legality and contributed to the solidarity which they have
achieved. The United Nations can properly insist that they are
not waging war in the old sense but are engaged in applying
sanctions against aggression.

As Dr. Stoner points out, Levinson did not entirely anticipate
all these results of his efforts. He refused to support the League of
Nations because it attempted to organize sanctions. His love of
peace stood in the way of his seeing that his own principles led to
the need of international organization to compel recalcitrant
states to observe law. In his last years he was moving toward this
understanding. In his demand for a world governed by law
rather than by arms he led the American public to realize the
international implications of their own constitutional experience;
but he, like that public, was slow to perceive that those implications included a more perfect union of the states of the world.
The logic of principles, however, have a way of fulfilling themselves in history beyond the expectations of their initiators. The
prolonged shadow of Levinson's movement may bring American
and world opinion to full acceptance of a world organization
strong enough to outlaw war.

QUINCY WRIGHT

UNIVERSITY OF CHICAGO
October 14, 1942

PREFACE

AT A time when the problem of the prevention of war is paramount to all others, any movement aimed at its solution deserves attention. One purpose of this study is to throw light on the American outlawry-of-war movement and its relation to the Treaty for the Renunciation of War, frequently called the Pact of Paris or the Kellogg Peace Pact. The second purpose is to explore the means and techniques whereby ideas and men come to influence. Numerous minute studies of leaders, of their procedures and methods, will be required to find the general pattern which makes for success or failure in the political process.

In the preparation of this work the correspondence of Salmon O. Levinson and the extensive documentary material which he produced and collected were examined. Many of the letters he wrote and received between 1913 and 1941, of which it has been estimated there were more than forty thousand, and much of the documentary material, which consisted of memoranda, diaries, reports of interviews, clippings, etc., and of which there were probably more than one hundred thousand, have been deposited with the University of Chicago Library for the use of responsible scholars. Another source of information was the oral testimony of many persons connected with the outlawry-of-war movement either as participants or as observers.

Owing to the voluminous source material and to the importance of intensive study of the techniques of influence, no attempt was made to evaluate the contribution which other individuals and movements made to the Pact of Paris. The definitive narrative of the forces and events leading to it cannot be told until both other sources and other leaders have been analyzed with painstaking detail. This study of Salmon O. Levinson and his dominant role in this movement is one contribution to the history of one phase of the long struggle of mankind to learn to live in peace.

[xiii]

PREFACE

The author's debts to Mr. Levinson for opening his files without reservation, for his tireless explanations, for his willingness to let the author tell the story without interference as it developed; to Mrs. Kelly, Mr. Levinson's secretary, for her diligence in searching through files; to the Levinson family for making possible and permitting this publication; and to Professor Wright, for his counsel, guidance, and example in scholarship are debts of a nature which may be only gratefully acknowledged but never repaid.

JOHN E. STONER

INDIANA UNIVERSITY
September 28, 1942

TABLE OF CONTENTS

TABLE OF CONTENTS

CHAPTER I

EARLY LIFE[1]

IN LAUNCHING his crusade to end war by outlawing it, Salmon Oliver Levinson was striking at an old enemy of his family. His grandfather Philip fled from Germany with the Carl Schurz emigrants in 1848 to escape the Prussian militarist regime. Newman, the son, who was then eighteen and who must have been the one most benefited by the escape from the rigors of conscription, accompanied the family to Cincinnati. Shortly thereafter he left the family circle to establish a home of his own at Noblesville, Indiana. He had very little money but an abundance of energy, ability, and good judgment. Before long he moved his wife and babies out of the back of the upstairs room, where he worked as a tailor, into a comfortable home; and the tailor's shop in the front of the room was expanded into a general dry-goods store. There in the last third of the nineteenth century "N.D.," as he was known to all in Noblesville, carried on his business, participated in the building of the community, and created for himself a high place in the esteem of his fellow-townsmen.

He first bought the building in which the store was located, and later he acquired the other buildings in the block. His was the best clothing store in the city. A third of a century after his death the reputation for durability of the goods he sold was still high. One old fellow, who obviously looked forward to the Utopia in the past, "calculated" that the "suits of clothes which N.D. sold for ten or fifteen dollars would cost you now pert nigh a hundred sixty dollar. He wasn't no scaly Jew, you understand. What N.D. told you about his goods or anything else you could depend on. It would be that way or he would make it good."

[1] Much of the information for this chapter was gathered from personal interviews with friends and former neighbors in Noblesville, business and professional associates in Chicago, and friends of the family. The picture derived from their accounts, impressionistic though it may be, nevertheless establishes the background from which Levinson came.

His store was the local meeting place for the discussion of the affairs of the community and of the nation. He was a source of advice for the city fathers and for men intrusted with public affairs. These latter came in to talk over their speeches and to get "points" for them. Congressmen in those days were very impressive to the boy, Salmon, and as a man he recalled the awe he felt for the one tall congressman who came frequently to consult his father. Not only did Newman Levinson talk to those who came to his store, but he kept up a running comment in the *Noblesville Ledger* under the nom de plume of "Citizen." These articles were said to be clear-cut, lucid discussions of contemporary issues, both local and national; and they must have been influential, as many of the older people recalled them years later.

The elder Mr. Levinson created for himself in the hearts of his fellow-townsmen a permanent place of high respect. When he died in 1899, the business houses of the city closed, and the circuit judge recessed his court to deliver the funeral oration. A later judge, who was practicing before the bar at the time, described the sense of loss that all walks of life felt at his passing and approved of the sitting judge's recessing his court on that occasion. No matter whom one asked, whether the circuit judge or the old fellow, quoted above, at the other end of the social ladder, there was a unanimity in the spirit of the testimony borne to the genuineness of Newman D. Levinson's character.

While the father was respected, the mother was loved. She was an "indefatigable worker among the poor," always caring for the needy, lending a hand to the down-and-out, "feeding the hungry, and clothing the naked." The record is not clear as to whether she entertained any angels unawares, but to those who knew her it is clear that she was herself an angel. One retired neighbor, who must have idolized this mother in Israel, remembered how she went "at all times, day and night, wherever she was needed to tend a squawling baby at birth or to smooth the sunset pillow of an ebbing life." Once she was asked if she were not afraid to go alone late at night. Her answer was, "Why should I be afraid? God will take care of me." But it seemed that she had nothing to fear, if the testimony of a hard-looking former bartender could be taken as evidence of the feeling among those who might have molested her. When I asked some questions which he interpreted as a little too prying, he very freely offered to knock the "damned block off" my shoulders if I said anything disrespectful of her. This affectionate devotion to her memory was not only shared most approvingly by his colleagues, the Knights of the Cuspidor, but it was also echoed in forms appropriate to his station in life by every person I could find in Noblesville, from the circuit judge to a clerk in what had been a competing store. One "rugged individualist," when discussing her activity as permanent head of the ladies' aid society until her death in 1901, suggested that she might have been a bit impractical, for "there have been and always will be a lot of professional deadbeats who ought to starve that put it over on her," but he added hurriedly, "no better woman ever lived than Minnie Levinson."

In the Levinson family there were five children who grew to maturity—three daughters, Sarah, Sophie, and Daisy, and two sons, Harry and Salmon. According to old neighbors they were early taught the lessons of industry and frugality. There were no maids in the home; the girls helped the mother, and the boys worked in the store.

It was Salmon's job to open the place of business every morning at 6:30. He had begun to sell goods before he started to school, and he was expected to buy some of the stock for the store from the traveling men by the time he was eleven or twelve.

His work in the store threw him a good deal with grown men. He listened to the discussions of current affairs which were always going on, and he heard his father conferring with the politicians, who were always coming in for counsel.

Sometimes, after affairs of politics had been disposed of, the men would play chess. Once, when the boy Salmon was very small, his father was playing with the banker—a Mr. Locke—and, as sometimes happens in other affairs, it appeared that the banker was getting the best of the storekeeper. Whereupon the little Salmon slipped around and whispered in the ear of his father, "Check him, check him again, and checkmate him."

There was a good deal of amusement among the spectators that a six-year-old boy should try to give advice in a chess game; however, the advice turned out well, for it was an inevitable mate in three moves. Salmon, the future lawyer, had done well in his first encounter with a banker—better than he anticipated, for the banker took him out and bought him a large sack of candy.

Some of the characteristics of S. O. Levinson which were partially responsible for his great influence may have had their origin in his boyhood experience in the store. As a man he had a deferential attitude toward persons like judges, lawyers, bankers, doctors, business people, and any persons in positions of influence or responsibility. This is not to imply that he was unduly awed or uneasy in their presence or bowed to their judgment; but he liked them, respected them, and treated them so that they were at ease in his presence; perhaps he encouraged them by his manner to indulge in private feelings of superiority. Another characteristic was his desire to work with and influence the chief actors on the stage without getting on the stage himself. He had no craving for public recognition; it was sufficient for him to know that the chief movers of the public got their tactics from him. As a child he had seen a procession of influential persons file into his father's store. Years later he thought of them as important, and no doubt his parents impressed their importance on his tender mind; hence his deference. He had seen his father controlling the actions of these persons and through them the community, hence his satisfaction later at himself controlling their successors. And, as will become clear in the story of his relation to the peace pact, he succeeded in controlling some of the most uncontrollable actors on the national and international stage.

His driving energy and his managerial ability found early outlet in sports—a fact emphasized by all who knew him. He was one of the mainstays of the baseball team. They never made him captain, but rumor has it that this was because by electing someone else they could have two captains. Young Salmon would run the team regardless of who the titular leader was—a characteristic which he never lost. Once he went to Indianapolis when the great Pop Anson was playing; and, not having enough money to see the hero from inside the field, he achieved perhaps a greater thrill by seeing him through a knothole. In another sport, croquet, his playing skill won him a considerable local reputation.

This interest in sports was as intense during his mature years as it was in boyhood. Pressure of business prevented him from spending as much time on the bleachers of the ball park as he liked, but he always found time to play golf and to go to one or two football games each year. During his young manhood his knowledge of how to handle a "kicker" and when not to bluff appeared to result in frequent losses to his poker friends.

One girlhood friend wrote to him after the peace pact was signed, recalling a walk in the long ago down a country lane. His feats of prowess such as jumping mud puddles had been a source of wonderment to her. Whatever her appreciation may have been, it is certain that he was not the object of open affection on the part of all the young girls. One, called Flo, by her silent, unapproving observance of his feats reminded him, he declared, of the all-seeing eye of God.

In general the testimony is that he did whatever he did with wild abandon; he played hard, studied hard and enjoyed himself strenuously. "I usually want to fight hard or not at all"— "Drink deep, or taste not the Pierian spring" of battle—is as good a characterization of his childhood as it was of his part in the titanic struggles he was referring to in his letter to Professor John Dewey in 1930, when he stated this creed of action.

His ambition was to go to Yale on finishing high school. But he had no Greek; and, even though he was able to surmount all other obstacles, it appeared that Greek was the *sine qua non* of eligibility as far as the admission authorities of Yale were concerned. This was the bitterest of disappointments to him. He then went to the old University of Chicago during the years 1883–86. After a year out of school to earn money and armed with some knowledge of Greek, he made another assault in the fall of 1887 on the citadel whose doors opened only to Greek scholars. They would admit him as a Junior—but as a Senior, as he insisted—never! In all her one hundred and eighty years Yale had admitted but three transfer students at a higher standing than as Juniors. Adamant refusal on the part of the university was met with increasing insistence on the part of the young Lochinvar from out of the west. Finally, a way out was hit upon. They would give him a series of examinations to convince him of the impossibility of his joining the Senior class—the class of '88. And what a series it was, from logic to geology! The memory of them was vivid in Levinson's mind nearly a half-century later, when it seemed that he "must have been examined in at least twenty-five subjects." And what significant questions were asked—the date, for instance, of the second edition of *Hamlet!* In spite of the nightmare of entrance examinations and baffling regulations, it is a matter of record that S. O. Levinson, along with such persons as Irving Fisher, A. A. Stagg, and Henry Stimson, was a member of the Yale class of 1888.

He then came to Chicago to study law in the firm of Moses and Newman. Even though Mr. Newman was his uncle, Levinson was recognized only on his own merits. For a time he received no pay at all. He tried to get a little income by teaching night school; but discipline was as difficult as it was distasteful to him, so he concentrated his energies on the law. His rise was rapid.

He was still one of the minor lawyers of the firm when the settlement of an important insurance matter came up. The older heads looked into the facts and decided nothing could be done. Not so Salmon. Some millions of dollars were involved. He went into the facts, concluded that he might be able to arrange a settlement, and set to work. When some of the firm's money had been spent working up the case, the older members raised a hullabaloo. That did not deter him. He went to New York to talk over the procedure. The question of the fee came up:

I said I would want $50,000. The man whistled and turned clear around in his chair, and wanted to know if I didn't think that was a lot of money. "Well," I said, "Remember, I don't get anything unless I settle the case, and if I do, don't you think it is worth it?" He said that he didn't know but what it was.

When the case was settled, the fee plus some expenses was turned over, making a total of about $55,000. That was said to be one of the largest fees any lawyer had received in those days. Though his position in the firm was materially improved, he was not made a partner.

When a case was submitted to him, he looked into it and came to a decision as to what should be done. Frequently he came to a different conclusion from that of his seniors, but it was his own conclusion on which he acted, not theirs.

Presently he became a junior partner, but before long he and Benjamin V. Becker organized their own firm. Mr. Becker had begun working in the same office with Levinson in 1891. The two were associated, as office workers, lawyers, junior members of a partnership, and as senior members, until Levinson's death on February 2, 1941. Their professional and business association was cemented by a very close personal and family friendship for more than fifty years. Later they took junior members into their partnership. These have included such persons as former United States Senator Otis Glenn and Federal Judge Jerome Frank.

The type of professional experience through which Levinson grew up had significance for his peace activities. He had some practice in court. On the occasion of the birthday celebration of his seventieth year, Governor Horner of Illinois wrote recalling how he himself as a beginner in law had been impressed with Levinson's industry, thoroughness of preparation, and cogent arguments before the court. Trial practice, however, formed a very small part of Levinson's experience. He had early come to the conclusion that if lawyers were reasonable men they should be able to get together and settle disputes without a trial. A lawsuit, he declared, was a miniature war; there was so much waste of every kind—of energy, time, and money. This conviction, he used to say, was the real origin of his interest in war; his feeling was that lawsuits were futile and could be prevented; war was futile too, so why could not war be prevented?

It often fell to his lot, also, to find a way for a business which had become insolvent to come to an arrangement with the creditors and make a new start. At that time there was no bankruptcy law under which a distressed debtor could get sufficiently free of his creditors to continue in business. The only thing he could do was to make some kind of arrangement with each individual creditor. This was sometimes a tedious, almost endless, job and required great skill in negotiation. After working in cases of this type, Levinson began to like the work and, consequently, was more and more frequently called upon to handle such matters. Before 1898, when the Bankruptcy Act went into effect, he had become an expert negotiator. While his dislike of lawsuits inspired him with his later dislike of war, it was in financial reorganization that he acquired the skill in negotiation which he later used to a superlative degree.

His chief professional concern continued to be financial reorganization. He helped in larger and larger cases. In 1908 he reorganized the personal affairs of George Westinghouse and began to work on the Westinghouse companies, one of the great cases of its day; another was the St. Louis and San Francisco Railroad. Fees from such work dwarfed that first large fee of his, and investments in the companies he had reorganized served as the basis for the fortune he later spent so freely in peace work.

The titans of the financial and legal world became his intimates. Otto Kahn knew him well enough to call on him for advice without remembering that he made a living by getting paid for such advice. Julius Rosenwald and James A. Reed were "Jules" and "Jim" to him. This is not to say that such persons were ever taken as a matter of course; they always were "big fellows" to him, even though many a man so-called would have liked to be as "big" a fellow as he was. But this type of acquaintance was much to his advantage. He knew famous men well enough not to be awed, but rather to be stimulated to his full powers in their presence. Furthermore, his acquaintance was so wide that, if he did not know a person of influence to whom he wished access, he seemed nearly always to have a friend who did and who could arrange for the meeting under favorable circumstances.

No preliminary sketch could serve the purpose of giving a basis for understanding Salmon Levinson, unless some indication were given of his humanitarian interests and his home life.

He shared his mother's compassion for the "weak and friendless

[8]

sons of men." He distributed many thousands of dollars among charities of all types. The education of the Chinese in China, outings for underprivileged children, the Women's League for Peace and Freedom, Hull-House, the poor in Noblesville, relatives and old friends who could not make ends meet, persons persecuted for political reasons—all alike came in for generous portions of his time or money or both. For many years he was very closely associated with the Abraham Lincoln Center of Chicago, and for much of this time he acted as its president. To this institution he not only gave a great deal of money, but he also secured large donations for it in the La Salle Street neighborhood.

No business, professional, or avocational interests ever prevented him from being a family man. He was a tender, even an indulgent, father. When his children were away from home, long letters went to them written in his own hand, full of comradely comment on all matters of mutual interest. These letters, suited to the age of the recipient, might be a request for advice, as well as an offer of it, or a gentle reminder of an opportunity for filial thoughtfulness. For example, to one son recently gone to college and therefore much engrossed with the interests of a different world this telegram went: "This is mother's birthday. Don't forget to wire her. Papa." The home at 4049 Lake Park Avenue in Chicago and the summer place in Maine, presided over by the gracious Mrs. Levinson, radiated good cheer, comfort, and cordiality. A procession of intimate friends, celebrated personages of the literary and cultural world, and the powerful princes of the financial, intellectual, and political worlds enjoyed the Levinson hospitality.

In the summer of 1914 Levinson's life must have been a singularly happy one. He had accumulated a comfortable fortune; he had a business partner in whom he had complete confidence and with whom he shared a lucrative influential business; of his two sons, one was just entering college and the other already there; the break in the family circle had been repaired by the new Mrs. Levinson's coming into the home to be a mother to his little daughter and a companion to himself. Life was comfortable, stimulating, luxurious—for him. But a young man in the un-known town of Sarajevo had an uncomfortable feeling about the tyranny of a foreign monarch; and, following the sharp crack of his pistol, came the duller throb of the war drum and the sound of hobnailed boots marching; the shadow of death fell across the land, and a new page was turned in the life-book of Salmon Oliver Levinson.

CHAPTER II

THE WORLD WAR: THE BACKGROUND OF THE OUTLAWRY IDEA

To find the original stimulus for an idea, to watch the complex influences in its formulation and development, to examine the techniques by which it is brought to acceptance, is to throw light on the dynamics and controls of our society. While it is impossible to pick out each thread in the cloth of any fully developed and accepted project, the outlawry-of-war movement will be subjected to a careful analysis.

Outlawry had its origin in Levinson's efforts to stop World War I. Consequently, it will be well to glance at his reactions to the hostilities at their outbreak and to trace in some detail his attempts to terminate them. The sources of information are his letters and his oral reports made two decades after the event.

About the time hostilities began, he recalled having read in the *New York Times*[1] how the rules of warfare had been fixed in the Geneva Conventions: fighting would be confined to the

[1] The kind of thing he was recalling is illustrated by an editorial in the *New York Times*, August 1, 1914. Some relevant excerpts from it are:

"The mass of these 800,000,000 [the population of the belligerent states] and their property are protected by the rules of modern warfare.

". . . . The chief safeguards lie in respect for family honor and rights, the lives of persons, and private property, which can not be confiscated, and for religious convictions and practices.

". . . . But war between actual belligerents is also much circumscribed. They can not declare that no quarter will be given. Elaborate safeguards are made for the rights and humane treatment of prisoners of war. The Geneva Convention permits the comprehensive activities of the Red Cross in the care of the sick and wounded on both land and sea. Unusually cruel weapons are proscribed. Towns must be amply warned before siege or bombardment, and occupied territory may be compelled to supply only the actual needs of the invading armies.

"All these rules were ruthlessly violated in the conduct of the Balkan wars. . . . . The Balkan States are not fully civilized. War provokes savagery, but a war involving the great powers would be fought with due restraint."

Would it be facetious to inquire after the manner of Homer if this last statement was not enough to provoke the inextinguishable laughter of the gods?

armed forces; noncombatants would be safe; property would not be wantonly destroyed. War had been civilized. There was no reason to worry. But his first shock came during a trip to New York, when he found the Stock Exchange closed.[2]

It appeared from his letters that he felt America was insulated; and, once the economic adjustment was worked out, there was no danger of this country's becoming involved. In a letter written September 15, 1914, he lamented the rise of interest rates; he could not see the reason, since it was "against the rules of neutrality to lend money to any of the belligerent nations. . . . ." This is the first reference to the war, indirect though it is, that is to be found in his correspondence. It was the reduction of the "infernal tariff" at the "wrong time" rather than the war which caused the financial strain, because the deficit had occurred by July 1 before the "elephantine brain," Wilson, could have figured "out the immediacy of an European struggle." "If the tariff had been left alone the government would have $200,000,000 more in its Treasury which is now in the hands of foreigners, and would not be taxing us in every conceivable way as if we ourselves were at war," he complained in a letter to his brother Harry. In this second reference to the war he was irritated because there was ". . . . entirely too much financial intimacy between the United States and foreign countries. Even a little Balkan war for six or eight months upset financial conditions in this country. We will have to get an international divorce from these Christian nations who are cutting each other's throats." But in a letter of October 9 he consoled himself with the reflection that "after a lapse of a few months we will begin to work out the advantages to this country of having its competitors at war."

This traditional American attitude toward European wars reached its climax in the letter of October 9. The flow of humanitarian effort to stop that war and all war was soon to set in and increase under the impetus of a driving energy and an indomita-

[2] The *New York Times*, July 31, 1914, reported the Stock Exchange as standing the strain, despite the heavy, almost unprecedented selling of the day before. But the next day, August 1, the *Times* stated that "for the third time in history the Stock Exchange had been compelled to close to protect the solvency of hundreds of firms."

ble, imperious will, though there is no direct quotation from the letters which shows exactly what it was that turned Levinson into the way of the peacemaker. He did, however, write the following letter to his intimate friend, the Rev. John Haynes Holmes of the Community Church, New York City:

DEAR MR. HOLMES:

If available, I will thank you very much to send me a copy of your yesterday's talk on Peace. Mrs. Levinson and I are very anxious to read it, believing that you have views that are more frankly and vigorously expressed than most of those that are expressed here.

Trusting you and your family are well, I am

Sincerely yours,

(*Signed*) S. O. LEVINSON

This letter was written October 5, and on the ninth he wrote thanking Holmes for the copy. The sermon has been retained in the files. It is a moving description of evil days to come, of the losses human and material, and a strong appeal to hold fast to the "law of love as the rock upon which to rear the new society that must some day rise out of the ashes of the old."

During the latter days of October a death occurred in the immediate family. This sorrow, along with other extremely important family matters, such as the birth of a son, and the press of business affairs, engrossed his attention so that there were no references to the war in his letters, except once when he wrote in response to a request for charity that if he were down for an annual contribution he would try to make it "if the European war does not last too long."

The *New York Times* of November 22, 1914, carried an interview of Jacob Schiff, an influential financier of New York City, born in Germany but a naturalized American citizen. When this interview was published, President Emeritus Charles W. Eliot of Harvard wrote to Schiff. A lively correspondence between these two leaders of pro-German and pro-Ally sentiment in America ensued. The pro-Ally view was trenchantly put by Eliot, while Schiff maintained that the belligerents might listen to a strong American appeal to stop fighting.

This correspondence, beginning on November 24 and lasting

to December 14, was all published in the *Times* on December 20. It was this appeal of Schiff's for the neutral world-opinion to be gathered in one voice and to be hurled in one cosmic "thou shalt not" at the maddened nations, which caught the fancy and stirred the restless energy of Levinson. If by some means Eliot, representing the pro-Ally sentiment, and Schiff, representing the pro-German sentiment, could be brought together—perhaps—he wrote to his partner, "there is a chance in a million of something coming of it"—perhaps, he might help to get the movement started; the question of Mordecai—"Who could tell but that he had been raised up for just such a time as this?"—gives the key to his attitude. So he made bold to write to Schiff on January 5, 1915.

"Your published utterances regarding the War have created such a favorable impression upon those of us who do not fully share your views, that I take the liberty of offering a suggestion." The suggestion was that, since Germany, "whether rightly or wrongly," had "incurred the ill-will of the neutral world," it was up to Germany to make the first move to restore that world's confidence in her.

He was surprised to get a favorable reply from Schiff. Several of his friends advised him to go on; and, while he still thought that there was only one chance in a million, he decided to see what could be done by getting Eliot and Schiff together. His first meeting with the financier was on January 15 in the latter's office in New York City. This interview "was not satisfactory"; "however," Levinson wrote to his partner, "he suggested I go to Cambridge and confer with Dr. Eliot and see him afterwards." Acting on this suggestion of Schiff's, Levinson secured a letter of introduction from Mr. Jenkin Lloyd Jones and another from Dr. John Haynes Holmes, men whom he regarded as being "only second to Dr. Eliot as Unitarians in this country," and proceeded to Cambridge to try to meet "one of the hardest men to get to" in America. This interview was most "delightful" and "satisfactory." Within an "hour's time" a working plan which was designed to give voice and volume to neutral opinion against the war had been agreed upon. This interview was summarized in a letter to his partner, Benjamin V. Becker:

I cannot refrain from adding that Dr. Eliot said at the close of our interview that if it came to him in the right way—as to the terms of which we had no
difference—he would accept an undertaking. I felt about as big as a balloon
when I left the house.[3]

The next step was to see Schiff again. Out of this interview
which left Levinson exhausted physically, because the great New
York banker was so "brief, business-like, to the point, and you
had to make every word count," came a plan for Eliot to head a
nonofficial, nonpolitical committee of ten representative Americans picked by the chairman to work without publicity. Various
names were suggested for Eliot's consideration, such as Chief Justice White, David Starr Jordan, Arthur T. Hadley, Andrew D.
White, James J. Hill, Cardinal Gibbons, and Felix Adler.

While Eliot wrote that he was doubtful of any good coming
from this plan, he appeared to be willing to work on the lines
suggested to him by Schiff under the instigation of Levinson.
Eliot drew up a list of peace terms that could be used as a working basis, such as withdrawal of the German forces within the national boundaries, indemnification of Belgium, and a plebiscite for
Alsace-Lorraine; and commented on the men suggested for his
committee. This letter was written to Levinson on February 2,
1915. Nothing happened for a fortnight, and Levinson became
impatient. On February 16 he wrote to Eliot, suggesting Robert
Lincoln as a member of the committee and then "urged action at
once." Again on the nineteenth he wrote, pleading that something be done immediately, since it appeared to him that Germany was bent on forcing the United States into the war. In addition to the fact that making haste slowly irked and irritated and
exasperated him, he feared that if the movement were not speeded
up his principals might "lie down on the job." For, he wrote to
his confidant, John Haynes Holmes, Eliot was as radical on one
side as Schiff was on the other, and he was constantly trying to
"moderate" the former and stop the latter from "attitudinizing."
The "constitution of the Committee was pretty well agreed
upon." He could see no reason for delay, and Holmes advised

[3] Levinson to Becker, January 1, 1915.

haste, because if the Allies got through the "Dardanelles, they won't listen to peace then."

The next day, March 2, after receiving this exhortation to hurry from Holmes, Levinson wrote to Eliot to arrange another meeting with him. This interview was necessary, he insisted, because, "we will have to hurry, for if the Russians get in sight of Constantinople our work will be next to impossible." But Eliot, in the meantime, had decided that the peace plans he had formulated ran no chance of realization; furthermore, in view of his "ideas about the ultimate interests of Europe and America in the right settlement of this War," he could not "make a satisfactory statement on behalf of the immediate cessation of hostilities," and therefore, he concluded, "I feel that I must retire from the undertaking which you interested me in."[4] By this time, while Levinson still may have doubted that the war could actually be stopped, he had decided that the proposition would have to be put up to the warring nations; the responsibility would be theirs, not his, if they chose to continue. He was not going to die until he hit the last ditch, he wrote to Holmes. To say that he was "disappointed was to put it mildly," he wrote to Eliot, and arrangements were made to meet with the latter again. After this meeting the President Emeritus agreed to revise his paper for submission to the warring powers; but later, after conferring with some of his friends, he decided to drop the matter again.

Levinson met Eliot's "off-again" tendency with a many-sided attack. In dealing with men whom he really wanted to see things as he saw them, he appeared to go on the assumption that, if they changed their minds and were against him, they might just as well change their minds again and be for him. To the "good Doctor" he wrote a letter of mingled praise and pressure. The three great documents of liberty, he declared, were the Magna Charta, the Declaration of Independence, and the Emancipation Proclamation. The fourth would be the "Declaration of International Interdependence"—the peace aims drawn up by Eliot.

[4] Eliot to Levinson, March 1, 1915.

The "timorous or partisan" advisers who were against issuing the document should receive the same "burning words" Lincoln gave those who opposed the Emancipation Proclamation:

"Gentlemen, I have called you together to state to you what I propose to do. I do not ask your advice as to the doing of it, but I shall be very glad to hear from you as to the best method in which it may [be] done, but I intend to issue this Proclamation."

. . . . Many men of fine judgment have agreed that you have the power and ability to achieve this great result.

Levinson communicated personally or by letter with the friends of Eliot who had advised against the project. He telegraphed about the situation to Schiff and asked what to do. The banker appeared to take an "I told you so" attitude and advised dropping the matter. Influential persons such as Dr. John Haynes Holmes and Mr. S. S. Gregory wrote to him, using the arguments suggested by Levinson. And Levinson himself went again to see Eliot. After his return he sent a memorandum covering the points agreed upon in their conversation, which shows Eliot "on again."

On April 24, Eliot wrote a five-page letter setting forth the seven conditions for suspension of hostilities.[5] Just as it appeared that the writer was back in the fold, Schiff telegraphed to Levinson that he had great admiration for his efforts but felt that nothing could be done.

The answer to this was a long telegram of patient explanation and an appeal to the sporting spirit to play the game. Levinson pointed out how he had had to wait for the effect of the adverse counsel given by Eliot's friends to wear off, that he had finally been able to win over Professor Munsterberg, and that he had seen Eliot again and "persuaded him to go through with it—provided your side of the house makes agreeable answer." This telegram appears to have reawakened Schiff's interest.

Eliot's feeling that Germany was the culprit apparently permeated most of the group. Levinson had written to Schiff early

[5] This letter was subsequently expanded and published in the *New York Times*, May 3, 1915 (for a résumé of it see below, p. 19, n. 7).

in January that the "English people whose homes are still being daily devastated will not allow England to play the role she now ascribes to Germany." This feeling became more pronounced as the spring wore on. Consequently, when Levinson by the middle of April had finally persuaded both Eliot and Schiff to push on with the peace plans, he had decided that the idea of inducing Germany to make the first overture was preferable to that of sending identical notes to all the powers and hoping for a favorable reaction. Through Schiff he had got in touch with Dr. Bernard Dernberg, who was then living at the Ritz Carlton Hotel in New York City. There was a general impression that Dernberg had very intimate and confidential relations with the German government.[6] The plan was to get him to use his influence with his government to accept the terms of the Eliot peace proposal. On May 5 it appeared that the preliminary arrangements were being carried through. Levinson wrote to Eliot: "D. promised me last Friday afternoon to send an urgent cable to his Government recommending the recognition or acceptance of the proposal as officially as possible. He even told me the proposed wording of the cable."

In the meantime the intention had been to prepare the American public to bring pressure on the warring nations. Some of the most important correspondence between Levinson and Eliot was published in the *New York Times* on May 3. Levinson had written to Eliot, asking for his views "as to the basis upon which this destructive conflict can be halted and the millions of European youth saved from destruction, so that the Angel of Peace and not the Angel of Death may hover over the suffering people of these distracted nations." Eliot, foreshadowing Wilson's longer list of peace aims, set forth at length what he considered "the feasible

---

[6] According to the report of the Judiciary Committee on Brewing and Liquor Interests and German Propaganda and Bolshevik Propaganda (*Congressional Record*, LVIII [June 16, 1919], 1133), "Dr. Bernard Dernberg was sent by German Government to the United States ostensibly as a private citizen, but in reality to have general supervision of the publicity propaganda in the United States." For a fascinating account of Dernberg's activities, as well as of others, see George S. Viereck, *Spreading Germs of Hate* (New York: Horace Liveright, 1930).

grounds on which preliminary negotiations for peace might . . . .
be opened with some prospect of a satisfactory result."[7]

Many commendatory letters came to Levinson, and he wrote
to nearly everyone he knew who might have an important German friend, urging that pressure be brought on these friends to
use their influence on their government. To Schiff he wrote:
"You can be of great service now—for now is the time for Germany to make good"; to a Mr. James Speyer, who, he said, was in
the confidence of the family of Dr. Dernberg: "You can now render a great service to the Fatherland by seeing that Dr. D. makes
good. This is an opportunity of a century for Germany to get by
shrewd diplomacy on this opening what she cannot get even by a
successful war"; to Dr. Dernberg: "Our end of the contract carried out, how about yours?"; and to Charles R. Miller, the editorial writer of the *Times:* "If any pressure is needed . . . . kindly
advise me," and so on.

But there were two difficulties that not even Levinson with all

[7] These grounds were: "1. . . . . Every nation should recognize the fact that no
nation in the world can establish rule or dominion over any other civilized nation,
large or small. . . . .

"2. . . . . A general agreement that the small States in Europe shall have firmer
securities . . . . no European population shall be held to an unnatural allegiance
contrary to their wishes, and that the national aspirations of the peoples of Eastern
and Southeastern Europe shall be satisfied to some reasonable measure.

"3. . . . . General acceptance of the proposal that the freedom of the seas . . . .
be placed under international guarantees.

"4. . . . . General acceptance of the policy of the 'open door' as the best means of
promoting the trade of all manufacturing peoples.

"5. . . . . The abandonment of the policy of seizing either distant colonies or ad-
joining provinces by force and holding them against the will of their populations,
and the recognition of the principle that the only enlargements of territory . . . . are
those which are brought about by consent and good will, and are bound to the central or parent State by the sense of mutual service and advantage.

"6. . . . . Belgium [must] receive adequate compensation for the losses which the
German invasion and occupation have caused, the nature, scope, and amount of
that reparation to be determined by an impartial arbitrator.

"7. It should further be generally understood before any suspension of hostilities
is attempted that the main object of an international conference or council called to
settle terms of peace will be to devise such a reorganization of Europe that national
armaments can be safely reduced . . . . [by] the establishment of a supreme international tribunal, the maintenance of an international military and naval force, and
the stable development of international law" (*New York Times*, May 3, 1915).

his finesse and tireless energy could overcome. In the first place the German armed forces were making advances. Miller lamented the fact that the correspondence published in the *Times* was followed by German military victories, and Schiff thought that, in view of the "splendid military successes" of Germany, she was probably not in the mood to do anything. In the second place the "Lusitania" was sunk. Levinson felt that "the shot fired from the Submarine into the 'Lusitania' was much more fatal to Germany . . . . " than to the ship. He had, indeed, hoped when the news of the disaster first appeared that it would turn out to have been not a torpedo but a mine which had sunk the great vessel; but, even though this tragedy stirred neutral opinion deeply against Germany, he was not yet willing to give up his efforts to get immediate peace.

To his prodding of Dernberg the latter replied on May 10: "I have been as good as my word, but I have not seen any reply from Germany, very likely it has not been passed by the censor." Schiff's response pointed out that Germany was evidently in bad odor since the sinking of the "Lusitania." He had dealt with Dernberg, and he hoped that Germany would keep her promises and take advantage of her opportunity. This was on May 10; but the next day, May 11, he was less optimistic. Owing to the "most unfortunate Lusitania affair," they would simply have to let matters rest. He hoped something would be done a little later, or there would be a relapse to "crudest barbarism."

But Levinson, undaunted, started another round of strong letters. Miller was to use pressure; Schiff must help the country of his birth out of a bad situation, for "as to Germany, it is now or never"; and an importunate letter was sent to Dernberg. These letters were written May 12. The next day he received Schiff's letter of despair of May 11. The answer to this letter is memorable not only as a sample of Levinson's unconquerable, undiminishable tenacity but also because it contains a suggestion that he was beginning to think of the outlawry of war. He pointed out that Germany had got herself into an acutely critical situation, out of which, with the whole neutral world against her, she could emerge only in defeat and humiliation. If Germany attempted to justify the destruction of the "Lusitania" "the condemnation of the entire independent world" would be upon her.

. . . . On the other hand, if she endeavors to formulate a general program and, with proper disavowals of both the desire for world domination and war itself, will appeal to the United States to bring about the consent of the belligerents for a general adjustment of grievances and settlement of salient international rights, it seems to me that order may be brought out of impending chaos.

He closed the letter by stating his faith in Schiff's ability. ". . . . if you will assert your full measure of power," you may "accomplish much, if not everything."

Asking Germany for a "disavowal" of "war itself" may have been only a reflection of the general feeling that this was to be the "last war"; however, this hardly seems probable since the "war-against-war" campaign had not been begun by May, 1915. More plausibly, this disavowal of war itself may be taken as an indication of the genesis of the idea of outlawing war as an instrument in international affairs.

Schiff could not be induced to do anything more. He felt that there was simply no help for the situation, unless, perchance, the President of the United States would use his powerful voice. That might avail something. But still Levinson was undismayed. Initial action by the President he felt to be impossible; but, if the peace proposals were launched privately, then the President could add the weight of his authority. Next, he advised Schiff to make a public pronouncement of his views. He followed this by writing to Miller, suggesting that the financier be interviewed concerning Eliot's peace proposals and that his interview be published. But no one would fall in line with his plans; and even Levinson began to feel that peace could not be had just then by willing it. On June 14, 1915, he wrote to Eliot: "The torpedo that destroyed the Lusitania knocked the bottom out of our peace plans and my optimism in that line is laid up for repairs." But "hope springs eternal in the human breast," and he closed his letter by saying something might yet come of the plans.

During the next two years Levinson devoted his attention to other matters than stopping the war, though its destructiveness appalled him. "It is a terrible thing," he wrote to Mr. J. S.

Bache, ". . . . to watch the destruction of men and property go on at such an endless rate." But references in his letters, such as the observation that arbitration was merely a form of temporizing and comments on the attitudes of Germany and England with regard to blockades and submarine warfare, indicate the trend of his thought. He examined several volumes of United States diplomatic correspondence in February, 1917. He also procured a copy of Eliot's *Road toward Peace*[8] and sent it to a United States senator.

His first efforts had been aimed at reconciling leaders of opposing views and at getting them to act on principles of their own choosing, his ideas as to the substance of peace proposals being incidental. But during the period between the sinking of the "Lusitania" and the entrance of the United States into the war he began to ponder the similarities of war and lawsuits. This brought about a shift in his attitude toward would-be peacemakers and their proposals. He began to insist, gradually at first but later with obdurate inflexibility, that his principles be followed. He tried to understand all proposals from whatever source they came, but he did not accept them *in toto;* rather, he tried to fit them into his own ideas, so that when the assimilation was completed they were his. Another shift occurred in his attitude toward Germany. As long as the United States was neutral he had hoped for peace without victory; but, when neutrality gave way to belligerency, peace was to be sought only after a German defeat.

Early in August, 1917, Levinson had a talk with Eliot about possible bases of peace. After this meeting Eliot wrote two articles for the *New York Times*, in which he suggested that the use of force be barred as a means of gaining territory or of protecting investments in foreign lands; that a comprehensive world organization, including a parliament, a court, and a police force, should be formed; and that an official conference to consider these proposals be called.[9] Levinson wanted to have the second article reprinted for wide distribution; but Eliot, mindful of the criticism

[8] C. W. Eliot, *The Road toward Peace* (Boston: Houghton Mifflin Co., 1915).

[9] These articles appeared in the *Times* for August 5 and August 27, 1917. Eliot wrote a third defending the objects of the first two; it was published on October 7.

resulting from the proposal for a conference, demurred. Levinson, however, was so much impressed by the article that he insisted on reprinting it and distributing copies among his friends.

Two other moves that Levinson made toward peace deserve mention because of the light they throw on his developing thought. On August 25, 1917, he again wrote to Schiff that since Germany was already defeated it was time for a new departure. The military caste must give up its hope of domination by force. The way to peace, he continued, was not by the sword

but by high-minded and big hearted conciliation, by constructive statecraft that makes due allowances for the heated and brutal passions of bloody strife, and that recognizes the fact that war as an institution to "settle disputes" and establish "justice among nations" is the most barbarous and indefensible thing in civilization. Diseases are cured by ascertaining and eliminating the causes, not by merely palliating their manifestations. The real disease of the world is the legality and availability of war as the Court of first and last resort to protect criminal nations in their . . . . aggression. Morally we are all accessories before the fact of recognizing and sanctioning wars as lawful. Must we not face this stupendous fact? Must we not get rid of the monster for all time? As has been recently said, we should have, not as now, laws *of* war, but laws *against* war; just as there are no laws *of* murder or *of* poisoning, but laws against them.[10]

The other and last effort to get the war stopped took the form of a telegram of two hundred and thirty words, which Levinson wrote and which he induced Mr. John A. Lynch and Mr. W. T. Fenton to sign with him and to send to President Wilson on December 28, 1917. The President was urged to use his personal skill upon the proposals of Austria-Hungary. If they could be properly modified by the addition of his "indispensable plan for an international system that will substitute a powerful international court of justice for the bloody decisions of war, the world can be reorganized in a real spirit of democracy." Though this was the last of Levinson's efforts to halt the mad career of the warring nations, he still constantly looked for peace "in thirty to sixty days."

[10] The phrases "settle disputes" and establish "justice among nations" are similar to those used by Charles Sumner, *Addresses on War* (Boston: Ginn & Co., 1904), pp. 15–16. However, according to the evidence which will be adduced below (pp. 30–32), Levinson did not see this book until the following February. It seems, therefore, that Levinson was using the quotation marks for emphasis.

In the meantime he had been reflecting on the implications of the suggestion for delegalizing war which he had made to Schiff in August. But the idea of putting war outside the law had not as yet become sufficiently important in his mind for him to make it the nucleus of the memoranda that he was in the habit of drawing up. One such contains ten paragraphs, of which only the last dealt with the idea of outlawing war, while the others set forth the conditions under which the war might be immediately terminated and the advantages that would result. One of the conditions which he thought should be the basis of peace was that there should be no "so-called war indemnities" but each belligerent should pay all actual damages caused by its violation of international law. To determine the amount of these damages an "independent tribunal" was to be provided. This is the first reference to an international tribunal. The second reference to such a court was in the above-mentioned telegram sent to President Wilson. The tenth paragraph—that concerned with the outlawing of war—is longer than any of the rest and appears to have been carefully considered. It is the same idea that was expressed in the letter to Schiff but in different terms. An analogy is drawn between dueling and war. Dueling lasted as long as an "affair of honor" could be made the occasion of a duel. But, after many failures to regulate and moderate dueling, it was called by its right name, murder, and then it met its proper legal fate. "Vital interests" and "national honor" in the affairs of nations are like the "affairs of honor" in the relations of individual men. War, not sanctioned by an international court, must, like dueling, be called murder. The main difficulty is that three-fourths of international law is the law of war. Besides, militarism—the direct offspring of war—must be legal if war is; therefore, the way to get rid of militarism is to abolish war. This paper shows him moving away from the demand that the war be brought to an end at once to the insistence upon the definite and specific outlawing of war as the *sina qua non* of peace.

During the early winter of 1917 he continued to work on this idea. Finally he got it ready to try out on his friends for their criticism, as was his practice with every new idea and every new angle that an old idea had taken in his mind during the whole history of the outlawry movement. The person whose criticism he most desired was the close friend of the family, Professor John Dewey. He and Mrs. Levinson were entertaining Professor and Mrs. Dewey at dinner in New York when he showed him the preliminary draft of his plan. The professor was very favorably impressed with the idea; sometime later Levinson wrote:

I am enclosing the memo on the war and peace subject discussed with you in New York. I sincerely trust you will be able to make something out of it although I will have to rely much more upon your ability than upon the material offered.

There is one comfort in experimentation of this kind: matters cannot be worse than they are internationally now.[11]

He also sent a copy of the memorandum to Holmes, asking for his criticism too. Was the matter "fully covered," or had he left "something out that was of importance"?

Why Levinson chose Dr. Dewey as his chief critic and adviser at this time when he had been working with Eliot cannot be answered with certainty. He had, however, been sensitive to the vagaries of the public, and no one knew better than he the suspicion with which the public regards a reformer—especially the peace worker. He, perhaps, did not want to have his idea discounted because it came from the pen of Eliot, whose peace proposals by that time were legion, nor because it came from his pacifist friend, Dr. John Haynes Holmes, who already had written a book[12] in defense of the philosophy of nonresistance.

However that may be, he wanted the article published over Professor Dewey's name, and he tried hard to get him to consent. At first the professor refused flatly; later, however, he reluctantly agreed. But in January on a scrap of yellow paper he wrote to Mr. Herbert Croly:

On a visit to Chicago I met my friend Mr. Levinson and we have gone over in detail the memorandum on the legal status of war which I recently showed to you. As a consequence there has emerged the article which seems to me both highly significant and timely, and which, I hope will secure your approval for

[11] Levinson to Dewey, December 18, 1917.

[12] *New Wars for Old* (New York: Dodd, Mead & Co., 1916).

publication. In case of publication of Mr. Levinson's article it suggests a possibility of a follow-up article which I might like to prepare. Mr. Levinson has withdrawn any objection to the use of his name in connection with the publication of the article.[13]

This article appeared in the *New Republic* for March 9, 1918, under the title, "The Legal Status of War."

The follow-up article which Professor Dewey had referred to in his letter to Mr. Croly was part of the understanding between Levinson and the professor. If the lawyer agreed to his idea's appearing in an article over his own name, then the philosopher should lend the weight of his great name by commending it in another.[14]

Levinson's article, "The Legal Status of War," was the first publication of the idea which had been hammered into shape in his mind during the preceding six months. No longer was the outlawry idea subordinated to devices for attaining the immediate cessation of hostilities, it was now advocated as the nucleus of any peace plan.

In the opening paragraph of the article the point was made that any attack by any nation on any other in the form of a war was legal; and regardless of how unjustifiable and regrettable the attack might be, other nations were as strictly bound by the laws of neutrality as if it were the most "benign enterprise."[15] War

[13] Dewey to Croly, January 28, 1918.

[14] Dewey's article entitled "Morals and the Conduct of States," was published in the *New Republic*, March 23, 1918. In it "The Legal Status of War" was highly commended, and a strong case for international organization was made by pointing out that, since individuals are moral only by virtue of their being "partakers in modes of associated life which confer powers and impose responsibilities on them," states could not be "moral in their activities just because of the absence of an inclusive society which defines and establishes rights."

[15] There is some question whether this statement was not too sweeping. A war against a state which had been neutralized by treaty, e.g., Belgium or Switzerland, by parties to it could hardly be said to be a "benign enterprise" from the standpoints of other parties to the treaty. Also from a strictly technical standpoint it seems that the weight of authority was against considering war either legal or illegal. Rather, it seems that the majority of jurists held war to be nonlegal, like a storm or an earthquake, though its occurrence might have displaced the normal law which prevailed in peacetime and substituted another set of legal relations, as, e.g., after a flood martial law may displace normal law, though the flood could not be considered legal

was claimed to be a perfectly legal way of settling disputes. This was the thing which tied the hands of those who would improve international relations. "If it is lawful to do a thing, why make such a cry about its being done?" Consequently, the obvious thing to do was to make it unlawful. The plan of the League To Enforce Peace would be of no value unless war were made illegal. There should be no loophole left for a clever minister to make a dispute nonjusticiable because it was an affair of "national honor" or "vital interests"; "the matters which reasonably constitute points of vital interest and honor to the respective nations are precisely the matters to be formulated and safeguarded in the proposed International Code." The analogy between war and the duel was developed in considerable detail. International law, as far as it was concerned with the rules of warfare, was similar to the old dueling codes—both were meant to mitigate, and neither had succeeded in abolishing; the outlawry of war must be the foundation of the peace structure. Trials before international courts must not be an alternative to war but an absolute substitute for it, and there must be sufficient force to execute the decisions of the court. An underlying assumption was that a code should be prepared for the court and war should be pronounced a crime by the code. When once war had been made illegal, then many of the old questions such as those of contraband, blockade, etc., which arise out of war, would be automatically solved.

The first article, the "Legal Status of War," contained the theory of the outlawry of war in all but one important particular. But for that it could be used as the text of the whole movement. The work of the many who since have written and talked about the outlawry of war has simply been to develop, expand, clarify, and illustrate what Levinson put into this original article, even though in some respects the emphasis has from time to time shifted. The one important change—the elimination of force from

---

(see Q. Wright, "Changes in the Conception of War," *AJIL*, XVIII [1924], 755). The examination of the authorities in this article shows them to be more than fifteen to three in favor of this view of the status of war. This, however, does not destroy the concept which Levinson was trying to set up—namely, to make war and any changes brought about by it illegal.

the plan—came about as a result of the controversy in the United States over the League of Nations, which will be discussed in chapter iii.

It is of interest to find, if possible, where Levinson got the idea of delegalizing war.

Writers on international law had long regarded war as a relation which existed between states when the law of war supplanted the law of peace in governing the conduct of the states toward one another. There was no distinction in international law between a good and a bad war, the law was concerned only with certain formal declarations made by the state wishing to begin war on another state and with certain rules to be followed in the conduct of hostilities. These rules for the declaration and conduct of war had been agreed upon by common consent in the interests of humanity. It is true that a state was not expected to go to war unless it could not in any other way secure satisfaction for a wrong done to it or prevent a wrong about to be done to it; but since each state was the sole judge of what the situation demanded and what action it should take, if it chose war, such a course was not open to question from a legal standpoint.

Levinson's studies of international law and the history of diplomacy had been enough to show him that this was the existing condition. He said that it was a real shock to him when he found that a great beast occasionally got loose and destroyed hundreds of millions of dollars worth of property and millions of lives but that "nothing could be done about it because it was legal—the most legal thing in the world." One of the things that led him to think about the legality of war, he used to say when he recalled the years in which the idea was born and developed, was that, as he read international law, he failed to find the word "crime" anywhere. That was a surprise to him as a lawyer; for surely war itself was a crime; he thought it must be against the law. In the "Legal Status of War" he quoted from Woolsey:

International law assumes that there must be wars and fighting among nations and endeavors to lay down rules by which they shall be brought within the limits of justice and humanity. In fact, wars and the relations in which nations stand to one another as belligerents or neutrals form the principal branch of international law, so much so, that in a state of assured and permanent peace there would be little need of this science.[16]

Being a lawyer, he would deem it logical, when once this situation became impressed upon his mind, either to accept the situation as it was and try to make improvements in the law which would mitigate still further the suffering resulting from war or to use the law itself against war.

This latter alternative had occurred to others besides Levinson. Charles Sumner glimpsed it as early as 1845. In an address entitled "The True Grandeur of Nations," which he delivered on July 4 of that year "before the authorities of Boston," he made an attack on war. From its context the speech seems to have been occasioned by the desire to prevent the United States from going to war with Mexico over the Texas territory.

A few relevant excerpts from this address show that Sumner was thinking of war as legal and claiming that it should be made illegal. A man in making an appeal to put down the animal instincts within his nature, he predicts, "will be startled as he learns, that, while the municipal law of each Christian nation, discarding the Arbitrament of Force, provides a judicial tribunal for the determination of controversies between individuals, International Law expressly *establishes* an Arbitrament of War for the determination of controversies between nations."[17] He goes on to point out that here is a gigantic evil "which, instead of proceeding from some uncontrollable impulse of our nature, is *expressly established and organized by law.*"[18] And again: "we have beheld War, sanctioned by International Law as a mode of determining *justice* between nations, elevated into an *established custom*, defined and guarded by a complex code known as the Laws of War. . . . ."[19] The remedy that he suggests is to get rid of war by agreement between states:

If nations can agree in solemn provisions of International Law to establish War as Arbiter of Justice, they can also agree to abolish this arbitrament, and to establish peaceful substitutes. . . . . A system of Arbitration may be instituted,

[16] *New Republic*, March 9, 1918.

[17] Sumner, *op. cit.*, p. 13.   [18] *Ibid.*, p. 14.   [19] *Ibid.*, p. 121.

or a Congress of Nations, charged with the high duty of organizing an *Ultimate Tribunal*, instead of "these battles."[20]

In another address, "The War System of the Commonwealth of Nations," delivered in Boston in 1848, he went into greater detail as to how war could be abolished. If the states of the Swiss Confederation or of the North American Union or the German Confederation could "divest themselves of the *right of war with each other*, and consent to submit all mutual controversies to Arbitration, or to a High Court of Judicature, then can the Commonwealth of Nations do the same."[21] Furthermore, if war is criminal in these several states, "then it is criminal in the Commonwealth of Nations to continue it."[22] "In the light of reason and religion," his conclusion was, "there can be but one Law of War,—the great law which pronounces it unwise, unchristian, and unjust, and forbids it forever as a crime."[22a]

But to say that others had thought of the idea before is not to prove that it was from them that Levinson got his idea. According to his own testimony and other evidence, he had developed his "Legal Status of War" article before he found that Charles Sumner had been thinking along the same line. As has been shown by the letter to Schiff, the idea seemed to be dawning in his mind in August, 1917. A conference was held with Professor Dewey early in December, and a memorandum was sent to him later the same month. A very few minor changes were made in the article in late January, when the professor visited Levinson in Chicago.

The letter which the professor wrote to Mr. Croly on January 28 was quoted in full above.[23] The next day Levinson wrote the following letter to Croly:

I enclose herewith paper on "The Legal Status of War" concerning which Dr. Dewey has had some correspondence with you.

I trust the idea conveyed therein may be of some service in working out the solution of permanent peace.[24]

---

[20] *Ibid.*, p. 51.

[21] *Ibid.*, p. 221.

[22] *Ibid.*

[22a] *Ibid.*, p. 222.

[23] Above, pp. 25 f.

[24] Levinson to Croly, January 29, 1918.

According to his own statement it was not until the Lincoln Birthday observances on Sunday, February 10, 1918, that he received the first clue to Sumner's ideas of peace. He went to hear Dr. Jenkin Lloyd Jones preach on "The Satellites of Lincoln." Sumner was one of three discussed in this connection. There are two reasons why he recalled this sermon vividly eighteen years later. In the first place during the course of the sermon the minister said: "Be ashamed to die until you have done something for your fellow-men." This sentence, which the Rev. Mr. Jones attributed to Horace Mann in an oration to a graduating class of Oberlin College, had a profound effect on Levinson, for it burned itself into his memory; and he used to say that nothing could stop his peace activities, for he could always hear the challenge ringing in his ears. In the second place, the reference to Sumner aroused his interest. Shortly afterward he found Storey's biography of Sumner.[25] A little later he was hunting through some books which had been stored in the barn, and there he found Sumner's *Addresses on War*.

His own personal statement is corroborated from two sources: the correspondence in his files and the testimony of his wife. Mrs. Levinson recalled clearly the events connected with the Lincoln Birthday sermon of 1918. Levinson brought the Rev. Mr. Jones home with him for dinner, and she remembered the discussion about Sumner and the search for the books regarding him. And she particularly emphasized the driving effect on her husband of the statement attributed to Horace Mann.

A letter written to the second son, Ronald, supports the essential points in Levinson's oral statement. "I have been reading Charles Sumner lately," he wrote, "and found his volumes out in the ex-barn. He is certainly an ideal scholar. His views on almost all subjects he touches, appeal to me very strongly." He went on to comment on what a great peace man Sumner was and how well his oration of 1845 "fits the day and age. He comes much the nearest to the views I have been thinking and writing about of anyone I have seen. In fact, I think anyone familiar with Sumner's orations would be sure that I had gotten my 'in-

[25] Moorfield Storey, *Charles Sumner* (Boston: Houghton Mifflin Co., 1900).

spiration' from them."[26] Another letter of still stronger support is the one he wrote to Moorfield Storey, the author of the biography of Sumner. The relevant part is as follows:

> By strange coinciden[ce] after my article was sent to the New Republic, I heard a sermon on Charles Sumner. I immediately took up your life of him and read it and then read his anti-war speeches, particularly the ones of 1845 and 1849. I was delighted to find this high confirmation of my theory that war is a "legalized institution" and a "duel of nations."[27]

It is a fact that Sumner's definition of war was quoted and attributed to the senator in the article, "The Legal Status of War." Levinson accounted for this quotation by saying that he had seen Sumner quoted in some of the books he was reading and thus had taken the definition from a secondary source.

As Levinson indicated in his letter to Mr. Storey, he was highly pleased that the idea of outlawing war had been held valid by such an eminent person as Charles Sumner, a former chairman of the Senate Committee on Foreign Relations. Surely with such support as this people would not think him "so crazy after all." Consequently, he frequently called attention to the little volume of *Addresses*, and he also bought a large number of them for distribution among persons interested in outlawry. Once he wrote to Elizabeth J. Hauser: "The volume is one that I would put in any select galaxy."

That publicizing Sumner might rob him of the credit for originating outlawry bothered him not a whit. He appeared to want the idea adopted and acted upon regardless of where the praise went. Once when Dr. Holmes objected to his not receiving some honor, he replied: "I believe that no one can be thoroughly devoted to a great cause and at the same time worry whether he is going to get sufficient reputation and glory."

The weight of evidence indicates that with regard to the legality of war and the desirability of delegalizing it Levinson came independently to the same conclusion which Sumner had reached more than seventy years before. However, in his later writing, it seems that he did borrow from Sumner, for there are many strik-

[26] Levinson to Ronald Levinson, February 19, 1918.
[27] Levinson to Storey, March 21, 1918.

ing parallels in language and illustrations. This may be shown by a few citations.

In reference to the duel Sumner said: "In calling the terrible war now waging a Duel, I might content myself with classical authority, *Duellum* being a well-known Latin word for war."[28] Levinson: "The closest historical analogy to war is the duel, 'duellum' and 'bellum' both originally meaning war."[29] As to the method by which war could be abolished, Sumner after explaining how St. Louis had rid France of the trial by battle by the simple expedient of issuing the decree, "These Battles we abolish in our Dominions Forever," wrote:

These at the time were great words, and they continue great as an example. Their acceptance by any two nations would begin the work of abolition, which would be completed on their adoption by a Congress of Nations, taking from war its existing sanction.[30]

Levinson: "The program for Outlawry of War could be largely effected by a general treaty among nations agreeing to abolish the institution of war as the method of settling international disputes. . . . ."[31] Both Levinson and Sumner regarded war as an "institution." The latter said:

I prefer to characterize it as an INSTITUTION, established by the Commonwealth of Nations as Arbiter of Justice. As Slavery is an Institution, growing out of local custom, sanctioned, defined, and established by Municipal Law, so War is an Institution, growing out of a general custom, sanctioned, defined, and established by the Law of Nations.[32]

Levinson wrote: "War is an institution. An institution is a custom not contrary to law, established over long periods among peoples and races. The church is an institution; marriage is an institution; slavery was an institution."[33]

[28] *Op. cit.*, p. 243.

[29] *Senate Doc. 115* (67th Cong., 2d sess.).

[30] *Op. cit.*, pp. 308 f.

[31] "Can War Be Outlawed?" *Forum*, January, 1924. It is interesting to note that this, written in 1924 four years before the Kellogg Peace Pact which did take this very form was signed, is the first of the three principles of outlawry. The other principles are: (1) codification of law, and (2) adjudication of disputes.

[32] *Op. cit.*, p. 151.   [33] *Senate Doc. 115* (67th Cong., 2d sess.).

Some among Levinson's disciples placed considerable emphasis upon the point that war is an institution. It is probable, however, that the idea was derived in the first instance from Levinson and, through his recommendation of the *Addresses on War*, from Sumner, since many of the persons who helped to popularize the outlawry-of-war plan appeared to take an attitude toward him such as Ruth took toward Naomi; for, indeed, where he went in the peace effort, they went; his arguments were their arguments, his thoughts, their thoughts; and his god—outlawry of war—was their god. Dr. Charles Clayton Morrison makes the idea of war as an institution one of the themes of his book, *The Outlawry of War*.[34] Morrison, according to his own words, placed such a high value on Sumner's *Addresses*, that if anyone came to town with the intention of making a speech on peace and had not read the *Addresses* he would sentence him to a half-day of solitary confinement in the public library while he did read them.

There were differences between the two. Sumner appeared to think that arbitration could be made to coexist with war,[35] whereas Levinson never agreed that any pacific means of settlement could successfully compete with war, if war were recognized as legal. His contention was that you never could have a real opportunity to try out arbitration as long as one or the other parties to the dispute was free to take his case out of the hands of the arbitrators and appeal to the arbitrament of war. Another instance of difference was with regard to self-defense, though on this matter Levinson after a time moved to the Sumner position. Sumner had insisted that the delegalizing of war had nothing to do with the right of self-defense.[36] The two were entirely separable.[37] But it was not from reading Sumner but from talking with Mr. Oswald Garrison Villard and Mr. John Bassett Moore that

[34] Chicago: Willett, Clark & Colby, 1927, p. viii.

[35] *Congressional Globe*, XLV, Part V, 4106 f. (*Res.* May 31, 1872 [42d Cong., 2d sess., 1871–72]). There is question as to the accuracy of this statement. Levinson thought the language of the resolution meant just that. However, another interpretation of it appears reasonable and results in Sumner's abolishing war legally just as Levinson did. The language of the resolution is so lacking in precision that one cannot be sure what it means.

[36] *Op. cit.*, p. 147.   [37] *Ibid.*, p. 168.

Levinson came to the same conclusion more than two years afterward. This point will be discussed more fully later.[38]

The use of the term "outlaw" in connection with the idea of delegalizing war is, of course, logical. Its value as a slogan has been great. The term was used by Levinson in connection with war in his first published article, "The Legal Status of War." First, in discussing militarism he said: "Outlaw war and militarism is out of a job." Later he said: "The Outlawry of War is manifestly the primary condition under which the League To Enforce Peace can be made effective." And in summarizing the article, he demanded, among other things, "the specific outlawing of war by the code of nations." In a paper entitled "War Is Hell—but Lawful" which Levinson prepared sometime in December, 1918, but which was never published, he again used the term. "The basic idea of the League [to be created] should be the outlawry of war." He was evidently the first to apply the word to his own idea, and he apparently coined it himself. Although he quoted a similar usage by William James[39] in his earliest writing—"War Is Hell—but Lawful"—it is declared by his son, Mr. Ronald Levinson, in a letter to the author that it was his father's previous employment of the term which prompted him to call James's essay to his father's attention. This last sentence was quoted in the unpublished article.

An international court, from the decrees of which there could be no appeal to arms, has been part of the outlawry idea from the first;[40] but the method of enforcing its decrees has undergone radical modification as the idea developed. At the beginning, force was the key to the execution of court decrees. Levinson's telegram of December 28, 1917, to President Wilson referred to a "powerful international court of justice" as being essential. In his

[38] See below, pp. 195–96; see also p. 196, n. 33.

[39] "The Moral Equivalent of War"; the phrase quoted by Levinson from James is: "and I look forward to a future when acts of war shall be formally outlawed as between civilized peoples" (in *International Conciliation* [Bull. 224], p. 495).

[40] There is no attempt to find the origins of the court in Levinson's thinking, since the demand for one was quite general at the time (see Eliot, *New York Times*, August 27, 1917).

first published article, "The Legal Status of War,"[41] he was emphatic about such a court. "We must not," he said, "indulge in the absurdity of committing ourselves to the proposition that we may use force to compel a nation to submit its cause to arbitration, but shall not use force to execute the decision of the international court in such arbitration."

Eliot was a firm believer in the efficacy of force in international affairs. In a paper which he read before the Lake Mohonk Conference of May, 1910—afterward published in his book, *The Road toward Peace*—he advocated a "Supreme Court with a force behind it."[42] Levinson had become acquainted with this book at latest by 1916, for he had sent a copy of it to a United States senator. He was closely associated with Eliot during this period and had a great respect for his learning and judgment. It may have been the influence of Eliot that led him at that time to place so much emphasis on a court with teeth. Three years later he placed one of Eliot's hobbies in his plan. Levinson's own explanation of Eliot's reliance on force for the execution of the decrees of an international court was that he thought in the European way and was influenced by the logic that the Europeans used in thinking of peace as maintained by bayonets.

The outlawry idea was born of the efforts to stop World War I. The techniques of propagating the idea can be best analyzed by tracing Levinson's efforts to influence the making of peace, to which we may now go.

[41] *New Republic*, March 9, 1918.

[42] Chap. iii. His strong belief in force was evident in most of his writings during the war. Once, after arguing that so long as men desired liberty they must be willing to fight for it, he said: "So long as there are wolves, sheep cannot form a safe community" (*New York Times*, August 5, 1917).

CHAPTER III

THE LEAGUE: THE FIGHT FOR A LEAGUE BUT NOT THE LEAGUE

AFTER the preparation of the article, "The Legal Status of War," a period of "all quiet" on the Levinson front followed. He was somewhat disappointed that his analysis had not attracted more attention; and in his letters to his sons in the army he continued to hope for peace in "thirty to sixty days." He was encouraged, however, by finding in Lloyd George's war-aims speech of June, 1918, that one of the aims was "above all, making sure that war shall henceforth be treated as a crime punishable by the law of nations." He wrote to Lloyd George, warmly commending this statement and pleading for a strong league of nations, for which, he added, they would have to "look to you and President Wilson."

In December, 1918, another period of intense, almost feverish, activity began. Levinson proposed to himself a big undertaking. He wanted to join whichever peace organization would adopt his ideas or to get the various peace organizations to agree on two basic points: the outlawry of war and a strong league of nations. He wanted to agitate and educate the public to demand that these basic ideas should be the foundation of the peace. He wanted to convert Wilson to the outlawry of war, and he hoped to coax or cudgel or shame the Senate into supporting the President.

As between the two chief peace organizations, he preferred the League of Free Nations Association to the League To Enforce Peace, even though he suspected the former of being a reflection of Wilson. Holmes, however, investigated and assured him that it was in no sense official. Levinson hoped to get both organizations to fuse on a basis of outlawry, "for if people don't want war why don't they outlaw it?" But, if that were impossible, he determined to join the one which would adopt "our ideas." If neither would accept outlawry, he was prepared to form a peace organization of his own. This last step, however, appeared unnecessary, for after a talk with Norman Hapgood of the League of Free Nations Association he felt sure that organization was on the verge of accepting his ideas.

Another method of putting his peace ideas before the public was to get the *Chicago Daily News* to advocate outlawry in its editorials. After a couple of satisfactory interviews with representatives of the *Daily News*, he saw a good chance of converting the whole staff if only Lawson, the owner and publisher, could be won over. Levinson made several unsuccessful attempts to arrange a conference with Lawson, for he felt sure that the publisher would succumb to outlawry, if once he could get an "eye-to-eye" argument with him. By December 17 a hostile editorial had appeared in the *Daily News*, which Levinson attributed to the publisher and which accounted for Lawson's unwillingness to see him. He regarded this editorial as very unfavorable to permanent world peace and sincerely regretted seeing the paper lining up with the "hopelessly reactionary" *Tribune*. However, he continued to din outlawry into any available newspaper ear and on January 20 wrote to Holmes that Strong of the *Daily News* thought material in one of David Lawrence's cables from Paris was "traceable to my work."[1] In the meantime the *Chicago Evening Post*, which he characterized as "Republican and Roosevelt," had "accepted Outlawry." To insure that this material was read by important persons, he had the *Post* sent to them, at the same time mailing cards from his office calling attention to what the *Post* was doing.

In his efforts to stir up public opinion in Chicago to demand a league of nations from the peace conference, he had found "great ignorance of [the] League among business men, bankers, and some members of the bar." In order to reach the lawyers he proposed to print and distribute an address which Justice Clarke of the Supreme Court of the United States had delivered before the American Bar Association on the subject of world-peace machinery. A group of people like Miss Jane Addams of Hull-

---

[1] See *Chicago Daily News*, January 15 and 16, 1918; the pertinent part of a cable for January 16 is quoted below, p. 41, n. 2.

House, Professors Dodd, McLaughlin, and Clark of the University of Chicago was called together, and plans were laid for working the Chicago area.

In all this Levinson put little emphasis upon the details of the peace machinery. "I want to stick to the fundamentals and let the experts of the world, when they get together, work out the highly important details, only limiting them to doing nothing that will destroy the efficacy of the utter abolition of war as a legalized institution and a civilized tribunal," he wrote on December 26, 1918. "A ridiculous example" of confusing the main point of handling international controversies in a civilized way with subsidiary questions, he wrote to Mr. Norman Hapgood the next day, "is Senator Lodge. He bitterly complains that if we enter a League of Nations, [the] United States will lose its right of reciprocity with Cuba. If this be true, can a tinier calamity be imagined?" Many people he had found were "willing to do something but . . . . have nothing definite in their minds." And he felt it necessary to "put something concrete in the hands" of such people.

It was partly for this purpose of putting "something concrete," namely outlawry, into their minds—something to which all their ideas and aspirations about peace could adhere—and partly for the purpose of getting American public opinion heard at the peace conference, that he planned and held a great mass meeting at the Abraham Lincoln Center in Chicago on January 12, 1919. He felt that with "President Wilson out of the country public opinion [was] leaderless," and his only hope of providing a shepherd for the milling flock lay in "monster mass meetings." He first planned to have Justice Clarke address this meeting, but no amount of insistence that peace work was of greater importance at that particular time than judicial duties could induce the Justice to leave Washington. Finally, arrangements were made for a number of short talks. The speakers were Judges E. O. Brown and M. W. Pinkney, Professors A. C. McLaughlin and Shailer Mathews, and Mr. Norman Hapgood. A resolution pledging support to President Wilson in his fight for a league of nations in which war would be abolished was introduced and passed by this meeting and immediately cabled to Paris. "The conscientiousness and voice of American people must be hurled at Versailles from every direction to prevent a hopeless compromise—as usual in these European meetings," Levinson wrote in urging that similar meetings be held in other parts of the country and that similar resolutions be adopted and cabled to Paris.

Copies of this resolution were broadcast far and wide to stimulate and solidify public opinion. Through co-operation with the *Chicago Evening Post* the resolution was sent to each United States senator and congressman, to each state governor and lieutenant-governor, to the members of the Cabinet, to the justices of the Supreme Court of the United States and of each state, and to a large number of the mayors of cities. The Abraham Lincoln Center, of which Levinson was president, sent a copy of the resolution to all Chicago churches and to key churches throughout the United States.

Levinson himself answered numerous calls to make speeches. At first he appeared to be reluctant, but it seemed as if it would save time to make the speech when he was asked rather than to try to get someone else and make the necessary explanations. On these occasions he spoke chiefly about the outlawry of war. The great interest shown in his subject surprised him. He was convinced of two things: that people were very enthusiastic about the idea of getting rid of war and that the outlawry-of-war program had great propagandist possibilities because it was simple and understandable and seemed to provide the public with an outlet for its inarticulate opposition to war. He had found that the words "outlaw war" struck a particularly responsive chord; and when Miss Breckinridge, of the University of Chicago, suggested to him that "wager of battle" would be more analogous to war than dueling, he showed his eye for making his ideas understandable to the man in the street by replying: " 'Wager of battle' brings no picture in the minds of ninety-nine out of a hundred people, whereas the parallel between duelling and war grips the intellect of the 'average' citizen."

Levinson was not content with the program of stirring up and converting the public to his cause. He wanted outlawry to be given a more direct access to the President than through the resolutions being cabled from the mass meetings. He looked for some person who was influential with the President and who could reach him through Colonel House. That person was Professor William E. Dodd, of the University of Chicago, with whom he got in contact on February 9, 1919. The professor agreed to cosign with him, and he sent the following cable to House the next day:

Tested middlewest sentiment by numerous mass meetings and interviews. Feeling strong for outlawing war. Believe with encouraging word from President entire country can be quickly won for League with good effect on newspapers and Senators. Sentiment now ripening fast. Popular slogan outlaw war timely. Writing.

In accord with the cablegram Dodd was urged to write a long letter to House giving a detailed and explicit argument for, and explanation of, the outlawry-of-war program.[2]

The next step was to get the Senate back in line. By the first of December, 1918, the Senate, encouraged by the congressional elections, which had gone Republican against Wilson's advice, was already determined to have done with the "autocrat," the erstwhile "Wobbly Woodrow," even though to ruin him would mean losing the peace. On December 9 Levinson wrote to Holmes that the "attitude of the Senate seems very bad," and again to Professor Dewey he complained that the Republicans

[2] According to David Lawrence, it appeared that Levinson's ideas or similar ideas were being seriously considered in Paris. He said in a report from Paris: "The trend of opinion inside the American delegation is toward the most drastic of plans. If as under the British scheme, war be postponed for one year while disputes are being investigated, then Americans ask why cannot war be postponed entirely? If to engage to postpone war for a year is yielding sovereignty temporarily, then there is no objection from the American point of view to permanent agreement prohibiting war. The objection raised to General Smut's plan is that a League permitting recourse to hostilities or leaving loopholes for war at the end of the year, legalizes war. . . . . There is a strong feeling among Americans in absolute finality of decision of the League and the necessity of bringing to bear the power of all the component parts to insure respect for its decisions" (*Chicago Daily News*, January 15, 1919; see also Lawrence's cable in the *Daily News* for January 16, 1919). It would be interesting to know to what extent the resolution cabled on January 12 from the meeting at the Social Center was responsible for the feeling reported by Lawrence on January 15 and 16. It may be added that a search of Lawrence's dispatches during the succeeding six weeks shows no further trace of Levinson's ideas.

had failed to catch the league idea. The Republicans were worse than Democrats, he said in a letter to Holmes on December 18. On December 3 he had written to Professor Dewey saying that a "man of influence" in New York had suggested that he should spend a couple of weeks with the senators. He had hoped that the public, if sufficiently aroused, would help to keep the recalcitrant senators from kicking over the traces, but there were two other ways of getting at them. The first was to see Mr. Will H. Hays, the chairman of the Republican National Committee, and Mr. Upham, the treasurer, who perhaps could use political persuasion; the second, to adopt the suggestion of the "man of influence," who was Mr. John E. Milholland, and see the senators himself. He decided first to try reaching the senators through their party officials. Accordingly, on December 20, just as he was starting for the East, he sent a telegram to Upham requesting an appointment with Hays. His correspondence does not reveal just what occurred at this meeting. All that it indicates is that he did have interviews with both Upham and Hays.

However, the situation in the Senate did not improve—from his viewpoint—and he and his correspondents continued their caustic comments on matters senatorial. He thought Lodge "ridiculous" in his failure to discriminate between major and "subsidiary" questions. When he found that Lodge in a speech delivered in 1916 had advocated a strong league of nations as part of the peace settlement, Levinson wrote, "I presume the political pressure has become too strong for him." Professor Dewey, while he felt that the masses were with Wilson and his principles, had begun to despair of a just peace because "the imperialists assisted by Knox, Lodge, and Roosevelt" would "dictate the settlement." During January, Levinson was so engrossed with the arrangements for the Chicago mass meeting and the follow-up work that he had little thought to give to other things, although he did make arrangements for conferences with some of the middle western politicians. However, on February 7 he was ready to think about the senators again. On that date he wrote to Senator McCormick of Illinois, asking why, being "surely for riddance of war," he objected to the proposed league of nations.

He himself was writing as a party man, for he always had been and still was "a devoted Republican," but on this matter of world peace he took pains to explain in other letters that he was strictly nonpartisan. The time had come when he "must get after the senators," he wrote to Dodd; he went on to predict a partisan fight about Wilson and urged the professor to see the President when he returned and to get his program put on a nonpartisan basis, "because the Republicans have fearfully resented his constantly ignoring their party."

On February 11 Levinson sent a telegram to John Haynes Holmes, saying that he was starting for New York. He had decided to take the advice of the New York "man of influence" and spend a couple of weeks with the senators, for he went from New York to Washington and remained there until after the first of March. At this stage of Levinson's career one is reminded of the marshal of France who vowed that he would capture Napoleon on his arrival from Elba and bring him back in an iron cage but returned from Grenoble wearing the colors and bearing the arms of the "Little Corporal." Levinson may have gone east vowing vengeance on the irreconcilables, but he returned one of the captains in command of the "battalion of death."

The occasion for this sudden and, to some of his Chicago coadjutors, such as Jane Addams and Professor William E. Dodd, wholly inexplicable about-face was the publication of the tentative draft of the Covenant of the League of Nations. But besides his feeling that the proposed Covenant was worse than nothing, there were other factors in the background which made a break with the President easy. Levinson had distrusted the leadership of the Democratic party. He had always thoroughly disliked William Jennings Bryan. In a letter to Eliot he had insisted that the "Commoner's" only *raison d'être* was popularity with the public; and early in the war he had said that the only thing Wilson had ever done that he approved of was to say that Bryan ought to be knocked into a "cocked hat." In common with his political brethren he had criticized the handling of the United States relations with Germany before the entrance of America into the war; and in 1918 he had said that the President tended to view things as they appeared at the moment, without regard to his previous utterances. However, from December, 1918, right up to the evening of February 14, 1919, he had supported the President, and in a letter to Justice Clarke he had expressed complete agreement with the President's peace views as far as they had been published. But during this period he had confided to close friends his doubts. He was afraid that Wilson's League would be "an improved and polished Hague Tribunal" and that the great nations would dominate it. He wrote to Professor Dewey: "I am so afraid that the Versailles Conference will end so far as a League of Nations is concerned, in some 20th century rhetoric, which may be an improvement upon the diction used in the 19th but when the test comes there will be a laugh on the 'radicals' again." There are two statements which, if read in the light of his subsequent shift on the league issue, may indicate that he felt the inclusion in any league constitution of a specific legal ban against war to be an absolute essential. They are:

The abolition or prevention of war is the essence of the objective of all League and movements, but when it comes to the final action the fundamental thing is compromised, which to my mind is fatal.[3]

Even if the disputes are reduced to a minimum by various suggestions of reform, we can still be precipitated into a cataclysm by the remaining disputes so long as war is the arbiter.[4]

According to Mrs. Levinson, her husband first read a copy of the Covenant of the League in the evening press in a hotel in New York,[5] shortly before they went to Washington, on what the correspondence shows to have been February 15. He then announced to her his opposition to it. The first documentary evidences of Levinson's deflection are a telegram to Professor Dodd and a letter to Eliot. The copy of the letter in the files to Eliot is written on stationery bearing the Vanderbilt Hotel letterhead.

[3] Levinson to Hapgood, December 19, 1918.

[4] Levinson to Holmes, January 20, 1919.

[5] Mrs. Levinson's memory of this point is supported by the fact that the Covenant was, in fact, first published in the United States in the afternoon papers of February 14, 1919, e.g., the five o'clock edition of the *Chicago Daily News* carried it. It first appeared in the *New York Times*, a morning paper, on February 15.

The date is February 15, 1919. In this letter he characterizes the League as a "compromise unworthy the sacrifices," "a system without machinery, a court without power, a body without a head," "more of an Alliance than a League." Nations retained "two chances to fight—either in limint [*sic*] or three months after arbitration defeat." The procedure would be so slow "that a death blow might be struck before the World-Machinery could be coordinated for action. . . . . No court is created wherein a single International law suit can be compulsorily tried." War was still "a legal institution for the settlement of International disputes . . . . the super-sovereign of the World." The provision for majority and minority reports on controversies was "a joke," since neither could be enforced. He ended his complaint by predicting that, unless the "venture" was "invigorated" and "clarified" in order to "abolish" the "bloody institution" of war, the American people would refuse to become involved in "European entanglements (WARS)."

On his arrival in Washington he went to see the senators. Of his first meeting with Senator Knox, he reports: "I plainly told him that our views were bound to be in serious conflict on the international question." But the Senator professed to be a great lover of peace, and Levinson found to his surprise that they were in "general accord on basic principles for world peace."

During the two next weeks Levinson, to use his own words, "did much work there regarding the League of Nations, especially with Senator Knox." It appeared from the argument he used on the Senator that, like the great Christian philosopher of his race, he was willing to be all things to all men that he might win some to his way of thinking. To Senator Knox and his fellow-planners for party success in 1920 he appeared as a party counselor and champion. The Republican prospects for 1920 were highly promising—unless a split should occur in their own ranks over the League or the League should give "the Democrats [Wilson] sufficient prestige to overcome the other handicaps." There would be a "cry for a substitute constructive program or else accept Wilson's plan as the best ever tendered the world." The large newspapers were gradually coming around; "the Republican party and specifically its Senators have been berated as personally hostile and partisan; to offset this they must take a humanitarian attitude," which they could do in their speeches by offering a constructive program, for the people wanted riddance of war. This argument must have appealed to the Senator, for Levinson later wrote to Mr. Edward Cummings of the World Peace Foundation: "Together we got up a preliminary program on one page. . . . . You will find in Senator Knox's speech March 1st, 1919, the essence of these ideas. We worked together on this branch of his address for several days before its completion."

In saying "together we got up a preliminary program . . . . ," Levinson seems, as often, to be sharing the credit for ideas of his own with a collaborator, whom by dint of relentless argument he has forced or enticed into accepting and using them.

Eight of the ten paragraphs of the first draft of the plan that "together we got up . . . ." were on stationery of the Hotel Lafayette where Levinson always put up when he was in Washington—and underlined in pencil in his own hand. The last two paragraphs were written with pencil in his own hand on the back of the sheet. The wording of them is characteristic. The plan is as follows:

1. Creation of international law through the instrumentality of a comprehensive code binding upon all nations.

2. Provision in this code, among other things, that aggressive war shall be outlawed and made a crime punishable as murder.

3. All nations to agree to submit all purely international disputes to the international tribunal created by the code, and all nations [to] agree to acquiesce in and aid in the enforcement of the orders and decrees of this court.

4. Universal membership of all nations in the League, the international court to have full jurisdiction over all nations for the purpose of enforcing the code.

5. General disarmament to a point consistent with domestic safety and a force adequate to fulfil the obligation of each nation to aid in the enforcement of the orders and decrees of the International Court.

6. The Monroe Doctrine, and all purely domestic questions enumerated as far as possible in detail, to be excluded from the jurisdiction of the International Court.

7. Abolition of all secret treaties and rights of conquest.

8. The alternative of arbitration to be open to the nations, if arbitration is preferred by the parties to the dispute to the processes of the International Court.

9. Each nation to report fully every six months (?) as to all armaments, military and naval, and committees to be formed by the League to check up and verify every such report. Provision to be made covering violators of armament limitations.

10. International tribunal to sit in hemisphere of defendant nation. United States to confine its military and naval aid of the international court to the western hemisphere, except in emergency when Congress may extend our aid to the eastern hemisphere.

The plan which appears to have finally resulted from the conference with the Senator[6] was very similar to the first draft, quoted in full above. It showed more polish; the first article was made into a preamble, and it was made more definite by stating that the Hague Conference should provide for the proposed codification. Less emphasis was placed upon force and more upon the good faith of nations. The plan bears a very close resemblance to that published more than a year later.

The speech, referred to above, which Senator Knox made before the Senate on March 1, 1919, and which contained the first public reference made by any government official to the outlawry of war, was an attack more vicious than logical on the Covenant of the League.[7] Among the tests the Senator proposed to apply to the Covenant,[8] the first was: Did it outlaw war? In his question: "Do its provisions abolish war and make it hereafter impossible?" and more particularly in his answer to it, Levinson's ideas were clearly visible. "In the first place," said the Senator, "the League plan still regards war as legal and as possible in the following more obvious cases: . . . . , [and] in all these cases the Covenant recognizes the legality of a state of War." After disposing of the League to his own satisfaction, he proposed alternative plans to secure the peace of the world. The first was "to provide for the compulsory arbitration of all disputes under some such plan as that provided for in the international prize court, or the unratified American-British . . . . arbitration trea-

---

[6] Identified as such by the typing, which is unusual and identical with that of the machine used by Senator Knox's secretary, Mr. Warren F. Martin.

[7] *Congressional Record*, LVII, 4687. [8] *Ibid.*, pp. 4690 ff.

ties of 1911. . . . ." At this point occurred the first suggestion that abandonment of the use of force in the execution of the court's decrees which was later to become one of the leading features of Levinson's outlawry plan. "We need not worry," said the Senator, "about the enforcement of the awards of the arbitral court, for I recall no case between great powers in which an award made has not been carried out as given or has not led to an adjustment mutually satisfactory to both parties. We may forget armed force in this and look to the reign of law and order."[9] Another alternative—that which Levinson said they had worked together upon for several days before its completion—was a new league. Said Knox:

Among the first articles of the Constitution which shall create this league shall be one which shall provide that war is thereby declared an international crime, and that any nation engaging in war except in self-defense when actually attacked shall be punished by the world as an international criminal.

Disputes involving international questions were to be adjudicated by the court; war itself and aggressive and offensive war were to be defined in the code; no nation could summon another before the court except in matters of international concern; the court was to sit in the hemisphere of the defendant nation; and "the international court shall be authorized by the League Constitution to call upon the powers signatory to enforce its decrees and awards as against unwilling states by force, economic pressure, or otherwise." Decrees against powers in the Western Hemisphere were to be enforced by countries of that hemisphere and decrees against countries of the Eastern Hemisphere were to be enforced by such means and methods as the court and the countries of that hemisphere devised.

Levinson was pleased to get his ideas coming thus from an official mouth. He would have much preferred that the Senator had confined himself to the outlawry of war, but perhaps the Senator might be induced to forget his own other peace pro-

---

[9] It was partly due to Senator Knox's influence that Levinson changed his position with regard to force. During the year following his first meeting with the Senator in February, 1919, the change started to take place, though he did not reach the extreme position against organized force as applied to states until in 1924.

posals and concentrate on the third alternative, that to which Levinson had referred in his correspondence as the "Knox plan." He told his acquaintances that Knox aimed at making the third alternative, the outlawry of war, the chief proposal. He wrote to many of his influential friends telling them of the speech and urging them to write to Knox, praising the speech in general and the proposal to outlaw war in particular. His way of commending the Senator was to wire to him, asking for a large number of copies of the speech for effective use.

Levinson's attitude toward the Covenant on March 1, 1919, was not yet one of utter irreconcilability, as he hoped that through Knox's efforts it might be amended in the Senate to include outlawry or that, perhaps, there was yet a chance that it might be rewritten in Paris. As it stood then, he considered it nothing but an "alliance plus . . . . a constitution without power and a system without machinery." It was not a "solution of the war problem but merely a compromise which kept war legal and supersovereign of the world." However, his hopes that the Covenant would be changed at Paris were never very sanguine, for, when his friend, S. S. Gregory, had written to the President suggesting that there be a straight-out declaration in the Covenant abolishing war, he declared: "The only point I am doubtful on is the willingness of President Wilson to take advice from people who know." But by March 29 he had come to the conclusion that "if war is not outlawed in the Covenant we must stay out," and by June 13 he had decided that the Covenant was irredeemably bad and should be separated from the treaty. If the Covenant were not severed from the treaty entirely, he wrote to both Knox and his secretary, Martin, then it should be amended with "your irreducible minimum" proposals: outlawry of aggressive war, codification of "real international law," creation of a court, compulsory arbitration of all disputes, universal membership in the League, and disarmament. "This will make Japan shake and France and Italy will be very little more inclined to accept these propositions that make for riddance of war."[10]

[10] Years later, in 1936, Levinson disclaimed responsibility for the failure of the Senate to approve the League. He placed the burden on those who refused to out-

Levinson had begun a campaign as thorough and intense against the League as that he had carried on for a league. He was not in the least squeamish about entering the lists in defense of the same persons whom he had been ruthlessly attacking a few months before. To the erstwhile political puppet, Henry Cabot Lodge, he sent a telegram of two hundred and thirty-six words, supplying him with arguments for a debate against President Lowell; with the editor of the "hopelessly reactionary" *Tribune* he held a conference; to Knox with whom he had so recently thought himself at odds he was writing, saying that his candidates for the Republican presidential nomination of 1920 were Knox and Robins. He watched for any and every opportunity to make active enemies of the League. To Frank A. Munsey, after an interview, he wrote: "I was exceedingly anxious to see you because I believe the New York Sun is the most influential newspaper in the United States on the League of Nations subject"; and to Herbert Croly of the *New Republic:* "You can be of great influence in backing up Senator Knox's proposals." In this campaign he had become, in his own words, a "shuttle-cock between Chicago, New York, and Washington." He raised thousands of dollars to help finance anti-League meetings and to send broadcast anti-League propaganda; and he wrote innumerable letters to friends and to enemies of the League, bolstering up the courage of the latter and attacking the Covenant bitterly to the

---

law war in the Covenant. It was his opinion that the Senate would not have "dared" to add reservations if outlawry had been included, for then it would have been a straight issue of the "riddance of war." However, the question arises as to the nature of the opposition. Was it genuine opposition to the League or was it opposition to Wilson? Lodge is reported to have said to three or four senators, "Gentlemen, we will have to change the League or we will make Woodrow Wilson king." And Taft wrote a letter to Will Hays, July 20, 1919, in which he expressed himself as highly favorable to the Covenant without any changes whatsoever, but because of a "condition of personal antagonism toward [Wilson] among Republican leaders" and "the general tendency to oppose anything that he might bring home," Taft didn't think the necessary votes for ratification could be "secured except by relieving their consciences through reassuring interpretations." Levinson may have been right in thinking that the inclusion of outlawry, assuming that was politically possible in Paris, would have secured the acceptance of the Covenant, yet one wonders if a fight would not have been made on it, regardless of what it contained.

former. He actually wrote a parody of the witch scene in *Macbeth*. In his version of it the three witches were Lloyd George, Clemenceau, and Wilson dancing around the boiling caldron, mixing up the hell broth—the peace settlement. He distributed ten thousand copies of this parody to a "probable Shakespeare-reading public." The whole peace treaty itself had become in his mind as iniquitous as the first twenty-six articles, which were the Covenant of the League of Nations. In the opinion of William Hard, all this activity was not in vain, for he wrote Levinson after one of the latter's many trips to Washington: "I certainly compliment you on the staunchness with which a certain Senator seems to be living up to various things you have told him. You have been apparently a highly successful missionary."

During all the fight on the Covenant and the treaty in the summer and fall of 1919 and spring of 1920 Levinson became more and more impressed with the necessity for the Republican party to have a substitute to offer for the "Wilson League." In July he was urging Martin to get his chief to prepare an amendment to the treaty which would provide such a substitute. If this were not done, there was danger of "our Senators weakening on the issue," which "would be fatal." But when Knox did not act, Levinson was led to believe during a visit to Washington in September that Senator Norris might prepare and submit the Republican plan for peace. He urged his friends to use their influence to this end. About the first of October, 1919, there was a rumor in the air that a compromise was going to be made between those who would ratify the treaty without "crossing a *t* or dotting an *i*" and the "mild Americans," those who would favor the treaty if a few mild reservations were made. This caused consternation in the camp of the "irreconcilables." Levinson then wrote to his friend, Milholland, urging that something be done. He thought it absolutely "vital that the Norris-Knox-Milholland-Levinson constructive program"—the outlawry of war—should be got into shape at once so that, if the suspected compromise were made, it could be incorporated in it. But it appeared that his friends in and out of the Senate were more interested in changing or destroying the handiwork of Wilson than in establishing any peace plan of their own, for nothing was done in an official way toward putting the outlawry program before the Senate or the country.

Knox had early proposed that peace be made first, and then, after the "boys" had come home, it would be plenty of time to make leagues of nations. Consequently, he had begun to push his peace resolution in December. This gave Levinson another opportunity to urge that his outlawry idea should be put forward. "I hope," he wrote to the Senator on December 27, "you are preparing an appropriate speech for the launching of a program which fits perfectly as a corollary to your peace resolution." He mentioned, as a gentle hint, the "alarming rumors" that the mild reservationists were weakening. During the holiday season he had seen Senator McCormick of Illinois and learned from him that Knox was expecting to have a "field day soon on the League of Nations." Thereupon he wrote to Dr. Holmes that he hoped this meant the adoption of the "program we agreed upon" and that he was going to Washington sooner than he expected for that reason. But again nothing happened, owing possibly to the illness of Mrs. Knox. While he was in Washington he had a conference with Senator Poindexter to try to get him converted to the outlawry of war. He gave him a copy of his peace plan. Then on January 24 he wrote to Poindexter, commending him for his fight on the League and urging him to see Knox with reference to the paper he had left with him. And again, on January 30, 1920, he was writing to Senator Knox as if the matter had never been mentioned before, praising the Senator for his statesmanship in handling the League and hoping he could soon adopt a "constructive program." "I shall not be happy," he added, "until I can spread the gospel of the Knox program for Peace." That was the only possible way of throwing out the Wilson treaty.

On the same day he had written to Senator James A. Reed, lauding him for mentioning the codification of international law in his "great speech" of January 19. He felt free to make the suggestion that an alternative to the League should be drawn up on the lines of that speech. He was being asked, he said, to collect funds to carry on the campaign against the League, and the money could be more easily raised if they had something to offer. Again on February 10 he urged Reed to have a program of his own. It "could be gotten from the last Hague Conference and Scott's points. . . . . You and I can get this up in a few days with materials before us." Then after a short conference between trains with Reed he wrote to Martin on February 10, suggesting that the stormy Missourian was ready to work out a constructive program, and to Knox two days later, suggesting that it might be a good time to make concessions, since the League issue was a political bugbear. If something were not done, the Democrats might make concessions, such as the codification within a given time of international law and the setting-up of a court, whose decisions would be binding in purely international disputes.

He next turned to Senator Borah to champion his alternative to the League of Nations. Borah had sent out a letter to the aspirants for the Republican nomination for the presidency, asking them what their stand on the League of Nations was. Governor Lowden and General Wood replied in a way which was not satisfactory from the irreconcilable viewpoint. Levinson took advantage of this occasion to write to Borah telling him that, if he could have pointed to an alternative proposal such as "Senator Knox and I have prepared," neither Lowden nor Wood could have dodged the issue. Such a constructive program issuing from the Senate he felt to be necessary for the Republican convention and the presidential campaign. Senator Reed was in favor of such a program, and he thought it likely that William Randolph Hearst was forming a third party. If this were the case, he would be quick to take an alternative which would leave the Republican party in a weak position of compromise. "If they should run Reed," he said, "I should vote for him, the first time for a Democrat." Then he suggested that he or Knox should present a plan. "You can storm the country with the kind of a proposal that you, Knox, and I have been considering." And then he played his trump card:

Let me add something which you may think I ought not to say but it does not call for an answer. It may easily be that with the League question injected, as it should be, into the campaign, you or Knox will be the only available candidate. You know my admiration and affection for Knox, but he may not, in view of his age and illness of his wife, feel himself at liberty to run. My judgment is that it is only a question of time when you will be the nominee for President, and although I would hate to see you out of the Senate in the next four years, the necessity for your running on a platform of freedom of speech and American traditions and independence may be inescapable.

This constant dinning was kept up with many of the other senators, and every turn of events was made the occasion for a new appeal. He wrote to both Knox and McCormick offering to send copies of a speech made by either of them setting forth the "constructive proposals" to "substantially every family in the United States"; and finally on May 5, 1920, Knox did make another speech, in which he went part way in announcing the "constructive program" that Levinson had been hoping for so actively and ardently. It was a partial statement of the plan quoted above.[11] Briefly it consisted of the three planks of the outlawry plan: codification of law, creation of a court, and outlawing of war.[12]

When Senator Harding was nominated instead of Senator Knox as Levinson had rather confidently hoped,[13] he set himself to the task of converting Harding to the "constructive proposal" —the outlawry of war. His first step was to find a friend of his who was also on close terms with Harding; Mr. L. W. Landman of New York was this person. At Levinson's request Landman wrote to Harding, suggesting that the Knox program be included in the acceptance speech and that Harding confer personally either with his colleague, Knox, or with Levinson. There were

[11] See above, pp. 46–47.

[12] *Congressional Record*, LIX, Part VII, 6556. This speech occupies ten pages of the *Record;* in it the resolution for peace with Germany is proposed, and the reference to outlawry occupies one paragraph.

[13] His hopes were close to realization, for Daugherty's "smoke-filled room" came near to producing a different candidate, according to Levinson's information. "I really believe if Penrose had been here Knox would have been nominated. As it was he came very near to it anyway. The convention adjourned Saturday noon to four o'clock and it was to decide between Harding and Knox. Senator Borah was very strong for Knox but they had waited too long, and in the absence of Penrose it did not seem to be possible of accomplishment. If Knox had only had some real workers the thing would have been easy" (Levinson to Emil Berolzheimer, June 14, 1920).

advantages in taking a definite stand in this matter, since the plan was favored by such an extreme irreconcilable as Senator Borah; and Levinson felt sure that with his close connections with liberal papers he could secure their support of the Republican nominee if he would take such a stand. The reply to Landman was genial and gracious, if noncommittal. Among other things, he wrote: "You may say to Mr. Levinson I shall be very glad to have his suggestions at any time and I will very greatly appreciate all that he does in my behalf." This provided Levinson with the opening he wanted. Accordingly, he went to Marion near the end of August to see the candidate and to appeal in person for him to adopt outlawry and to be wary of the pitfalls of the League. Harding's answer to the Levinson plea is indicated by the following letter:

> I have a very clear idea of what I think we can do and should do in working out an international agreement, but as a candidate of a party I do not want to make my plan an issue in a campaign which I am waging upon the theory that international agreements ought to be made a concerted agreement of the executive and the congress.
>
> I believe that the people are disposed to trust the Republican Party to find a way to an effective international agreement looking to the promotion of universal peace and a judicial arbitrament of international differences without a surrender of national independence.[14]

But still Levinson was not satisfied, and he wrote the following insistent letter, which is typical of many other letters with the arguments tempered to suit the occasion, urging that outlawry of war was the best peace plan:

> Thanks for your kind letter of the 20 ult.
>
> I think you are doing yourself a great injustice in not regarding it as your right to formulate a proposal for an international arrangement which would be subject to changes in conference with the Senate. After all, the President does initiate treaties and it is only when he autocratically resists all change and opposition from the Senate that he goes astray.
>
> Your announcement of the "outlawry of war" was used as a headliner in many newspapers throughout the country and aroused great comment. Your recent pronouncement, if correctly quoted, that you have "no constructive program for an association of nations" has been utilized by Cox, his orators and press with, I fear, considerable effectiveness. The Republican Party has always

[14] Harding to Levinson, September 20, 1920.

been characterized by constructive policies and has never been content to rest in pure negation.

This is the only weak spot in our armor; I don't see why it should not be repaired. Some simple, effective and understandable international program, even if not emanating directly from you, based upon your announcement of the "outlawry of war," ought to be made and made promptly. Take articles published in this month's "Atlantic Monthly," particularly Dr. Eliot's: They could not have been written with any plausibility or effectiveness if the Republicans had adopted and announced a constructive proposal looking to the abolition of war.

At the very least, this question should be seriously considered and disposed of one way or the other. It would be criminal negligence to take the slightest chance of Democratic success this year.[15]

However, Harding was so sure that the people were "disposed to trust the Republican Party to find a way" that he was not going to run any risks of getting into trouble by championing new-fangled ideas. The nearest he ever came to taking up the outlawry-of-war idea was in a speech on September 4, 1920, when he said: "If I catch the conscience of America, we'll lead the world to outlaw war."[16] Levinson later, in explaining what happened in 1920, said: "The Republican Party got very near to adopting this general program but somehow got shunted off."[17] But he was not stopped, "only chocked," in his efforts to get official recognition of his "constructive program." He continued to plead and exhort and to hammer for this particular thing in season and out until Senator Borah introduced it in the Senate in the form of a resolution in February, 1923.

[15] Levinson to Harding, October 1, 1920.

[16] The *New York Times* (September 4, 1920) version of it is: "We would lead the world to outlaw war."

[17] One of the events which justified Levinson in thinking the party was "near to adopting" his peace plan was the request of Senator New that he go to Knox and persuade him to make a public pronouncement on peace for the party. He went to Valley Forge to confer with Knox, who did give out a statement in which the Senator called for the "formation of a true League of Nations under which controversies may be judicially determined and the curse of war outlawed and made an international crime" (*New York Times*, October 24, 1920).

CHAPTER IV

HARDING AND THE DISARMAMENT CONFERENCE

EVERYONE was sure in 1920 that Governor Cox favored the United States entering the League; likewise, it appeared that nearly all Republican voters were sure that Senator Harding would do just exactly what each one wanted done about the League, regardless of whether that was to enter it, to stay out, or to find some other way of dealing with it. While Lowell, Taft, and Wickersham were looking forward to a speedy entrance into the League with Harding, Levinson was thankful the country would be saved from it. Shortly after the election he wrote to Senator Knox's secretary: "All I can say is that the figures are stupendous and that the little band of courageous patriots mostly in the Senate have grown into so many millions . . . . it is almost too good to be true."[1]

But no chances were to be taken. After the election had been won, the fight against the League might still be lost if the "mild Americans" got the ear of Harding. Consequently, the day after the election Levinson suggested in a letter to Borah that he and Knox should be included in the new cabinet. Borah's response was not enthusiastic as to himself, but he agreed that Knox should be the secretary of state. During December no information leaked out as to the intentions of Harding, and Levinson began to suspect that a cabinet favoring the League was being selected. This suspicion was contagious; Borah began to investigate, and in January wrote to Harding to make known his opinions "on the question of the Secretary-ship of State."[2] First came information that Knox was to have the premier place in the cabinet, then inside circles began to talk about Hughes. This shift was attributed to League pressure, and Levinson wrote to Borah that it was an

[1] Levinson to W. F. Martin, November 3, 1920.

[2] Levinson to Cora Rubin, secretary to Borah, February 23, 1923.

outrage that "Harding should be over influenced after the tremendous verdict from the people."[3] Hayes and Taft were evidently "messing up" the situation. His source of information was the president of one of the largest banks in Chicago. Both he and the banker thought Otto Kahn should have a place. He next discussed the situation with Senator McCormick. He impressed it on the Senator that if Hughes were appointed to head the cabinet it would be "the beginning of the breakup both of the administration and the party."[4] He hoped, when the Senator conveyed this to the president-elect, that Hughes would be transferred to some other post. But how had Hughes got this lead over Knox anyway, when the latter had been "practically agreed on"? The answer was "infernal league propaganda." It must be, he wrote to the editor of the *Forum*, that the "pro-leaguers" were trying to "snatch victory from defeat."[5]

"The distressed appointing power" at Marion finally "went along the lines of least resistance" in filling his cabinet positions; not Otto Kahn but Mellon was selected to be the "greatest Secretary of the Treasury since Hamilton"; and, when it was finally decided that a supporter of the League, Mr. Hughes, was to be secretary of state and another, Mr. Hoover, was also to be in the cabinet, the irreconcilables began to doubt covertly if Harding could be trusted in international matters. These private doubts found public and alarmed expression after Harding was reported to have said publicly, "after all, it matters little what flag we owe allegiance to in the North American continent."[6] Levinson inquired of Borah: "Has his desire to please gone to that dangerous length?"

It was in the interest of outlawry that Levinson watched appointments to the cabinet. Once they were made, he accepted them as accomplished facts and turned his efforts toward convincing Harding that Harding's proposed "Association of Na-

[3] Levinson to Borah, January 29, 1921.

[4] Levinson to Borah, February 3, 1921.

[5] Levinson to Payne, February 3, 1921.

[6] Levinson to Borah, April 27, 1921.

tions" had possibilities beyond serving as a red herring in the campaign. He would try to get outlawry accepted indirectly by getting it attached to the peace resolution which Senator Knox had sponsored and directly by getting it officially adopted as the President's peace policy.

Knox's peace resolution was of first importance since, until peace was restored, the pressure to ratify the Versailles agreement would be strong. Consequently, he suggested to Knox, as a means of stopping the League momentum and at the same time of restoring normal arrangements with Germany, that the substance of the following declaration should be added to the resolution:

(a) For the Western hemisphere: No colonization or conquest—this is, the Monroe Doctrine; (b) For the Eastern hemisphere: No political alliance *at any time* with any foreign power; no military alliance with any foreign power *in time of peace;* and the ever readiness of the young giant of the West to make an alliance for conference and defense with foreign nations representing the cause of justice and right whenever another powerful nation runs "amuck."[7]

This "greatest step in the preservation of peace ever made," would redeem the promise of the party, as well as prevent "any treaty folly." When Borah showed signs of being more interested in disarmament than in the peace resolution, he was urged to work with Knox first; the way would then be open for his own projects. "Keep your artillery in shape," Levinson pleaded, "but keep it until after the Knox resolution is passed."[8]

To get outlawry officially adopted by the President, he worked out a "condensed statement of the basic conception of President Harding's 'Association of Nations,'" which he planned to have taken to the White House. It was:

A meeting of the nations to be called, either as the delayed Third Hague Conference, or otherwise, or a special association, to

a) Codify international law;
b) Abolish the institution of war and outlaw it by making it a crime punishable as murder under the law of nations;
c) Create a permanent international court for the settlement of international

[7] Levinson to Knox, April 7, 1921.

[8] Levinson to Borah, April 13, 1921.

disputes, which court shall possess inherent and specified jurisdiction over all the nations, with power to summon them in and hear and decide the controversies.[9]

With this condensed statement went a longer one explaining it.

He urged the propaganda value of basing any peace move on the phrase "outlawry of war" and the advantage to the administration of putting itself at the head of such a popular movement. If the President would adopt it,

> I will undertake to organize the people of this country, both Pro-League and Anti-League of Nations factions, in favor of it. I could get up a group of perhaps fifty or a hundred speakers and connect with various clubs, particularly Women's Clubs, chambers of commerce, Rotary, Kiwanis, etc. . . . . I can get the plan approved by such widely divergent classes as officials of the League to Enforce Peace and the "irreconcilable" group of Senators to prove its worth for harmony on fundamentals.[10]

He doubted if anything would come of this, "but I thought," he explained, "I would try a homeopathic dose of basic simplicity." Nothing did come from it; but far more stringent, allopathic doses were administered in connection with the disarmament conference.

Harding, under the goading of Borah, or in spite of it, was set on making his contribution to peace by securing a reduction of armaments. The disarmament conference would provide a good opportunity for Levinson to focus attention on outlawry. A threefold plan worked itself out. The primary object was to sell the idea to Harding; but, in view of Harding's absorption with the conference, Levinson decided the best way of pushing outlawry was to help organize public support for the conference. A liberal amount of outlawry would be infused into this campaign, but the President could not help being more friendly to him if he helped the President roll some logs.[11] Once the campaign got well under way, Harding could be drawn into it for one speech and, perhaps, be induced to make a statement indorsing the outlawry of war

[9] Levinson to Jane Addams, May 21, 1921.

[10] Levinson to Landman, April 29, 1921.

[11] It may be added parenthetically that he soon turned this campaign into more of an attempt to capture the conference than to support it. This will be dealt with later.

specifically, since he had used the magic phrase during the presidential campaign. Levinson's second object was to get the proper kind of delegates chosen to represent the United States at the conference; his third, to induce the President to pledge the United States to outlawry in the address at the formal opening of the conference.

The women's organizations of the country were beginning a big drive in support of the conference. Levinson got in touch with Mrs. James Morrison to help her and her group to organize a "monster meeting" of women in Chicago. Plans were made to give it the widest publicity; delegates were to come from far and wide; the railroads were to be induced to arrange excursions; and Harding was to be persuaded to come for the opening address. Mrs. Morrison was sent to Washington to secure the President. Levinson had been in communication with Attorney-General Daugherty, urging him to lend a hand. This bosom friend of the President appeared to be enthusiastic; he visioned his chief holding the public spellbound with outlawry orations. In spite of this elaborate preparation Mrs. Morrison failed to persuade the President to address the meeting, though she did extract some vague promises.

Meantime Levinson had started to bombard the President and others with letters emphasizing the advantages of having Borah, "the author of the movement," and Knox as delegates. Great was his satisfaction when it seemed that they were to be included. But greater was his disappointment when neither was chosen. It was the "greatest negative humiliation of Knox's career,"[12] and the omission of "the mover of the resolution" was "unprecedented." Sometime later Levinson learned the reported cause for the apparent slight to the two senators. According to his oral report to the author, the English had asked Ambassador Harvey who would be on the delegation. He had said: "Of course, the mover of the resolution, Senator Borah," to which the astonished reply was: "What! That radical!" And when Harvey suggested Knox, he received the still less encouraging reply: "He is too pigheaded; we can't do anything with him." If this

[12] Levinson to Borah, September 13, 1921.

[61]

was true, it was English preference plus "New York influence" that upset Levinson's plans.

However, at the time he attributed the omission of the senators to the machinations of the secretary of state.[13] Hughes appeared to be in full command of the situation, for he had found Seward's prophecy fulfilled: the head of the Cabinet table had become the place where the secretary of state sat. Levinson's hopes sank with Hughes's elevation. He thought "Senator Borah's original idea of a simple reduction of naval armaments by the three commanding powers was a stroke of genius"; but "Secretary Hughes, who is riding rough shod over Borah, has to my mind seriously jeopardized the work and result of the meeting by injecting questions of the Far East and the Pacific which will precipitate diplomatic clashes, jockeying and

[13] Apart from the influences operating to prevent Borah from serving on the American delegation, it would seem that the purpose and scope of the conference were changed so radically from what he had proposed as to raise a question of his usefulness as a delegate. His settled conviction appeared to be that the United States, Great Britain, and Japan should enter "into an understanding agreement by which the naval expenditures and building program of each of the said Governments . . . . shall be substantially reduced annually during the next five years . . . ." (*U.S. Statutes at Large*, XLII, Part I [67th Cong.], 141). He first introduced a resolution on December 14, 1920, calling for this simple tripartite conference, which was to be concerned only with naval reductions; and again on April 13, 1921, and on May 4, he offered it as an amendment to the naval appropriation bill. The bill with this amendment was approved July 12, 1921 (*ibid.*). Harding was reported as being opposed to this amendment (C. O. Johnson, *Borah of Idaho* [New York: Longmans, Green & Co., 1936], p. 266); and apparently to avoid being committed morally by it to the single consideration of naval armaments, the administration through the State Department issued the statement on July 10 that Great Britain, France, Italy, and Japan had been "approached with informal but definite inquiries." Thus the number of nations was extended beyond Borah's plan; and by this time the purpose of the conference had been extended to include Pacific and far eastern questions and Harding's association of nations, in addition to the limitation of naval armament (Quincy Wright, "Washington Disarmament Conference," *Minnesota Law Review*, March, 1922, p. 279). Professor Wright, who was in Washington during the autumn of 1921 serving as a technical adviser to the Navy Department on questions pertaining to the conference, is of the opinion that the objects of the conference were so differently understood by the administration and Borah, because of the inclusion of matters other than the limitation of naval disarmament, that only with difficulty could the Senator have served officially on the United States delegation.

compromises."[14] "The diplomatic dickerings" would, as usual, end in nullifying the expectations of "the good people."[15]

But he did have hopes that Harding would either make outlawry of war a part of the conference agenda or inject it into the conference atmosphere. Mrs. James Morrison had received a "fairly good promise" for a commitment by the President in January; and she reported that there was a good chance of getting him to announce his acceptance of outlawry in a keynote speech, for "many influential people" were urging him to do so. Levinson was "on tiptoes with interest" and not far from the toes of Harding's friends.

This is a sample of one of his allopathic doses, which he "tried" upon Attorney-General Daugherty:

> I understand the President will deliver the keynote speech at the virtual opening of the conference on November 12th. If he will incorporate in his speech the general idea of the outlawry of war and thereby pre-empt that proposition, it will enable us to manage not only the Chicago meeting, but all further auxiliary meetings in a most satisfactory way all around. Unless he so pre-empts this Outlawry proposal (which is so basic and so easily understood and gripped by the minds of both women and men) it is certain to be snapped up by Lloyd George or some other shrewd statesman and the effort to make [Harding] the champion of this movement will be thereby lost.[16]

And to Martin, the former secretary of the now deceased Knox, who was close to Daugherty in the Department of Justice, he administered a dose still stronger:

> If only the President will re-announce and advocate this proposition in his forth coming speech to the conference, the foundation will be solidly laid for future activities. If he does not do it and the opportunity passes, it will probably never come again. Wilson lost his opportunity at Versailles but Harding should not miss his now. The failure of one is the stepping stone to higher things by the other. But he must take time by the forelock.[17]

But the President did not "take time by the forelock," and his advisers turned down other "plain facts" urged in many direct conversations "by a plain person."

[14] Levinson to Gordon, October 7, 1921.
[15] Levinson to Von Behren, November 26, 1921.
[16] Levinson to Daugherty, November 5, 1921.
[17] Levinson to Martin, November 5, 1921.

Levinson then turned to the leading foreign delegations to the disarmament conference. He was not able to make direct personal contact with any one of importance in the British delegation. Horace J. Bridges, an Englishman living in Chicago, wrote to Balfour in his behalf. The only response was a telegram of acknowledgment.

With the French he was more successful. During a call at the French Embassy in Washington, he had a two-hour conference with a M. Casenave, who was the financial adviser to the French delegation. He tried to explain the idea of outlawry and he argued the advantages to France of adopting the outlawry program. In the first place, it would throw confusion into the camp of her enemies. What France really wanted was security. There was no selfish motive in insistence on large armaments as long as war was legal. France could say to the world, "outlaw war, demolish the institution and thus give us security, or let us keep our armaments so that we can defend ourselves."[18] This would refute the charges of imperialism and militarism which were being made; and, secondly, French prestige, which had been damaged during the course of the conference, would be restored. Casenave expressed himself as favorable to this, but Levinson went away doubting if the Frenchman really understood,[19]

first, because the whole thing is probably new to him, and not being a lawyer it would probably take him somewhat longer, especially with his mind full of other things. Secondly, the political situation in France is now so confusing that it would be difficult to expect a representative of the old regime several thousand miles away to go into details in a matter of this kind.[20]

After his return from Washington, Mrs. Langworthy, the secretary of his Committee for the Outlawry of War, which had been organized less than a month before, wrote a letter in line with Levinson's arguments at the Embassy and also sent a telegram to Casenave, urging that some statement be made by the French

[18] Levinson to Eliot, January 31, 1922.

[19] This conversation was significant, because it was the first connection which Levinson had with French officials and because shortly a multilateral treaty for the outlawry of war was mentioned—a treaty not unlike the peace pact, see below, chap. xiii and Appen. F.

[20] Levinson to Hard, January 20, 1922.

in favor of outlawry. Such a pronouncement, she said, "would have an electric effect in this country."[21] Three days later a dispatch appeared in the *Chicago Daily News* which represented the French as favoring outlawry. Said the French, as quoted by the dispatch:

You want to outlaw the submarine and poison gas. We do not object. What we want however to get rid of is not this or that particular atrocity but the one great atrocity namely war itself. What France wants is to outlaw war, not this or that phase of war.[22]

Levinson immediately sent a long telegram, urging the French to repeat this statement and address it to the American people. He and his committee would have it reprinted and distributed widely. This would refute the charges of imperialism and militarism made against France and also "restore her to the pinnacle of admiration and affection which she held with the American people all through the war. France would thus be the first nation to propose to the world a universal treaty or law by which war would be made criminal and outlawed."[23] At the same time he approached William Hard to take up the French statement in his articles which were widely published in the daily press. Harding, from his use of the phrase in the campaign, could be linked with the French as desiring outlawry of war. France could be put in a better position by defending her sincerity in "demanding security either by large arms or by abolition of [the] war system." Hard replied:

Our French friends were absolutely not in earnest in the matter. They would not go to the point at which they were willing to make any statement that would really bind them to the idea. They were concerned only to use it as a sort of oratorical flourish in some manner as: If war could be abolished, which of course we favor, we would behave quite different from how we are behaving now but now of course we have to behave as we do.[24]

The French statement was Levinson's signal to start another campaign to induce the Harding administration to adopt outlawry. It was futile, he argued, at that point to try to regulate the

[21] Langworthy to Levinson, January 6, 1922.
[22] Levinson to Casenave, January 10, 1922.
[23] *Ibid.*   [24] Hard to Levinson, April 6, 1922.

weapons of war, while leaving war legal. The thing to do was to get rid of war; the rules of fighting, gas, and submarines would no longer be a problem when there was no longer any use for them.

He had published and broadcast his *Plan To Outlaw War* in December. Copies were sent to all the delegations at Washington. Follow-up work had been done to get comment from responsible persons and insure that the pamphlet was read.[25] It was on the basis of this and his conversation with Casenave that the French had made the statement about outlawry, and it was on the basis of this statement and the letter of acknowledgment which he received from the Japanese delegation that he made a futile attempt to secure an acceptance of outlawry in that quarter. If "your country would join with France in this demand, it would refute the charges of imperialism being made against your country and France," he wrote to Major General Haraguchi, military attaché of the Japanese Embassy.

At the beginning of the disarmament conference, Levinson's object had been to get outlawry adopted and publicized by the United States or, failing that, then by some other state. As one means of doing this he started a campaign of public education. Once started, this campaign spread so rapidly that by the end of the conference its gargantuan proportions overshadowed his failure to gain anything substantial at Washington. We must now trace its course.[26]

[25] This activity will be discussed in more detail below, pp. 73 ff.

[26] The treaty results of the conference were not to Levinson's liking (see Levinson's letters to Eliot, April 8, 1922, and to Holmes, February 11, 1922). He appeared then to share the view which Borah had always held, namely, that arms could be dealt with separately from political matters, if indeed the latter were ever dealt with at all (see above, p. 62, n. 13). Levinson then agreed (see above, pp. 62f.). Levinson later took a different position, e.g., he worked long and hard to get a solution of the war-debt tangle as a necessary foundation of peace. The sterility of subsequent disarmament conferences, when attempts were made to stack arms without corresponding political arrangements, compared to the success of the Washington conference is rather conclusive testimony of the necessity for political arrangements as a basis for disarmament. It would seem to be in line with human experience that men set up means of safeguarding themselves without arms and then disarm rather than to throw away their arms first, as Senator Borah had proposed for the nations, and later to make other arrangements if necessary.

CHAPTER V

SPREADING THE GOSPEL OF OUTLAWRY IN THE HOMELAND

Before the Washington disarmament conference was well under way, Levinson had "almost reached the conclusion, particularly noting the forecast . . . . of a quadruple alliance, that it is impossible to get governments as at present constituted to take any interest in the outlawry of war. In the end the appeals will have to be made to the peoples of the various countries and through them by new governmental officials or otherwise, to compel the adoption of a policy that amounts to the abolition of warfare."[1]

The necessity of making appeals to the people was not a new idea with him; he had planned and to some extent carried out numerous appeals of one sort or another, in 1915 to stop the war, in 1918 to get outlawry made a part of the peace aims, in 1919 to generate sentiment for a league of nations, and in 1920 against the League. In the summer and fall of 1921 he had helped to win popular support for the disarmament conference. During these campaigns he had felt the need of something definite and concrete around which opinion might be organized. It was to meet this need for a "constructive plan" that he decided to prepare a pamphlet which would contain the outlawry-of-war program.

This conclusion was justified also by the results of several previous campaigns undertaken to furnish various officials with an alternative to the League of Nations. In 1919, after conferring with Knox, he had produced a short plan in the Senator's office; he had tried to get Harding to use this plan in the campaign of 1920, and he was trying again to get him to sponsor it for the disarmament conference. In 1919, after revising it, he had put the plan into the hands of Attorney-General Daugherty and presented it to the group with whom he was working to organize

[1] Levinson to Hard, December 10, 1921.

[67]

women's groups to support the disarmament conference. Suggestions were now made to him that it be published "in a very wide way."[2]

The pamphlet as published contained the following: (1) An introduction signed by Levinson's newly formed Committee for the Outlawry of War. (2) A list of quotations, three from Harding, in which he used the word "outlaw"; one from Knox, in which he had stated the three main points of the outlawry plan— viz., outlawing of war, codification of international law, and the setting-up of an international court; one from Lloyd George, in which he had used the word "outlaw," and one from Foch in which he had used the word "crime" in connection with war. (3) A foreword by each of the following: Professor John Dewey, Raymond Robins, and E. O. Brown, a justice on the federal bench in Chicago. (4) A restatement of the plan to outlaw war which had been formulated in 1919 with the assistance of Knox and which was now elaborated to twelve planks instead of the original ten. The chief changes were: (a) judicial means of settlement were emphasized to the exclusion of political; (b) the basis for the doctrine of nonrecognition was included; (c) war of any kind was to be declared a crime, whereas in the first plan only aggressive war was to be put under the ban; and (d) a citizen soldiery on the Swiss model was included for defense. (5) A detailed analysis of the plan by Levinson himself.

While the pamphlet was being prepared, plans for its widest possible distribution were being considered. It was agreed that it would have a much better reception if it should appear as coming from an organization rather than from a single individual. For the same reason a foreword of indorsement from each of a number of prominent persons seemed admissible, and likewise the citizen soldiery idea on the "Swiss model" was included. All this is typical of Levinson's procedure.

In view of the fact that the organization formed at this time was to provide the stage setting for so many of his activities during the ensuing years and that his eagerness for the forewords to his

[2] Levinson to Holmes, November 11, 1921.

pamphlet and his inclusion of the Swiss soldiery proposal were typical of his method, it is worth while to examine these matters in some detail.

He had conferred with a number of people in October, 1921, and before, to make plans with regard to the women's disarmament activity. On the twenty-fifth he wrote to Mrs. James Morrison: "I really believe that if several of us could devote an evening to this matter and develop and think it out, it would be reciprocally helpful." After a dinner party in Levinson's home, December 9, 1921, the American Committee for the Outlawry of War was organized. This fact was not for publication, just yet, he wrote to Dr. Holmes. "Confidentially we have organized. They insisted on me being made chairman. . . . ." At this meeting all the persons in attendance were "brought into unanimous accord as to the soundness of the theory and the necessity for its promulgation world wide."

The personnel of the committee consisted of S. O. Levinson, chairman, Mrs. B. F. Langworthy, secretary, Margaret Dreier Robins, F. R. Moulton, Raymond Robins, E. O. Brown, Mrs. W. S. Hefferan, Mrs. A. G. Becker, J. M. Artman, M. F. Goodman, and Mrs. Russell Tyson.

Goodman was elected treasurer at an early meeting. The seriousness with which he undertook his duties of raising money among his and Levinson's acquaintances and the gravity with which contributions were made is shown by the following letters:

DEAR HARRY:

Here is a copy of [a] letter written Milton S. Florsheim and Henry X. Strauss. If you will send me your check for $100.00 it will be very much appreciated and it will avoid the necessity of listening to us for a half hour.

Yours very truly,[3]

And the answer:

DEAR MILT:

Your argument appeals to me—especially if Sol was coming with you.

Gratefully,

[3] Goodman to Stern, April 14, 1922.

[69]

Another answer, from A. G. Becker:

> Here is my check for $250.00 to help advertise Mr. S. O. Levinson. I always thought he was able to advertise himself. I did not think the time would ever come to pass when we would have to help him. Please understand that this is not sent willingly. It is done for Outlawing War at home.

These early attempts to make the committee serve a real purpose—that of raising money—soon failed, which is not surprising in view of the vigor with which Levinson went at other things and the lack of energy he exhibited in getting contributions for his own cause. He began to pay more than 95 per cent of the expense of the campaign out of his own pocket, and he continued to do so even when it was costing upward of fifteen thousand dollars annually.[4]

Several members of the committee—some who were in it at its formation, like Mrs. Langworthy, Raymond Robins, and F. R. Moulton, and others who became members of it at a later date, like Horace J. Bridges, Francis X. Bush, and William B. Hale—testified that the committee never performed any real function except to provide a stage for the chairman. When he wrote letters to strangers, as he did many times daily, it lent authority for him to sign his name as chairman of the American Committee for the Outlawry of War, and it appeared less presumptuous to distribute the millions of pieces of literature which were broadcast during the next few years or to bargain for terms with other peace groups in the name of the committee than for one man to do all these things on his own responsibility. There was still another advantage in having a committee. If some member of the outlawry group had to travel in the interest of the cause and could ill afford to pay his own traveling expenses, he could submit a bill to the American Committee for the Outlawry of War with more grace and dignity than to Salmon O. Levinson, even if the money

---

[4] This estimate is based upon the references in letters in which checks for traveling expenses or publication of literature, etc., were sent to other persons. The figure does not include any money for Levinson's traveling, communication, secretarial, or other direct expenses. When I asked as to the substantial correctness of this estimate, he dismissed the matter with the comment that no one would ever know what outlawry had cost him.

did come out of the same pocket. And such expense items were not infrequent.

One could hardly have a better illustration of Levinson's desire to secure the prestige of great names for his proposal than his effort to get them on this pamphlet. Those whom he asked to write a foreword for his plan were Justice John H. Clarke, Professor John Dewey, Colonel Raymond Robins, Senator Borah, Mr. Otto Kahn, Justice Brown, Mrs. James W. Morrison, Assistant Attorney-General Martin (secretary to Knox until the death of the Senator), and President Emeritus Charles W. Eliot. It finally turned out that he used only three contributions—those of Brown, Robins, and Dewey—but the arguments which he used with Borah and Eliot show how important he thought them. Several letters went to Borah, each one increasing the pressure. There were eleven reasons cited in one letter why the Senator should comply with the request. Finally, after another letter and telephone talk, by which he extracted a "general commitment in principle," he agreed not to press for a foreword if there were a likelihood of involving the Senator in a large amount of correspondence and study, for which he would not at that moment have the time.

With Eliot, Levinson was, if possible, still more insistent. He was determined to get his approval, and early in November he had paid him a visit at Cambridge. A few days later he wrote his thanks for the two-hour talk he had had and declared: "I believe we have succeeded in blending our views, at least substantially." This blend involved more particularly the inclusion of Eliot's pet project, "the Swiss model of citizen soldiery." This was one of the last times that Levinson provided for the use of organized force as between nations; consequently, when persons began to object to it, he was more than glad to call on Eliot to defend it, for, after all, it was not his own project. In fact, he believed in it less and less. He would drop the citizen-soldiery idea if Eliot would not defend it. But he would still try for Eliot's indorsement. His next suggestion was that Eliot should write an article, to be published in the Chicago papers, showing how the program could be carried out. And when some of his close friends, like Miss Hauser of the National League of Women Voters, attacked it, he wrote to Eliot, "Here is your irresistible opening to aid our cause by protecting your own. I hope you will be able to write an article either for the Nation or some other paper and I will expect you to support the pamphlet generally as much as you consistently can."

But the old gentleman wrote a letter in his own hand with his broad-pointed pen refusing to move. He lamented the "downfall into timidity and selfishness" which the country had suffered in 1920. The League of Nations, he thought, was the way out, not the outlawry of war. Well might Levinson confess to Holmes after a visit to Cambridge: "I have never been able to feel sure of his aid in this matter after I leave his august presence." But he kept on pressing Eliot for a foreword, and not until his plan was on the way to the printer did he reluctantly give up.

It was decided to start distributing the *Plan To Outlaw War* on December 25, 1921, thus "making the whole thing a Xmas affair." According to one of the members of his committee, he was genuinely and deeply moved by the significance of this gift of peace to a war-weary world. For it was his belief that peace is the quintessence of the Christmas spirit.

The first release of the *Plan* went to all the members of the delegations to the disarmament conference—eleven hundred of them—and to the newspaper correspondents; then came the turn of the congressmen, the Cabinet, government officials, federal judges, governors, university and college teachers, librarians, ministers, lawyers, chambers of commerce, and women's societies. Later on, public school teachers and farmers were included among the recipients, Senator Capper's mailing list being used for these. Lists of merchants, businessmen, and heads of manufacturing concerns were found and covered in the distribution. Publishers, editors of magazines, small country newspapers and religious periodicals, peace organizations, and other propaganda groups, such as the Anti-saloon League, were furnished with single copies of the *Plan* for individual use and with parcels of it for distribution to interested persons. Mrs. Robins distributed a few of them to key women in Europe. A number were sent to Central and South America, Japan, and Europe.

The pamphlet was first privately printed and mailed out, and a good start on this wholesale broadcast was made with the privately printed edition. In January, 1922, Borah offered it for printing in the *Congressional Record*.[5] After that it was printed by the Government Printing Office at Levinson's expense. Many copies were sent out under the franks of Borah and Capper. By the end of February, 1922, two months after the pamphlet had been released, two hundred and fifty thousand had been distributed; and a steady stream, though in a diminished volume, was maintained for more than a year. Later other materials were added, and it was again put into the *Congressional Record*.[6] It is likely that more than a million copies of the *Plan* in various reprints were distributed.

Levinson was not content with simply sowing the seed and letting it lie on stony ground or fertile soil, to perish or grow wherever it fell. He furnished the sunlight of personal interest to help it to bring forth fruit. He persuaded the advertising firm which was to address and mail the pamphlet to write to two hundred and fifty important newspapers, urging publication of the pamphlet because of its news value and because of the intrinsic merit of the principle involved. He followed this initial effort with hundreds of personal letters to encourage the asking of questions to clear up doubtful points and to stimulate the voicing of opposition or approval.

One example of the way he pushed for comment and met opposition is found in his letter to Professor Reeves of the University of Michigan:

Perhaps I should add we have had more adverse comment from the University of Michigan than from any other of the scores of universities that have favored us with their reactions. This is an additional reason why I should like to hear from you at length.[7]

One man returned the pamphlet with "criminal childishness" written across it; another copy had written across it in large blue pencil: "Why not join the League of Nations whose primary pur-

---

[5] January 19, 1922, p. 1384.

[6] *Senate Doc. 115* (67th Cong., 2d sess.).   [7] January 17, 1923.

pose is to abolish war?" One person wrote to him anonymously: "Doctor Levinson, you are a damn fool," which called forth the comment, "I always knew I was a damn fool, but this is the first time I ever knew I was a doctor." A Dr. DeGaris from Mississippi inquired: "Why not codify federal laws, compelling all men to be honest men?" A long letter of explanation went to this gentleman, who answered saying that the greatest weakness in the plan was the refusal to use force. "If your laws must remain only . . . . a 'priest-like task of pure ablution round earth's human shores' then pardon me if I seem to smile." Another typical Levinson letter, three pages of single-spaced, narrow-margined argument, was the answer. It started with "I knew that further discussion would dissipate most if not all of our difference. In the main, I agree with your statements." DeGaris was for the League, so was Levinson—if it would incorporate outlawry. No factor which could be taken advantage of to establish a favorable mental attitude on the part of his correspondents did he miss. To a Miss Della Lehman, student in Manchester College in Indiana, he wrote discussing her criticism and then closed his letter with "As I was born in Indiana I have a sentimental interest in having the largest number of adherents in my home state." But if persons whom he regarded as influential in their respective communities did not comment or merely acknowledged the receipt of the pamphlet, they would probably receive a polite reminder, such as:

I have been expecting a further and more comprehensive critique of the pamphlet as promised which I still await.

or

This is to remind you of the promise contained in your letter . . . . to give our pamphlet on Outlawry of War comprehensive study and, I take it, your comprehensive criticism of it.

He answered the letters of all, high and low. Jacob Gingerich, teacher in an elementary school in Johnstown, Pennsylvania, wrote to him for material which was sent; he had a question, and there was another two-page answer. Two high-school boys were going to take part in an "important" debate and wrote asking him to send them material and explain how they could answer a certain argument about the League. The million-dollar lawyer on one of the world's greatest financial streets sent the material and wrote a long letter showing how various other arguments also could be answered, even when the answers were against his own views on the subject. And he wound up by offering to give them more information if they needed it!

Not only did he answer the letters addressed to himself, but he also answered great batches of similar letters which were forwarded to him from Borah's office. He suggested to Capper that if he were receiving such letters they be forwarded to Chicago for the same purpose.

On one occasion, when the pamphlet first began to go out, he thought a "broad side of criticism" might perhaps be leveled at his idea, and he suggested to Dewey: "I might have to call upon your powerful talent in reply." Though Dewey and others did engage in debate for him later, the answers were the result not of their "powerful talents" but of his own.

When people expressed approval of the outlawry of war, he asked them to write to their senators and representatives; and, also, frequently he suggested that they should write to Borah and Harding as well, the latter "already being committed in principle to it."

He continually sought statements of approval which could be used to show the growth of the movement, so that he could attract the sort of people who like to board bandwagons. For example, he asked Hugh S. Magill to write a letter of recommendation "which we could send out" or even a "few quotable words." He never failed to make the most of any news of some important person's using the term "outlawry" or indorsing his movement or giving it any encouragement, however trifling. He had met Justice Florence Allen early in 1922. She had become enthusiastic over outlawry almost immediately and started to speak for it.[8]

---

[8] Justice Allen early formulated an epigrammatic summary of outlawry which Levinson prized. It was: "Outlawry merely asks nations to renounce the right to do wrong."

Various senators were informed of her speaking engagements and of the receptions she got. In March, Dewey was apprised of the fact that "seven colleges had seen fit to use our pamphlet as a textbook in History and International Relations." Later in March he reported to Assistant Attorney-General Martin that his committee had received favorable responses from seventy-five universities and from both supporters of the League and opponents of it; that the leagues of women voters in Illinois and New York had adopted outlawry resolutions and in New Jersey and Wisconsin were asking for more information. Approval of outlawry was almost unanimous, for forty-nine out of fifty replies were friendly: "What pleases me more than anything else is the answers from the 'plain people' who say that it is the first proposal that they have been able to understand in terms of human experience."

A third means of spreading the gospel, in addition to the broadcast of literature and the writing of letters, was personal contact with important people. Persons in Chicago, Cleveland, New York, Boston, Washington, and other cities were visited for an eye-to-eye talk.

A fourth means was speaking. Levinson did not himself speak often. He felt the necessity of conserving his strength for the work behind the stage, but many of his converts spoke. Justice Allen has already been referred to. Ministers began to preach outlawry —ministers he had talked and written to and ministers he had never heard of. Shortly after his Christmas pamphlet of 1922 was broadcast, he began to get clippings about sermons on outlawry from a clipping bureau. To every such minister and later to any speaker who dealt with the subject he always wrote expressing an interest in his address and asking for a copy of it or, if it was not in manuscript form, for an outline.

The chief speaker for the cause was Raymond Robins—a remarkable man and one who played an important part in the outlawry-of-war movement from 1921 until after the ratification of the Pact of Paris in 1929. He was born in New York; as a boy he mined coal in Kentucky; when gold was discovered in the Yukon he joined the rush. In the "bitter night of the silent north," he "digged" enough "clean gold with [his] two hands" to free him from the necessity of manual labor. His life continues to read like a vivid page from a fairy tale. A political free lance and fluent orator, a friend of the elder Roosevelt, a Protestant missionary to "heathen lands," a private in the First World War (lieutenant colonel at the end), a member of the Red Cross Commission to Russia, a friend and adviser and admirer of Lenin, a social "uplifter," an enemy of political corruption—he was all these. In a Chicago political campaign he was slugged and left in the gutter for dead. He was a friend of Johnson, Borah, Harding, Coolidge, and Hoover. He had lived in a congested tenement district in order to understand its inhabitants. Finally, he had made Levinson's acquaintance and become an enthusiast for the outlawry of war. In January, 1922, he started a speaking campaign, which took him into nearly every state of the Union.

His power as a speaker seemed almost incredible. Audiences stood and cheered for ten minutes at the end of his speeches. After one such he reported "the Lord was with me and the juice flowed." He spoke to all kinds of audiences. Teachers' institutes, businessmen's luncheon clubs, leagues of women voters, religious gatherings, labor groups, farm organizations, political committees—these and many others heard him gladly preach the gospel of outlawry, of which Levinson was the prophet.

Sometimes out of one audience as many as twenty people would write to Levinson asking for literature. A sample letter is: "We have had the great pleasure of hearing Raymond Robins on Outlawry of War. We were profoundly impressed and want some literature. If there is anything women's clubs can do we want to know."[9] Letters came to Levinson from libraries in the cities where Robins had spoken, asking for more pamphlets. He left a trail of resolutions behind him; for example, from the War Mothers of Marion County (Indianapolis) came this:

Resolved: They enlist in this great . . . . the genuine "war to end war," by spoken word, written letters and resolution, uniting to outlaw war, thus liberating mankind from the agelong thraldom of the sword and proving that the countless dead upon the battle fields of the great war did not die in vain.

[9] January 22, 1923.

[77]

Half of the gifted colonel's value lay in his private oratory. He talked in private as eloquently, fluently, and persuasively as he spoke from the platform. And, wherever he went, he was sought out by the chief intellectual, social, financial, and political lights. Before and after the public speech there were long talks in which the listeners hung on his words and not a few of them came away convicted. William Hard attributed a great deal of the rapid spread of outlawry to this high-powered private oratory of Raymond Robins.[10] Most certainly Coolidge was one who knew its persuasive quality.

It must be added that part of Robins' effectiveness in spreading outlawry may have been due to the state of the popular mind. One gets the impression from the reports he sent to Levinson that the people quite generally had a feeling of frustration. The country had fought a war to end war; the United States had failed to go into the League; they—the people who attended meetings in the evenings and thought about things of that kind as a sort of relaxation from the hard grind of trying to earn a living—were hungry for something concrete. Here it was: outlaw war! It cost nothing, it involved no danger of entangling alliances or of being tricked by Old World schemes, no sending our boys to die on foreign soil, and it would get rid of war.[11] "It appeals to the average mind more quickly than any other issue I have discussed in twenty-five years," Robins wrote to his "Captain General."

However, the smooth-tongued colonel had his trials. Speaking of his missionary journey, "I know the name," he declared, "of every bed bug in four states, and have eaten worse food and traveled in more dirt and spoken to more hot, tired audiences than ever before in my young life." But the cause was worth to him all it cost. And he concluded: "I am ready to enlist with you for three years and give all my time. . . . ."

[10] William Hard, "The Nonstop Peace Advocate," *World's Work*, March, 1929, p. 76.

[11] As to the distinction between the popular version of outlawry as the end of the use of all force and Levinson's conception of the delegalization of war see below, pp. 185 f. and 190–93.

The gospel was making converts. A superintendent in a California school system wanted to put the literature in all his schools. At Seattle, Washington:

> The Shipyard Laborers, Riggers and Fasteners of local 38-A-2 of the A.F. of L. at their regular meeting held Friday night February 24, 1922, unanimously indorsed the principle and substance of your pamphlet, Outlawry of War. If any further action is deemed of value please inform me.

In July, 1922, Mr. Edward Cummings, general secretary of the World Peace Foundation, wrote for more literature. He explained:

> I am sending the last of our supply to some people at the International Institute of Politics at Williamstown, with whom I have just been discussing the project. . . . . I have been gratified with the enthusiasm with which some important organizations have endorsed the plan for the outlawry of war.[12]

Conventions were adopting outlawry resolutions. Among these conventions were the National League of Women Voters, the Young Women's Christian Associations, the Women's League for Peace and Freedom, the National Association of Parents and Teachers, and the International Trade Women's League. Other groups which indorsed outlawry were the National Committee for Reduction of Armaments, the Federal Council of Churches of Christ in America; and the American Legion put it in the agenda of its national convention.[13] This all happened within seven months after the Christmas pamphlet had been released.

In November Levinson wrote to his son, Horace:

> The greatest accession we have had recently is that of 9,000 of the Massachusetts aristocrats, members of the League to Enforce Peace, etc., headed by President Lowell of Harvard. On November 1st they petitioned President Harding to call a Convention of the Nations "to outlaw war as an institution and to codify international law. . . . ."

News items about the movement began to appear in the daily press. The *Chicago Herald and Examiner* for February 17, 1922, published a cartoon depicting the idea of outlawry. There were two pictures: the first was of Mars standing with drawn sword in

---

[12] Cummings to Borah, July 21, 1922.

[13] Levinson to Cummings, January 7, 1922.

a field of dead men, with the caption: "This is legal." The other presented an assassin in a mask with his victim lying near and the caption: "This is not legal—What is the difference?" The subject matter and title for the cartoon were inspired by Arthur Brisbane. It was accompanied by a Brisbane editorial indorsing outlawry. One of Levinson's converts in the press world would ask the President questions about outlawry in the semi-weekly conferences; Levinson had helped to prepare those questions before they were asked.

A latter-day Hebrew prophet was again calling on a people to "learn war no more" and "many were they who believed."

CHAPTER VI

THE START OF THE CONQUEST OF THE UNCONQUERABLE BORAH

IN FEBRUARY, 1919, Levinson went to Washington to put pressure on Republican senators to line them up for a league. But, instead of conquering the senators, he joined them.[1] He learned to know Knox, who incorporated a little of the outlawry doctrine in a speech in the Senate. It was then that Levinson realized the value of having a sounding board in that body. He continued to feed his ideas to Knox until the latter died, in the fall of 1921. After failing to commit either the administration or the disarmament conference to outlawry, he turned back to his earlier idea of finding a voice in the "greatest deliberative body in the world." Borah, the "Lone Wolf," was the man he selected to be his spokesman.

He first met Borah in December, 1919, when he came into Knox's office, where he read and commented on the "Knox-Levinson" plan as being "masterly." From that time on Levinson held up his hands in the fight against the League, supported him for the vice-presidency in 1920 and for a place in the Cabinet, and in general aided him in whatever battle he happened to be for the moment engaged. Their acquaintance had sufficiently ripened by May, 1921, for Borah to write to Professor Clarke, of the University of Chicago:

I note you say you are an acquaintance and friend of Mr. Levinson. There are few men for whom I have a higher regard than for Mr. Levinson. He is not only a man of very great ability—exceptional ability—but he is thoroughly broadminded and patriotic. I have derived a great deal of help from interviews with him.[2]

The first direct effort to draw Borah actively into the outlawry movement was Levinson's attempt to induce him to write a foreword for the Christmas pamphlet of 1921. His refusal and his sub-

[1] See above, pp. 43 ff.   [2] May 31, 1921.

sequent approval of the pamphlet as shown by his placing it in the *Congressional Record* and by permitting hundreds of thousands of copies to be mailed under his frank have already been mentioned.[3]

Levinson's methods with Borah deserve some attention, because of the intimacy and long association of the two men and because of the results flowing from the association. An examination of these methods will also throw light on those he used with others, for all had much in common, though it must be remembered that Borah was always a law unto himself. In dealing with the Senator the wind had always to be tempered to the shorn lamb. This Levinson well understood.

In the first place, if he considered a man of major importance to him, he would help him to fight his own battles. In 1921 Borah was interested in calling a disarmament conference; so was Levinson. Borah later wanted United States recognition of Russia; Levinson worked for it too. Borah wanted to draft a bill for the regulation of primaries in which candidates for national office were nominated; Levinson had a thorough brief worked out for the guidance of the Senator. Borah wanted to pay back the tainted money which Hayes had collected to elect Republicans; Levinson contributed. Borah wanted to find what legal power the State Department had to withhold diplomatic information for reasons of public interest; Levinson had an exhaustive brief prepared on the subject. Borah was interested in legislative aid for agriculture; while protesting that the farm problem was not within his own understanding, Levinson helped the Senator to gather information and to see persons who could offer constructive suggestions. He contributed to the Senator's political success in every way possible, distributed literature in Idaho, assisted in forcing the Republican National Committee to permit Borah's renomination in 1924 by the state convention without serious opposition, and distributed the Senator's speeches on other subjects than the outlawry of war. He started to back Borah for a place on the presidential ticket in 1920; he stopped pushing him in 1924 and 1928 only at the insistence of the Senator.

[3] See above, pp. 71–73.

It would be an exaggeration to give the impression that Levinson did as much as this to support other men, for with no other man in as high an official position was he so intimately connected for such a long period as he was with Borah; but the kind of support he gave to the Senator he gave to all other important persons, if the amount of it was not so great. One other observation should be made with respect to his support of his chief lieutenants. It would seem that he was all things to all men. He was certainly almost all things to all the men whom he chose as his chief lieutenants; but it appeared that, in singling out these key men, he chose only those whose general policies he could support, so that he was not forced to compromise his own views. However, there were many issues on which he parted company with his friends and associates. There was one case only in which it appeared that support of his champions led him to take a position which did violence to his own best judgment. His very close association with the antipeace, jingoistic Reed-Johnson-Hearst group led him to use language and arguments which at times smacked of William Hale Thompson.

The second method was to make his appeal on the basis of the inherent value of the cause. He wrote to Borah when he was pushing the Senator to write a foreword to his pamphlet: "I hope you may not feel that I am trespassing upon your friendship . . . . I am rather relying upon the quality of the cause."[4] Although he seldom stated it as bluntly as this, his reliance on his cause to win support was fundamental to his procedure.

The third method was one which he used more with others than with Borah. It was to dwell upon the popularity of the cause, the momentum which it was gaining, and the popular acclaim its adherents would certainly receive. It was spreading, he would urge, like wildfire; this organization and that had committed themselves to it; this man and that had espoused the cause; it was receiving support, more support than he thought possible; it was years ahead of time, etc. Support of outlawry would throw confusion into the camp of the supporter's political enemies. To Borah, for instance, "I feel in my heart," he wrote,

[4] Levinson to Borah, September 30, 1922.

[83]

"that this will furnish you a great constructive issue that will disarm such political enemies as you made in the League fight, and it will cut the ground from under the wrongful impression which even many of your political associates create concerning you."[5]

A fourth method was based on the principle that "molasses catches more flies than vinegar." He praised his lieutenants; they should be president, senator, member of the cabinet; they were the chief leaders of this or that; they were the most powerful preachers, orators, editors in America. He borrowed Goethe's maxim, "You must take people for better than they are." Elsewhere I have characterized this trait as a deferential attitude toward those who were successful in business, political, or professional lines. It could almost be said that he used flattery on those with whom he worked. But that would not be quite correct, since to flatter is to praise falsely. He could hardly be charged with flattering people, because, in the first place, he appeared to believe what he said and, in the second place, the people he chose to work with were really capable.

A fifth method was that of argument. He argued with everyone he met, he argued in his letters, he argued over the telephone, the telegraph, and the cable. His eye-to-eye talks were intense; Lord Robert Cecil is reported to have had a headache after being closeted with him for an hour. Said one of his intimates to me in regard to his talking ability, "for forty-eight hours Sol had been talking to me without ceasing, going over the whole thing time and again. . . . . He had just worn me out with saying it over and over—you just can't ever wear him down." He never tired of saying it all over again. The first time I met him, in 1930, he went into the theory of outlawry with the same relish and vehemence and with many of the same terms he had been using in his letters and presumably in conversation during the preceding ten years.

A sixth method—one which appeared to be particularly effective with Borah and may seem contradictory to that last mentioned—was to welcome criticism of his ideas and give it careful attention. Someone would find a weak place in his armor. He

[5] Levinson to Borah, July 17, 1922.

would talk it over with intimates and think about it. Presently he would either find an answer to it or make a change in his plan to eliminate the weakness. Very few people were aware of his eagerness for criticism or of his readiness to profit by it. The reason was that one seldom got a chance to make a full statement without interruption and some kind of an answer. And though he appeared neither to listen nor to understand, he usually caught the gist of the criticism before it was finished; and if it were germane his mind went to work on it for the real answer, though at the time his tongue might becloud the issue with a fog of words. A good example of his reaction to criticism and his relation to Borah is an excerpt from a letter to Dr. Holmes:

> I have been struggling the past ten days with the question of punishing international criminals without giving the power to one or more nations forcibly to extradite heads of other nations. This proposition was hurled at my uncovered head by Dr. James Brown Scott at Washington recently. The same question, however, has been raised from a great variety of angles. Indeed, the question of creating a crime that can be adequately dealt with without derogation of complete sovereignty is inherently the most difficult. . . . . I have been doing some intensive thinking along this line recently and I believe I have found the way out. This is quite important because, undoubtedly, some Senator will tackle Borah along that line and try to catch him in an inconsistency of position when comparing his position as regards the league to his advocacy of our plan. . . . .
>
> You do not know what a relief it is to me to have acquired even in the rough a way out of this exceedingly difficult proposition. I have felt that my job has been to reconcile radically different forces and to furnish a common platform for all . . . . and it is doubtful whether the program could be put through without a satisfactory answer to this question.[6]

A seventh method, which illustrates his ability to handle persons of high position like Borah and was probably of great importance in his relationship with the Senator, though there is no direct documentary evidence to substantiate the point, was his absolute refusal to derive profit for himself or friends from his intimacy with those in authority. He never asked for an office for

---

[6] Levinson to Holmes, June 5, 1922. This matter of enforcement was one which troubled Borah when he first began to work on the outlawry idea. After he had spent some "hot hours" in the summer of 1922 preparing for speeches on outlawry, he wrote, ". . . . there is one proposition, Levinson, which I have got to have some light upon and which I must settle in my own mind before I proceed further."

a friend[7] or for any personal favor of a material kind. Neither would he permit any of his friends to use his name in order to approach Borah or anyone else with the purpose of obtaining a material benefit. In appealing to people like Borah or Eliot, he did, it is true, occasionally plead the closeness of his friendship with them. An example is one of the eleven reasons he cited in the last letter to Borah, urging the Senator to write a foreword to the 1921 pamphlet. "After our close personal relations and great admiration with which I followed your fight against the League," it would be a "great personal disappointment to me not to feel that I had to some extent at least the momentum of your great power behind this effort."[8]

His methods were more effective because of his absolute sincerity. It rang in his voice, gave point to his gestures, sat on his countenance, and inspired a like sincerity in others. Coupled with this, he had sufficient wealth not to be cramped. A trip to Washington or New York; a telegram, cablegram, or telephone conversation; the reprinting and distributing of an article; a trip for one of his lieutenants in the interest of outlawry—all these things could be considered on their own merits. None of them needed to be ruled out by financial considerations.

Although by 1922 Levinson had settled on Borah as his mouthpiece in the Senate, he made one more effort to get Harding to espouse outlawry after snubbing it during the disarmament conference. He had come to feel pity, if not contempt, for the perplexed man in the White House—that puppet of powers beyond his understanding; but the prestige value of a presidential indorsement would be great, however incompetent the president. His plan was to induce Harding to "announce that the present treaties are stepping stones to the achievement of his ultimate objec-

---

[7] The only exception to this statement that I can remember finding in all his correspondence was his advocacy of a Cabinet position for Robins in 1928. However, this can hardly be called an exception, since Borah first suggested Robins for the place. His advocacy of persons for Cabinet posts in 1920, 1924, and 1928 were not exceptions, since his arguments were based upon the accepted qualities of the persons in question and never on his friendship for the proposed appointee or appointer.

[8] Levinson to Borah, December 8, 1921.

tive, thrice announced by him, that war must be outlawed, because such a ringing statement would 'swing the country behind him.' "⁹ If Harding refused, he believed that the Republican party would run a great risk of disruption.

But, while the President dallied with the idea, Levinson's plans continued to grow. Borah was to introduce an outlawry-of-war resolution in the Senate, and the administration was to give it official support. He urged this for the sake of harmony. If Harding gave an official blessing to Borah, then the widening breach between the two could be healed: ". . . . the president is in a position to retain leadership with B[orah] representing him in the Resolution and the work. It will bring back to the Republican vote vast bodies of dissatisfied citizens and will also enlist the largest possible women's vote."¹⁰ After trying to get a commitment out of the administration during March and April, he wrote early in May to the attorney-general's office: "While it seems almost inconceivable to me that the plan we worked out will not be highly acceptable to the Chief, I am able to make most effective alternative arrangements and time is the essence of such effectiveness."¹¹

It was nearly the end of May, 1922, before word came by way of the attorney-general's office that the administration would not at the moment make a public commitment to outlawry. The press of other business, such as consideration of the tariff and bonus bills, was so great as to prevent it just then. The alternative arrangements appear in a letter to Professor Dewey.

I have turned all the papers over to Borah, who is getting up a resolution based on our own, to produce in the Senate committing this country to the international purpose of outlawing war. I have told the administration people I have dealt with that the whole thing is in Borah's hands, and they are to deal with him in case Harding wants to lead the movement. But in any event I do not want Lodge or Watson, or some other chap not of our choosing, to make the speech. In any event Borah is slated for the job. He has been perfectly wonderful and generous in his attitude both towards the administration and towards Col. Robins and myself. All this in confidence.¹²

⁹ Levinson to Martin, March 15, 1922.
¹⁰ Levinson to Martin, April 28, 1922.
¹¹ Levinson to Martin, May 3, 1922.　　¹² Levinson to Dewey, May 29, 1922.

When Borah agreed to introduce a resolution in the Senate for the purpose of making the outlawry of war the basis of American foreign policy and to permit the administration to take it over there, Levinson was "thrilled with pleasure." To reverse a criticism which Harding had made of Borah, Levinson wrote to his Senator: "If the Chief could have overheard your willingness for teamwork with the Administration he might have said: 'Bill, I guess I am the man that needs practice in double harness, not you.' " On the occasion of the introduction of the resolution, Borah was to make a great speech on the doctrine of outlawry which was to be reprinted and distributed to nearly every family in the United States. It was the hope of Levinson and Robins that Borah would make this move before the first of July, 1922. It was the opinion of all three of them that the administration would be forced to get on the bandwagon once it was started rolling by the consideration of a resolution in the Senate.

But Borah's promise to introduce the outlawry resolution and to make a speech setting forth the outlawry faith was a long way from fulfilment. In fact, the voluminous correspondence that went to Borah and his shorter, less numerous replies may give one the feeling that the "Lone Wolf of Idaho" was more ready to promise than to perform. He had promised to introduce the resolution in May, 1922, and to make a speech on it. Nearly nine months elapsed before the resolution was introduced; though he made some remarks on outlawry in connection with the World Court controversy in 1926 and on the Pact of Paris when it was before the Senate in 1928, he never made the speech.

The outlawry resolution as originally conceived by Levinson was to be a simple declaration of the policy of the United States "to make aggressive war a crime, and to outlaw and abolish it."[13] But, toward the end of June, 1922, after the speech on Russia had been delivered and Levinson had distributed fifty thousand copies of it, when Borah finally found time to study the matter, he raised questions about the principles of outlawry and suggested that the resolution should include the whole concept. Some of the questions he raised and the answers Levinson worked

[13] Levinson to Eliot, June 20, 1922.

out may be of interest in throwing light on the relation of the two men, as well as on how the concept of outlawry developed under criticism.

Borah was squeamish about sanctions. How could they be applied? Levinson had been working on the problem. He had come to the conclusion that the enforcement of sanctions against a nation was the equivalent of war and that it was useless to try to outlaw and abolish war and yet keep it as a means of enforcement. The next step in the evolution of his thought was to provide for sanctions against individuals. James Brown Scott had thrown doubt on this when he asked Levinson if he could expect Germany to surrender the Kaiser. It was at this stage that Borah began to raise questions as to means of enforcement. Levinson wrote to Borah on June 12, 1922, admitting that this was the "only point of consequence brought against our plan." If a world court were empowered to punish officials such as the president of the United States, that would mean conferring the power of a superstate upon it. He recalled the power of Congress as stated in the Constitution, Article 1, Section 8, "to define and punish . . . . offenses against the law of nations." Since outlawry was a people's movement, "they should punish their own offenders." So "criminal jurisdiction over international law breakers can be allotted to the nations severally. Of course, the international code should also provide for the outlawing diplomatically and economically of a nation waging war in violation of the code."

Borah then suggested that the outlawry resolution as drafted by Levinson should contain something more than a simple declaration of policy.

In looking over the resolution relative to the outlawry of war, it occurs to me that we ought to have a more definite and concrete proposition with reference to action under the resolution. I believe in addition to the resolution left by you, there ought to be a provision similar to the provision in the disarmament resolution, to wit, authorizing the president of the United States to call a conference for the purpose of bringing about the desired result. It is altogether probable that ultimately it would take the form of taking the matter up at the Hague. But a definition proposition, [a] concrete proposition, is a good thing to have in mind of the public while you are organizing public opinion upon a specific question. What do you think?[14]

[14] Borah to Levinson, June 29, 1922.

The resolution was revised several times by Levinson to meet such objections as Borah was constantly bringing up.

Congress finally adjourned for the summer without any action from Borah. Pressure had been brought on him by letters from Levinson and visits from Robins. When the Senator appeared slightly huffed, Levinson wrote:

I ought to have known that conditions are such at Washington that it is not only merely impossible, but highly inadvisable for you to attempt to force through outside matters. I had understood you to say to Col. Robins and me early in June that you surely could get the thing through sometime in July. I know that man proposes and God disposes.[15]

In September, Borah was in Chicago for a series of meetings in the interests of amnesty for political prisoners and recognition of Russia. Promises again were given:

I met him at the train and have had considerable to do with him since. Colonel Robins and I had a splendid talk with him late yesterday afternoon for upwards of an hour, in which the Senator pledged himself absolutely to the theory of Outlawry and to the presentation of a Resolution at the coming session of Congress. . . . . He promised to prepare the best speech he is capable of in connection with the resolution.[16]

The Senator was able to explain to Levinson's satisfaction his failure to offer the resolution and make the speech before the adjournment of Congress. Everybody was worried with the tariff and bonus bills; and besides, with the mine and railroad strikes going on, a move by the outlawrists might have failed to get front-page space in the press.

Levinson had several more conferences with Borah before Congress convened in December. The resolution was worked over many times more to meet each new objection which the Senator raised. Finally, on December 7, Levinson reported to Holmes that it included "everything of basic importance"; he had been at "great pains to keep Borah's attitude logical and consistent"; and he was expecting Borah "to shoot any day now," because the Senator had promised Robins and himself on Monday of the previous week that he would make the address in about ten days.

[15] Levinson to Borah, July 29, 1922.
[16] S. O. Levinson to Horace Levinson, September 30, 1922.

But Borah stopped answering letters, and soon Levinson was asking Robins why. More letters were sent to Washington, and Levinson went there himself about December 20. Borah was stalling in regard to the enforcement of world-court decisions; and now, as later, when he wanted to balk, he would urge strategy as the justification. Suddenly he changed his tactics altogether and offered a rider to the naval bill which called for an international economic and financial conference. The justification for this shift as stated in a telegram to Levinson was: "Think if we can get this conference called we can force in our proposition."[17] Levinson at first accepted this strategy as it would cut the ground from under previous critics, despite his desire for the early introduction of the resolution so that he could base further popular education upon it. Soon the situation in Washington became more complicated. A controversy arose over the war debts, and he began to fear that Borah was being jockeyed into a position which would put off the resolution indefinitely. Harding had condemned Borah's rider, and a number of other senators had agreed to fight it. Levinson wrote two letters to Borah on December 26, and one each on the twenty-seventh, the twenty-eighth, and the thirtieth, urging that something be done about the resolution. He quoted Knox, editorials from the daily press, Washington's farewell address, played on Borah's dislike for some members of the administration, his hatred of the League, secret diplomacy, Old World chancellors, etc., and suggested how, with outlawry so popular, Borah could use the resolution to extricate himself from a difficult position. On December 31 he sent a long telegram to Raymond Robins, pointing out that their cause was in great jeopardy and,

. . . . I therefore earnestly request that you wire him [i.e., Borah] that conditions necessitate conference before you make western tour and that you have asked me to meet you in Washington naming date stop sincerely hope it is possible for you as I shall desert every thing here to meet you and him stop. . . . . Evidently there is big political move involved in background which demands your penetrating judgment. . . . .[18]

[17] Borah to Levinson, December 21, 1922.

[18] Levinson to Robins, December 31, 1922.

But before the colonel could arrange a meeting, administration spokesmen said in the Senate that the administration was favorable to an economic conference, whereupon Borah withdrew his rider calling for such a conference, and the "first act was terminated."

Another period of changing the resolution and gentle wooing of the balking Borah followed. Robins, Levinson wrote him, was just starting on another speaking tour in the West and was "exceedingly anxious" to put Borah's name at the head of their movement as its national champion. Robins had been very close to Hiram Johnson, but they had become partially estranged over the peace issue.

If you can give Robins the right to use your name, this will probably detach [him] and clinch his relations with you.

The presentation by you of the resolution seems now to be most pertinent and effective. Robins and I both agree that you need only one thing in this country and that is a great, paramount issue in addition to the many splendid but relatively subordinate principles you so splendidly advocate. We, particularly Robins, have demonstrated that Outlawry is the most popular and effective issue available. It strikes me as of the greatest importance to have you pre-empt this issue by presenting the resolution as early as possible during the present session of Congress which, of course, may be referred to the Foreign Relations Committee, make a speech on it, and let us get out at least half a million copies in this country and throughout the world. If necessary, we will get out a million copies. Then nobody can stop you or it.[19]

While he was thus nursing the temperamental Borah back into position for a start, Robins got out of hand. Why not drop Borah, get up a great campaign, evangelize the country, and organize a bureau of information and state and local committees? "If you mean," wrote the colonel from San Diego, "to put this idea over in your generation and become an immortal figure and personality in human history and to lead in making the greatest contribution to human welfare since Moses and the prophets then you will have to earn [these] results."[20] Levinson was making every effort to "earn" them, for as soon as the colonel began to snort and rear, he called up Borah on the telephone to find if the Senator

[19] Levinson to Borah, January 5, 1923.
[20] Robins to Levinson, January 23, 1923.

was ready to introduce the resolution and make the speech. Borah's reason for delay was a variation of strategy. ". . . . Owing to complications," he wrote, "the time was not ripe for presenting it"; he must "wait until the developments called for it." And when Levinson had urged some concession for the benefit of the colonel, who was speaking on the Pacific Coast, Borah said, "I am fully in accord with your movement and I am thoroughly in favor of it, and Robins can use my name as he pleases."[21]

But, however "fully in accord" and "thoroughly in favor" Borah was, he raised the question of what could be done if, after war was outlawed, "Japan wantonly or otherwise attacks Siberia." This stopped Levinson temporarily; and while he considered the question he threw dust and side-stepped; but shortly he reported to Robins:

. . . . My answers to him have been as follows:

a) Japan has been behaving about as well as any other nation connected with the war outside of the United States. She has returned Shantung which is more than any other nation has done with reference to any territory or concession.

b) Japan has been treated with such dignity and equality by the other nations that it seems inconceivable that she would defy all international law, agreements and treaties, and make herself the outcast among nations.

c) But if she does: I have suggested a provision in the code giving the international court summary jurisdiction to hear and decide at once whether such an attack, viz: Japan on Siberia, was justified or provoked; whether Japan had violated the code and international law; and if the court so found, which, of course, it would under the case suggested, all the other nations signatory to the code would have the right (not the duty) to join in the defense of Siberia. You will recall in the plan Knox and I prepared under the amendment suggested by John Bassett Moore himself, we said: "The right of defense against actual and imminent attack shall be preserved."

It will be comparatively simple to elaborate this right of defense in the code and to make it available to all other nations to join in this right of defense provided the international court held that a given attack was unjustified and illegal.

The foregoing marks the extreme limit to which I think it is possible to extend the use of force in international relations. I think, however, there is no objection to it, first, because it merely constitutes the right of defense, and secondly, because it would be a right of defense supported by force in support of

---

[21] Levinson to Robins, January 13, 1923.

a finding and decree of the international court. I feel very much pleased to have been able to work this out, at least to my own satisfaction, better than I have ever done it before. You know you have been a large factor in influencing my judgment altogether away from the concept of force, and your judgment has been fortified by my researches in history and political philosophy. I want you, therefore, to give this matter your best thought and your honest conclusion.[22]

In addition to answering Borah's questions, Levinson kept trying to spur him on, both directly by writing himself and indirectly by getting various persons of influence to write also.

An example of the direct approach is a letter of January 26. In this Levinson used four different arguments. Borah, he urged, had the administration, and Hughes in particular, "on the hip." A combination of Borah's skill and Hughes's, "secrecy, and his stupid Senatorial spokesman" had "maneuvered" the secretary into a "hopeless hole." The press, particularly the New York press, had deserted Hughes and seemed to be practically all Borah's. Viviani was making an effort to get the League to make some specific step with regard to disarmament. Borah's program would "dwarf this pretentious effort of the League to pull itself out by its boot-straps . . . . ," and, finally, outlawry was the "one fascinating appeal to the women as against the League," as was shown by the "ovations" which Robins was getting wherever he went. "I am in daily receipt," the writer added, "of requests for hundreds of pamphlets, on the aftermath of his work."

Examples of the indirect approach can be seen in letters to Justice Allen and Elizabeth Hauser and an unknown person on the west coast.

Meantime, I wish you would snatch enough time from your new busy life to write a letter to Senator Borah. Among other things, I venture to suggest that you tell him you have become interested through the pamphlet that he promulgated through the Senate and have lectured and are lecturing on it to the universal enthusiastic reception by your audiences. . . . . Be sure and stress the importance of an early official pronouncement from him as the situation warrants, the earlier the better. Please avoid reference to me except, if you prefer, a general one, as I want the letter to be as effective as possible and to be what I know you would feel like having it, a voluntary statement from yourself to one to whom we look for leadership in the great cause. I am most anxious for the momentum of a letter from you.[23]

[22] Levinson to Robins, January 18, 1923.
[23] Levinson to Allen, January 17, 1923.

To Miss Hauser he wrote: "I am reluctant to make suggestions to a literary woman of quality as to the contents of the letter [to Borah] but . . . . ," he wanted four things mentioned: what she had seen in the press about outlawry, the importance of its being announced as the public policy, the fact that women like it as a substitute for the League, and her own consuming interest in the issue. "You will, of course, write on your letter head so that he will know that he is corresponding with the secretary of the National League of Women Voters . . . . send me a copy of the letter. . . . ."[24]

A president of a women's club on the west coast, after hearing Robins, wanted to know what she and her club could do. The answer went back immediately: get her club to adopt a resolution favoring outlawry and send it to Borah.

But the strategist in the Senate still waited. And Levinson had already written to Robins: "You write to Borah saying you have heard from me regarding the use of his name and also, among other things, say that you will be in Chicago February 8th and will try to come to Washington with me shortly thereafter."[25]

And to Washington they went, "invincible in every respect." What happened there may be recorded if it is permissible to lift the veil behind which men live their home lives. On February 15 Mrs. Levinson telegraphed:

Last night[']s *News* and this morning[']s *Herald Examiner* give account of Senator Borah[']s resolution in Senate Yesterday. *Examiner* with picture of Senator Borah on front page. Rejoice with you over accomplishment of this great epoch making step in civilization[']s progress. . . . .[26]

There was reason for rejoicing, for had not the uncertain Borah begun to perform what he had promised?—yet not too great rejoicing, for he had only introduced the resolution,[27] he had not made the great speech.

[24] Levinson to Hauser, January 25, 1923.

[25] Levinson to Robins, January 13, 1923.

[26] Mrs. Levinson to Levinson, February 15, 1923.

[27] See Appen. A for the outlawry resolution presented to the Senate, February 13, 1923.

CHAPTER VII

OFFENSIVES FOR OUTLAWRY
ON WIDER FRONTS

FROM 1914 until February 14, 1923, Levinson's peace activities had tended to crystallize around some immediate objective. These objectives had successively been to bring Eliot and Schiff together to unite the American opinion against the continuance of the war, to give voice to pro-League sentiment, to defeat the League, to elect Harding, to distribute the pamphlet, *A Plan To Outlaw War*, to put outlawry in the program of the disarmament conference, and, finally, to prevail on Borah to introduce an outlawry resolution in the Senate and make a great speech in support and explanation of it. In the last case Levinson had been only half-successful: he had got the resolution but not the speech. Using, however, the broader base of prestige which the resolution provided, he immediately enlarged the scale of his operations to secure what was his ultimate objective—the universal acceptance of outlawry. And now, instead of concentrating on one immediate task at a time, he had several in mind. Later on, events so shaped themselves that his activities again tended to center on one project. It is with the in-between period, when, to change the analogy, the main current had spread out and the whirlpools and the eddies seemed to be more apparent than the current, that this chapter is concerned.

The "great speech" to canonize outlawry was the next step; but pressure for it was eased, for had not the lion-maned Borah promised that it would be forthcoming when "the Senate proceedings permitted"? Although the Senator had said "it was impossible even to guess at the day when he would speak . . . . ," there was every reason to expect that he would keep his promise within a week or so. The resolution had been proposed "substantially" as Levinson had drafted it. It had received a good press in the United States and evoked a cablegram of praise from five members of the English parliament, who proposed that the resolution should be made the starting-point for disarmament and for a revision of the Treaty of Versailles. Borah had declared, "The die is cast," in reply to Levinson's greeting: "Senator, how would you like to shake the hand of the happiest man in the United States?" after the introduction of the resolution.[1] But what is a promise among friends, especially when one of them has senatorial immunity? After Congress adjourned, Borah declared as an excuse for his failing to speak: "There was really no opportunity for me to do so and do it adequately. I felt that to do it inadequately, that is not to the best of my ability, would be a great mistake. . . . . But nothing in my opinion has really been lost."[2] He tried to ease the pain of disappointment by promising to do a great deal of speaking on the subject during the spring and summer when he had more fully digested the concept. "I am now," he said, "giving some time to a more thorough study and consideration of the whole proposition and the arguments in support of it." He admitted that it would be "impossible to consider it as it was entitled to be considered," but he hoped "to be shortly more completely a master of the subject. At least I ought to be as I am endeavoring very earnestly to be."[3]

Though Levinson was "tickled to pieces" and was "too elated to express [him]self coherently" and the Rev. John Haynes Holmes "nearly turned hand springs" when Borah introduced the outlawry resolution, Levinson felt that "the real crusade to end war" had only just started. Unfortunately, from the standpoint of dramatic symmetry, there is no record to show how the philosopher of the pragmatic way of life expressed his jubilation, but he was sufficiently aroused to send a telegram to Borah a few hours after the introduction of the resolution, asking for a copy of it.

Whatever pleasurable excitement Levinson and his co-workers enjoyed did not deter them long from the "real crusade." Before leaving Washington, Levinson had seen Senators Couzens and

[1] Levinson to Albert Loeb, February 23, 1923.
[2] Borah to Levinson, March 6, 1923.
[3] Borah to Levinson, March 6, 1923.

Capper with a view to co-operation with Borah, and he had discussed at some length with Mr. James G. McDonald of the Foreign Policy Association the advisability of Borah's going to Europe. McDonald was much in favor of such a trip, but Levinson demurred. There were two dangers. Borah's activities might by reason of press censorship be "ignored and butchered." And, "while Borah was away from this country, his enemies might sow tares in the wheat."[4] Two months later, when it was found that Lloyd George was coming to the United States, it seemed advisable for Borah and Robins to go to Europe to saturate him with the outlawry idea. This plan was only partially carried out.

The tares which Levinson most feared were the renewed signs of another campaign for collaboration with Europe, by supporting either the League or the World Court. His attitude toward the Court and that toward the League were slightly different, although the position he assumed for bargaining purposes was much the same in each case. In general, his techniques as a bargainer for outlawry when dealing with advocates of the Court and the League involved at least five tactical principles. The first was to give evidence of a great amount of strength and point out that the weight of authority or public opinion or history or sound logic or practicability, etc., was on his side. The second was to indicate persons on the other side who indulged in cheap tricks, whose motives were mixed, who had failed to carry out their promises, or who were obstructionists. The third was to exhibit, generally, a warm personal feeling for the particular person on the other side with whom he was dealing and expatiate on the desirability of conciliation. Their differences were not fundamental and could be composed if they would get together. They both wanted the same thing—the riddance of war. So why not adopt outlawry as a starting-point and then co-operate? The fourth was to let the other side make the first move toward compromise. If he attacked strongly enough, the other side would have to make offers, and he himself would then be in a much better position to lay down the terms. The fifth was to reject all compromises on the subject of outlawry. Let it be the core of any peace

[4] Levinson to Robins, February 23, 1923.

plan. Illustrations of these techniques will appear as his attitude on the Court and the League is made clear.

The Court became an issue when, in Levinson's words, Harding "made a political [error] under the auspices of Root, Hughes and Hoover"[5] by asking for United States adherence to it.[6] One of the three principles of outlawry was adjudication; consequently many people expected Levinson to favor the Court. But to his thinking there were many fatal errors in it. His immediate objection was:

There isn't any doubt that once we enter any kind of scheme with the European diplomats there will not be enough energy left in the people to change it for the next fifty years. Therefore we must get it right as an indispensable condition of entry.[7]

Some of the essentials of "rightness" appeared in various letters. When Lord Robert Cecil sent a telegram to Justice Florence Allen, asking her the changes necessary in the peace machinery to secure United States support, she called Levinson by telephone to find what the conditions should be. With regard to the Court, he said:

The League court might be used for our world court if the League were utterly detached from the Treaty. Otherwise, it would be vastly better to use the present machinery of the Hague Conference where there is a Hague tribunal of the same general character as the present League court (although not so well developed in details of machinery). The advantage of the world court at the Hague would be that all nations are automatically members and the question of the admission of certain nations would be obviated.

Give it inherent and affirmative jurisdiction over all international controversies as defined by the code; . . . . .

Create a comprehensive code of law based upon equality and justice and let this code state in detail all of the controversies over which the court has jurisdiction, thereby destroying the possibility of the diplomats destroying the

[5] Levinson to Holmes, March 5, 1923, and Levinson to Dewey, April 27, 1923.

[6] Levinson was certain that Harding hastened to submit the Court protocol to the Senate as a means of offsetting the outlawry-of-war resolution submitted by Borah. The fact that the President's message went to the Senate within a few days after the introduction of the resolution lends plausibility to Levinson's belief. The message may be found in the *Congressional Record*, LXIV (February 24, 1923), 4498. The resolution was submitted February 14.

[7] Levinson to Holmes, March 6, 1923.

317289

court's jurisdiction by distinguishing between justiciable and non-justiciable disputes. For any dispute is justiciable that appears in the code. In fact, the main difference between these two classes of disputes would be whether they were in the code or not in the code. . . . .

Of course the code would provide as its major premise that the institution of war be abolished and made a crime under the law of nations. The right of defense, of course, shall be strictly maintained.

The court should be wholly independent of the League and of all influence. No court is of value unless it has complete independence in every respect.

. . . . In order to make the nations equal before the law we must create a world court as nearly as possible on the model of our Supreme Court in its jurisdiction over our sovereign states. Here Rhode Island enters the court the exact equal of Massachusetts, New York, Texas or California. All politics, intrigue, diplomatic trading and secret diplomacy must be thoroughly and exhaustively eliminated.[8]

Besides these conditions he suggested others in other letters in regard to the Court and the code:

There must be no super-powers given to the Court and no form of superstate whatever. The independence of each nation must be maintained and its sovereignty must not be destroyed. The nations must all yield of their sovereignty to the International Court the right to be sued, to have their international disputes heard and determined. The right of self-defense must be preserved and the international court shall have summary power to hear and decide an emergency case of a claimed breach of international law in the nature of an aggression, or an attack, and all signatories shall have the right of defense the same as the nation attacked; this right of defense shall not be compulsory but a voluntary and optional right. . . . .

The vicious doctrine of force shall be forever laid at rest, because that is merely a nom de plume for war. The decrees of the court shall rest upon the good faith of nations, on the specific agreement by general treaty to abide by and to carry out the decisions, and the effective force of international public opinion functioning upon an open court where all disputes and law suits shall be manifested in writing both complaint and defense.[9]

All the "infernal expressions" relating to war, e.g., military necessity, retaliation and reprisal, etc., were to be "plucked out by the roots from the present body of so-called international law."[10] The code should be "comprehensive and the wisdom of

[8] Levinson to Judge Allen, April 19, 1923.

[9] Levinson to Frances Kellor, March 23, 1923.   [10] *Ibid.*

the ages should be distilled and all good things that have been developed in international law should be preserved and the evil cast out."[11]

His attitude toward the League was somewhat different. His distrust of diplomacy and his faith in legal processes led him to discount the League. "The cumbersome machinery of a League of Nations," he wrote, "is not necessary, but personally I believe it would be conciliatory, and we could get at Outlawry more quickly, by preserving the maximum machinery of the League that does not conflict with the paramount principles of Outlawry."[12] This feeling toward the League, however, changed somewhat, so that, while he felt it was distinctly second in importance to the Court, he came to feel that as a "conference room, it [was] not only desirable, but invaluable."[13]

The conditions which he laid down in the above-mentioned letter to Justice Allen—conditions which she was to suggest to Lord Robert Cecil as a basis for United States support of the League—give a very good idea of his opinion.

The objections to the League of Nations are so numerous that those of us who are trying to regard merely the essentials prefer to emphasize the major operations needed to be performed on it before it will become healthy for America. Here goes an extempore try. . . . .

The League is either based ultimately on force or it is not. If it is, it is in the nature of a superstate (possibly with conditions) and it therefore should be rejected on that ground alone. Articles 10, 11, 15, 16 and 17 construed together have convinced many of us that the League is unmistakably an instrument of force. . . . .

If, as Lord Cecil contends, the League is merely a meeting place of the nations; in effect, a conference table where differences are threshed out in a friendly way and good will developed among the nations of the world, then the following things should be done:

a) All of the articles of force mentioned above (except article 11), should be eliminated.

b) There should be no Council, but only the Assembly, unless the Assembly cares to have something in the nature of an "executive committee" for certain specific purposes. But the League must not ham-string the Assembly by any such requirement as the unanimous assent of all members of the Council being necessary to the Assembly's acts.

The League is all tied up with the Treaty—the worst treaty in history. . . . .

[11] *Ibid.*   [12] *Ibid.*   [13] Levinson to Allen, April 21, 1923.

We must utterly detach the Versailles Treaty from the League. The peace of the world will never be brought about until some of the rank injustices of the past few years have been remedied. . . . .

The Labor section of the League, as I understand it, is very objectionable. The attempt to regulate, from Geneva, Labor conditions of the world will be very strenuously resisted by the American people. Take the south for example. They very greatly resent any attempt by our federal government to regulate the labor conditions in the various states. How will it work when an international group in Switzerland attempts to bring into an economic straight jacket the vastly diverse labor conditions of the various nations?

Then, above all, there must be inserted in the League the essential provisions of the outlawing of war, plucking out of the present League all of the provisions that are in any sense inconsistent therewith. This would take out Article 10. It would thoroughly revise articles 12, 13, 14, and 15. It would take out articles 16 and 17. Of course, if, ultimately, the nations thought best to set up a blockade or boycotts against a resistant nation, or one that has run amuck, then suitable provisions in that regard could be inserted. Also, prohibitions against the sale or delivery of arms, munitions, etc., to a recalcitrant nation.[14]

Perhaps his real feeling about the Council is not sufficiently indicated by the above. Two days later he wrote:

. . . . There can be no justification . . . . for the stranglehold of a Council. Suppose a corporation has a Board of Directors and an Executive Committee, the latter to act while the board was not in session, covering emergencies, etc. Then suppose the Board of Directors was powerless to act or pass any substantial resolution without the consent of every member of the "Executive Committee." What an unbusiness like and unheard of thing this would be. The idea that an Executive Committee would supersede and destroy the power of a Board of Directors is a perfect business demonstration of the real character of the League. For all the power is, in effect, in the "Executive Committee," or Council and none in the "Board of Directors" or assembly.[15]

It should be noted that these quotations have been taken from letters to persons close within Levinson's confidence. As a general rule his position in public was one of independence of the peace machinery or of bitter and critical hostility to it. Professor Zueblin, "a paid advocate and coach of the League of Nations," invited him to dine and discuss outlawry. "I finally told him that it was not our business to make propositions; it was not our League; that if the nations that were controlling the League

[14] Levinson to Allen, April 19, 1923.   [15] Levinson to Allen, April 21, 1923.

wanted us to enter, the proposition should emanate from them."[16] He and Justice Allen had agreed when the conversations were being held with Lord Robert Cecil that a "premature offer to compromise on what we would retain of the League might be ingeniously used against us. There is a time to adjust and there is a premature time."[17] Consequently, it was necessary "to be careful and not prematurely attempt to make an adjustment that many people would misunderstand that might result disastrously for our cause."[18]

In the spring of 1923 in addition to the overtures from Lord Robert Cecil there was another move on the part of a League group. It resulted in a debate in March between Manley Hudson, on one side, and Raymond Robins and Levinson, on the other, before the Foreign Policy Association in New York. Robins was first invited to debate with Hudson. He immediately sent an SOS to Levinson:

> Hudson is a very able seaman I am told and I am doubtless in for a trimming. I want to get as good a price as possible for the fleece! . . . . McDonald will preside and he will try to be fair I am sure, but the crowd will be with Hudson and I will get the hot end of the stick from start to finish. . . . . We will make our Cause the only alternative to the League of Nations or absolute isolation. . . . . Any decent price is worth paying for the result. . . . .[19]

Levinson not only got up the brief but participated in the debate. Both sides were satisfied that they were pretty close together and that further talk without the handicap of an audience might unify them. Hudson wrote, "We really are not far apart. . . . ." And Levinson's answer was almost verbatim the same. To one of his confidants he wrote:

> We had a wonderful time in New York. It developed that the crowd was largely pro-League and favored the Court, principally because they thought it would get us into the League. We smoked them out on this. I then got them into a good humor and from a condition of apparent hopelessness, we substantially won out.[20]

[16] Levinson to Allen, May 21, 1923.
[17] Levinson to Borah, April 20, 1923.
[18] Levinson to Dewey, April 20, 1923.
[19] Robins to Levinson, March 1, 1923.
[20] Levinson to Allen, March 15, 1923.

Hudson was anxious that he and Levinson should get together for a day. It was finally arranged that they, together with others, should meet the last of May. The results of this conference were not so very happy. The outlawrists stuck by their guns, and they were charged with being obstructionists. To which they retorted that the other side were the real obstructionists, for Levinson's ideas had been launched before the League and Court had been founded.

I think after all, while the meeting was a bit stormy, it cleared the air. It certainly should have removed the last doubt in the minds of pro-Leaguers that we are looking for the substance and not the form, and that while we have no vital principle to compromise, we are not obstructionists in any real sense.[21]

A campaign was constantly going on to attract persons of importance. Every time any event occurred, such as the introduction of the outlawry resolution in the Senate or the appearance of a dispatch in the daily press referring significantly to the movement, Levinson was not slow to use it as the basis for appealing to men he had failed to win over before or for approaching new men. He wrote to Charles W. Eliot again and again. Once Eliot replied:

. . . . I remain unconvinced. . . . . Have you ever read or heard of a reform in government, industries, or social structure which was brought about without self-sacrifice? To declare war outlawed and aggressive war a crime costs nothing. Therefore in my opinion it will bring nothing to pass.[22]

Levinson wrote to Mr. Luther Day, the son of Justice Day and an eminent member of the Cleveland Bar. He wanted to put Day on an enlarged committee for the outlawry of war. He wrote to Professor Charles E. Merriam, of the University of Chicago, expressing a desire to discuss the whole matter with him in order to test his reactions. Mr. Charles H. Levermore, afterward author of the prize-winning Bok Peace Plan; Professor Ruopp, the speech teacher of Miami University, Oxford, Ohio; and Senator Shipstead of Minnesota were some of the others who received attention of one kind or another. More attention was paid to Senator Pepper of Pennsylvania. Someone found a speech that the

[21] Levinson to Christina Merriam, June 9, 1923.
[22] March 24, 1923.

Senator had made in London in 1920 on much the same lines as those of Levinson's outlawry idea. If they could find a time for a discussion it would be of much value. Someone found a statement of Elihu Root, which was favorable to outlawry. Levinson laid "much store by Root's high approval of outlawing war because he is a God to so many people interested in international affairs."[23] Therefore in the letter of appreciation which he wrote to Root he suggested:

Sometime, at your liberal convenience, I should like very much to discuss some phases of our work with you. We feel that your two great propositions for the codification of international law and the clothing of the court with jurisdiction over all justiciable controversies, which were rejected by the Council and Assembly, are incorporated in our own program and are invaluable. Therefore, we feel, rightly or wrongly, that our program is largely built up on your two great propositions, plus the specific outlawing of war, ... which really is a corollary to your proposition.[24]

Root, according to J. Reuben Clark, was the real power behind the Court movement and to win him over would be the easiest way of winning such men as James Brown Scott, who idolized him. But Levinson also wrote to Scott directly, asking for a conference.

Every opportunity was used to get outlawry into the newspapers and the magazines of the country. Mr. Herman Waldeck, vice-president of the Continental and Commercial National Bank of Chicago and very influential with the *Chicago Tribune*, was urged to have that paper feature the program before the Hearst papers took it up. William Hard was constantly being urged to work outlawry into his syndicated articles. He was also subjected to pressure to speak on the subject. Occasionally he did both. From George Henry Payne, editor of the *Forum*, a promise was extracted to publish an article on outlawry if Borah would write it; and this it became Levinson's task to try to persuade Borah to do, but all in vain.

However, when he was successful in securing comment on peace matters, the result was occasionally disappointing. Mr.

[23] Levinson to Borah, April 27, 1923.
[24] Levinson to Root, June 14, 1923.

Oswald Garrison Villard, editor of the *Nation*, consented to give some space. A letter appeared which discussed outlawry, but in the same issue there was an editorial favoring United States adherence to the Court project. Immediately Levinson protested: "I must say that I am surprised a man of your progressive mind and your thorough grasp of Old World diplomacy should fall for this proposition. . . . ."[25] To which the editor replied: "I knew that editorial would bring the wrath of God down upon me, with you in the role of God."[26] Villard favored the Court on the whole, despite several admitted weaknesses, because the *Nation* had taken a stand for it a year before and he did not feel free to change that stand. Then followed a flood of letters pleading the justifiability of a man's changing his position in the light of more information if he found he was wrong.

Will a man of profound and emotional judgment like yourself, allow a little obstacle like this stand in the way of a great objective? Why don't you come out in a burning editorial recanting the past and rise to the dignity and courage of the present? Surely your first judgment is not always and invariably your last.[27]

But Villard would not yet recant entirely, though he went so far as to say, "I am not going to change our policy on the Court, and do not intend to push it, as I consider the issue a dead one."[28] With Senator Capper and his farm journals Levinson was more successful. Capper published the outlawry resolution and an outlawry article by Levinson. It was estimated that these journals reached at least three million farmers. The Senator also began to use the phrases of outlawry, although there were doubts as to whether he had the faith, because he also talked in terms of aggressive war. Borah was urged to see him and saturate him with the outlawry idea, for he was now, said Levinson, "available for great work in our behalf."

Professor Dewey had been roused to action by the introduction of the Borah resolution. He wrote an article for *Foreign Affairs*

[25] Levinson to Villard, March 6, 1923.
[26] Villard to Levinson, March 8, 1923.
[27] Levinson to Villard, May 14, 1923.
[28] Villard to Levinson, May 11, 1923.

for March, 1923.[29] And he also wrote two articles on the "Outlawry of War" for the *New Republic*. The *Foreign Affairs* article caught the attention of Walter Lippmann, who wrote a strong editorial for the *New York World* of Sunday, March 18, 1923. In this editorial he called attention to the significance of the outlawry resolution, but he refused to commit the *World* to its unqualified support. In addition to writing, Professor Dewey did some speaking for outlawry. Whether he spoke or wrote, he frequently conferred with Levinson before preparing his article or speech, although, he said, he could not always tell what an article was going to contain when he sat down to write. An illustration of his relation to Levinson is found in a letter he wrote asking for the answers to certain questions which he had been asked concerning outlawry. He was to speak to a group of lawyers in Newark, so, "Please," he wrote, "give me any points you think will appeal to the legal fraternity especially." And he went on to report of a previous meeting: "I made your point that this was a condition of serious consideration of social and economic reforms . . . . and that it was fantastic to suppose that the various reform issues would ever make any headway as long as we live under the war system."[30] There was little hostile reaction to this. If the occasion for a speech were of sufficient importance, Dewey might even write out his address and send it to Levinson beforehand for suggestions. Levinson was anxious for Dewey to do more speaking, especially at the colleges and universities; but the philosopher did not like to speak often, and he would not be pressed into such a tour.

Levinson had reprinted and distributed thousands of the *New Republic* article and the *World* editorial. He wanted the *World* editorial especially sent to supporters of the League. He also used these reprints and others, such as his own Capper farm-journal article, to strengthen Senator Borah with his own constituents, by sending fifty thousand reprints to Idaho. Arrangements were made to send material to England. Dr. Holmes, who was personally acquainted with some of the British Labour Party

[29] Dewey, "Ethics and International Relations," *Foreign Affairs*, March 15, 1923.
[30] Dewey to Levinson, March 30, 1923.

leaders, wrote: "The more I think of it the more I feel that the next great big step is to get these men converted. I know Morel and Snowden, and with your permission will level my guns at them."[31]

Occasionally, Levinson became disturbed by the cost of the crusade and cast about for assistance. He tried charging a small price for printed material that he had been sending out gratis, especially when large batches were called for. But, when Amy Woods of the Women's International League for Peace and Freedom asked for fifty thousand pamphlets and insisted that there was no money to pay for them, he made an exception. In point of fact exceptions were made in nearly every case, so that very little money was raised from that source. He wrote to the treasurer of the Committee for the Outlawry of War:

> When are you going to do something about helping me out? There is so much to be done and so many calls for money in all directions that it seems a pity not to be able to finance the project after we have got it launched to the point that a year ago we were merely dreaming it might get. Please get a move on yourself as Treasurer.[32]

And he wrote a few letters directly to persons who he thought might contribute, such as Mr. Frederick P. Keppel of the Russell Sage Foundation, who was also president of the Carnegie Corporation, and Mr. James Brown Scott. It was Levinson's hope that through contacts with these men an opportunity might occur "to break into the stronghold as well as the strong box of both the Carnegie Endowment for Peace and the Carnegie Corporation. We ought to be able to get all kinds of material aid from this quarter."[33] But these and other attempts to get outside assistance were in vain.

There are perhaps several reasons why he was never able to attract much financial support. In the first place, Levinson himself, engrossed in outlawry, really never made any but scattered and sporadic attempts to raise money. He much preferred to give what was needed out of his own pocket rather than be dis-

[31] Holmes to Levinson, March 15, 1923.
[32] Levinson to M. F. Goodman, April 21, 1923.
[33] Levinson to Robins, February 23, 1923.

tracted from his main object. In the second place, he wanted no interference with his authority. Few people of financial substance were likely to give substantial amounts without some voice in the expenditure, and Levinson was not the man to hand over the control of his outlawry movement in exchange for any amount of financial consideration. He made his helpers concentrate all their energies on the main object, and no one had any time for a diversion like raising money. He summed up the situation himself by saying: "I would like assistance all right, but am not going to beg for it. . . . ."[34]

One of the best evidences that outlawry was a "one-man show" was the result of the attempt to organize outlawry-of-war committees elsewhere. Levinson tried to get them formed in Idaho, Ohio, Kansas, Massachusetts, New York, New Jersey, and in some foreign countries. A Mrs. Ida Mueller, of Vienna, wrote that she was translating some of the papers into German. He urged her to organize a committee. The dean of Kansas University, Dr. Olin Templin, was urged to organize. He offered to send printed material to Kansas and even to send Miss Frances Kellor with it to help at the beginning. He suggested to Justice Allen and Miss Elizabeth Hauser that they form an Ohio committee. They both demurred. He agreed with Miss Hauser that it was "not up" to her "and Justice Allen to form a Committee" but it seemed to him that it was perhaps necessary either that she do it or see that it was done so that it would be done right.[35] The only committee actually formed elsewhere was in New York. Mrs. Willard Straight under the guidance of Professor Dewey invited a group to her home in May, 1923. Mr. J. Reuben Clark was selected as chairman. He had been a close friend of Senator Knox and was considered by him to be an exceptionally able man. He had been in the State Department, and he was at the time general counsel for the American International Corporation. A full-time secretary for the committee, Joseph Mayper, was chosen and sent to Chicago to read some of the Levinson correspondence to get better acquainted with the ideology. But this com-

[34] Levinson to Holmes, April 2, 1923.
[35] Levinson to Hauser, May 24, 1923.

mittee, though some of its members were relatively wealthy, started out under the subsidy of Levinson. He was to, and did, contribute $250 a month for three months, but within the next few months there is no more reference to the New York Committee in his correspondence. Outlawry did not thrive except near the original source.

While some of the outlawry lieutenants were making plans to get into touch with leaders of foreign thought, "Captain Outlawry" sold his wares in important quarters. The preparation for one such sale is reported in a letter to Mr. Albert Loeb:

> Last Tuesday I took my courage in both hands and went to the Playhouse to hear Philip Kerr, who was Lloyd George's private and confidential secretary all through the War, and with whom I had a slight correspondence over my original article in the New Republic in 1918. I was as surprized as delighted when he set forth his plan on the "Prevention of Future War," to hear him utilize about two thirds of our material. He kept insisting as the basic proposition in grappling with this problem, that law and the courts offered the only possible alternative to force, that is, to war.
>
> I spoke to him after the lecture and he invited me to breakfast with him at the Drake Wednesday morning. We spent two hours together and you will be glad to hear that he approved of our entire plan and of all the extensions and developments thereof that I have been able to make in the past few months. He said he wanted to keep in close touch with me and altogether I think the interview was one of the most important and effective I have had.[36]

Kerr was not entirely won over at this meeting. During the year a running argument went on by letter; then Kerr was to lecture at Williamstown, and Robins and Levinson went to see him. In the course of three and a half hours of talk he said, as reported by Levinson:

> I have been won over to your plan and I am convinced that even you yourselves do not at all appreciate what a big proposition you have. The Outlawry of War is the most gripping thing from the point of view of the moral will of the people that exists in the world and is bound to win its way to success and consummation.[37]

The association with Kerr was close and cordial during the whole period, although his belief in outlawry never prevented his continued support of the League and the Court. His indorsement

[36] Levinson to Loeb, October 20, 1922; Kerr, later Lord Lothian, subsequently was the British ambassador to the United States.

[37] Levinson to Allen, October 5, 1923.

of outlawry was used with great effectiveness by Levinson in pro-League circles.

Another contact which Levinson established was with Lord Robert Cecil. The opportunity to talk with him was the result of a studied plan; the consequences were, on the surface, not so personally gratifying, but, from the standpoint of favorable publicity and official influence, much more impressive. Lord Robert was coming to the United States to speak to the Des Moines meeting of the National League of Women Voters in the spring of 1923 and to make other peace speeches. Levinson put out his "lines for him." To prepare Lord Robert's mind, he had printed material, like Lippmann's editorial in the *New York World*, put into his hands when he landed in New York. Presently, James G. McDonald was writing to ask Levinson to meet Cecil. Levinson could not meet him in New York as McDonald suggested; he was going to Atlantic City for a few days' rest. Perhaps Lord Robert would be in Chicago, and, if so, he might himself be back from his vacation in time to see him then. Meantime Levinson had hasty consultation with Borah, Holmes, Robins, and others, getting ready for the interview which he appeared so indifferent about having. After Lord Robert had spoken to the Chicago Council on Foreign Relations, Robins and Levinson were closeted with him for an hour. As a speaker he had made a very negative impression on Levinson, but as a conversationalist he had scored rather heavily. Levinson, on the contrary, had not made such a good impression as a conversationalist on Lord Robert. He said later that Levinson gave him a headache. Robins' part in the conversation is reported thus: "Raymond went along but the time was so limited and between Cecil and myself he didn't have much chance even for his interpellation."[38] A report of the interview, as nearly verbatim as possible, was prepared and circulated among the inner circle of the outlawry group. Levinson was somewhat disappointed that they did not get an unqualified indorsement; but

having thought the matter over for twenty-four hours I think we did pretty well to get a pronouncement in favor of an international law outlawing war

[38] Levinson to Kellor, April 17, 1923.

without ourselves having made any concession or having been asked to make any. Therefore it was not a trade.[39]

Though, "of course, [one] must always make allowances for the astute diplomats."[40] In his final interview before he sailed for England, Lord Robert referred to the League as the only alternative; and Levinson concluded that neither he nor Justice Allen, who also had talked with him, had had any success with this "diplomat of the first order." Consequently, he "felt very much set up" when he saw in the *Chicago Daily News* and the *Chicago Tribune* that Lord Robert on landing in England said that he was compelled to give first place in the United States to the outlawry proposal.[41] However, Philip Kerr, according to Levinson, was of the opinion that "Cecil thinks he understands Outlawry, but doesn't get the idea at all. He merely plays with it."[42]

The official recognition which outlawry was to get as a result of Lord Robert's experience in the United States was in the Draft Pact for Mutual Assistance. Cecil told Justice Allen when she met him in Europe later in the summer of 1923 that "he intended to include in the mutual guaranty pact a statement that aggressive warfare is a crime."[43] When aggressive war was condemned in the pact, Levinson said to Justice Allen: "I, too, was somewhat thrilled to find that Lord Robert induced the Sub-Commission of the Assembly to introduce a declaration or preamble of limited Outlawry in his pet Guaranty Pact."[44] But he pointed out this was not outlawry at all, because there was a distinction in the kinds of wars to be outlawed, whereas he wanted war as an institution renounced.[45] His conclusion was that "Cecil has dressed up article ten [of the Covenant of the League] to make it resemble the Outlawry of War."[46]

The Geneva Protocol for the Pacific Settlement of the International Disputes (1924) was the second proposed treaty in which

[39] *Ibid.*
[40] Levinson to Holmes, April 18, 1923.   [41] *Chicago Tribune*, May 7, 1923.
[42] Levinson to Allen, October 5, 1923.
[43] Allen to Levinson, September 25, 1923.   [44] October 5, 1923.
[45] The validity of this distinction will be more fully discussed below, pp. 190 ff.
[46] Levinson to Allen, December 21, 1923.

it was claimed that outlawry was included. Professor James T. Shotwell and other New Yorkers had drawn up an "American Plan," which had an influence in the preparation of the Protocol. In one of the discussions before the Chicago Council on Foreign Relations Shotwell brought "out the fact that this idea which originated in Chicago was of great value in drawing up the Protocol. . . . ."[47] Shortly afterward Irving Fisher suggested: "It will be a tremendous triumph for you and Senator Borah if America can be induced to sign the protocol, outlawing war in fact as well as in name."[48] And while Shotwell did not advocate United States adoption of the Protocol, he did want recognition of the "work done recently at Geneva."[49]

But Levinson was strong in his denunciation of the whole affair from the first. William Hard asked for his first impression of the Protocol, and he replied in a long telegram:

New League Protocol conforms to diplomatic orthodoxy by using soft glove of Outlawry promise to conceal its iron hand of world control by force stop it revives reinforces and makes formidable the two dangerous articles of force namely ten and sixteen stop these two articles have been allowed to lie fallow and the Bok Plan supported by the prominent pro-Leaguers of America proposed that they both be plucked out by the roots stop now the reverse is taking place these articles are not only to be revived and made the heart of the Covenant but they are to be supplemented by special treaties and military alliances stop now comes the wily Jap and renews the fight for race equality which was compromised with Wilson for Shantung and the League respectively in nineteen nineteen stop now however Japan is supported by nations which are also chafing under immigration restrictions and debt obligations and they are proposing to make of Covenant article eleven a world super government by means of which all questions including domestic ones and of course the Monroe Doctrine can be dealt with on the pretense of preserving the peace of the world stop independently of Jap incident the Protocol at best is a scheme to outlaw war with war stop in short to control the world by force with the real power in the hands of three or four nations coupled with a potential threat to United States that unless she becomes member of League and submits to Councils jurisdic-

[47] Mary R. Collier, executive secretary, Chicago Council on Foreign Relations, to Rabbi Leon Fram, November 6, 1924. On the relation of Professor Shotwell to the Protocol see Alfred Zimmern, *The League of Nations and the Rule of Law 1918–1935* (London: Macmillan & Co., Ltd., 1936), pp. 387 ff.

[48] Fisher to Levinson, November 18, 1924.

[49] Shotwell to Borah, November 28, 1924.

tion we may find ourselves in war with all League nations automatically against us stop this is wonderful treatment of the real winner of the war and an unprecedented creditor by our bankrupt debtors.[50]

His attacks, if anything, became more bitter when overtures such as that quoted above from Fisher were made. These people are "pilfer[ing] our titles, our phrases and our symbols without giving anybody credit for them. . . . ."[51] They are "stealing the livery of heaven to serve the devil in."

In the meantime Mr. Edward Bok had offered a substantial prize for the best peace plan. Some of the group wanted a plan submitted in behalf of the American Committee for the Outlawry of War; Dr. Holmes was "skeered" by the Bok propaganda; but Levinson agreed with Borah "against submitting any proposal to the Pact Committee and Judges of the Bok Prize outfit."[52] He thought that the danger from the League was constantly growing less as a result of the Corfu incident and that the Democrats would probably avoid the issue completely. Levinson presently secured an advance copy of the prize plan from Villard, who telegraphed:

Pure League propaganda done in particularly indecent way. Even summary printed on ballot is misleading, featuring world court, whereas plan is really simple plea to enter League. Bok's peace referendum most gigantic hoax since Cook discovered Pole.[53]

But Levinson contented himself with observing that the Bok plan supporters were inconsistent. The plan itself, he said, called for easing down the force articles of the Covenant, while men like Justice Clarke, though claiming that sanctions were essential to the League, yet hailed the Bok plan. He noted with satisfaction that some of the outlawry phrases had been appropriated and later that the promoters of the balloting on the plan were disappointed because of lack of popular interest in it.

These plans—the Pact for Mutual Assistance, the Geneva Protocol, and the Bok plan—were in Levinson's opinion all European in origin or spirit.

[50] October 3, 1924.

[51] Levinson to Allen, December 12, 1924.

[52] Levinson to Holmes, October 5, 1923.

[53] Villard to Levinson, January 4, 1924.

The way in which they would outlaw war is by war itself. While we are gaining ground, we are always in a dangerous path when anything emanates from the war offices of Europe. I don't think we will ever get the real brand of Outlawry from the European diplomats and the officials of the war department. . . . .[54]

Another contemporaneous event illustrates the fighting effectiveness of the outlawry group. The *Atlantic Monthly* asked Walter Lippmann in the summer of 1923 to write a history and critique of the outlawry movement. He in turn asked Levinson for materials. Levinson was under the impression since the appearance of the editorial in the *World* earlier in the year that Lippmann would treat outlawry favorably. He accordingly provided papers and went to New York for a special conference with Lippmann. But the article, when it appeared in the September *Atlantic Monthly*, was anything but satisfactory to the outlawry group. Said Levinson: "Notwithstanding [my assistance] after the manner of a good many lawyers who feel that they are hired to be on one side and to strain every point to belittle and besmirch their opponent and the opponent's cause, he grossly misstated many of the facts of the origin and history of the movement."[55] Holmes said the article was so clever that it disturbed him more than, for fear of wounding Levinson, he had ever intimated. A conference was held at the Levinsons' summer home in Maine. It was decided that Levinson with the assistance of Dewey should answer the article. Accordingly, he wrote to the *Atlantic Monthly*, saying it was his understanding that it was "your custom to give both sides of an important question. . . . . If you can reserve the space in your December issue, I can submit manuscript for your approval in apt time. Doctor John Dewey may collaborate in the answer."[56] But the editor thought the Lippmann article was in itself an answer and that no answer could be written "without going over ground that is pretty familiar to our readers."

In the meantime Levinson was stricken with sciatica, and Dewey answered Lippmann through the pages of the *New Re-*

[54] Levinson to Faville, October 17, 1924.
[55] Levinson to Allen, October 5, 1923.
[56] Levinson to editor of *Atlantic Monthly*, September 8, 1923.

public in two articles which appeared October 3 and 24, 1923.[57] The first one was published without having been submitted to Levinson. In explanation the professor wrote:

> I should have sent you the article for criticism only I put off writing it till the last moment the NR would stand for and then there was not time. Anyway I thought there was some advantage in being able to say that you weren't in any way responsible in case of certain criticisms, and it might prejudice the cause less if a free-booter assumed all responsibility.[58]

But there was an exchange of letters in regard to the content of the second article.

The articles defined outlawry, what it is and is not, and discussed the possibility of codifying international law and the use which could be made of such law by a court with universal affirmative jurisdiction. Dr. Holmes said they were the most brilliant pieces of controversial writing he had ever seen, and Levinson described them as "masterful" and "smashing." They were reprinted in one pamphlet, and forty thousand of them were distributed. But it was a sore point with Levinson that he was not able to get the list of *Atlantic Monthly* subscribers in order to send each one the Dewey attack on Lippmann. He was disappointed also that the *Atlantic* would not mail the pamphlet to its subscribers at the expense of the American Committee for the Outlawry of War.

By the beginning of 1924 there were accessions to the outlawry movement which were not the result of a studied campaign. Dr. Charles Clayton Morrison, editor of the *Christian Century*, was one of the more notable of those who joined the movement in 1923. His magazine had a wide circulation among the leaders of the Protestant churches in America, and in his editorials he began now to advocate the outlawry of war. He had been opposed to United States adherence to the League of Nations; and, though his opposition resulted in the loss of a large yearly contribution to the support of the *Christian Century* and even though the League

[57] "Outlawry of War: What It Is and Is Not," *New Republic*, October 3, 1923, and "War and a Code of Law," *New Republic*, October 24, 1923.

[58] Dewey to Levinson, October 4, 1923. It should be added that this is what I think Professor Dewey wrote, for even his typewriting is sometimes almost impossible to make out.

was extremely popular in church circles, he had continued in opposition. Consequently, he must have been anxious to find an alternative to the League to support, in order to rid himself of the charge of being antipeace. His editorials were called to the attention of Levinson by Dr. Holmes. After a few days a meeting was arranged. Dr. and Mrs. Morrison were to go to the Levinson home for dinner on February 16, 1923, and they "stayed till midnight talking Outlawry." Levinson had found "one of [the] greatest acquisitions we have had,"a "real crusader, a wonder mind," a man of "human sympathies." So he wrote ten days later in a letter to Justice Allen, and a very close association during the rest of the year did not change his appraisal. For he wrote to Justice Allen again in December that Morrison was "one of [the] greatest assets in Outlawry," "brilliant," a "powerful and discriminating mind"; and, finally, that he was "flooring Shotwell."

Dr. Morrison was an interesting man. He had a great facility with ideas. No thought ever appeared to linger long in his mind before it found expression. He was a modernist in religion, but his manner was fundamentalistic and evangelistic. No evangelist who paints the tortures of hell or the beauties of heaven or the joy in the heart of a sinner saved by grace could talk with more certainty or earnestness than did Dr. Morrison when he dwelt on outlawry. Toward those with whom he disagreed he was direct and pointed. Truth was on his side, error on the other; those on the other side were misguided. They were to be defeated, shown up, not compromised with, for life was made up of all whites and blacks; there were no grays. Life was simple, the other side was lacking in keenness or had ulterior motives or was at any rate lost in a fog; the way out was easy when fundamentals were kept in mind. After a duel with him, his opponents gave the impression of having been outraged personally; and in their bitterness and exasperation they usually forgot the issue.

But his value in the crusade for the outlawry of war can hardly be overestimated. When Borah had one of his moody spells with Levinson, he would talk to Morrison; or when he would not take advice direct from the "Leader," he would get it indirectly through the editorial columns of the *Christian Century* and, as likely as not, congratulate the editor for his great service to the cause of peace by writing so lucidly. When it seemed impolitic to send any other emissary to the President, Morrison could go as a spokesman for the Protestant churches and be received with cordiality. But his greatest value was his access through the columns of his magazine to the Protestant leaders. Always in the closest touch with Levinson, except at rare moments, he carried on a propaganda campaign for outlawry which was up to date from the standpoint of information and timed to the strategy of the particular move then under way. And his power over persons with semireligious and intellectual inclinations was very great. Two typical examples may be cited. A dean of a small denominational college regarded him as one of the outstanding leaders of American thought. Morrison's pronouncement on a matter was likely with such a man to be conclusive. A certain doctor in a county-seat city of about seven thousand inhabitants, who has been a director of the chief bank and a Sunday-school superintendent in one of the largest churches in the little city, has read the *Christian Century* for years and years. When you mention Charles Clayton Morrison to him, a light comes into his eyes, and he may recall as one of the high points of his life an occasion when he ate dinner with the great editor.

In April, 1924, another Protestant minister, Dr. Melvin Verne Oggel, joined the outlawry ranks. He was a Presbyterian, influential among his fellow-ministers and for that reason a useful recruit. He was valuable also because he was a Woodrow Wilson Democrat and a very strong pro-Leaguer. It was this type of support which outlawry particularly required, since many of its own supporters had been vigorously opposed to the League. Dr. Oggel, as a believer in the League, would receive a better hearing among the churches, where the League had had a great proportion of its strength.

The earlier speaking of Raymond Robins, the "crusade" carried on in the *Christian Century*, and the writing and inside work of the Reverend Mr. Oggel had so popularized outlawry in church circles that by the summer of 1924 outlawry-of-war resolution's began to appear frequently in church conference resolutions.[59] By July, 1924, such resolutions were adopted by the Pacific Coast Conference of Unitarian Churches, the Chicago Presbytery, the Connecticut Universalist Churches, the Vermont Congregational Conference, the Lutherans, the Canadian Presbyterian General Assembly, and the General Presbyterian Assembly. By the end of 1925 Dr. Morrison reported that the Methodist General Conference, the Disciples International Convention, the Northern Baptist Convention, and the Federal Council of Churches of Christ in America, with innumerable state conferences and local groups of all denominations had passed resolutions calling for the outlawry of war.

All this was very gratifying to Levinson and his lieutenants, but they were not content. The support of the religious bodies was extremely important and welcome to them, but they were now out for higher game. They wanted to have a president in the White House of their own way of thinking and willing to champion their cause. They had already started to lay their plans for 1924. To this we must now turn.

[59] C. C. Morrison, *Outlawry of War* (Chicago: Willett, Clark & Colby, 1927), p. 25.

CHAPTER VIII

THE CAMPAIGN OF 1924

As early as 1920 Levinson had begun to mention Borah for a place on the presidential ticket, but the "Thunderer from Idaho" had been shy as a maiden at such talk. Though Levinson held on to this ambition for his "Hamlet," he was not unwilling to follow other leads to advance the cause.

With the introduction of the outlawry resolution in February, 1923, Borah suggested that they should embark on a nonpartisan campaign to force an outlawry plank into each of the political platforms and to "see to it that every candidate, actual and potential [be] made to declare himself flatly on the subject and if he doesn't come out squarely for outlawing war, God help him."[1] Levinson's reaction to this was enthusiastic:

> In reflecting upon our talk Thursday night, I am tremendously impressed with your proposition to present Outlawry as a non-partisan issue. I think this is not only the statesmanlike and humanitarian thing to do, but I think it quite the most effective politically, as well.[2]

These tactics were for public consumption. He was in the meantime discussing privately with Robins what effect a speaking campaign by Borah would have on his presidential possibilities. But before they had their plans laid, Harding began to forestall the issue in the minds of the irreconcilables by proposing the adherence of the United States to the World Court. In Levinson's estimation he had made a "political fool of himself under the auspices of Hughes and Hoover"[3] and "wrecked not only his candidacy . . . . but the Republican Party" as well.

There was consternation among the enemies of the Court, for "it was regarded as certain that the President [could] put the [Court] over in the next Congress." Several alternatives appeared

[1] Levinson to Hauser, February 28, 1923.

[2] Levinson to Borah, February 19, 1923.

[3] Levinson to Dewey, April 27, 1923.

[120]

open. One was a third party headed by Borah. It seemed that the Senator was openly flirting with the idea, and Levinson and Robins went over the possibilities very carefully. They found a "lot of important Republicans" were "almost unanimously against the League Court and many of them [had] a very great and growing interest in your [Borah's] personal candidacy." Consequently, they were

sure that if you would do your utmost, as you have in the past, to stick to the Republican ship, you would carry with you . . . . a very large section of the Republican party, whom otherwise you might lose. While the issue is great enough for a third party and while a third party may become inevitable, we think now, thirteen months ahead of time, that you ought to do all you can to remain steadfast to the party, particularly as you have been so viciously attacked by your unscrupulous opponents on this very theme.[4]

He added that if Borah jumped the party fences Johnson would probably try to rescue the party. In that case with no other issue separating them, Borah would lose. Besides it appeared likely that he could attract nearly as many of the independent voters by staying in the fold as by running independently.

As Harding "got more and more tangled up with himself and his party" and his lack of "mentality requisite for profound conviction or for continuity of purpose" became more apparent, Levinson felt that the President might be shelved without running the "League perils of a Democratic President." And Borah appeared almost willing to make an avowed bid for the nomination. He went to St. Louis in May to make a speech attacking the Court and for a discussion of the Russian question. Levinson went also to hear the "fearless humanitarian" and to see what the popular reaction would be. He considered it as a virtual announcement of the Senator's candidacy. But Borah did not quite start the race.

Another alternative which kept bobbing up for several months was the nomination of "Uncle Hi Johnson." Robins first suggested it. A bosom friend of Johnson's since Bull Moose days, he had been estranged by his refusal to favor any peace program. If Johnson could be converted to outlawry, he would be much

[4] Levinson to Borah, May 14, 1923.

stronger and more easily nominated and elected than Borah. During the late summer and fall Robins had been on a speaking tour which took him from the conservative East to the Progressive West and he found much sentiment for "Uncle Hi" everywhere. Levinson at the same time discovered that Otto Kahn was favorable and George Henry Payne of the *Forum* already actively working for him. The next problem was to find if the Senator could be induced to champion outlawry.

One of the close friends of Johnson was Senator Medill McCormick of Illinois. One day Levinson met him in a Chicago bank and was surprised at his interest in outlawry. McCormick's term in the Senate was expiring, and he was angling for the oratorical support of Robins and whatever assistance Levinson could give him. Levinson quickly suspected this and immediately set his price—though only in his own mind until he could confer with Robins. If the Senator would join the outlawry forces, then they would help him in his fight for nomination. A good deal of dickering went on, McCormick always appearing as much interested in outlawry, though never giving a straight-out avowal. Harold Ickes for reasons of progressivism wanted Robins either to enter or threaten to enter the race for the nomination against the Senator, and Levinson was at times also willing for outlawry reasons. Robins, however, preferred the original approach: "Perhaps you should see him again, and if he will say what you think is sufficient I will come into Illinois and help him. He is our best bet on the whole in that State. . . . ."[5] Finally Levinson and McCormick laid their cards on the table, and Levinson summarized "the finals" to Robins under nine points. (1) McCormick and Johnson felt there was some danger in the background if they avowed outlawry; they might lose their great asset of isolationism. Levinson dared them or anybody else to come forward with the dangers. (2) McCormick was anxious for Levinson to explain outlawry to Johnson.[6] (3) The irreconcilables in the Senate had "the

[5] Robins to Levinson, December 13, 1923.

[6] McCormick especially wanted Levinson to explain outlawry to Johnson, since the "Father of Outlawry" had made it much clearer to him than had Knox when the latter had discussed it.

idea that Borah was changing and had practically abandoned them when he offered the Resolution without even consulting any of them." (4) McCormick dwelt at length on the coldness between Johnson and Borah and brought himself into it, "indicating that the Johnsons had been very, very sensitive and suspicious of a great many of their good friends." (5) McCormick was anxious to see Robins and for him to try to patch matters up. (5) Levinson emphasized the danger of a negative policy in view of the women voters. (7) McCormick wanted Levinson to spend three days with the senators in Washington. (8) McCormick had misgivings about Coolidge; the President appeared in a two-hour conference to lack initiative. (9) And McCormick was willing to co-operate with the outlawrists provided, of course, that Johnson could be "convinced first."[7]

Robins had tried his siren voice on his former intimate while they were traveling in France during the summer. Johnson promised not to fight outlawry, though he did consider it a counsel of perfection, "because Europe wouldn't agree to it and wouldn't keep faith if it did agree." Later Mrs. Raymond Robins poured the virtues of outlawry into his ear at a dinner party, and it seemed as if he were going at least to leave room for it in his plans; but by the last of November Levinson had become disgusted at his demagogic tactics. None of his associates except Robins trusted Johnson, and another alternative had emerged.

The going had been rough for Harding. Government had proved to be not so simple a job after all; and a party eight years out of office, whose apparent reason for existing appeared to be an organized appetite, needed sterner control than could be found in the easy, good-natured soul of Warren G. Harding. As the most worthy act of the first Charles's life was the leaving of it, so the greatest service Harding rendered to his party was when he quit it.

What manner of man was the New Englander who had suddenly become president of the United States in the middle of the night? Was he safe on international issues? As to that, "I hope to let you know when I am in New York . . . . ," Levinson wrote

[7] Levinson to Robins, November 22, 1923.

to Holmes. If he was safe, then it would be simply a matter of finding a running mate for him, though Robins doubted if any Republican could win, especially if La Follette entered the race on a third ticket. The colonel went to see Coolidge, who asked for a full written statement on outlawry. Robins, then, by his own admission, wrote the "best letter" he had ever produced. The President made his commitment on outlawry in a letter to Robins, November 13, 1923.

MY DEAR COLONEL ROBINS:

Your favor of recent date has been received. I trust that our country is in theoretical harmony with the position you are striving to reach. It is exceedingly difficult, in fact almost impossible, to get any consideration of international questions in Washington at the present time. It would be especially so just before the Presidential election. Some of the things that you mention I am trying to do, in so far as I can find them practicable. You noticed, however, that when we made as mild a suggestion as that we take an inventory of what Germany had, the result of which was to be binding upon no one, we could not secure any agreement to that end. You will recall also the obstacle that stood in our path at the Washington Conference. These things are not hopeless, but they require long and painful effort. I am very much pleased that men like you who have the public ear are thinking of them and talking of them. You have expressed an ideal towards which I believe the world is moving.

When are you coming to Washington again? I hope next time I shall have a better opportunity to talk with you.

Very truly yours,

(*Signed*) CALVIN COOLIDGE

Said Robins to Levinson in comment on this letter, "if you can determine from Coolidge's letter whether he is coming or going you are a better man at interpreting dead languages than I am."[8]

Perhaps the President's "Hardingesque" language might be clarified in his message to Congress. And while they waited to see they maintained close touch with Johnson's promoters and endeavoured to keep the road open for Borah.

The President told Borah, the latter reported, that the outlawry scheme was the "real solution" but that it was impracticable because of the situation in the Ruhr; if he indorsed it, he would be acting totally alone, because "no government of importance to

[8] November 20, 1923.

the continued peace of the world was free" to accept the program at that moment. On other matters also the Senator approved of the President's attitude; he was satisfied "that his message upon taxation and the bonus will disclose a clear program and courage." This despite the fact that Borah also said that politics were so tense in Washington that he hadn't found a "backbone" in three weeks, although there were plenty of "dishrags," which were serving.[9] Borah then decided that he would not permit his name to be entered in the primaries. But, on the same day, November 30, that Robins gathered this information, he saw an advance draft of the President's message to Congress. To his sorrow he found that Coolidge would support the Court.

Robins was perplexed. "I'm in more trouble," he wrote, "than I have yet been in a political scrap." They would all be forced aboard the Johnson wagon or they would be silenced on the great international issue. Yet the opposition to outlawry of both Johnson and his lieutenants was becoming clearer. On the other hand, even though Coolidge had been led astray on the Court, he had accepted outlawry "in principle," and others high in the councils of the party were favorable to it. John W. Weeks was for it, if his "explicit statement" could be trusted. Hays had called up Harvey on the telephone in the presence of Robins and "argued for our position . . . . [and] made an excellent statement for the tactical advantage of a declaration in favor of Outlawry in the message of the President. Frankly I could not have asked for it to be done better." The situation was at a crisis. "Soon [we are] going to have to decide who [m] we are going to support."

Borah and Robins were both deeply interested in the recognition of Russia. In their visits to the President during November this matter had been broached. They were convinced that it was Hughes not Coolidge who opposed the re-establishment of diplomatic relations with the Soviets. On December 1 the President intimated to Robins that his message to Congress would contain an overture to the Soviets. Whereupon Robins immediately cabled in their cipher to Moscow what answer he thought they should make to the President. With Coolidge making friendly

[9] Borah to Levinson, November 30, 1923.

gestures toward both Soviet recognition and outlawry, it seemed a foregone conclusion where Robins' and Borah's support for the presidential nomination would go. Levinson was really far from being enthusiastic about Coolidge; but, with Johnson out of the question and Borah refusing, he seems to have decided that, as Coolidge was the man he would be forced to support eventually, he might as well accept him with what enthusiasm he could. Consequently, when Professor Dewey, always favorable to a third party, needed reassurance as to the progressiveness of the President, the strategist of outlawry took advantage of the seemingly increasing White House approval of it to write a most enthusiastic letter to Dewey. In the course of it he said:

(This I recite with great thrill.) The President has fully approved the Outlawry of War as the real solution of the war problem. His only hesitancy is that he is doubtful of being able as President to make any headway at the present time, and until the Russian and Ruhr questions are settled. (I have from two main sources representing two independent talks with the President that he has been won over completely to the theory of Outlawry.)

It is not necessary for the President to take the lead in Outlawry at this time. . . . . I cannot tell you how much moved and how I feel that our cause has been advanced by this news. While, as I said regarding the League Court, we are not able, especially as we have still to reckon with Hughes, to write our own ticket, I feel that we have made immensely more progress in the most powerful way possible than I could have expected a few weeks ago.[10]

The decision to support Coolidge was made in December, though not irrevocably, because Levinson was still talking with Robins about whom they were to support, though without much seeming encouragement from the colonel. However, the latter had made up his mind privately, although he still kept the politicians in Washington guessing, hoping that he could sell his support for more definite commitments than he had yet been able to extract.

Then came Teapot Dome, and the Republican skies for the moment went black. Before venturing into the oil madhouse, we must glance once more at the perennial struggle to induce Borah to make the great speech in the Senate on outlawry. Levinson began early in the fall to point out how such a speech could be

[10] Levinson to Dewey, December 3, 1923.

made the basis for most of the things which Borah was interested in. Something had to be done to stem the rising tide of internationalism due to the Bok Peace Award contest, which was receiving such a good press as "to make one's heart sink"; and, when it became clear that Coolidge intended to support the Court, the necessity for making such a speech became more imperative.

Borah had made so many absolute commitments to follow up the outlawry resolution that he was expected to perform what he had promised without urging. For instance:

.... He stated that Outlawry of War was the greatest proposition before the world and that he was willing to make any sacrifices, personal or political, that would help the cause. He said he would ignore questions of personality and party and would give the best there was in him in whatever way we saw fit.[11]

But Levinson and Robins were not in the habit of calling him "Hamlet" without reason. Consequently, Robins and Dewey and Frances Kellor were all three deputed to try their various hands at persuading him to speak. The Senator did reintroduce the resolution on December 20, 1923, but Russian recognition was uppermost with him at the time and nothing happened. On January 25, 1924, he promised Robins that if the colonel could bind Coolidge to outlawry he would make the speech. Robins was to see the President on the morrow; but, regardless of White House concessions, he thought an additional stimulant would be needed for their Hamlet. Consequently, he wrote to Levinson that if he got any encouragement from Coolidge he would wire his mentor in Chicago, who should immediately write to Borah,

saying that I wrote to you of *his wise idea* that this concession to *Outlawry* from the President, made the circumstances that warranted and required his speech on that Resolution . . . . that you want [to hear it and broadcast it] . . . . that it is an added evidence of *his statesmanship* that he has resisted our appeals for this speech until this supreme moment, etc., etc., ... [impress him with his] *greatest wisdom in the tactics of statesmanship* . . . . that he will be glad . . . . to accept parentage and even support the brilliant child.

It would be in accordance with custom for Borah thus to assume the parentage of the child of another, according to Robins,

[11] Levinson to Hauser, June 9, 1923.

for, "the older I get" he declared, "the more impressed I become with the fact of the woods colt character of the great ideas of the GREAT STATESMEN."[12]

The interview with the President was not so fruitful as it must have been colorful, if one may believe the colonel's report. Coolidge was evidently holding back on both Russia and outlawry because of Hughes's attitude. When the President intimated that it might be well for Robins to see the Secretary of State, the colonel flatly refused to have anything to do with Hughes. So, for lack of the complete commitment that Borah wanted, the great speech was put off again. A new series of pressures produced new promises by Borah amid the friction of oil.

Levinson's first reaction to the disclosures of the Teapot Dome scandal was surprise and shock. Then, true to his slogan of "turning liabilities into assets" and proceeding as before, he saw an advantage for outlawry. The President "ought to be looking for an overmastering issue that would entirely cast into the shade the awful disclosures of the recent past." Robins should stay on the spot in order not to "let this golden opportunity pass because the pressure is so strong and the scare is so great that they would be a set of fools not to swallow most greedily your entire program."[13] Robins thought that "if Coolidge will take our program he can't be beaten," but, if not, then the nomination would not be any good. However, as the seriousness of the disclosures developed, even Levinson began to feel that, though Coolidge was innocent, he and the party would have to suffer for "the errors and crimes of its chosen and trusted officials"; and, since Coolidge was too weak to handle the situation, there might be a chance of nominating Borah; or, if conditions continued to run against the Re-

[12] Robins to Levinson, January 25, 1924. It should be added that Robins always wrote very freely to Levinson. Most of his letters were marked confidential. During the first months of 1924 he spent much time in Washington doing political work. In a postscript to one of his letters in which he had been most free to make "the firstlings of his heart the firstlings of his hand," he cautioned: "Please regard all my letters of substance as confidential. In that understanding I can write in freedom. No other can really know just what ought to be confidential in another's correspondence. Matter that seems entirely harmless may contain dynamite. Please destroy or bury in the graveyard my letters" (Robins to Levinson, January 24, 1924).

[13] Levinson to Robins, February 1, 1924.

publicans, Borah could lead a third party. Almost the only compensation he could see for the disgrace was the evidence that McAdoo had been near oil. As the revelations got blacker and blacker, he wrote to Borah that he was rapidly getting the "political blind staggers."

Why did not Coolidge act swiftly and with an iron hand? If he did not dismiss the culprits from his Cabinet, the Democrats might start impeachment proceedings; and then the culprits could be ousted only at the conclusion of those proceedings or under such circumstances as to give the Democrats the sole credit for cleaning the Republican stables. One of the high Cabinet officers could apparently think of nothing more timely in the "tense atmosphere . . . . of fear and corruption" than to send Robins off to "whoop it up at a Lincoln celebration."

Borah at first appeared to have a good deal of confidence in the honesty and honor of Coolidge; but before long he, too, became impatient that Attorney-General Daugherty, in particular, should be permitted to remain in the Cabinet. Robins found the Senator "fighting mad" near the end of February after he had talked with the President. Borah said Daugherty must resign in forty-eight hours or he had been trifled with, but Coolidge was noncommittal. Mr. George Lockwood, director of publicity for the Republican National Committee, thought Daugherty innocent, and he expected the President to stand by him. This was on February 25. Ten days later, after seeing the President again, Borah insisted that Daugherty had to go before he would accede to any of the requests which the President made of him. Lockwood was beginning to weaken in his defense of Daugherty. Hughes, who had been called into the "game," according to Robins was in favor of ousting Daugherty but doubted the legality of the Senate investigation; it was "an invasion of the prerogatives of the Courts and could be . . . . stopped."[14] Mr. C. Bascom Slemp, the President's secretary, transmitted these views to Borah at his home and offered to give Borah a "brief which Hughes had prepared on the illegality of the investigation procedure." The Senator's reply was:

[14] Robins to Levinson, March 6, 1924.

Legal or illegal, the investigation which uncovered wrong-doers should proceed and the technicalities were not important where national morality was concerned. He also said that they had plenty of good lawyers in the Senate and did not need a brief from the Secretary of the State.[15]

Robins reported Borah as in the sulks. He even appeared to feel that Robins had been trying to inveigle him into a wrong position. Consequently, "for the moment," Robins wrote, "I have passed him up and am working with less gifted and brilliant but more workable materials."[16] But two days later Robins had a friendly dinner with Borah, who was completely disgusted with the President and would have nothing to do with him. Robins agreed. Why didn't Coolidge act quickly to purify his official household? "This," Robins declared, "is one of the rare nights I would like to get drunk, or go to a fire or start a riot—or most any old thing. The move seems so manifest and so simple and the issues so overwhelming and we are so helpless."[17] And in disgust he went to his home in Florida.

Levinson, however, worked on. If Daugherty could be forced out under conditions which could be interpreted as reflecting credit on Coolidge, perhaps even yet an advantage for outlawry could be found; accordingly he went to Washington. He stressed the necessity for Daugherty's dismissal to everyone he knew but no encouragement came from those close to the President. Daugherty was scheduled to appear before an investigating committee; in the meantime nothing could be done. However, during the undaunted lawyer's second talk with Assistant Attorney-General Martin in the Department of Justice he felt that the situation was changing. He accordingly postponed his departure from Washington in order to get into touch with the President's confidential adviser, Stearns, to discuss the situation again. Stearns could not be located, but Levinson eventually saw Slemp, another secretary. Levinson told him:

My particular point is this: that Mr. Coolidge has three capacities—as a man, as an official and as a titular and responsible head of the Republican party.

[15] Levinson to Robins, March 31, 1924.
[16] Robins to Levinson, March 7, 1924.
[17] Robins to Levinson, March 9, 1924.

As a man and as President he has the right within limits to protect and defend his appointee and his friend, but as the responsible head of the Republican party he is violating his sacred duty as trustee for sixteen million citizens by allowing his sympathies as a man and as an official to sway his judgment and to cause the wreckage of his own Republican party.

Slemp was impressed, and after making a few notes went in to see the President. When he came out, he said:

"I think everything will be straightened out." I said to him: "This is a novel situation in that no fixing up will serve the purpose unless Daugherty gets out. There can be no political deal or compromise that will help." He said: "I think, Mr. Levinson, you will be perfectly satisfied with what will be done."[18]

This interview was immediately reported to Borah, who refused to believe anything would happen. The next morning, however, Daugherty resigned, and Levinson sent a telegram to Robins in Florida to hurry back to Washington. Again plans were made for Borah's great speech. The time would be right, the Senator believed, in about three or four weeks—about the end of April.

The campaign for the Republican nomination for United States senator in Illinois had become complicated. McCormick had not yet given the commitment to outlawry, but Colonel Sprague, a former Republican, had entered the Democratic primary and had pronounced himself against the League and the Court and favorable to outlawry. This put Levinson in a dilemma. He was fearful of being maneuvered into a situation where he would be forced to support a Democrat. On the other hand, the administration was anxious for the nomination of McCormick as opposed to Deneen. Slemp had asked Borah to make a speech before Daugherty had resigned, but Borah had flatly refused. Levinson wanted Robins to aid McCormick, but matters were so pressing elsewhere that the colonel either could not or would not do so. Finally, Deneen was nominated over the sitting Senator.

The question of persuading Borah to speak on outlawry was again in order. He had been rather fulsome in his praise of the editorials which Morrison had been writing on outlawry in the *Christian Century*. Morrison seized the opportunity to write and to see him, arguing for the advantage of the expected speech. If he

[18] Levinson to Robins, March 31, 1924.

waited until the Court was being debated, it would have an unhappy effect, he thought, on the church people of America. They would consider it a "mere opposition idea." It was important for outlawry to get the support of the Wilson tradition in the church.[19] Borah's reply to this importuning was characteristic. There was a limit, he said, to human energy, and he was taxed beyond it already. He went on:

> The situation is such here that it is not possible for me to avoid being occupied with other things which interest me far less and are less momentous in every way, but nevertheless they must have attention under present conditions. When I can do the work and do it as it should be done, I shall take great pleasure and pride in doing it.[20]

There was indirect intimation that Coolidge wanted Borah as his running mate or to make the nominating speech; the outlawry fraternity, except Borah, were highly enthusiastic. The Senator absolutely refused to be enticed into support of Coolidge at that time, May 10; he was so set against having anything to do with the "Coolidge gang" that he appeared ready to run on a third-party ticket. Robins admonished Levinson: "Now is the time to see your friend Weeks and together with Martin and Slemp and Strawn you must win the President, or we are off the Republican map."[21]

But, instead of attempting to "win" the President, the play went the other way. Levinson with Robins' help won Borah's promise to run on the ticket with Coolidge in 1924.

It was assumed that because of oil and corruption Coolidge would have slight chance of winning the election. Levinson, after consultation with Weeks, went to the President to discuss the weakness and suggest the remedy—Borah. His fearlessness and honesty would be a bulwark of strength. Coolidge was willing and anxious, but he doubted if the Senator would accept the nomination. It was then the task of Levinson and Robins to persuade the Senator, who, when they approached him, could see no virtue in becoming the spare tire for any administration. But

[19] Morrison to Borah, April 26, 1924.

[20] Borah to Morrison, April 29, 1924.   [21] May 10, 1924.

after it was shown to him how he would be next in line in 1928 and how he could resign, if elected, and become Secretary of State, thus preserving his place in the line of succession and at the same time be active in directing the foreign affairs of the country, he consented. Attempts to arrange an immediate appointment for him to see the President were blocked by Slemp, the President's secretary, who said it was useless in any case, for he himself had asked Borah and had been turned down. The earliest possible appointment he would make was for the next morning at ten o'clock. The next morning the Washington papers, but not the New York, carried a story of a boom for Lowden for the vice-presidential nomination. (Slemp had been the manager for Lowden in 1920.) When Slemp was called on the telephone, he denied any knowledge of the news. Levinson and Robins waited anxiously for Borah to return from seeing the President. His answer, given with the innocent smile for which he was famous, to their question as to what happened was: "Nothing." Levinson and Robins, however, found later that Coolidge disclaimed any knowledge of the Lowden boom. But the golden moment was gone when Borah would accept the nomination. During the convention in Cleveland no amount of persuasion over the telephone could move him to accept. Levinson felt that the failure to get Borah on the ticket was one of the turning-points in the history of the country and especially in the history of the Republican party.[22]

Platforms, however, as well as candidates were to be watched. Levinson's first care was to get outlawry into the Republican platform, the plank he submitted being as follows:

We favor the codification of international law based on justice and equality between all nations, great and small. The U.S. should take the lead in promoting a general treaty between the nations abolishing and outlawing the use of war for the settlement of international disputes. But the right of defense against invasion shall not be impaired.[23]

[22] The popular rumor at the time concerning the Republican vice-presidential nomination was that Borah had answered Coolidge's inquiry as to whether the Senator would run with him on the ticket with "Which place?" But, according to both Levinson and Robins, Coolidge never actually mentioned the matter to Borah.

[23] Levinson to Slemp, June 9, 1924.

Only the part declaring for codification of international law was put into the platform. With the Democrats he was more successful. He sent his outlawry plank to Bryan, and the platform contained this statement: "we pledge all our energies to the Outlawry of War." But, following this, appeared praise of the League which spoiled the whole thing for him. The La Follette platform advocated an agreement to outlaw war. Coolidge threw a sop in the direction of the outlawry camp in his speech of acceptance:

I, personally, should favor entering into covenants for the purpose of outlawing aggressive war by any practical means. Those who are working out detailed plans to present such a policy for consideration have my entire sympathy.[24]

The inclusion of the word "aggressive" showed that Coolidge had failed to understand outlawry;[25] nevertheless Levinson treated it as a commitment by the President.

The activities of the outlawry group in the presidential campaign were characteristic. It was too much to expect such men as Dr. Holmes and Professor Dewey to support Coolidge. But Levinson's and Morrison's[26] Republicanism could be trusted when a national campaign got under way. It was a different matter with Robins and Borah. The Republican high command especially desired the support of the two latter.

Robins stated his price candidly and without reserve to men who approached him. Senators Butler and Pepper told him he was the best man to keep the progressives from going astray after La Follette. To them all he said his action depended upon Borah and that the Senator's action would be determined by the conditions of his nomination for the Senate in the Idaho Republican convention and by the measure of support accorded him by the Republican state and national organizations. The second demand Robins made was for the President to state his support of outlawry. Furthermore, they had asked that Robins should be

[24] Levinson to Hauser, October 7, 1924.

[25] Between 1919 and 1924 Levinson had changed his position with regard to distinguishing between defensive and aggressive war (see below, p. 194, for discussion of the point).

[26] By 1932 Dr. Morrison had deserted the Republican party.

put on an advisory committee. This he refused until he received satisfactory assurance of compliance with his demands.[27] The arrangement was made after a conference with Borah. At the end of August Robins reported that Butler had delivered his end of the contract and that they must get Borah out to do something; they just had to "deliver Borah." Robins' own activity in "whooping it up" for Coolidge put him, the erstwhile progressive, in strange company; he got something like a Bronx cheer from his former progressive friends. To prove his sincerity, he paid his own traveling expenses during the entire speaking tour he made for the President.

The next problem was to "deliver Borah." There is no record of any letters written to him by Robins. One reason may be that it is not common in our culture to use asbestos for letter-writing purposes. After his exasperation had been exhausted in a lament over the Senator, he philosophized: "Well, it's just another illustration of the aphorism, 'We can lick our enemies, but our friends are hopeless.' "[28]

The efforts of Levinson to coax the Lone Wolf into the fray were numerous and varied. He played on the hates, prejudices, loyalties, and honor of the Senator, but with only partial success. The Democratic candidate, Davis, had said something derogatory about outlawry in a speech in August, while Coolidge had been complimentary, so the patient lawyer concluded: "You now have irresistible momentum behind your Resolution provided always Davis, the Baker-like pro-Leaguer is not elected." He had just promised the President: "I would write you hoping that you would handle brother Davis in your own inimitable way." His letter ended: "Please be good enough to let me know that you will hurl a thunderbolt at Davis. We must eliminate this dangerous pro-Leaguer."[29] There being no sign of a thunderbolt for a month, Levinson telegraphed September 29, 1924:

Raymond [Robins] left last night on his extended itinerary stop he seemed somewhat disturbed about your delayed program which is so vital to us all stop

[27] Robins to Levinson, August 6, 1924.
[28] Robins to Levinson, November 13, 1924.
[29] Levinson to Borah, August 26, 1924.

He had fine reassuring talk with chief [Coolidge] at capital last week stop I sincerely trust nothing has changed the plans agreed upon here. . . . .[30]

The next day Borah answered:

I have your telegram before me of the 29th.

The situation in Idaho, Levinson, is such that I cannot leave here just now and I do not know just when I can. I do not want to be selfish about the matter, but I think under all the circumstances, I should make no mistake about this condition here before I leave the State. Furthermore, I think I can be of just as much service later as by going in at the present time. In view of Mr. Dawes' speech upon reclamation and some other things, I am very much embarrassed and just now I am interested in trying to counteract the effects in this part of the country to some parts of the national campaign. I am quite sure if you understood the situation here, you would fully agree with me.

In other words, I am doing the best I can to serve the cause particularly in which you and Robins and I are more interested—that is, serve it ultimately.

I write somewhat in haste as I am in the midst of the campaign.[31]

On October 3 Levinson answered, that, above all things he didn't want Borah to jeopardize his own election; but it was the understanding when the agreement was made that it would take about ten days to fix up the local situation, and "then you would be free to start out. I remember your winsome smile as you turned to me, when we three were dining together and said, 'Levinson, I am going to follow the Colonel.' " Clippings were included to prove the rumor that Borah would not support Coolidge. Besides, the agreement had been made, and "I consider the matter vital," Levinson went on, "from the standpoint of both you and the Colonel and therefore of myself for the following reasons." Here followed five reasons. The colonel had made arrangements only after consulting him:

The President had promised, among other things, to give us all the time and consideration we wanted for Outlawry after the election. In the language of the Col[onel]: "It is not so much the President's making good with us as our making good with him. I am absolutely convinced of his co-operation with us."

The presidential year, 1928, was coming, and Levinson had it in mind. It was true that Dawes was a liability on the ticket, but Coolidge ought to be protected from him. And Coolidge was going to win.[32]

[30] Levinson to Borah, September 29, 1924.
[31] Borah to Levinson, September 30, 1924.
[32] Levinson to Borah, October 3, 1924.

The next day, October 4, Levinson reinforced his argument by pointing out how "Wall Street interests" and the "International Bankers" might after all prefer Davis to Coolidge; and with La Follette dividing up the West they might throw New York and New Jersey to the Democrats, whereupon the fight against the League would have been in vain.

A few days later Borah granted an interview to the press, in which he paid a personal tribute to Coolidge. About October 20, Levinson renewed the pressure, only to receive this rather curt reply:

I have your letter of yesterday. I am very sorry you and the Colonel seem to be disappointed or dissatisfied with my work or attitude in this campaign. I think if you were more familiar with the situation with which I have to deal, particularly in my own State, you would not feel as you do.

I have done the best I could under the circumstances. I have managed not to say anything I didn't believe and not to refrain from saying anything that I did believe, so that I will have no retreating to do in the future.

I do not entertain the view that you and the Colonel do with reference to my most effective instruments of warfare after the campaign is over. Have been here a good while and I think I know pretty well how to get results on small capital invested.[33]

Levinson could be firm, too, though courteous. His reply was to the effect that he and Robins always had the Senator's political and personal welfare at heart; the action they had taken had been with his approval, and he would continue to be their inspiring leader until "we reach a point where free men cannot agree. . . . . I cannot resist saying in closing, that I have an abiding friendship and affection for you which I trust nothing can undermine."[34]

Then came the election. In the fellowship of victory the differences over tactics in battle were forgotten; and a statement by Coolidge commending outlawry drew forth so much praise from Borah for Levinson and Robins, on the one side, and from them for him, on the other, that personal differences were swallowed up by mutual admiration. The ranks of the outlawrists were united for the next battle—the fight for peace among the peace workers.

[33] Borah to Levinson, October 22, 1924.
[34] Levinson to Borah, October 24, 1924.

CHAPTER IX

THE FIGHT FOR PEACE AMONG THE PEACEMAKERS

THERE were two kinds of peace advocates in America in the 1920's; there were those who wanted peace but were not particular what road they took to reach it; and there were those who wanted peace but would consent to approach it only by a road of their own choosing. There was a good deal of internecine warfare among those of the latter group. And the warfare was frequently the more bitter because in many cases it became a clash of personalities rather than merely a difference of opinion. Among all the peace workers there was a feeling that there should be a common program and that they should stop wasting their energies in sniping at each other. Said Anna Garlin Spencer to Levinson:

> If I were a Czar, an ethical Czar (a very unAmerican suggestion) I would shut a few people into one room and keep them there until they could give us a united leadership. Senator Borah would be one, Ex Justice Clarke would be another, the President and Secretary Hughes would be others. You would be there and two or three Democrats who should be able to speak with some actual power for their party and also for Mr. Wilson's point of view (for he is still an influence of strength).[1]

The difficulty of reconciliation between the extremists of the outlawry group and those of the League group was great. The latter felt that they had been defeated by the sharpest kind of trickery. The claim that the election of 1920, when prominent Republicans had urged that the election of Harding would guarantee American entry into the League[2] had been a verdict against it, made them bitter. They were also outraged by the campaign of falsification which had been carried on against the League.

[1] February 26, 1923.

[2] For Taft's own statement in support of Harding see William Howard Taft, *Papers on League of Nations*, ed. Marburg and Flack (New York: Macmillan Co., 1920), pp. iii f.

On the other hand, Levinson was bitter because of the flippant dismissal of his idea by those favoring the League. They appeared to mistrust him in particular, not only because they considered his ideas visionary and as an attempt to solve the war problem by the magic-wand method, but also because of his association with some of the most jingoistic superpatriots, who obviously were not interested in peace at all. In the excitement of battle he had also repeated with a straight face some of the extreme arguments of the superpatriots.

Several abortive attempts from time to time had been made to get these two groups together. However, by the end of 1923 there were evidences of a more sincere willingness on both sides. The presentation of the outlawry resolution to the Senate in 1923 seemed to arouse a feeling among the League party that outlawry could attract sufficient public attention for it to deserve recognition from them. Levinson, on his part, grew less belligerent because of the extending use of the term, "outlaw war," the gesture in the direction of outlawry in Lord Robert Cecil's Treaty of Mutual Assistance, and in the next year the similar gesture in the Geneva Protocol. As his idea was being accepted, he felt less necessity for pressing the attack.

There were two other reasons why Levinson in particular was willing by 1924 to attempt a reconciliation with the League group. The first was his desire for support for the Senate resolution to outlaw war. The first step toward a general treaty against war, he thought, would be adoption of the Senate resolution. The second reason was the impending consideration by the Senate of the World Court, or "League Court," as he and his lieutenants insisted on calling it. "In view of the attitude of the large majority of Senators in both parties with respect to the entry into the Court it is almost hopeless to expect to compass the defeat of the Court directly."[3] If the United States was going to adhere to the Court in any case, the thing to do was to offer support of the Court in exchange for consideration of outlawry.

However, Levinson's willingness to co-operate was not to be advertised. "Never appear too anxious but let the other side

[3] Levinson to Robins, April 29, 1925.

make the first move," epitomized his method in the fine art of negotiation. Another rule was to overstate opposition to the other side so that there would be room for adjustment. His extravagant attacks, for instance, on the Court among its friends did not reveal his real attitude as shown when discussing it with Borah. "Of course, the Court doesn't amount to very much in itself, except as it represents deception and misrepresentation and is used as a part of the League crusade and for the manifest purpose of getting us addicted to the League until we swallow it whole."[4] But the adjustment usually took a form which is characterized by a statement he made to Borah in reporting a debate with Manley Hudson: ". . . . You see we handled the matter in a conciliatory spirit, but without giving . . . . an inch of ground. This, I take to be your method, as I have observed you the past four years."[5] Like the ordinary negotiator he was always cautious with those with whom he was bargaining. "They are willing to furnish the ocean if we furnish the ship and their ocean is always ready."[6] And when he was angling for support, he had an eye, too, on the importance of the supporters whom he was acquiring. He would not bother with the Bok Peace Award publicity because "the position of Coolidge will offset five or ten million people at one stroke." Here is his own statement of the technique:

You know this negotiating business is familiar to me. It is interesting that these large world compromises are merely horse trades on a colossal scale. Human nature must be watched closely and the tactics of common sense and effective common negotiation must never be lost sight of, otherwise, we will allow ourselves to get into a position with the Leaguers where they will complain that they have yielded and that we are unyielding.[7]

A move for peace among the peacemakers was made by Professor Shotwell in November, 1924. He and some other pro-Leaguers discussed the outlawry-of-war resolution with Levinson and then arranged for a visit with Borah. Those present at the meeting were Levinson, Morrison, and Borah for the outlaw-

[4] Levinson to Borah, December 3, 1923.
[5] Levinson to Borah, March 17, 1923.
[6] Levinson to Dewey, October 19, 1923.
[7] Levinson to Holmes, June 27, 1924.

rists and Shotwell, Keppel, and Hale for the League party. This meeting was held, Shotwell explained because,

the time has come for those who really want to get rid of war to join their forces in a common attack upon the enemy, rather than spend themselves, as has been too much the case in the past, in mutual criticism.

The result was that Shotwell pledged his support of Borah's outlawry-of-war resolution on two conditions:

In the first place, that it would be understood that there was to be not criticism but recognition of the work done recently in Geneva. . . . . The second point was that we should accept the invitation to the Disarmament Conference called by the League of Nations.[8]

The recognition of the work done at Geneva was to be in the form of a statement accompanying the resolution. Levinson at first appeared well satisfied with the outcome of this conference. He lamented that Shotwell was still in favor of the League, but he commended his love of peace, his sincerity, and his intellectual attainment. But soon suspicions of Shotwell began to creep into his letters.

Whether or not Borah was bound to push his resolution as a result of the agreement with Shotwell is not clear. Borah gave no indication of wanting the Senate to consider it, and Levinson saw bad strategy in pressing it, since its consideration would probably bring up the Court and he was unwilling for the Court and the Senate resolution to be considered in the regular session, preferring a time when there could be extended debate. "If the World Court is jammed through, our proposal may merely be a reservation or a fifth wheel on a wagon."[9]

Levinson was soon convinced that the League party were not yet ready for genuine co-operation. They would have to be trounced more soundly before they would feel the need for real conciliation; consequently, he proceeded to pick a quarrel at the first opportunity. Borah made a speech on outlawry in Philadelphia on December 17, 1924. The same issue of the *New York Times* that carried a report of the Senator's speech "had a nasty

[8] Shotwell to Borah, November 26, 1924.

[9] Levinson to Robins, December 13, 1924.

editorial" which was "unscrupulous . . . . and . . . . offensive."
Levinson called up Shotwell and Keppel and

raised Cain about it. I told them I would be charged with having been caught
in a trap. They each disavowed the editorial and were high in praise of the
manner in which Borah had kept faith in the terms of our conference, but I capitalized the thing to the top of my ability for present and future purposes.[10]

He did not expect any congressional action that session of Congress, and he wrote to Robins:

I am not in favor of any more meetings at the present time for conciliation
purposes. That is what I had in mind in raising a row about the Times Editorial. Borah has done all and more than they can ask, and I do not believe in
pushing this thing further for the present.[11]

Another reason why he did not "believe in pushing this thing
further" was the feeling that the efforts at conciliation were alien-
ating Borah. After the meeting in November, Borah stopped answering his letters. In December he complained to Robins about
Borah's silence. In the middle of January he wrote to Holmes:
"Confidentially, I fear Borah has taken offense at me because of
some of these developments. I can't account for certain things
otherwise."[12] These hunches of Levinson's were made more
plausible when Borah expressed his resentment to Robins because of the conference with the League party.

In the meantime Levinson wrote an article which appeared in
the *Christian Century* for January 8, 1925, entitled, "Can Peace Be
Enforced?" It was his contention that the use of sanctions meant
war; that, therefore, any force used by the individual states must
be applied only to their own nationals; and that in the last analysis dependence would have to be put on the good faith of the
states to carry out the obligation to punish their own war criminals. He thought this article would "draw the fire" of the League

[10] Levinson to Borah, December 23, 1924. The editorial to which Levinson objected was entitled, "A Lonely Statesman," and it was concerned with Borah's
record of talking for one set of ideas and voting for another. The speech in Philadelphia "illustrated what has been called 'the solecism of power'—which is vehement
advocacy of ends while rejecting the necessary means" (*New York Times*, December
18, 1924).

[11] Levinson to Robins, December 23, 1924.

[12] Levinson to Holmes, January 15, 1925.

party, "if they had any fire left." Another thing which hardly
made for conciliation was the question that he put to the advocates of the World Court. He asked what disputes the United
States would submit to the World Court that it would not submit to the Hague Tribunal. William Hard, at his behest, put this
question in the Hearst papers to embarrass the Court party; and
when Raymond Fosdick was scheduled to speak in Chicago in
February, 1925, Levinson wrote to him demanding that he answer it during the course of the address. At this time his attitude
with regard to the League party seemed to be summed up by
"We have been trying to sting these people into a debate on the
subject or at least an answer of some kind. None has yet appeared."[13]

As evidence accumulated that the senators opposing the Court
project could not postpone consideration of it, Levinson began to
feel the need for a program of attaching outlawry to the Court.
The cutting-out of advisory opinions, the provision that "we have
as many votes as Great Britain, to wit seven" in electing judges
to the Court, and some "provision which will require the Court
to be based upon the real brand of outlawing war" were planks
in this program. He made these suggestions after having spent a
weekend with Borah and Robins and was now ready for another
effort at conciliation among peace workers. That he was hardly,
however, in the mood for a love feast with all the League party
may be gathered from his comments on some of the "gross misrepresentation" which "the perfectly self-satisfied Mr. [Ray-
mond] Fosdick" had perpetrated upon him.

The first move for conciliation came from Mr. James G. Mc-
Donald, when he reported a four-cornered debate among Hard,
Senator Bingham, Robins, and himself. After describing how
"cruelly, heartlessly, and wantonly" Robins had pillaried Bingham and how they had all enjoyed it and how amazed the audience had been at the "audacity of a mere commoner like Colonel
Robins daring to treat so rudely a Senator of the United States,"
he concluded by "hoping that some day I, or someone else, may
be able to convince you and Mr. Fosdick of the good which is in

[13] Levinson to Oggel, January 26, 1925.

the program of the other [party]."[14] Levinson answered this letter three days later by saying that he had had McDonald in mind for two or three years as "one of the most effective and valuable men for the ultimate junction of the peace forces." Then followed three pages of explanation of why it would be a difficult job, "in short, ... Brother McDonald, there are two or three fundamental and vital propositions on which we would rather lose than compromise."[15] Another exchange of letters followed, in which Levinson stated the outlines of outlawry for bargaining purposes and made clear his objections to the League program.

The next move was a meeting in Cleveland on May 31 of some of the outlawry group to draw up their program for co-operation. Among those present were Levinson, Dr. Morrison, Justice Allen, and Miss Hauser. The paper they worked out was put in the hands of the other outlawrists. Then came a chance meeting of Robins and Morrison with Sherwood Eddy and Kirby Page at a conference which was being held for another purpose in Columbus, Ohio. There was an exchange of recriminations during which Robins and Morrison were told that they were "poisoning the peace atmosphere of the country and doing great injury to the cause of world peace" and Eddy and Page were asked "where they would have stood in the slavery question"—whether for some of the compromises or "for the outright abolition of slavery." After this passage at arms Robins produced the Cleveland paper. As a result of the discussion which ensued it was decided to call a meeting of a larger number of representatives from both groups at the Hotel McAlpin in New York City for June 3.

Present at this meeting were twenty-two Court partisans, among whom were such persons as Professor Shotwell and Justice Clarke, while the outlawrists were Robins, Dr. Morrison, Dr. Holmes, and Miss Dreier. Levinson was not present at this conference, it appears, for reasons of strategy. It would be easier for him to apply his independent judgment to an agreement after it had been formulated. The first half-day was spent in explaining outlawry. It might be added that this explanation was badly

14 McDonald to Levinson, May 20, 1925.
15 Levinson to McDonald, May 23, 1925.

needed, since much of the ground for misunderstanding between the two groups was the failure of the "pro-Leaguers" to understand what Levinson meant by the "institutional status of war"; hence their mystification at his refusal to make a distinction between aggressive and defensive war. In the afternoon a tentative agreement was worked out on the basis of the Cleveland paper. This agreement was to be explored further by a committee which was appointed at the time and which was to report back to the full group on June 26. The committee was composed of Justice Clarke, chairman; Holmes, Morrison, Norman Thomas, McDonald, Levinson, and Shotwell.

When Levinson entered upon the direct negotiations, it was his aim, if he failed in attaching outlawry to the Court plan, either to divide the ranks of the "pro-Courters" or to "alienate from them such sincere peace advocates as Kirby Page, Sherwood Eddy, et al."

An agreement was prepared by the special committee and accepted about June 26, 1925, by the full committee. In the preamble the signatories agreed to a "program for the outlawry of the institution of war in the adherence of the United States to the World Court Protocol." It was understood also that "each person signing this program commits only himself to its approval and that he is not limiting in any degree or manner his freedom to advocate methods or agencies for promoting world peace other than or additional to the Permanent Court of International Justice." However, United States adherence to the Court was declared the chief issue before the country, and United States co-operation with the rest of the world necessary to end war. There were three planks in the program. The first provided for "immediate adherence of the United States to the Court Protocol, with the Harding-Hughes-Coolidge reservations." The second plank provided that within two years the signatories to the Court Protocol should indorse the basic principles of outlawry and call an international conference for the purpose of embodying these principles in a general treaty. These principles were: (a) war as an institution for the settlement of controversies should be made a crime under the law of nations, (b) the law of peace should be codified, and (c) the Court should have affirmative jurisdiction. The third plank was a condition subsequent. It provided that should the above planks fail of materialization within two years, the United States might withdraw from the Court. And its withdrawal would become automatic at the end of five years if the outlawry provisions were not put into effect.

Influential people signed the agreement. Among them were Justice Clarke, Professor Shotwell, Colonel Robins, Dr. Morrison, Levinson, Miss Mary Dreier, Justice Mack, Mr. Bruce Bliven, Mr. Sherwood Eddy, Mr. Herbert Croly, Professor Carlton J. H. Hayes, Mr. Norman Thomas, and Justice Allen. The list with the proposal in Levinson's files contained twenty-seven names, though later he said that there were in all thirty signers.

From the standpoint of such outlawrists as had a sincere desire for peace the agreement represented a genuine triumph, since it was all gain for them and no loss. The essence of outlawry was all there—a treaty condemning war, codification of law, and a court with universal affirmative jurisdiction. However, for those who had been using outlawry as an effective means of attacking the existing peace machinery, it was a distinct setback. The reactions to it appear to separate the proponents of outlawry into these two groups. By this test William Hard and Senator Borah were of those who valued outlawry for its obstructive uses only.[16] Levinson appraised the "Harmony Plan" very highly: "The more I reflect upon the coalition agreement, the more I am convinced that it is the ideal method of laying the foundation for durable World Peace in the shortest possible time."[17] It was a "great constructive protective" arrangement, which he was sure the strongest irreconcilable would "approve, if not applaud."

The Harmony Plan was no gain from the standpoint of hastening United States adherence to the Court, for it was clear that there were votes and to spare in the Senate to approve the Pro-

[16] William Hard by inference placed himself in this group by indicating that he doubted the desirability of permanent peace (see his article, "The Non-stop Peace Advocate," *World's Work*, March, 1929). Levinson dissented most emphatically from this characterization of Borah.

[17] Levinson to J. H. Clarke, September 24, 1925.

tocol. Only from the standpoint of unifying the peace forces of the country, in so far as that could be achieved, was the Harmony Plan of benefit to the League party.

Its subsequent failure was not due to lack of public attention. Beginning on July 15, when the Harmony Plan was released to three thousand American newspapers, it was given extensive publicity during the remainder of the summer and fall. It received considerable notice in the New York papers. Copies of the plan were distributed widely in England and other foreign countries. Justices Clarke and Allen, Kirby Page, Sherwood Eddy, and Raymond Robins carried on an extensive speaking campaign. Much propagandizing was done in the colleges and universities; and there, when put to a vote, the plan received huge majorities over other peace projects.

It is difficult to give an accurate account of the maneuvering for support of the plan and of the final explosion which left the peace forces more estranged than ever. So much of the negotiation went on in the presence of nearly all the members of the outlawry group that Levinson did not have to do his usual amount of letter-writing to keep his lieutenants informed, thus reducing the amount of information obtainable from that source. The charges of bad faith and double dealing which soon crept into the correspondence make what little information they give partial.[18] Consequently, no attempt will be made here to set down the bitter recriminations exchanged between the Court and the outlawry groups. One sample may suffice and a brief mention of the chief source of friction between them, which was Borah.

Whether or not the support of Borah for the agreement was an essential to its consummation, there was a strenuous effort on the

[18] Levinson felt that the final breakup was due to the "pro-Courters" running out on their contract. His explanation is that they said, "Coolidge has come out for us, now we don't need you." Others of the outlawry group agree with him. Dr. Holmes, not caring to risk his memory for the details, said that when the harmony agreement was called to his mind he had a distinct feeling of having been "outraged." Pearson and Brown (*The American Diplomatic Game* [New York: Doubleday, Doran & Co., 1935], p. 15) give their conclusion in this manner: ". . . . Calvin Coolidge came out for the World Court without the outlawry-of-war reservation, and the Shotwell group, no longer needing the support of Levinson and Robbins [Robins], tore up the compact."

part of Robins and Levinson to line him up. They went to see him and gave him a full statement of the plan. Would he support it? Robins said he would answer this question, when the Court party put it to him, in this manner:

> I shall seek to put the issue of Borah's going along as resting on the effectiveness with which they get publicity and cooperation of the peace forces in behalf of the Statement agreed to by the conference. I shall say that the Senator was skeptical of their ability to unite behind the Statement and that our first task is to do this, then we will have a right to expect the Senator's support.[19]

Levinson, on his part, continued to woo Borah during the summer and fall and to make known his feeling that the Senator would support the Harmony Plan if the other side did. But no new maneuver in the perennial struggle to conquer the unconquerable Borah showed any signs of success, for in the midst of it all the Senator wrote a letter to Professor John Grier Hibben, attacking the Court because of its alleged connection with the League:

> . . . . The one object for which I shall strive is to separate and divorce this court from the League. . . . . The contest in the Senate . . . . will be largely, if not wholly, confined to the one proposition, that of divorcing this tribunal from the League of Nations. . . . . When that is accomplished, I will no longer oppose our joining the Court.[20]

To use adherence to the Court project as a means of getting war outlawed was of no importance to him, for he did not mention the Harmony Plan.

During the first week of December another meeting of some of the Harmony Plan signatories was held, where Levinson "upbraided them for not having carried out in spirit the agreement." A few days later Professor Shotwell wrote letters to Eddy and Levinson in which he indicated that, as result of the Locarno agreements, conditions had so changed that "looking back at the document we signed, it seems to me that there is too much of an element of threat directed toward those powers which have already done more than we have done and that the *wording* of our desire for co-operation in the outlawry of war is now unsuit-

[19] Robins to Levinson, June 28, 1925.
[20] November 30, 1925.

able."[21] The former wording had been made to attract the support of Senator Borah, but inasmuch as his insistence that "absolutism in international affairs would keep the world in anarchy forever," any attempt at future co-operation with him was useless. The Senator was "misleading this country by playing up those elements of democratic prejudice and nationalist exclusiveness which are the dry material of the conflagration of war."[22] Levinson had not "quite done justice to the honesty of purpose of the men on our side of the group. I know that both in money and time we have contributed fairly and honestly."[23] Though the plan should be revised, he did not think anything would come of a meeting for that purpose.

Some telegrams had been exchanged between the opposite sides, copies of which were not available in the files. On the same day that Shotwell wrote his letter, Levinson wrote to Borah: "I think this thing has worked out pretty well, all things considered" and Robins was writing to Levinson: "It seems to me that you have just the situation that you must desire—that the 'record' is made up and can be used effectively in the battles just ahead."[24]

Despite the joy of outlawrists at their freedom to return to the old war against the Court, they did not miss the opportunities to let fly some barbed shafts at their fellow peace workers. The nonresistant pacifist, the Rev. Dr. Holmes, still had a resisting, not to say, a belligerent, pen. His fellow-nonresister, Kirby Page, was the target of this shot:

> When we signed that peace program we made a compact, one with another, and it strikes me that most of that committee have made of that compact a scrap of paper. What did we think we were doing last summer anyhow? Why did we waste time, strength, words and personal honor if we don't propose to do anything with our work or carry out our plighted word?[25]

Levinson replied to Professor Shotwell in a letter which was a combination of a buzz saw and a camel's-hair brush:

[21] Shotwell to Eddy, December 9, 1925.

[22] Shotwell to Levinson, December 11, 1925.

[23] Shotwell to Levinson, December 10, 1925.

[24] December 10, 1925.

[25] Holmes to Page, December 16, 1925.

I want to say to you, Professor Shotwell, that I have highly appreciated many things you have done. I see that Senator Walsh and others have been compelled to take your view of the Court, namely, that it is the "feeblest possible step toward peace," and not in any sense a remedy for war.

I also think your prediction of the coming Locarno that you made to me a year ago and as to which we began to see a process of agreement, shows your profoundly analytical comprehension of world developments and a general willingness to perfect the Harmony Agreement with the Outlawry group.

However, I everlastingly protest against making and signing a binding agreement to do a given thing and to commit ourselves to a given program, and then because some parties think they can accomplish their original purpose better by abandoning that agreement and breaking it—to do so. To me that is inexcusable. It is especially inexcusable to those who, like you, have no great delusion as to the value of our entering the Court.[26]

And like the Irish at a picnic the peace workers had a fighting "good time" bruising each other's heads.

[26] December 23, 1925.

CHAPTER X

THE SENATE VOTES ON THE COURT

LEVINSON's attitude toward the World Court has been referred to in earlier chapters. He had suggested changes as tentative bases for discussion;[1] and, in connection with the Harmony Plan, he had agreed to support it under certain conditions. But with different people he appeared to take different attitudes. It is only when construed in the light of the outlawry of war that these apparently inconsistent attitudes toward the Court are seen to have a substratum of consistency. In brief, he wished to scare the friends of the Court into accepting outlawry as a means of attaining their desires and to soften the attacks of the enemies of the Court by showing them that outlawry would not only conserve all the benefits claimed for the Court project but add others and remove all its shortcomings; it was outlawry and as little, or as much, of the Court as would help to get the maximum amount of outlawry.

Senator William M. Butler of Massachusetts, chairman of the National Republican Committee, one of the chief champions of the Court in the Senate, was constantly reminded of the political risk he ran in supporting it, of the popular suspicions of it, and of the charge that the Republicans were pulling Democratic chestnuts out of the fire. To Mr. J. Reuben Clark, avowed enemy of the Court, Levinson wrote in explanation of his support of the Harmony Plan shortly after it had been drawn up:

If the Court must pass, it would be infinitely better to clothe it with constructive conditions for peace upon which our permanent membership would depend, changing the basis of international relations and the theory of the League itself—constituting the difference between compromise with the Court and League and revolutionizing them.[2]

Levinson had had "a sickening feeling" when he had heard the President in his inaugural address devote twenty minutes "to the

[1] See above, pp. 99–101.   [2] October 1, 1925.

[151]

adherence of our government to the League Court with the 'thin-as-gruel' Hughes reservations"; but, since the Court forces were well organized and their opponents were not and since Coolidge considered himself bound to the Court by the platform pledge as well as by the Harding and Hughes commitment, Levinson felt that the only thing to do was to attach outlawry to the Court plan as a condition of his support of it.

His relation to Borah led him to voice very strenuous objections to it. Even though he was supporting it under the Harmony Plan agreement, he rejoiced at the discomfiture of the Court party when he thought that "Billy Hard" had had a "great victory" over them in a debate. And he reported with considerable glee a debate that he himself had had before a Republican club of Chicago, in which he had "stirred the animals up." He appeared to fear that his support of the Harmony Plan might alienate his chief leader in the Senate. Consequently, he was anxious to shiver a lance against the internationalists in order to demonstrate his fidelity to the Borah tradition.[3]

When he felt himself free from the obligations of the Harmony Plan in December, 1925, he began using extreme language publicly once more in his attacks on the Court. He was irritated beyond measure to find his name appearing on the advisory committee of "the World Court committee of the council of Christian associations." This "ghastly finding of my name" was somewhat softened at seeing the name of his lieutenant, Justice Allen, heading the list. This use of names without authority was the occasion for the exclamation: "This whole court campaign has been conducted on the basis of misrepresentation, exaggeration, and falsehood. This is the reason it has so roused my ire."[4] He considered the claim of the League group that United States adherence to the Court did not create any legal relation with the League a particularly vicious falsehood. "One might as well say that a contract may be made with a subsidiary corporation of a

---

[3] This paragraph may be a misinterpretation of his action. He may have been attacking the "League Court" proponents, as he called them, not to keep in good standing with Borah as is indicated, but rather to force them to support the Harmony Plan as he claimed.

[4] Levinson to Brown, December 8, 1925

[152]

parent corporation and yet that one has no legal relation with the parent corporation."[5]

While the adherence of the United States to the World Court was under consideration, the settlement of the French war debt to the United States came up. The war-debt problem was of peculiar interest to Levinson in addition to its connection with his peace activity.

I have not often in my life been so wrought up on a subject. You see it hits me home. I have spent thirty years of my life in corporate banking and finance in connection with legal matters in reorganizations, and I feel that I am at least partially qualified to pass upon those things in somewhat self confident fashion. In short, I am on the war path.[6]

He was quick to realize that the debt issue could be used as a scare against the Court. The "Hearst people hugged" this idea to their bosoms, and Senator Reed was delighted when Levinson suggested this argument:

We enter the League Court. . . . . We claim it is a vast improvement over any other court. . . . . Thereupon the French tender us a dispute in the form of the state of the indebtedness between the two countries. . . . . They will offer, big heartedly, to go to the League Court, this great judicial institution. How can we refuse?[7]

His first major blast was the publication of an article, "Capacity To Pay," in the Hearst press in the latter part of October, 1925. The plan of scaling down the obligations of a debtor to what he was able to pay under the principle of capacity to pay he considered to be the rankest type of financial heresy.[8] Who could tell how much France could pay? What were the criteria? Besides, "this 'Capacity to Pay' proposition, if it gets into economic affairs generally, will, in my humble opinion, destroy all the sound principles of banking and common honesty with which I am familiar."[9] In short "this infamous and damnable 'capacity to pay' [was a] subterfuge for cancellation."[10] Besides being published in the Hearst press in Boston, Washington, New York, and

[5] *Ibid.* [6] Levinson to Holmes, November 17, 1925.

[7] Levinson to Oggel, April 1, 1925.

[8] *Congressional Record*, LXVII (December 16, 1925), 916.

[9] Levinson to J. A. Lynch, December 11, 1925.

[10] Levinson to J. R. Clark, November 19, 1925.

Chicago, the article was placed in the *Congressional Record* by Senator Reed of Missouri;[11] and then Levinson had it reprinted and broadcast widely in financial and official circles.

Aside from other issues, the debt settlement would be a staggering loss for the American taxpayer. He telegraphed to Borah:

> Over fifteen thousand million dollars of the taxpayers['] money has just been given away by our administration to pave way for payment of existing bankers['] loans and to enable the placing of additional huge bankers['] loans at eight per cent with millions of dollars of commissions to bankers stop hypocritical excuse made in defense of Belgian settlement that Wilson's promises by letters were compelling moral commitments utterly lacking in Italy's cases where far greater concessions were made without such false pretence stop thus our government granted substantial cancellation to dictatorship government based on force with its secret military pact with soviet government stop all this is done under the treacherous and damnable doctrine of capacity to pay stop here we have situation in which public opinion except only soft headed pro-League section is being denied expression because of press silencers and infamous propaganda and far reaching power of administration stop as Washington says in his farewell address real patriots who resist intrigues of favorable [foreign] nations are liable to become suspected and odious while its tools and dupes usurp the applause and confidence of the people to surrender their interests.[12]

The arrangements were a double-barreled theft. In the first place, the settlements were claimed to conserve the principal, but the rate of interest was greatly reduced and the time for payment was extended to a long period. A loan to Italy of six hundred and forty-eight million dollars would amount to about a six-billion-dollar loss to the United States under the arrangement proposed. To one of his banker friends he wrote:

> It seems almost staggering to say that the government can lose eighty billion dollars on debts of twelve billion. But, as a banker, you are familiar with the cumulative loss attendant upon a transaction covering a period of sixty-two years in which the creditor carries the load at a normal rate of interest and the debtor proposes to pay one-fourth or one-fifth that rate of interest. What Italy is proposing to do is this: She owes us one hundred cents on the dollar, which is due, and she proposes to give us an I.O.U. for twenty-three cents on the dollar, payable through sixty-two years. If you made such a settlement for your bank the next step probably would be a hearing as to your financial sanity.[13]

[11] *Congressional Record*, LXVII, 916.

[12] Levinson to Borah, November 13, 1925.

[13] Levinson to William Riggs, February 16, 1926.

He was shocked at "the idea of Coolidge, who had won his spurs by frugality, and economy, being a major party to the greatest gift and swindling settlement of all time."[14] But, he argued, if the foreign countries actually were unable to pay more than the settlements call for, "then in God's name let us stop the international bankers" from selling a lot more of these worthless foreign bonds to the helpless American investors. If the French, for example, could not pay, let them cede islands to the United States, thus honorably discharging the debts. He was at a loss to understand why the debts could be scaled down to twenty-three cents on the dollar in the case of Italy and at the same time why the government should permit the loaning of large sums of new capital to Italy. The administration was in reality playing the game of the international bankers, who were profiting by the huge commissions and discounts on the new loans. France and Italy were filching money from the United States in two ways, "first, by virtual repudiation of the debt, alias long range extension, alias 'capacity to pay' and then by getting a license from the administration after this miserable funding, to tap the investors of the country through international bankers."[15]

The debt settlement could be used to defeat the World Court in two ways. A reservation could be made to the entry of the United States, providing that the Court had no jurisdiction in any case affecting war debts owed the United States. He hoped that the "European masters" would never consent to such a reservation, thus killing the Court. Or again if the Court debate could be prolonged, he thought the public could understand "the unpatriotic graft of the House of Morgan" and would turn against not only the proposed settlements but the Court also. He wrote to leading Democratic senators, such as Reed and Hull, suggesting how they could make great political capital of the debt issue by siding with the taxpayers against the administration. He urged William Hard to help the Democrats to take partisan advantage of the situation. Why, he asked, did the "poor prunes" not seize this their last vestige of an issue?

[14] Levinson to Villard, March 13, 1926.

[15] Levinson to Villard, March, 8, 1926.

In connection with the initial fight against the debt settlements in 1925 it occurred to Levinson that the United States might use the debts owed to it by the European states as a leverage to obtain outlawry or, later, after the signing of the Pact of Paris, disarmament. It might be said here that after 1928 the use of debts to secure peace became the center of his activity as outlawry had been during the preceding fourteen years. The first clear statement of this use of the debts, which was to play such an important part in his thinking, is contained in a letter to Harrison Brown in December, 1925. "The worst of it all is that we are giving up our hold on the nations . . . . without getting a single commitment for peace or without getting the benefit of charity, humanitarianism or liberality."[16]

But during the fall of 1925 and January, 1926, the debt settlements were for Levinson only a side issue. His main effort was concentrated on the fight over the Court project. To this we must now turn.

Miss Frances Kellor suggested that one of the best means of fighting the "present and future attempts to encroach upon American independence" would be to establish an International Research Bureau, "which would be prepared at all times to assemble and furnish information." The services of such experts as Hard, Flynn, and of Miss Kellor, herself, could be utilized in this bureau. She had come to this conclusion after consulting with Mrs. Longworth, Mrs. McCormick, Hard, and Borah. Ten days later Levinson sent her five hundred dollars for expenses in December. His last monthly check went to her on February 1, which ended the venture for him. Her chief duty was legal research for Borah.

Levinson attempted to make the Court a partisan issue with those who could be appealed to on a partisan basis. One of the reasons for supporting the Harmony Plan was to "intrinsically revolutionize" the Court as a "Republican proposal for peace" rather than to leave it "a mere Democratic resolution to enter this subsidiary of the League." A good example of this partisan use of the Court was a debate in which he took part with Mr. S. J.

[16] Levinson to Harrison Brown, December 8, 1925.

Duncan-Clark before the Hamilton Club of Chicago. Duncan-Clark complained that though they both wanted peace it was too bad that they should be placed in a position of antagonism "to the delight of such ignorance and prejudice as was displayed" by their audience. Levinson's tactics, he thought, were unfortunate:

> To call a proposal which has been approved by at least three Republican secretaries of state and as many or more Republican presidents a Democratic proposal, particularly when it was made a definite plank in the Republican platform, appears to me an utterly unjustifiable position on any basis of reason. Of course on the basis of prejudice, before a Hamilton Club audience, it was clever.[17]

Evidently the sentiment of the club as reflected during the debate was overwhelmingly against the Court. This was a surprise to Levinson, since he had supposed the members of the club would be following the lead of Coolidge. He reported the reaction of these Republicans to as many of the party leaders in Washington as he could. In view of such strong Republican sentiment he hoped the President and his leaders would not resort to any strong-arm tactics such as limiting debate. The country had existed one hundred and thirty-eight years without being in two courts, and he thought it could "worry along a few months more."[18]

Another maneuver in the fight against the Court was the supply of anti-international matter to the Hearst press. Levinson persuaded Mr. Victor Polachek of the *New York American*, whom he considered to be the most intimate with Hearst of all the Hearst editors, to run the following question conspicuously in every Hearst paper every day: "What dispute can the United States get into with another nation that it would be willing to submit to the League Court that it would not be willing to submit to the Old Hague Tribunal and why?"[19] He had used this question in debates with leaders of the League party, and he had considered that none of them had given a satisfactory answer.

[17] Duncan-Clark to Levinson, January 12, 1926.
[18] Levinson to Senator Butler, January 12, 1926.
[19] Levinson to Borah, December 26, 1925.

Levinson also used his influence with the Hearst press to get publicity through it for Senator Shipstead. On January 13, 1926, William Hard sent the following telegram to Levinson:

Following very important. Shipstead likely to speak in Senate today. He is being attacked on World Court by almost every newspaper in Minnesota. He needs favorable publicity in Minnesota. Will you explain situation to Herald Examiner and implore editor to give Shipstead's speech as much space as possible. Herald Examiner reaches Minnesota. Will you acknowledge receipt of this telegram and do what you can for Shipstead.[20]

Levinson telegraphed back at once: "Telegram received matter fully covered with Herald also expect speech featured in other papers."[21]

The crisis of the main battle was the debate on the floor of the Senate on the resolution to adhere to the World Court Protocol. Levinson went to Washington to stay two days and remained there for thirteen to aid in "the gallant fight [which] was made against the double steam roller, one from each party." When Mr. Becker casually observed his partner's protracted absence, Raymond Robins telegraphed him "to try to get along," because Levinson's leadership at Washington was indispensable.

One of the obstacles which neither Borah nor Levinson had planned for was the limitation of debate.

It was a dastardly move. The statute of the Court had not been discussed, three of four important speeches were in the making and immediately after the petition for Cloture was presented the Swanson resolution was greatly amended. This resolution did not reach the senators until Monday morning and all the reservations had to be filed in the Senate before one o'clock of the same day. . . . . Indeed, it was the signs of weakening within their ranks and the very unmistakable manifestation of a change in public sentiment as against propaganda that decided the Administration to take the anti-court senators by the throat.[22]

It was the view of Levinson and Borah that the League of Nations could enforce decisions of the World Court by whatever means thought necessary. Levinson told the editor of the *Nation*, Mr. Oswald Garrison Villard, that, were the United States a member of the Court, with a "judge sitting on the bench partici-

[20] Hard to Levinson, January 13, 1926.
[21] Levinson to Hard, January 13, 1926.
[22] Levinson to Villard, February 1, 1926.

pating in the decisions," then this country could not escape its "moral obligations" to assist in enforcing the decision, especially when "big banking houses who think and deal in terms of Europe overwhelm and dominate public opinion."[23]

Senator Borah voiced the same kind of argument in a long speech before the Senate on January 22, 1926. It was his contention that the American view—which was also Wilson's—of the method to keep peace was founded upon the principle of pacific settlement, which was sustained by organized public opinion, whereas the European concept of peace was based upon the "old balance of power," which was in essence supported by brute force. These two systems of thought had been in conflict when the Treaty of Versailles was drawn up, and the European system had triumphed over the American. The Court by virtue of its "advisory-opinion" function was the "legal adviser and counselor of a stupendous military combination (the League of Nations), now in process, either by construction or amendment, of being completed." Since the Court was an integral part of the League, the League had the same right to enforce a decision of the Court and a decision of the Council. He was unalterably opposed to the "recognition of the right to employ force against a sovereign nation in any contemplated plan of peace." Force had failed for two thousand years. What had been the result of the worship and teaching and practice of force? "If any one is familiar with the vernacular of Hell, let him undertake to paint the picture. Human tongue is inadequate to the task." The alternative which he had to propose was to turn "to a different plan and a different people and to a class of leaders of broader vision and of a profounder faith, the fathers who framed the Constitution of the United States." They had taken the "boldest step ever taken by any body of men in favor of peace between sovereign states or sovereign nations." They had substituted law between governments for violence and force, and they had said that "they would rest the execution of judgments against a state upon the power of public opinion." This could be applied to governments as well as to states. Governments made treaties to employ force, and the

[23] Levinson to Villard, February 6, 1926.

only guaranty of the performance of their obligations was their promise. When governments made treaties to submit their controversies to the decision of a court and to abide by that decision, they should be depended upon to keep that solemn pledge and no other guaranty should be asked.[24]

It may be noted that this idea of depending upon the plighted word of a nation and the power of public opinion was set forth in an article entitled "Can Peace Be 'Enforced'?" written by Levinson and published in the *Christian Century*, January 8, 1925. He had emphasized the point made by Borah that all agreements in the last analysis rest upon the good faith of the parties involved. This idea had appealed to Borah, and he had congratulated Levinson on having found the solution to the problem of sanctions.

Levinson had been apparently unable to find any senator who would introduce and sponsor the Harmony Plan as a reservation to the Court proposal. However, after Borah's speech on January 22 the idea of sanctions that stopped short of force became more popular. Even "Hell and Maria" Dawes went to the Senator and congratulated him on his profound analysis of the problem of force in international affairs. "Senator," he said, "you have utterly convinced me of the futility of force as the mainstay of international relations."[25] Levinson then prepared something a little different and persuaded Senator Moses of New Hampshire to introduce it—the so-called "Moses reservation." It was: "That the adherence of the United States to the statute of the World Court is conditioned upon the understanding and agreement that the judgments, decrees, and (or) advisory opinions of the Court shall not be enforced by war under any name or in any form whatever."[26]

[24] *Congressional Record*, LXVII (January 22, 1926), 2555. This argument of Borah shows him at his best and worst; at his best in moving oratorical appeals, at his worst in moving logically from one *non sequitur* to another. To say that force in all circumstances had always failed and then to cite the organization and continued existence of the United States as an example of government without force is quite startling. For Borah's own statement as to the necessity for organization as an alternative to war see below, pp. 244 f., and as to the rise of the United States as an example see below, p. 204, n. 64, and esp. p. 205, n. 67.

[25] As quoted by Levinson to Oggel, February 2, 1926.

[26] *Congressional Record*, LXVII, 2677; also *Nation*, February 17, 1926. The reservation was offered on January 25, only two days before the final vote on the Court.

Though this reservation was considered to be a "corker" by such persons as Villard, it did not receive the support Levinson had hoped.

If I could only have induced the boys to come out on the Senate floor with the proposition that they would accept the Court if the Moses reservation were added to the amended Swanson resolution—the result would have been sensational. Probably this was too much to expect all at one gulp. But gradually it is being pounded into the heads of the people that Outlawry is not only sound philosophy of international relations but is the only effective antidote to the poison peace plans that emanate from and are acceptable to the war offices of Europe.[27]

The reservation was debated on January 27. Borah prefaced his remarks with ". . . . It is unfortunate, I presume, that this reservation had to be offered by those who are in opposition to the World Court. It would be difficult to have the offering accredited with sincerity or the reservation with soundness."[28] He then retraced to some degree his argument against force to execute the decrees of the Court. Others of the stamp of Reed and Moses supported the reservation. It was generally considered to be part of an obstructionist plan to smash the Court proposal rather than a bona fide effort to improve it. The Rev. Mr. Oggel complained to Levinson that Borah had seen fit only to push this feature of outlawry in a negative way, when he could have presented the whole outlawry concept in a constructive role.

Levinson had one of the most exciting times of his life listening from the gallery of the Senate to this debate. He afterwards spoke of Borah's speech as the "first speech on the Outlawry of War in the United States Senate" and declared that, if Demosthenes in his palmiest days "had done any better than the Senator on this occasion, it was no wonder he had his matchless reputation through the ages."

The foundation is now laid and the Senator will, within the next few years, immortalize himself in international history. . . . . Now, for the first time in human history, a comprehensive and sane basis of international relations, ... has been advanced and championed by Senator Borah. If he perseveres as he will . . . . he will deserve and receive, when he and we have passed on, a monument between that of Washington and Lincoln at the Capitol, and no less recog-

[27] Levinson to Robins, February 1, 1926.

[28] *Congressional Record*, LXVII (January 27, 1926), 2808 ff.

nition and gratitude in other peace loving nations. For the Christian World, the absolute Outlawry of War is the second coming of Christ, indeed.[29]

One wonders what the "Captain of the Hosts of Outlawry's" state of exultation would have been had the "Thunderer" from Idaho really discussed outlawry instead of merely touching on it.

Even though Levinson had lost his fight to stop the debt settlement and had failed either to stop the World Court or to get any outlawry reservations made to it and though Borah had failed to make the speech he had hoped for, he found the

possibilities of the situation . . . . greater than ever before. You know I am an incorrigible optimist; it is my life's philosophy to turn liabilities into assets. I can therefore easily see a tremendous moral victory in the apparent defeat we had last week. To me it is the stepping stone to the highest.[30]

First arrangements were made for the broadcast of Borah's speeches of January 22 and 27. He ordered six hundred thousand copies of the first speech and five hundred thousand copies of the second. He raised seven or eight thousand dollars from his partner, Becker, and from friends and paid ten or twelve thousand dollars out of his own pocket for this purpose. It seemed that the distribution of these speeches stimulated considerable interest, for Miss Cora Rubin, Senator Borah's secretry, reported having received thirty-four thousand letters from Illinois alone.

The next steppingstone by which a liability was to be turned into an asset was the organization of a "come-out-of-the-Court" campaign.

What is running in my mind is something like this: That we get our good people and candidates committed to the proposition that unless the signatories to the Court agree to eliminate war from this alleged peace tribunal by 1928 we will make withdrawal from the Court an issue in that campaign. Now that the Republican Senators have done their partisan duty as they think they see it, they are free to get aboard the peace bandwagon.[31]

He thought that as a result of this strategy they were really ahead of the Harmony Plan. But, alas, his lieutenants declined to follow

[29] Levinson to Mrs. Borah, February 3, 1926.

[30] Levinson to Holmes, February 6, 1926.

[31] Levinson to Oggel, February 5, 1926.

the lead of their commander. Oggel refused to participate in such a campaign. The time must surely come, he objected, when the peace forces should get together if they really desired to be effective. To start a come-out-of-the-Court campaign would serve to embitter the League party. Any attempt to snatch this meager victory from them would necessarily postpone the day of the unification of the peace forces. If Levinson insisted upon such a campaign, Oggel would have to be content to sit on the side lines for a while; but he would much prefer for Levinson to part company now with Reed, Hearst, and Johnson and the *Tribune* and Klan crown, with whom he had been consorting. Mr. William B. Hale, who was a member of the committee for the outlawry of war, wrote to Levinson, saying that he was utterly opposed to any attempt to reopen the Court issue and that if that was Levinson's purpose he would resign from the committee.

Robins was not at first opposed to such a campaign, though after a while he arrived at the same conclusion as had Hale and Oggel. The beginning of the campaign was to be the reintroduction of the outlawry-of-war resolution by Borah in the Senate. The Senator was also to make the great speech on outlawry which he had promised so many times before. On February 13, 1926, Robins wrote that he had lunched and had had a long talk with the Senator at the latter's invitation. He was not sure whether he had succeeded in convincing him of the necessity of making the speech, but he had convinced himself that if they went ahead "Borah will take the easiest way and we will wait another two years for the speech that is now two years overdue." Therefore he would have nothing to do with the come-out-of-the-Court campaign, nor did he want to be considered as in the battle until "Borah has drawn a clear line between himself and the Hearst, Thompson, Cohalan, Reed, Johnson group of narrow nationalists who are in fact American Militarists."[32]

But, undaunted by the failure of his plan for a come-out-of-the-Court campaign, Levinson next started plans to elect Borah president in 1928. The Senator's reaction to this was anything but friendly:

[32] Robins to Levinson, February 13, 1926.

I wish these who are talking about Presidential booms would leave me out of the picture. I am sure it will not help the cause in which I am so deeply interested. I do not want to be placed in the position before the public of using a great issue like this to advance personal ambitions.[33]

But Levinson assured him that it was impossible for a man to be identified with great issues and not to be thought of in connection with the presidency, because that was the way a republic had of expressing itself; furthermore, a man burning with desire to aid his country should seek the presidency to further his issues. "Lincoln, with all his character and genius, could not have abolished slavery if he had not been president. . . . . Even if he had been a Senator, like yourself, he could not have done it."

Borah made a speech in Chicago later in the spring, which Levinson regarded as the virtual announcement of the Borah candidacy. He and Robins set to work to find issues for the "Lone Wolf"; but, when Robins interviewed the Senator near the end of June, Borah refused to plan any definite program until after the fall election. Then he wanted the colonel to see all the "anti's" and progressives to get them interested in rescuing the party from the "interests." He had no lists of people who had written to him nor could he suggest persons who would be willing to give money. He was not yet ready to come out in the open as a candidate. The only definite things he had in mind were an America-first war cry, law enforcement, and an anti-international banker and anticancellation program. In June, 1926, Borah was promising a plan of action for the winter of 1926 and 1927; the gifted colonel and the imperious lawyer had found it easy to corral Wild Bill "in the future"; but the future had a tendency to remain the future. Soon events were to occur in the regions with which the Senator had such a horror of entangling alliances—events which took the attention of Levinson far from the White House aspirations of his senatorial spokesman, even though Borah, when the fateful moment arrived at which he had to decide whether he would "choose to run" or not, chose not to run.

[33] Borah to Levinson, March 5, 1926.

CHAPTER XI

SPREADING THE GOSPEL OF OUTLAWRY IN FOREIGN LANDS, AND THE REPERCUSSIONS AT HOME

IN EARLIER chapters some reference has been made to sporadic attempts at acquainting the rest of the world with outlawry. Correspondence from overseas was always answered with more than the usual care. Important articles, beginning with the first, "The Legal Status of War," were sent to influential personages abroad, and personal letters frequently were written to them asking for comment. The contacts of the outlawry brotherhood with Philip Kerr, the wartime secretary of Lloyd George, and with Lord Robert Cecil and its attitude toward the first official adoption of some of the outlawry phraseology in the Pact of Mutual Assistance and the Geneva Protocol have also been indicated.

While the outlawrists continued to pay occasional attention to the propagation of the gospel in foreign minds and lands, it was not until the summer of 1923 that more concentrated efforts were made in this field.

Raymond Robins spent July and August, 1923, in the capitals of the great powers of Europe, where he met important political leaders. In Paris he talked with Stephen Lusanne, of *Le Matin*, the counselor of state and the secretary of the Protestant Federation of France, and with the secretary of the French Federation of Labor. They listened but would do nothing more until the reparations were settled. In Berlin people could think of nothing but the situation at the time. They said: "Yes, yes, ... but what will America *do now* in relief of the hungry and to force France to keep faith with the Fourteen Points?"[1] In London he got both a worse and a better hearing. When he arrived in July, though he preached outlawry as the healing elixir for the wounds of Europe,

[1] Robins to Levinson, August 9, 1923.

[165]

no one seemed able to fix his attention on the musical voice of the silver-tongued colonel. The imminence of war was only a question of days if not hours. Some of those to whom he tried to explain outlawry at that time were Lord Robert Cecil, Gilbert Murray, Sir Hugh Bell, Miss Bondfield, Sir Charles Trevelyan, Captain Grenfell, and Lord Haldane. Later the tension seemed to be easing a little and the reaction improving. He dined at the Liberal Club with a group of the more important members. Between group meetings of this type, he saw a number of people, singly or in twos and threes—some of them several times. Maude Royden, Lady Rhondda, J. St. Loe Strachey, of the *Spectator;* J. A. Hobson, Ramsay MacDonald, H. N. Brailsford; J. L. Garvin, editor of the *Observer;* E. D. Morel, editor of *Foreign Affairs;* Lord and Lady Astor, C. R. Buxton, Arthur Ponsonby, and other members of parliament were some of the more important persons. Some of them seem to have given him a good hearing but others not. Cecil, he reported, felt that what the British wanted was not "no more war" but rather "good war," that is, "a war system in their control to be used against the lesser breeds who know not the master's law."[2] However, in most circles he felt there was "a general acceptance of the Outlawry of War as a remote ideal worthy of moral endorsement, but far removed from immediate usefulness to prevent [the] Next War."[3]

Justice Allen went to Geneva in September, 1923, for the meeting of the Assembly. Robins had agreed that this would be advisable, provided "her conversion to Outlawry is certain." It was perhaps due to her work there that agreement had been reached with Cecil, for it was then that he told her that he was going to include outlawry in the Pact of Mutual Assistance. During the summer of 1924 Charles Clayton Morrison was in Europe partly in the interests of outlawry. In 1925 Miss Frances Kellor, the woman whom Levinson characterized as having a masculine mind, also went there.

The efforts of these emissaries—Robins, Allen, Morrison, and Kellor—along with what have been called the sporadic attempts

[2] Robins to Levinson, July 27, 1923.
[3] Robins to Levinson, July 21, 1923.

at foreign conversion, were perhaps more in the nature of seed-sowing than of immediate production of fruit. Taken together they filled the European press with references to the outlawry of war; and soon in Europe as in America, though two or three years later, the phrases of outlawry were on the lips of many, though probably, as in America, there were only a few who understood the idea.

It may be suggested that the reason for the popular acceptance of the terms of outlawry was probably different in Europe from that in America. In America, as one reads the letters and newspapers and public speeches of the period, one gets the feeling of a kind of a guilt complex. People felt, so to speak, that Uncle Sam had hardly played the part of a sportsman in suddenly backing out of the game after forcing upon it a new set of rules. They were anxious for an opportunity for him to slip in again without any of the subsequent risks of participation, and outlawry seemed to be ideal for the purpose. It was all gain, and as for risks—the very point of outlawry was that it abolished them. While Europe, on the other hand, stunned by Uncle Sam's sudden departure, could not believe that he had so suddenly and entirely lost his nerve. She preferred to think that he was only "spoofing" and that if he were humored a little he would soon return to take the place he had deserted in a moment of "winner's jitters." So Europe, too, began to talk of outlawry.

It was a mention of outlawry in the European press that led to Levinson's acquisition of his chief European lieutenant. Early in March, 1924, Levinson received a letter which began: "I recently read a long extract in the London 'Public Opinion' of a remarkable article you wrote for 'The Forum,' Can war be Outlawed?" The writer went on to say the purpose of the letter was to ask for permission to translate the article into "french" [sic] for publication in one of the Paris "revues." He then mentioned a campaign which was going on between the "intellectuals and the gun-metal group." "As an Englishman living in France, and one who has had his life considerably torn by the war, I am all for the campaigners, and it seems to me that your fine article is just the kind which would be welcomed here and which would prove of

[167]

great help." He explained that he could not afford to buy any rights; but any substantial returns he would be glad to share.

I trust that you will excuse such a request from a total stranger, and in event of your granting permission, I would ask you to kindly tell me in what issue of The 'Forum' the full article appeared, as my extract does not give this information and I should of course require the full text to work from.

Thanking you in anticipation of a reply I beg to remain sir

Yours faithfully,

(*Signed*) G. HARRISON BROWN.[4]

Thus Harrison Brown made known an interest in outlawry. When the war began, he had been on the stage, touring England with one of Arnold Bennett's plays. He went directly to a recruiting office to enlist but was refused because of bad eyes. After several attempts, however, he was accepted; but, after the "damn fools had spent several hundred pounds training me," they again found his eyes were bad and let him go. The whole process of getting re-enlisted and retrained, only to be dismissed because of his eyes, was repeated two or three times before he finally got to France, where he saw "a lot of the rotten business." Though army life was onerous to an extreme degree and army discipline had made him a revolutionist, he still believed the "bally rot about patriotism," until he tried to get back on the stage after the war. Then he found himself outdistanced by his competitors who had stuck to "hard work on the stage." Subsequently he secured a position in France representing an English exporting firm. It was then he began to read and develop ideas about war. His salary of five or six hundred pounds was not satisfactory; and within two years after his first letter to Levinson, he was getting ready to throw the thing over and "clear out for the colonies," perhaps Australia, where he could get away from the "whole mess."

He had a passion for peace, and he worked for it with abandon. As a speechmaker he was not extraordinary; his special ability lay in letters. His letters were soon as long as Levinson's or even

---

[4] Mr. Brown at one time used the initial *G;* but early in his association with the outlawry movement he dropped it, wishing to be known simply as Harrison Brown.

longer and were written in his own hand. He wrote easily, racily, and picturesquely. He had a refreshing bluntness of expression; his characterizations of political leaders were penetrating, sometimes bitter, but always iconoclastic. He appeared to view political institutions with a natural cynicism turned sour by war experiences. On one occasion he wrote:

> There is only one thing I find it very hard to forgive the Germans and that is they killed none of our old school politicians. . . . . The present conservative government . . . . what a bunch! headed by Baldwin, the business man. Camouflaging the smug satisfaction of stupidity, under the mask of an honesty so boomed that it is in danger of being believed. As a specimen of the brilliant intellectual ability of the party we have Austen Chamberlain, now in his fifth or sixth Continental trip this year, from all of which, he has returned bewildered and bamboozled and faced with the task of explaining that he did not mean what the other fellow claims to have understood. . . . .
>
> The Frenchman is a cynic in his bones—when he is not a bigoted worshipper of superstition, or when by mental acrobatics peculiar to this country of so called lucid thinking he does not amazingly manage to combine the two.

Levinson was happy to have outlawry material translated into French, and he not only gave Harrison Brown permission to use the *Forum* article but also encouraged him to use other outlawry material. He liked the information in the letters of his new correspondent and urged him to write more and often. Levinson appreciated the running comment coming direct from Paris and, especially, the clippings which Brown sent him from both the British and the Continental press. He was so impressed with the activity of the new convert by February, 1925—less than a year after he had received the first communication—that he wrote:

> I enclose check for $500 which I wish you would use in connection with your publicity work for our Committee. I would like very much to have my article of January 8[5] . . . . reach the eyes of the important peace and war people of Europe and if necessary have it translated for use in more important countries. You can use this money at your discretion.[6]

Harrison Brown did a good deal of traveling in France, and he was always making contacts with any important person he could reach. To those he could not meet personally he wrote letters.

[5] Levinson, "Can Peace Be Enforced," *Christian Century*, January 8, 1925.

[6] Levinson to Harrison Brown, February 5, 1925.

He generally sent one of the translated articles; and in the covering letter he passed on information, supposed to be of a semiconfidential nature, which Levinson had sent him about the events behind the scenes in Washington or elsewhere. Sometimes he got a personal letter in reply, as he did from Gilbert Murray; sometimes it was only an acknowledgment, such as he received from Herriot's secretary; but many people in official or influential positions thus got a chance to read about outlawry. He went to peace meetings whenever possible and talked with the leading peace workers about outlawry, and he kept up a constant bombardment of the editors to get them to write on outlawry. When he went to London during the holidays in 1926, he found that many of the persons with whom Robins had talked were thinking about outlawry. It is interesting to note that in 1926 he expected Mac-Donald, whom "nobody knows . . . . from a bale of hay," to land sooner or later in the Conservative party. He joined the Union of Democratic Control in order to get in close contact with the people who controlled the London *Foreign Affairs*.

By April, 1926, Levinson was so greatly impressed with his correspondent that he began to think of Brown as a representative in Europe for the American Committee for the Outlawry of War. Arrangements were not made to this end until Levinson's visit to Europe in 1927. Brown later described orally his first meeting with "Captain Outlawry" and his decision to work for him in this manner:

Then Sol came over. I met him in London and my life was changed. You can have no idea my surprise at meeting Sol. I didn't know anything about Americans and here was a super-American. He wanted me to go over Europe with him. I did. We went to the best hotels and saw important people and Sol talked all the time. Then he wanted me to represent him. Silly as it sounds I hesitated. Sol said, "Try it for awhile, then if things don't go, you can clear out for the colonies—to Australia." I had my mind on the colonies and I didn't want to stay in Europe. But after awhile I decided to stay.[7]

Levinson did not depend solely on his lieutenants to win foreign converts. He used every opportunity both by letter and by

[7] From interview with Harrison Brown in Levinson's office, 1 N. La Salle Street, Chicago, June 20, 1934.

personal confrontation to spread the evangel himself. His effectiveness with Harrison Brown has just been noted. Israel Zangwill was another on whom he tried his powers. Levinson had met him in Chicago. He thought Zangwill was favorably impressed, but he failed later to win him completely, for Zangwill had his own way of abolishing war; therefore, he remained cold to "any of your moral nostrums."[8] J. C. Maxwell Garnett, secretary of the English League of Nations Union, was another. Garnett inquired of Levinson how he proposed to deal with a nation that refused to abide by the codified laws of peace and how he would enforce the affirmative jurisdiction against a state that refused to accept it. The answer to these two questions went in a six-page letter to Garnett in March, 1924. Briefly, it was (1) to depend upon the good faith of nations and (2) to create a court with the kind of jurisdiction which Levinson contended the United States Supreme Court possesses. His court would be empowered to hear and pronounce judgment in any case submitted to it, regardless of whether the defendant state appeared or not.[9] The only apparent effect of these and subsequent letters was to confirm each writer in his own convictions.

Others gave him a respectful hearing and occasionally signs of belief. J. L. Garvin, the editor of the *London Observer*, a man said by Borah to be one of the world's greatest editors, became interested in outlawry, as a means, at any rate, of getting America to engage in more active international co-operation and possibly even as an idea valuable in itself. Robins had talked with him, and Harrison Brown had written to him and supplied him with outlawry material. On August 31 and September 7, 1924, articles appeared in the *Observer*, which Levinson thought "were of tremendous importance." One sentence ran: "The absolute outlawry of war is the attainable ideal of the world." Levinson wrote to him expounding outlawry, and Harrison Brown kept hammering away at him. He promised the latter that he would write "a whole-hogging" article against war; but Brown hardly

[8] Zangwill to Levinson, March 13, 1924.

[9] These answers were later reprinted in pamphlet form for wholesale distribution.

expected any such thing, as the great editor "had close friends among and was a great admirer of many in the old school." In January, 1926, Garvin wrote one of his usual letters to Levinson about the necessity of German and Russian adherence to the League and American co-operation. Then he added: "If the time ever comes when the United States, not necessarily joining the League, proposes to co-operate with it in securing the Outlawry of War, one of the greatest things in history may be achieved."[10] And in March he wrote in a strain still more pleasing to the outlawrists:

I do not believe that the world will ever be safe until the United States summons a World Congress for the outlawry of War. That would in no way constrain the United States to change its relations to the League, but outside the League would do more than that organization by itself can ever accomplish to save the supreme cause.

Harrison Brown received this without lifting an eyebrow. In his opinion Garvin represented the official mind. He doubted if there were any really sincere politicians in Europe; all of them were hypocrites; and Garvin was not great, only unusually competent in contrast to the expanse of mediocrity around him. But Levinson was elated. "I think," he wrote to one of his intimates, "you will agree with me that, perhaps, all things considered, this is the most formidable word of encouragement for the general acceptance of Outlawry we have had."[11]

Another leader of English peace thought was the Oxford professor, Gilbert Murray. He, too, had heard the persuasive tongue of Raymond Robins and had read the picturesque letters of Harrison Brown. Levinson's first contact with him came indirectly. Murray had written to Mr. James G. McDonald, asking his opinion of what the American reaction would be to a universal compulsory arbitration treaty, which would also include a sanctions provision that, should any nation resort to war, it would *ipso facto* be deemed to have committed an act of war against all the members of the League, who would undertake to confer immediately as to the means of restoring peace. McDonald sent a copy

[10] Garvin to Levinson, January 28, 1926.
[11] Levinson to Mrs. Robins, March 26, 1926.

of the letter to Levinson for his opinion. Levinson, as usual, decried "this clinging to the god of force." McDonald forwarded this to Murray, who was much surprised at it. After disavowing any intention to trap Levinson, he asked him the same question directly because he thought there was some chance of Europe's making such an arrangement. Would Levinson oppose this as he did the League? In other words, did he insist on Europe's remaining exposed to the war danger until the very long and problematical task of codifying law had been performed? The answer to this was that arbitration could not be successful so long as the institution of war remained a legal alternative to judicial settlement. This exchange of letters in 1925 led to others, and in 1926 the writers met for the first time. Levinson reported of this meeting: "I have just returned from Boston where I had one of the greatest interviews of my life. . . . . We had straight four and one half hours of animated discussion of international questions."[12]

In general Murray commended the outlawry movement in the United States. He pointed out that practically all the civilized states except Russia and the United States had bound themselves with strict covenants of peace, while these two states had retained their freedom with few exceptions to "attack anybody at any moment for any reason"; he was, therefore, heartily in favor of the Borah outlawry-of-war resolution. After a critical analysis of the resolution, he said: "Thus I bless without reservation the Borah Resolution." He warmly commended Levinson's idea of a general treaty for the renunciation of war. Much of what Borah and Levinson wanted was "both consistent with the Covenant and practice of the League, and in some respects represented improvements. . . . ."[13] His final words of approval at that time were:

I must send you a line before I sail. . . . . I think your movement very important, and I will warmly support it when the moment comes. But I feel clear that before I can act either usefully or consistently the movement must have reached a state at which it visibly has national or official backing. That is: I cannot say to my friends: "Cease to press for America's co-operation with the

[12] Levinson to F. A. Seiberling, December 14, 1926.

[13] Murray to Levinson, December 10, 1926.

League and put your strength in to this other plan" until I am also able to say: "This other is backed by the Administration, or at any rate by public opinion. It has definitely a good prospect of being carried through."

My own policy at present, and for some years past, has been: "It is not for us to give advice to America. Our business is to develop our own peace system, and let America do what she likes." But as soon as there comes any move from America—from America as a whole or as a Government—then of course we shall all pay the greatest attention to it. And if it should take the form of an Outlawry of War Treaty nothing could please me more.[14]

Levinson had long been fully conscious of the necessity for official support of outlawry at home in order to make it usable in Europe. In March, 1925, after refusing to comment on a private French peace scheme, he wrote:

I do not want to make any mistakes abroad especially as it is our present intention not to begin any active campaign ourselves in any foreign country until we have put the United States, by declaration of the Senate and possibly by further announcement of the President, at least in principle behind the Outlawry movement. We can then go, not as reformers and cranks, but, as representing basic official opinion in the United States. This is purely a matter of tactics but vitally important.[15]

It therefore becomes necessary to take up again the story of the continuous campaign to conquer the unconquerable Borah. It will be recalled that in June, 1926, Borah had agreed upon a line of action for the next session of Congress. Thus encouraged, in November Morrison and Levinson called on the Senator to persuade him to reintroduce and debate the outlawry resolution and try to get it approved by the Senate.

We had an hour or so with the Senator, at the conclusion of which he decided to offer the resolution to outlaw war—We had a very long argument involving almost everything on the subject and he gave us to understand that he was being overruled and that he was following the judgment of yourself [Robins], Morrison, and myself. It was against his judgment, he said, because of the danger of not doing anything with it and as the head of the Foreign Affairs Committee he wanted to be able to aid the cause and not let it be snuffed out as by defeat. However, he has been working with Congressman Porter; also with Tinkham, etc., and he virtually said that he had been trying for months and months to work out a program that would greatly advance our sacred cause.

[14] Murray to Levinson, December 26, 1926.
[15] Levinson to Harrison Brown, March 31, 1925.

Morrison seems to think that he was not so against re-presenting the resolution and perhaps it is his reluctant and Hamlet-like nature working.[16]

It was during this visit that the Senator first called Levinson, "Sol."

The first time he called me by my given name I thought I misunderstood him, but he repeated it again and again. This is the first time that has happened and must have some significance, especially as neither you [Robins], nor Morrison, nor any other person with whom I have called has that habit.[17]

However Borah's judgment did not prove to be so badly over-ridden, for, though he did reintroduce the resolution, he let it lie.[18] Other matters were pressing at the moment. Levinson was so occupied with a special outlawry-of-war number of the *Christian Century* that neither he nor any of his lieutenants had time to walk the ramparts to haunt their Hamlet into action. Levinson was disgusted with the administration attitude toward Nicaragua —a disgust which was fully shared by Borah; and Levinson was urging the Senator to give the administration "Hell."[19] And Kellogg's handling of the relations with Mexico at the time was weak and disappointing. "Indeed, the President and Kellogg ought to be for the Outlawry of War; for, what in God's name would they do with a war if it came except to cry out: "Help me, Cassius, or I sink.' "[20]

But eventually the *Christian Century* had been distributed; Levinson had exhausted his vocabulary against the "inconsistent" President and the "helpless" Kellogg, and he was satisfied that Borah had given them all the "Hell" the Nicaraguan situation deserved. Then he began to plan for his Hamlet to make "the great speech," which they had been expecting for more than three years. The first step was to arrange, if possible, a three-cornered talk between Borah, Robins, and himself.

[16] Levinson to Robins, November 23, 1926.

[17] *Ibid.* His given name was not "Sol," but some of his intimates used it because it was formed from his initials.

[18] *Congressional Record*, LXVIII, 106. It was referred to the Committee on Foreign Relations.

[19] Levinson to Borah, December 27, 1926.

[20] Levinson to Hard, January 21, 1927.

S. O. LEVINSON AND THE PACT OF PARIS

On January 26, Borah's secretary telegraphed: "The Senator is so busy he can't fix any definite hour to see you, but of course he will be glad to see you and Colonel Robins whenever you are here at sometime during the day or evening."[21] Before they arrived in Washington, Borah himself telegraphed: "Lets defer the conference until after the fourth of March. Every moment occupied just now."[22] It will be recalled that, nearly a year before, Robins had lost patience with Borah and had begun to act like a prima donna, as Levinson would say, by threatening to have nothing to do with the Senator unless there was some start in the performance of senatorial promises. But now even the patience of Levinson was a trifle frayed by the above telegram. The following telegrams, which are arranged in the order of their sequence, tell their own story:

Telegram received. I deeply regret to have to say what I would vastly have preferred to talk over with you at length personally and alone namely that the manifest course you have adopted may prove fatal to colonels wholehearted co-operation—we both saw him absolutely break with Californian [Hiram Johnson], in somewhat analogous situation—knowing him so intimately, I am grievously alarmed at this possibility of disaster—I am wiring him in Florida your telegram and asking him to communicate with you direct.[23]

Borah wire says he wants to defer entering resolution this session—time too rushed. Wired him this might break off your friendship for him—as you broke with Californian on same kind of matter.[24]

Do not understand your telegram. If it merely involves the matter of seeing you and colonel of course I will see you regardless of conditions here. But if it involves my surrender of judgment upon matters then its beyond my power to remedy it. Dear and vital as colonels friendship is my convictions must still be my guide.[25]

Telegram received colonels position of course does not involve surrender or even modification of your convictions stop he feels that after three years constant campaigning on resolution some statement however brief should be made by you before adjournment so as to keep it alive in some form which will serve

[21] Cora Rubin to Levinson, January 26, 1927.
[22] Borah to Levinson, February 11, 1927.
[23] Levinson to Borah, February 11, 1927.
[24] Levinson to Robins, February 11, 1927; this is a condensation.
[25] Borah to Levinson, February 11, 1927.

[176]

to answer the serious charges he struggles with among peace and church people stop I am convinced that full open talk between you two will bring friendly adjustment acceptable to all stop we must not allow anything to becloud our sky now stop am therefore taking liberty of wiring copy of this message to colonel asking him to meet you next Friday alone and reach agreement as friends and comrades stop am now working on brief covering history and status of congressional right to withhold information from departments which grows more luminous and important the more we delve into it.[26]

Then Levinson sent a long telegram to Robins; after quoting in full the two preceding messages, that from the Senator and his reply, he said:

Because of developments Morrison with my approval not going stop in my sincere judgment matter is now in such shape as to produce results between you two stop owing to strange personality and otherwise perfect prospects you will know how best effectively to handle situation stop hope you will therefore wire or write him for conference next Friday stop I honestly think conference more effective without me but will do as you wish regarding attendance stop there are interviews at which any third person is hurtful stop is not this such an one stop I propose for your serious consideration following compromise, that he announce before adjournment his intention to have made extended remarks in view of the clouded international situation but that press of closing days will not permit and also stating that when they reassemble he will not only reintroduce his resolution but will bring it up for debate and vote stop this will take five minutes and he can cast it into any diplomatic or strategic form he desires stop this will save entire situation from both your and my viewpoints offsetting death of resolution end of session.[27]

Borah telegraphed:

It would be unjust to Colonel Robins to ask him to cancel his dates and come here on the theory that anything can be done as to a statement prior to adjournment—under conditions here it is not practicable and I would not want him to come here on theory that it is possible as I feel I would be doing him an injustice.[28]

To this Levinson replied:

Telegram received colonels engagements will be finished and he intended anyway to be in Washington next Friday stop you can certainly convince him that it is not practicable for you to carry out his minimum wishes during session and can suggest some other way mutually satisfactory to cover situation stop I

[26] Levinson to Borah, February 12, 1927.
[27] Levinson to Robins, February 12, 1927.
[28] Borah to Levinson, February 13, 1927.

feel terribly distressed over this matter and would consider it extreme personal favor if you would get seeming difference adjusted so that we can go forward with great momentum stop after all I can't help feeling matter entirely exaggerated in light of tremendous prospect.[29]

Levinson telegraphed to Robins:

Borah wired injustice to you to have you break your engagement—told him you be in Washington D.C. anyway, told him either to do what you want or convince you its impracticability. Ponsonby here said he would introduce similar resolution in House of Commons when he sure it being considered in our Senate. Think debate in two great houses wonderful—after I hear from you will write him again emphasizing your loyalty suggesting compromise in view of Ponsonby's proposal. Making great progress underwriting him [i.e., Borah's candidacy for nomination for president]—find friends among wets.[30]

The reference to Ponsonby in the last telegram quoted referred to a promise which this English member of Parliament had made in person to Levinson while in Chicago. He had been one of the signers of the cablegram sent to Borah on the first introduction of the outlawry resolution in 1923, and he had been in some contact with outlawry through Robins or Harrison Brown ever since. His promise to offer a "like resolution and arrange with Premier Baldwin to stage a debate in the British Parliament at the same time"[31] was one of the reasons for the added pressure on Borah at this time. If the Senator would only perform for them, the moment was right for the outlawrists to get a toe hold for their propaganda in foreign lands. Another reason was the desire of Levinson to repel the insistent charge of the League party that he was being used by insincere politicians, who had "resorted to the well-known political trick of offering substitutes as a red herring across the trail." In a debate with Dr. Holmes, Professor Irving Fisher had said that Senator Knox first used outlawry only to defeat the League, and

it is now being again drawn across the trail by Senator Borah for the same purpose. Senator Borah has introduced his Outlawry of War resolution three times. . . . . But nothing has been done about it. Not a particle of political progress has been made toward even passing the resolution through the Senate. *It is politically dead.*[32]

[29] Levinson to Borah, February 13, 1927.

[30] Levinson to Robins, February 14, 1927; this is a condensation.

[31] Levinson to Borah, February 15, 1927.

[32] Levinson to Borah, February 15, 1927.

There was so much plausibility in this argument as to make it devastating, and Levinson felt that it was hamstringing his efforts abroad and at home.

An agreement was made with Borah, but its nature is not recorded in the correspondence, since Levinson went to Europe before reporting to his other conferees. He did write to Borah, rejoicing that an agreement had been reached:

> I really enjoyed our visits very much. I feel so much more comfortable about the situation, and yourself, than I did before. I am so eager to do the right thing, to do it in the right way, and I have so little patience with myself in making blunders, that I rejoice that we reached a practical agreement among ourselves. I know as time goes on and you develop these burning issues through speeches and intervals of thought you will satisfy every morsel I crave.[33]

When the Harmony Plan fell through in December, 1925, Levinson was breathing anathema against the League people. After the Senate had approved the Court project in the January following, some of the outlawrists thought it was time to break with enemies of peace like Johnson and Hearst and try to effect a reconciliation with the League party; but Levinson was still characterizing them as unscrupulous, lacking in faith, and hypocritical. Soon, however, he saw the need of an armistice with the other peace forces.

It was decided to devote the 1926 Christmas issue of the *Christian Century* "to a special consideration of peace on earth in terms of the outlawry of war."[34] The first few pages were given over to normal *Christian Century* matter, although there were two editorials in these pages setting forth the purpose of that number and stating Dr. Morrison's idea of outlawry. Then came the resolution to outlaw war which Borah had introduced in the Senate for the third time on December 9.[35] Following this was a letter from Morrison to Levinson, asking him as his part of the symposium to provide a treaty for the renunciation of war suitable for the general signature of the nations. Then appeared Levinson's answer along with a draft treaty.[36] The Borah outlawry resolution to-

---

[33] Levinson to Borah, March 18, 1927.
[34] *Christian Century*, December 23, 1926, p. 1573.
[35] *Congressional Record*, LXVIII, 106.
[36] The draft treaty will be found below, p. 223.

gether with the two letters above mentioned were sent "to some twenty leading peace advocates in America and abroad asking them to comment on the situation thus created."[37] Among the articles by these "leading peace advocates," Professor Dewey's led all the rest. He found "America's Responsibility" to be for the United States to do the "one thing that Europe most needs and the one thing which is most in harmony with American traditions and aspirations . . . . ,"[38] namely, to share in delegalizing the war system. Then came Gilbert Murray's article, "From the League's Point of View," in which he commended both the resolution and the draft treaty highly. The League was already doing much that was contemplated by them, but in some respects they called for advances over the existing arrangements. He concluded by saying that the will to peace and the habit of peaceful international intercourse were more important than peace treaties and courts. John Haynes Holmes discussed the "Simplicity of Outlawry" in the usual outlawry style. William E. Rappard's article was "A Promoter and Preventer of Peace." He found that the United States had done more in the preceding ten years than any other country to deserve that title. He praised the Borah resolution, he hoped that Borah and his friends would not be baffled by the practical obstacles, and he asked that they should consider others who were working for peace as friends and not as rivals. Ernest F. Tittle, Frederick Lynch, Frederick W. Norwood, Henry A. Atkinson, Frederick F. Shannon, and Melvin V. Oggel gave ministerial exhortations to peace. Others who contributed were Florence E. Allen, Stephen S. Wise, Raymond Robins, Patrick H. Callahan, and A. Maude Royden.

Levinson was jubilant over this joining of the League party and the outlawrists in a common effort, along with others who were for any proposal which would make war less likely. In reporting that he had secured Murray's promise to write an article in this symposium, he wrote F. A. Seiberling that it "will be the greatest move for a new approach to international cooperation ever made."[39] And to a nationalist like Hard he said:

[37] *Christian Century*, December 23, 1926, p. 1582.

[38] *Ibid.*, p. 1584.   [39] Levinson to Seiberling, December 14, 1926.

Perhaps it will influence you to know that there is ill-suppressed enthusiasm here that this is the greatest thing for world peace that has ever been done. When you consider the different points of view of the writers and see that they are now making an approach to peace, it may perhaps satisfy a "hopeless" irreconcilable like yourself.[40]

He used his usual means of securing publicity for this Christmas number. Arrangements were made for press releases with the Associated and United Press services; influential people were encouraged to ask questions and to comment; the attention of the clergy was especially called to it; and above all a special effort was made to circulate it. Lists of over a thousand influential persons in Britain and France were prepared for the purpose and copies sent to them. Gilbert Murray declined to have his name used publicly to help the circulation in Europe, because, as he explained to Levinson, he did not want to support outlawry until it had received official recognition in the United States; but privately he called the attention of Sir Eric Drummond and others to it. Some idea of the extent of its circulation may be had from the bill which Levinson paid for it. This came to $5,295.47.

Levinson had been anxious for some time to have one of his lieutenants write a book on outlawry. Frances Kellor had written a two-volume work[41] dealing, among other matters, with the World Court. Senator Thomas Walsh had considered it the chief authority of those opposed to American adherence. Robins had been able with its assistance to cool the ardor of Coolidge for the Court. "Captain Outlawry" now wanted a book on outlawry for acquainting Europeans, especially, with his movement. He had suggested several times that Dr. Holmes should write it; but Holmes, with his church and the editorship of *Unity*, did not seem to see his way to this. Morrison and Oggel had both toyed with the idea, and Levinson encouraged them. Oggel set to work and completed his manuscript during the summer of 1926. After reading it himself, Levinson wanted Holmes and Morrison to criticize it. By October Oggel was becoming impatient to put it in the hands of the publishers, but Morrison was critical. Though

[40] Levinson to Hard, December 17, 1926.
[41] *Security against War* (New York: Macmillan Co., 1924).

Levinson considered it "replete with genius," even he felt it needed lightening and shortening for propaganda purposes and reported Morrison as insisting that the first book should be "nearly
perfect" because it would be severely criticized. After long discussions between Levinson and Morrison, during which Morrison lamented such passages in the manuscript as the sarcastic remarks at the expense of Hudson and Fosdick and other advocates
of the League, it came to light that Morrison himself had a manuscript, nearly half-completed, to substitute. Between them they
"decided that it would be best for Morrison's book to come out
first. I am now trying to arrange my feeble mentality so as to develop Oggelian arguments to that end. Please pray for me. This
will be a good test of the efficacy of prayer," wrote the embarrassed Levinson to the colonel.

But the colonel's prayers, if offered, were not granted, for Levinson failed to get the news broken to Oggel. All he succeeded in
doing was to write that he liked the book, thought it was "really
excellent," and, being full of research and historical citation,
would make an excellent work for reference, but that he had some
suggestions to make which would require a little discussion. In
the meantime Borah and Robins had both agreed that Morrison's
book should appear first. So Levinson pushed Morrison's book
along as rapidly as possible by getting office help for him. He also
began to spend six or eight hours a day or night with Morrison.
When he began to write to Oggel again, it was clearly assumed
that Morrison's book was to come out first and Oggel's was to
follow. Finally, in January came an admonition to Oggel to use
care lest he and Morrison should get their wires crossed or the
books cover the same ground. Then Oggel caught on. His reaction
was: "It's complicated business, isn't it, holding up the first book
on Outlawry till the second is ready so it can be the first one?"
But he added quickly, lest the wrong impression be conveyed,
"Don't tell Morrison." Morrison might think he was "peeved"
—but he wasn't—he was "writing this grinningly."[42] And, when
Morrison's book did appear, he wrote that he was glad Morrison
got ahead of him. One chapter especially was "beyond praise."

[42] Oggel to Levinson, January 26, 1927.

However, Oggel's health became frail; and after a trip to Mayo's, financed in part by Levinson, he was unable to revise his manuscript; and soon the world situation had so changed as to make it useless except for historical purposes.

By the middle of February, 1927, Morrison's book was nearly ready for the galley proofs. Levinson thought Morrison's powers of analysis and statement were "masterly."[43]

We are going to have a great piece of work. However, I have to do a lot of thinking and checking to avoid vulnerable spots and both unjust and plausible criticism. Morrison is in the seventh heaven of delight over the way—highly satisfactory to himself—the material has been moulded into book form.[44]

Morrison kept revising and revising; and, even though Levinson was able to take a galley proof of it to Europe with him in April, Morrison held back from publishing it until the following autumn. Its title was *The Outlawry of War*, and it was brought out by Willet, Clark, and Colby, Chicago.

Levinson had been planning to go to Europe for three years, but each time, before the sailing date arrived, something occurred to postpone his departure. However, in April, 1927, he actually got started. But before we set off to Europe with him, it will be convenient to examine in greater detail the project of which he was the originator and the principles on which it was based.

[43] Levinson to Robins, February 15, 1927.
[44] Levinson to Robins, February 16, 1927.

CHAPTER XII

THE THEORY OF THE OUTLAWRY OF WAR

BEFORE attempting to set out the principles of outlawry, some preliminary observations should be made as to the conditions under which the theory was developed, because it proved to be indigenous to its background.

Levinson was a controversialist; except possibly in the writing of his first article,[1] his thinking was done in the atmosphere of debate. He knew the tricks of the debater: how to claim everything for his own side and admit nothing and how to use arguments with a straight face which could be dismissed later as "provincial peanut idea[s]." He always attacked, and occasionally it was not only the arguments of his opponents that he attacked but his opponents themselves as well. Consequently, his ideas, stated as they usually were, with the winning of a particular battle in view, can sometimes be interpreted only in the light of the occasion of their utterance. It must also be kept in mind that his crusade for the outlawry of war was the self-imposed task of a busy lawyer and that, therefore, his letters, from which a knowledge of his ideas is chiefly to be gained, were usually actually dictated under heavy pressure for time.

The debate milieu and the lack of precision in the use of language due to haste in dictation explain inconsistencies which might have been avoided in a more deliberative atmosphere. He insisted, for instance, on the necessity of legal equality for all states, big or little;[2] yet he opposed any definition of an aggressor, because some major power like Great Britain might be found to come under it.

A second element which makes for confusion in understanding outlawry was Levinson's avowed shifts in his position over a period of years. At one time he believed the use of force in international

[1] "The Legal Status of War," *New Republic*, March 9, 1918.
[2] "Can War Be Outlawed," *Forum*, January, 1924.

affairs to be absolutely necessary. Later he espoused openly and belligerently what he had previously called the "absurdity"[3] of refusing to admit the use of force in international relations. There were other shifts also, if of less importance. So that any statement about the theory of outlawry, if it is to be strictly accurate, should always indicate the date to which it refers.

A third confusing element which in some respects accounts for both his conscious shifts and his unconscious inconsistencies was what he termed his deductive development of the theory of outlawry. In his first article, "The Legal Status of War,"[4] he set forth the three major principles of his theory. All questions of peace and war as they came up for the next ten years and more were approached and dealt with in the light of these principles. The details of the theory of the outlawry of war were not unified into a harmonious whole as a result of long observation and philosophic reflection as were the theories of Bodin and Montesquieu; but, rather, certain basic principles were laid down before the complexity of the problems of war and peace had been quite realized, and new ideas, information, and conditions had to be fitted into the structure erected upon them.

A fourth element which was the source of endless confusion was the double character of outlawry. In the first place, it was a definite legal concept. In the second place, it was a popular movement. The confusion came about by the frequent failure to use the appropriate vocabulary according as the legal or the popular concept of outlawry was being discussed. Often there was a shift without any warning from the popular to the legal concept or vice versa in the same paragraph or even sentence. It is probably just to say that part of this was due to a lack of clear thinking on the part of the outlawrists, and it is also probably one of the reasons why men like Professor Shotwell never seemed quite to understand what Levinson was talking about. In addition to this, even Professor Dewey, who understood Levinson better than most of his disciples, never seemed quite to comprehend what Levinson's legal concept meant. Illustrations of this, especially of the difference between Dewey and Levinson with regard to

[3] *Ibid.*   [4] *Op. cit.*

war in a legal sense and self-defense, will be given later, when self-defense is discussed. With these preliminary observations we may proceed to examine the theory of outlawry as of the period 1927–28, unless another date is specifically indicated.

The fundamental premise of outlawry was that war was accepted by international law as legal. Albert Bushnell Hart and others objected to Levinson's contention that war was so accepted. One authority, a secretary in the League of Nations, insisted that international law did not recognize war as legal but that "it simply accepts war as a fact antecedent to international law and gives it certain legal powers intended to regulate its operation and effect." It would seem that the weight of authority is on the side of this type of view, namely, that war is neither legal nor illegal but rather nonlegal in its status. Like a storm or an earthquake, it displaces the normal law of peace, as martial law may do after a fire or an earthquake. Professor Wright concluded from an examination of the authorities that they supported this view in a ratio of more than fifteen to three.[5] However, this point does not affect the object which Levinson was seeking: the making of war and any changes effected through it illegal. His grounds for insisting that war was legal appear to have been twofold. In the first place he quoted Woolsey to the effect that the greater part of international law was concerned with the law of war and its corollaries, neutrality, etc.,[6] and, in the second, he maintained that war was legal because there were certain legal consequences which followed from it.

In general, outlawry is abolitionist in nature:

The [Outlawry] group believes that civilization has arrived at a crisis when war must not be compromised or temporized with; that there is no time like the present, and that the legal institution of war for the settlement of international disputes must be abolished, and destroyed root and branch. . . . .

Let us outlaw war once and for all, without equivocation and without conditions.[7]

[5] Quincy Wright, "Changes in the Conception of War," *American Journal of International Law*, XVIII (1924), 755; hereafter cited as *AJIL*.

[6] "Legal Status of War."

[7] Levinson, "The Draft Treaty and the Outlawry of War," *New Republic*, August 27, 1924.

THE THEORY OF THE OUTLAWRY OF WAR

Outlawry was to produce a sudden and abrupt about-face:

The chief difficulty which people have in comprehending the proposal to outlaw war is due to their failure to envisage the new situation which will emerge directly upon the establishment of the outlawry system. . . . . Their trouble is due to their failure to conceive the outlawry proposal as the profoundly revolutionary thing it really is . . . . . *This book is dealing with nothing short of a world revolution.*[8]

While a great deal of emphasis was placed upon the abolitionist nature of outlawry up to the signing of the Pact of Paris, after that time there was less insistence on it.

But there was something more than the fervor of a William Lloyd Garrison in Salmon Oliver Levinson. When he fastened his dark eyes on you and his fist beat a staccato on the table and his voice, filled with intense sincerity, rose in thunderous intonations, you recognized a new Hebrew prophet castigating the race, like Moses of old, for bowing down to a strange god—the god of war; and, like Moses, he, too, brought new commandments, only three in number and not graven on tablets but forged out of the realities of his own experience in the living fire of a dynamic personality.

Justice Florence E. Allen stated the three commandments of outlawry in this fashion:

1. That war be outlawed and declared a crime, under the law of nations, and that its use as a means of settlement of disputes be abolished.

2. That a conference of civilized nations be held for the creation and codification of international law on the basis of equity and right.

3. That a court be established with jurisdiction over all purely international disputes as defined by the international code.[9]

[8] Charles Clayton Morrison, *Outlawry of War* (Chicago: Willett, Clark & Colby, 1927), pp. 101 f. Italics his.

[9] Address delivered at the Fourth Annual Convention of the National League of Women Voters, Des Moines, Iowa, April 19, 1923. John Dewey added a fourth ("Outlawry of War," *Encyclopaedia of the Social Sciences* [New York: Macmillan Co.]), namely, that each state is to make provision for punishment of its own war criminals. However, this seems to be a part of the means of enforcement and will be discussed along with the other means of enforcement in the section devoted to the third commandment of outlawry. These three points plus the one called a fourth by Dewey form the proposal for action in the resolution offered by Senator Borah at intervals from 1923 until 1927. The dates and references for each time it was offered are: *Congressional Record*, LXIV (February 14, 1923), 3605; LXV (December 20, 1923),

S. O. LEVINSON AND THE PACT OF PARIS

The use of the transitive verb "outlaw" to indicate what should be done with war was purposeful. It is a term which has a particularly long history, having originated in primitive law. It was the most extreme of the penalties which could be pronounced against an offender. According to Plucknett,

> Outlawry is the withdrawal by civil society of all legal rights and protection from one of its offending members. The device of thrusting out of the group those who have broken its code is very ancient and constitutes the most fearful fate which primitive law could inflict. The offender was cut off from the ancestral cult and so deprived of divine protection. His house was demolished and his goods were destroyed or confiscated, and he was driven forth naked into the wild. If he were slain no price could be demanded and no feud could avenge him, and thus his life was at the mercy of anyone who came upon him.[10]

By virtue, perhaps, of its long legal use, the word "outlaw" had become pregnant with meaning in the popular mind. It had great value as a slogan word, as Levinson found from its quick adoption when his movement began to grow and as he pointed out to Kellogg and others when the term "renunciation of war" was largely substituted for it in the official peace pact negotiations. Harrison Brown often lamented that he could not find a French equivalent which carried both the technical and the popular meaning of "outlaw."

The legal meaning of the word and its possibilities as a slogan were both present to Levinson's mind when he adopted it at the very beginning of his movement. It appears in his first published article.[11] However, his early use of the term was more for its symbolic character than for its legal sense. He then expected to declare war illegal and to organize pains and penalties to be applied to those who used it.

440; LXVIII (December 9, 1926), 106; LXIX (December 12, 1927), 477. For the complete resolution see Appen. A.

[10] T. F. T. Plucknett, "Outlawry," *Encyclopaedia of the Social Sciences* (New York: Macmillan Co., 1933). For reference to outlawry in England see F. W. Maitland, *The Constitutional History of England* (Cambridge, 1909), p. 475; also D. J. Medley, *A Students Manual of English Constitutional History* (2d ed.; Oxford: B. H. Blackwell, 1898), pp. 40 and 345.

[11] "Legal Status of War."

War, though made illegal, might still conceivably occur but it would be branded as a crime and the force of the world would be organized to deal with the criminal.

To sum up, two things are indispensable to the reorganization of the world: The specific outlawing of War by the code of nations and the ability by force to execute the decrees of the international tribunal.[12]

"Outlawing" is not here used in its strict legal sense, which assumes a condition of society antecedent to its organization of a system of pains and penalties and of adequate legal machinery for enforcing them. If the offender could not be brought to trial and punished by society, society could only withdraw its protection and leave him to whatever punishment any of its members might choose to inflict. Anyone, in other words, could take a "pot shot" at him.[13] "Generally speaking, the weaker the system of law enforcement the more rapidly it resorts to outlawry. . . . . "[14] However, after Levinson came into contact with Senator Knox in 1919 and he began to reflect on the difficulty of using force in international affairs, the trend set in toward the use of the term in its legal sense. In fact, he began to think of the problem of war on the plane of legal development which existed at the time when outlawry was in wide use as a legal device; and, what is more significant, he became opposed to any collective organization of pains and penalties in international affairs.[15] This meant that if there were to be any force used, it would be under the conditions in which outlawry was employed in ancient and medieval law. The trend continued toward the legal use of the term, so that, in a sense, it may be said that the peace pact itself is an expression of outlawry as used in primitive law systems.[16] No system of pains

---

[12] *Ibid.*   [13] Maitland, *op. cit.*   [14] Plucknett, *op. cit.*

[15] While his letters begin to show evidence that he opposed the use of force in international affairs in the early twenties, his first published article dealing with the matter was "Can Peace Be 'Enforced'? A Study of International Sanctions," *Christian Century*, January 8, 1925.

[16] It may be said that by 1927 Levinson began to move toward permitting the organization of pains and penalties on a regional basis. Let the nations outlaw war; and then, if in a region some states still felt insecure, they could make arrangements to protect themselves against a "mad dog."

and penalties is provided whereby an outlaw nation is to have punishment measured out to it according to the degree of its offense; but, rather, in keeping with outlawry practices of the old system under conditions mentioned in the preamble to the Pact, all the other states are released from their obligations toward an offender and are free to take pot shots at it at their pleasure, as far as that treaty is concerned.[17]

However, the analysis which has just been made of the analogy between outlawry in its original sense and in Levinson's sense is not one which Levinson consciously made. He wanted to outlaw *war*, not a nation which used war, although, when his theory of the use of force is examined, it will become evident in the last analysis that he did outlaw a nation which insisted on attacking its neighbors.[18] But he wanted to do to war what the older outlawry did to a person, that is, to take away all its legal protection, first, by a formal multistate declaration that the further use of war was illegal and, second, by removing the legal advantages which had hitherto resulted from war. No legal title to territory could be secured by conquest; no change in the legal relation of states could occur by the use of violence.

The language which Levinson and his lieutenants used to discuss war in its legal sense always turned on the word "institution." He began using the term "institution" in his first published article in 1918, and he continued to use it in season and out. A number of quotations are gathered at random to indicate the sense he attached to it.

[17] Professor Shotwell takes just the opposite view: that outlawry implies an act of power directed against the lawbreaker or requires the organization of pains and penalties and, since there are none in the Pact of Paris, it is not outlawry in the original sense (see Shotwell, *War as an Instrument of National Policy* [New York: Harcourt, Brace & Co., 1929], chap. x, esp. p. 113; also "The Pact of Paris," *International Conciliation* [Bull. 243; October, 1928], p. 455).

[18] "Can War Be Outlawed?" Professor Reeves in the debate in the *Forum* objected to the use of the term "outlaw" when applied to a thing. He held it was applicable only to a person. Levinson answered by quoting James's use of it in connection with war in his "Moral Equivalent of War," *International Conciliation* (Bull. 224), p. 495, and Root's proposal at the Washington Disarmament Conference to outlaw submarines and poison gas. This answer is found in a letter to the editor of the *Forum*.

The further use of war as an institution for the settlement of international disputes shall be abolished.[19]

Resolved, that it is the view of the Senate of the United States that war between nations should be outlawed as an institution or means for the settlement of international controversies by making it a public crime under the law of nations. . . . .[20]

If the people would only give a little time to its study they would learn that war is an *institution* in the same sense that a university or college is, or the church, or marriage, or the League of Nations itself. War is in the nature of a court, a bloody court to be sure, but the only one that can *compel* the settlement of international disputes. Of course courts are institutions—war being the only bloody one.[21]

Whatever else war is, it will not be disputed that it is an established institution, respectable, legal, authoritative. It is an institution in precisely the same sense that marriage is an institution, or the church or the school.[22]

Now, as you well know, we outlaw all war. That is to say, we outlaw the institution of war. The use of war as a policy or a means of adjustment ceases, is prohibited, abolished.[23]

We are attempting to get rid of an institution in the nature of a court used to settle disputes between nations.[24]

Now it would seem that the abolition of legal advantages resulting from war is implicit in this language and follows inescapably from it. However, it did not convey this meaning to everyone, as it was intended by the outlawrists to do. Many people took "war" in the popular sense of violence, whereas the word was being used in the technical sense of a source of rights. When

[19] From the plan formulated by Levinson and Knox in 1919, "Plan To Outlaw War," printed in *Senate Doc. 115* (67th Cong., 2d sess.).

[20] From the resolution to outlaw war offered by Senator Borah first in 1923 (see Appen. A).

[21] Levinson to Garvin, December 28, 1925.

[22] Morrison, *op. cit.*, p. 91.

[23] Levinson to Dewey, February 8, 1928.

[24] Levinson to Fisher, March 31, 1928. This style of talking about war as an institution crept into the language of the notes in the negotiations which led up to the peace pact (see below, p. 276). It had also been impressed on Briand (see below, p. 313).

Levinson said he would "abolish the institution of war," he did not mean that there would be no resort to violence but rather that changes resulting from its use would have no status in law. An international robber might still take a city at the point of a bayonet, but it would not, as a matter of law, be his city.

For some reason or other many people did not see that to declare war illegal would necessarily destroy the legality of advantages gained by means of war. Some persons grasped this idea better when Secretary Stimson called it the "non-recognition doctrine" and applied it in 1932 in the Manchurian affair. Part of the responsibility for the misunderstanding lies with those persons who condemned outlawry as "a Pope's bull against a comet" or as "buncombe." But in all fairness it seems to me that Levinson did not make clear in the early twenties the difference between war in the legal and war in the popular sense and that he did not connect the declaration of the states against war with the legal consequences as clearly as he did in 1928 and after. On the other hand, if one had the idea in mind as he read Levinson's earlier letters and writings, he could find all of it there. For example, in the plan that he prepared for Senator Knox in 1919 this statement occurs as the fourth point: "All annexations, exactions, or seizures by force, duress, or fraud shall be null and void."[25] Though this declaration appeared as one of the statements of the plan, in the discussion which followed there was no mention of it. Nearly always in his letters he stressed the institutional character of war and the conception of war as a court, which was really coming very close to the idea, but not close enough, apparently, to prevent misunderstanding. However, by 1928 he was definitely distinguishing between war as a source of rights and war as violence and making clear that a title secured by a means which was outlawed would not be legal. He wrote to James G. McDonald:

> You cannot be sure that you are abolishing force and violence in international relations. You can be sure, however, if the nations so agree by treaty . . . . that if force or violence comes in international relations it will be in violation and contempt of the law and not as a recognized and legalized institution . . . . this

[25] *Senate Doc. 115.*

theory of trying to establish right, justice or title by brute strength and scientific engines of destruction has been banished from every aspect of civilization except the international where it truculently lingers.[26]

Elsewhere he wrote that "as long as the outlawing of war remains the keystone of international law, violence may indeed break out, but it will not come as the legal institution of war, as a method recognized by international law to 'settle' disputes, or an instrument of national policy."[27] A still clearer statement with regard to the source of rights is contained in his "Sanctions of Peace." The first sanction—an enlargement of his 1919 null-and-void plank—is: "In the future all annexations and territorial acquisitions by means of war or under the menace of war, or in the presence of armed force, and all seizures or exactions by force, duress or fraud shall be null and void."[28] In the comment on this sanction he said in part:

> If it is unlawful to wage war, conquests by war should furnish no legal title. . . . . Never again can a nation bent upon conquest acquire indefeasible title to anything. . . . . In short, hereafter no title shall pass by any kind of war except the title of a pirate.

His application of the idea of the invalidity of a title secured in an illegal way is the statement which he handed to Briand in December, 1931, relative to the Manchurian crisis.

> Japan was one of the original or charter signatories of the Briand-Kellogg treaty of August 27, 1928. By this treaty Japan pledged itself never to seek the solution of any dispute or conflict with another nation except by pacific means.
>
> By this signature Japan bound itself among other things not to seize, occupy or annex the territory of another nation by means, or under threats, of force. In short, Japan committed itself completely to this new law of the nations which outlawed the use of force for purposes of acquisition or occupation against the will of a possessor nation.
>
> China also signed this treaty as a cosignatory with Japan. On July 24, 1929, this treaty was proclaimed operative by President Hoover. Having been signed by practically all the nations of the world, the treaty thereby becomes an integral part of international law and, in fact, the supreme law of the world.

[26] Levinson to McDonald, of the Foreign Policy Association, April 7, 1928.

[27] Levinson, "Abolishing the Institution of War," *Christian Century*, March 22, 1928.

[28] Levinson, "The Sanctions of Peace," *Christian Century*, December 25, 1929.

Therefore, if Japan has violated this treaty, this supreme law of the nations, its occupation of Manchuria and its claimed rights thereunder are clearly in violation of the law and are legally and juridically null and void.[29]

This, then, is the fundamental concept of outlawry: war in the sense of an institution for settling controversies is declared by the nations of the world to be illegal, and changes resulting from the use of war have no legal validity.

On the basis of the legal concept of war, Levinson refused to accept any distinctions among wars, especially such as that between aggressive and defensive war. If aggressive war were put under the ban and defensive war were not, then title could pass in the latter case. That would not be destroying war as a source of title, the essential object of outlawry.

> I told Shotwell . . . . [his definition of the aggressor] had absolutely no place in our scheme. Our plan contemplates the abolition and ending of the use of the institution of war for the settlement of international controversies. We do not say that war can be used on this occasion but not on that; we say war cannot be used to settle any kind of a dispute.[30]

He frequently tried to make this point with regard to offensive and defensive war clear by comparing war in the legal sense to dueling. He wrote:

> Suppose this same distinction had been urged when the institution of duelling was outlawed. . . . . Suppose then it had been urged that only "aggressive duelling" should be outlawed and that "defensive duelling" be left intact. . . . . Such a suggestion relative to duelling would have been silly, but the analogy is perfectly sound. What we did was to outlaw the institution of duelling, a method theretofore recognized by law for the settlement of disputes of so-called honor.[31]

[29] Paul Scott Mowrer's cable to the *Chicago Daily News*, December 10, 1931. It is of interest to note that this action by Levinson was followed in January, 1932, by the notes to Japan and China in which Secretary Stimson announced the nonrecognition doctrine and the resolution of the Assembly of the League in March to the same effect.

[30] Levinson to Holmes, January 15, 1925.

[31] "Abolishing the Institution of War." This kind of argument seemed to be conclusive with Kellogg, as shown by his insistence on the renunciation of war without any qualifications as to whether it was aggressive or defensive (see below, pp. 269 f.). He, however, in his notes based his contention on the ground that the right of

The matter of offensive and defensive war was intimately connected with self-defense. Levinson would tolerate no distinctions as to war, but the question was then asked him, "Are you a complete nonresistant pacifist? Won't you let us defend ourselves?" His answer was:

Our point is simply this: the right of defense cannot be plucked out of human nature as to any unit from the individual to the nation. If there were a hundred laws depriving a person or a state of the right of self-defense, such laws would be perfectly inoperative. . . . . While we think it will be next to impossible to get war started once Outlawry has been thoroughly adopted . . . . yet it is conceivable that some nation may run amuck and if so any involved nation that might be attacked would have the God-given right to defend itself. . . . . In our scheme the word war becomes obsolete as an institution. . . . .[32]

---

self-defense could not be alienated, so that a renunciation of all war had no effect on it, following the same line of reasoning as Levinson had been urging, as will be seen in the next paragraph. It must be added that Levinson also urged that no distinctions be made between offensive and defensive war, simply because no such distinction could, in fact, be made with sufficient precision. The only definition which he thought had any reality was: "An aggressor nation is the nation you are at war with." It seems to me that this argument of the difficulty of definition weakened his case quite materially—a case which, as resting on his legal concept of war, appeared strong enough. Especially is it an attack on his plan to achieve such perfect codification of international law that the states cognizant of this law could repair with confidence to a world court where most of their controversies could be adjudicated. How, if it is impossible to provide for determining an aggressor in a treaty, can a code a thousand times more difficult be set up? He himself suggested one way of finding an aggressor whom he at other times said could not be found, namely, by referring the whole matter to a court with power to issue a summons and hear the case (see below, p. 198). The fact of the matter was that in many of Levinson's arguments with Shotwell over aggressive and defensive war they were both talking about the same thing, self-defense. But they managed to misunderstand each other perfectly by using different terms for it, the one calling it defensive war and the other using the word "war" in a legal sense. The difficulty was that Levinson thought Shotwell was trying to distinguish between aggressive and defensive war, but Shotwell was really trying to distinguish between the aggressor and the victim.

[32] Levinson to McDonald, May 28, 1925. Levinson might have supported his position by citing the Constitution, Art. 1, Sec. 10, clause 3: "No State shall . . . . engage in war, unless actually invaded or in such imminent danger as will not admit of delay." The point that he made with regard to the right of self-defense is so axiomatic in both municipal and international law that it hardly need be stated to be accepted (see John Bassett Moore, *International Law Digest*, Vol. II, sec. 217; H. Lauterpacht, *The Function of Law in the International Community* [Oxford: Clarendon Press, 1936], pp. 257 f.).

John Bassett Moore had given him the idea about letting the word "war" become obsolete.[33] He quoted that great authority as saying "after you outlaw war do not use the word 'war' any more but refer always to the inherent right of self-defense."[34] So he reasoned that when war in the legal sense was outlawed, the initiation of *de facto* war would be like murder in the legal sense; for a nation to use every means at its command to beat back an unprovoked attack would no more be war than killing an assailant to repel him would be murder. "Such a defense against an aggressor," he wrote, "although almost inconceivable after war has been outlawed, would not be war any more than a defense by an individual, after duelling was outlawed, would be called duelling."[35] In fact, he concluded, "when people get it through

[33] It seems that two persons made this suggestion to Levinson about the same time, Oswald Garrison Villard and Moore, as will appear from excerpts of letters quoted. However, Moore was the one generally cited as the authority. "You may recall a pleasant discussion we had en route New York to Washington on an International program prepared by Senator Knox and myself. You suggested a change, namely, that after war had been outlawed, no nice distinctions of kinds of wars be made, but that the right of self-defense be inserted instead of the expression 'defensive war.' This was done and has been of great advantage in the consideration and discussion of the subject" (see Levinson to John Bassett Moore, February 21, 1922). "Recently I met Mr. Moore on my way from New York to Washington and showed him the paper. He made a similar suggestion to yours" (see Levinson to Oswald Garrison Villard, June 1, 1920).

[34] Levinson to Borah, June 20, 1924.

[35] Levinson to Miss Alice Henry, February 7, 1928. It seems to me that this reasoning makes almost necessary a means of determining an aggressor. While it is true that there would be no reason for distinguishing aggressive from defensive dueling, yet, with dueling legally abolished, it would seem that the law should provide for distinguishing the murderer from the victim in a shooting affair. It would seem that Levinson's point is well taken that in international law as in municipal law it is difficult to lay down a rule defining an aggressor ahead of time, since the matters to be determined are questions of fact and not of definition. Such a definition might prove to be a "sign post for the guilty and a stumbling block for the innocent," but to agree ahead of time upon a procedure for determining an aggressor is a wholly different matter. Such procedure works in municipal law, and it would seem to be more readily applicable in international matters because of the continuing nature and public character of the events involved. The practice of the League of Nations has shown that there is little, if any, difficulty in determining an aggressor (see Sir John F. Williams, "Sanctions under the Covenant," *British Year Book of International Law* [1936], p. 130; also Q. Wright, "The Test of Aggression in the Italo-Ethiopian War,"

their heads that war has been and is used as a 'court,' as a lawful method of settling disputes, they will see that the right of self-defense is as irrelevant to the question of abolishing the institution of war as it is inherent and ineradicable as a naked right."[36]

While Kellogg and Borah insisted that each state should be a judge of the occasion and the means needed for self-defense—the Senator going so far, in the opinion of many, as to destroy the treaty—Levinson was quick to agree with them, though he knew the maxim, "No man is a good judge in his own case." Here is his agreement with his star performers, his justification for this agreement, and his mature judgment:

It is claimed by cynics and others that so long as each nation has the right to decide for itself that the occasion for the exercise of this inherent right of self-defense exists, it is a law unto itself and war will be prevalent. This is nonsense. Once we have war condemned and abandoned by officialdom, the power over its return will be in the hands of the people who ought to have that power. It is too much for the masses to pass upon war when war is presumptively legal and regular; the people cannot find a needle in the haystack. But when war is cast out of the law, is abolished, is abandoned, is outlawed, then the burden of proof

---

AJIL, XXX [1936], 45). For a discussion of tests of aggression see Q. Wright, "The Concept of Aggression in International Law," *AJIL*, XXIX (1935), 373.

[36] Levinson to Kellogg, August 9, 1928. While the inalienability of the right of self-defense was accepted widely, forming the basis of Kellogg's argument on the matter (below, p. 290) and of Borah's defense of the peace pact in the Senate (below, p. 330), Levinson's conclusion that the use of violence is not war in the legal sense was not accepted by Borah or by Kellogg or, as far as I know, by any of his other lieutenants. This point which, it seems to me, is of the utmost importance has, as far as I have been able to find, either not been understood or not been considered worth commenting upon by the jurists, with the exception of Professor Wright (see his "Neutrality and Neutral Rights Following the Pact of Paris," *Proceedings of the American Society of International Law*, XXIV and XXV [1930], 86; also "The Meaning of the Peace Pact," *AJIL*, XXVII [1933], 39; and "When Does War Exist?" *ibid.*, XXVI [1932], 362). It is a question how far Levinson would want to follow the implications of his idea—that the use of violence in bona fide self-defense is not war—since he excoriated the League as a war-making alliance because it provided for a means whereby collective violence could be used against a state running amuck. This kind of violence could come under the meaning of self-defense and therefore not be war in the legal sense. However, apart from theory and as a matter of practical politics, he was willing for European states to have military alliances after the signing of the peace pact—regional alliances which would be in a state of suspension until the Pact might be breached.

shifts and the nation attempting to use force will have to convince public opinion that it is soundly within an exception to the general and universal rule.

Sooner or later I favor, if necessary, the jurisdiction in the international courts, to hear the facts on petition and to decide whether or not the treaty has been broken, whether a nation has resorted to the use of force in self-defense or otherwise.[37]

The outlawrists had little patience with those persons who wanted to solve the war problem by removing its causes.[38] The real causes of war were not the admitted causes.[39] And "while law and courts have never attempted to remove the causes of disputes, outlawry would provide the conditions for a much freer and more energetic educational campaign against economic injustice than now exists. . . . ."[40]

This contention that the simple outlawing of war would change the whole atmosphere of international relations by removing the constant threat of war was shared by all the outlawrists and used to justify their indifference or opposition to other schemes for peace.[41] It was Professor Dewey who carried it furthest and provided the philosophic basis for others to build coherent arguments on. It was his belief that

law has always served the purpose of condensing and defining the moral wishes and expectations of the community. No matter how much it is behind the highest moral aspirations of the developed members of the community, law has precipitated average moral sentiment in a way that has rendered it more effective than it would otherwise be. It has canalized moral emotions so that they may flow to a purpose.[42]

He went on to say that, as long as law either in a positive, or even in a passive, sense was on the side of war, moral sentiment was in

[37] Levinson to Senator La Follette, December 13, 1928.

[38] "Plan To Outlaw War," *Senate Doc. 115.*

[39] John Dewey, "War and a Code of Law," *New Republic*, October 24, 1923.

[40] John Dewey, "Outlawry of War," *New Republic*, October 3, 1923.

[41] If one reads carefully the first article, "The Legal Status of War," with this claim in mind, it is not incomprehensible why Levinson could suddenly shift from support of a league to opposition to the League.

[42] John Dewey, "Ethics and International Relations," *Foreign Affairs*, March 15, 1923.

a self-contradictory position. The way to remove this contradiction was to outlaw war, and until that time

there is no opportunity for existing moral sentiments to function effectively in international relations, and next to no hope for the speedy development of a coherent and widely accepted body of moral ideas which will be effective in determining international relations. . . . . Till this move is taken I do not see much chance that any other improvement in international relations will win general assent or be practicable in execution.[43]

The second commandment of outlawry was the codification of an international law of peace. Some attention must be given to the meaning which Levinson put into the word "codification" when he used it. It is certain that he was not using it in the legal sense of improving the form of the law but not the substance—the "re-expression of the pre-existing law," as Austin puts it—for he admitted that the greater part of the substance of existing international law was the law of war, all of which would be of no use after the advent of outlawry; and he lamented the rudimentary nature of the law of peace and its total impotence.[44] On the other hand, he was much opposed to the creation of a true legislature—a superstate, he called it—a sovereign body with power to alter the substance as well as the form of the law. It was with the substance of the law that he was concerned, and in using the word "codification" to include changes in the substance as well as in the form of international law he had good authority in contemporary usage.[45]

[43] *Ibid.*

[44] "The Legal Status of War." Sir Henry Maine says there are two senses in which codification is used: (1) "the conversion of unwritten into written law" and (2) "the conversion of written into well written law" (*Village Communities in the East and West* [New York: Henry Holt & Co., 1880], pp. 362 ff.). Lobingier agrees with this definition in his "Codification of Law," *Encyclopaedia of the Social Sciences.*

[45] James W. Garner, "The Codification of International Law," *Christian Century,* February 12, 1925. Also see Elihu Root, *Addresses on International Subjects,* ed. R. Bacon and J. B. Scott (Cambridge: Harvard University Press, 1916), pp. 57 ff. and 405 ff.; "To codify international law is primarily to set in motion and promote the law-making process itself in the community of nations . . . ." (*ibid.,* p. 59). It was decided at the Hague conference for the codification of international law that it "was not to be an attempt to study merely the pre-existing law" (M. Hudson, *Proceedings of the American Society of International Law,* XXIV and XXV [1930], 230).

[199]

His plan for securing such a code and the means for keeping it up to date are suggested in the following excerpts from his own comment on the plan prepared in 1919:

The code should be prepared by the leading statesmen and jurists of the world, with all civilized nations represented in an international conference called for that purpose. It may take two years to prepare such a code. Senator Knox thought it would take five years. Therefore, a commitment in principle to a plan for the codification of international law, the creation of a court with affirmative specified jurisdiction and the criminal outlawry of war is all that is necessary at this time. The code conference will do the rest.

That the international code when prepared must be submitted to each civilized nation and be by it approved. As each of such nations will participate in the preparation of the code, general harmony may be expected. Besides, it is also proposed that every five years the code may be amended and brought down to date, so the freshly discovered points may be covered.[46]

There was little disposition to say what the code should contain, for it was to be part of the plan for the leading jurists to draw it up and no one could tell in advance what their conclusions would be.[47] The futility of previous attempts at codification was no proof that a conference for codification after the threat of war had been removed would fail. "Unconsciously we tend to project into the future situation all the attendants of the present system of legalized war and thus fail to recognize the extent to which difficulties spring from the legalizing of war and would disappear were war outlawed."[48] The objection that the codifiers could not

---

[46] *Senate Doc. 115.*   [47] Dewey, "War and a Code of Law."

[48] *Ibid.* It would seem that Levinson and Dewey were advocating the impossible —a conference in which international law could be codified. "So I say, considered as a conclusion, there can be no codification, but, considered as a process, there must be codification . . . . " (Root, *op. cit.*, p. 407; also see G. W. Wickersham, "The Codification of International Law," *Foreign Affairs*, January, 1926, p. 237). The failure of the first international conference held at The Hague in 1930 for the purpose of codifying law, although it was limited to three matters only, showed the very great improbability of any conference ever being able to codify law to the extent which Levinson hoped for (*Proceedings of the American Society of International Law*, XXIV and XXV [1930], 213 ff.; also A. Alvarez, "The First Conference for the Codification of International Law," *Transactions of the Grotius Society*, XVI [1930], 119). Codification of municipal law, even in the code countries like France, has scarcely reached the perfection which the outlawrists were hoping for in international law (Lauterpacht, *op. cit.*, pp. 60 ff.).

get at the real issues, the basic reasons for war, such as immigration and the control of monopolies in China, was answered by Dewey. The code would not need to cover such things. Nations never admitted that they were going to war over such matters. They admitted going to war only over such matters as could be covered by law, such as the murder of nationals, etc.[49]

Later, when a demand was put forward for making the Pact of Paris more explicit and adding explanations, Levinson sidestepped it with "ultimately we must have a code and the code can contain all the distinctions and niceties of legal protection that human ingenuity and expert voluminousness can command."[50] Frequently he could answer troublesome questions by referring the inquirer to the wisdom of the world's chief jurists, who could iron out the difficulty in the conference.

He would have nothing to do with attempts at codifying the rules of warfare. "It has seemed to me that it would be crossing my own wires, impairing and undermining my own work, to give time, thought and expression to the kind of maritime code we should have now relative to 'the conduct of war against an aggressive state' etc. I do not go along these lines," he replied to Buell when the latter sounded him on the subject.[51]

It may be said in conclusion with regard to the second commandment, that it played no very significant role in the outlawry concept. The first commandment was that which drew the fire and received most attention in the correspondence.

The third commandment was the creation of a court with affirmative jurisdiction over international disputes:

In creating a real international court the subtle and mischievous distinction between justiciable (triable) and non justiciable (non triable) controversies must not be permitted to defeat its jurisdiction. . . . . The new code must itself state what causes are within the jurisdiction of the court and what are not, and must not allow an individual country to decide the matter for the court. The proposed plan covers this by excluding from the jurisdiction of the court all domestic and protective questions (like revenues, immigration, Monroe Doctrine, etc.) which shall be agreed upon for all countries and enumerated

[49] Dewey, "War and a Code of Law."
[50] Levinson to Brown, June 1, 1928.
[51] Levinson to Buell, October 8, 1928.

in the code. In this way the jurisdiction of the court over all purely international disputes can be protected and maintained.[52]

This court was to be modeled as nearly as possible on the United States Supreme Court, because, in Levinson's opinion before 1928, the latter was the only international court that had ever been set up. All nations were to come into the court on the same basis of legal equality. "We claim that when San Domingo comes into the court against Great Britain, San Domingo should stand on an exact parity with Great Britain so far as justice and right are concerned,"[53] precisely as little Rhode Island had come into the United States Supreme Court on an even footing against Massachusetts.[54] And, like the United States Supreme Court, the new court on petition of a complainant state was to have power to issue a summons to a defendant state and to hear and decide the matters in controversy, whether the defendant state appeared or not. This is what he meant by "affirmative jurisdiction."[55]

Levinson had great confidence in the judicial method of settling disputes. And he said very little about other methods of international intercourse. But, when Walter Lippmann said the "central fallacy" of outlawry was its "refusal to acknowledge the necessity of diplomacy for just those war breeding disputes which are not within the competence"[56] of a court, Dewey answered

[52] "Outlawry of War."   [53] "Can War Be Outlawed?"

[54] *Rhode Island* v. *Massachusetts*, 37 U.S. 657 (1832).

[55] To advocate an international court with compulsory jurisdiction and, by inference, United States membership in it would seem to lack political realism in view of the constant opposition of the Senate since 1897 to any agreement which would provide for the submission of a dispute to any competent international body without the concurrence of the Senate at the time of submission. For a review of the Senate's attitude see letter of Secretary Hughes to the President (*Congressional Record*, LXIV [February, 1923], 4499; also Chandler P. Anderson, editorial, *AJIL*, XXVI [1932], 328). There is one exception in the record of the Senate. It "voted unanimously to make the United States a member of the International Labour Organization under which it [The United States] will be subject to the compulsory jurisdiction of the [World] Court in certain cases" (James W. Garner, "Acts and Joint Resolutions of Congress as Substitutes for Treaties," *AJIL*, XXIX [1935], 482). In view of the intransigent attitude of a minority of the Senate with respect to international matters, it would seem that this vote occurred without a knowledge of the implications involved.

[56] "Outlawry of War," *Atlantic Monthly*, August, 1923.

hotly that outlawry did contemplate political as well as judicial means.[57]   However, the outlawrists continued to emphasize the judicial means to the neglect of the political in international affairs.   And in the spring of 1928 Professor Shotwell and his group insisted that Levinson had admitted the efficacy of the political means in his conversation only but not in his writings and that Dr. Morrison had so stressed the judicial means as to give the impression that he was entirely excluding all others.   Since his book[58] was taken as authoritative by the interested public, Shotwell and his group wanted some statement by Levinson to correct this impression, if it was a mistaken one.   In response to this request, which had been transmitted through Dewey, Levinson wrote an article in which he said:

> Let it be said once and for all that conferences are vital to every process of making and maintaining peace.   But the conferences should be held under the reign of peace and not under the reign of war.   The conference table must not be decorated with loaded revolvers.[59]

It was, however, a judicial organization of the world which Levinson wanted; he was usually opposed to any attempt to organize it politically.   Less than a month after it had been recorded in print that he was willing for political as well as judicial procedures to be used, he wrote to Dewey:

> I am a great believer in the ultimate resort to the judicial.   That is the way, and the best one that civilization has yet discovered.   It is by no means perfect because human nature is imperfect and judges are fallible, but we can reach the nearest approach to perfection in that way.[60]

When he first conceived outlawry, the use of force was essential to it.   "The power to enforce any law must always be adequate. . . . . We must not indulge in the absurdity of committing ourselves to the proposition that we may use force to compel a nation to submit its cause to arbitration, but shall not use force to execute the decision of the international court in such arbitration."[61] But shortly after 1920 he began to waver on the necessity of force.

[57] Dewey, "Outlawry of War: What It Is and Is Not."

[58] Morrison, *op. cit.*

[59] "Abolishing the Institution of War."

[60] Levinson to Dewey, April 7, 1928.   [61] "Legal Status of War."

It was then that he began to read the debates in the Constitutional Convention. He decided that "the makers of the Constitution knew that the physical enforcement of a decree against a state meant war, or the . . . . equivalent of war."[62] In many letters he quoted Madison and Hamilton to support this point. Borah agreed thoroughly. He quoted Hamilton as saying: "It has been observed to coerce the States is one of the maddest projects that was ever devised. . . . . This thing is a dream. It is impossible."[63] In keeping with these sentiments the outlawrists insisted that the "fathers made no provision in the Constitution for the enforcement of the judgment of the Court against a State."[64] Therefore, neither should the proposed world court have any power to enforce decisions against any state.[65] The Supreme Court, he claimed, had never enforced any decisions in the eighty-six cases which had been tried before it involving disputes between states.[66]

[62] "Can War Be Outlawed?"

[63] Borah, "The Fetish of Force," *Forum*, August, 1925.

[64] *Ibid.* They cited *Rhode Island* v. *Massachusetts* to support this contention. No attempt can be made here to examine this point, though it does seem that there is a question as to the validity of this view. There is a case in which the Supreme Court of the United States speaking through Chief Justice Marshall issued a mandamus to a lower court to enforce a decision of that court even though the governor of the state of Pennsylvania had been authorized by the legislature to resist (*U.S.* v. *Peters*, 5 Cranch 115 [1809]). The marshal of the court appointed a day for the service of the writ and summoned a *posse comitatus* of two thousand men; the governor in the face of overwhelming force failed to resist. Though this case is not exactly in point, since the action was not against a state, it does provide an example of enforcement in the presence of physical force. The case of *Virginia* v. *West Virginia* (246 U.S. 565 [1918]) is exactly in point, the Court declaring that a state could be coerced, though here West Virginia complied with the decision before any further threat of force was made (W. W. Willoughby, *The Constitutional Law of the United States* [New York: Baker Voorhis Co., 1929], Vol. III, Secs. 923–26). Professor Wright is of the opinion that the power to coerce a state will be found in an emergency. "The very fact that active corecion of states has seldom been necessary, far from proving the absence of a sanction, proves its effectiveness" (Q. Wright, "The Outlawry of War," *AJIL*, XIX [1925], 76, and *The Control of American Foreign Relations* [New York: Macmillan Co., 1922], p. 157).

[65] The fear that the decisions of the World Court might be enforced by the Council of the League was one of the reasons why he opposed the Court so bitterly until the Senate approved it in 1926.

[66] "Can War Be Outlawed?" (see above, n. 64, for cases in which the threat of force was present).

Neither would an international court need to enforce a decision against a nation.

When it was urged that the analogy between the Supreme Court and a world court was not good, since the Supreme Court operates with a strong political federal government in the background, whereas the other would be operating against a background of political anarchy, Levinson answered:

To me the concept of the United States of the World is a babel of tongues and an utter impossibility. Our program calls for no such thing. We are merely trying to get the various countries to agree to a juridical system to supplant the war system in the settlement of international controversies. Our particular reliance is upon a treaty which will provide that neither side will go to war about a dispute if it never gets settled. We do not claim that every dispute, particularly domestic matters, can be or will be submitted to an international court. But we do say that war is so futile and destructive that it is infinitely better to let a dispute go unsettled, as individuals constantly do, rather than to pursue such an insane method. This does not require any federalization or any general governmental machinery. It is very little more than the process of treaty making, somewhat amplified to carry out the purposes of the treaty. The power and jurisdiction of our federal supreme court in handling disputes between states has nothing to do with the executive, nothing to do with congress, nothing to do with legislation, and nothing to do, strictly speaking, with the United States as a federalized government. The colonies could have made the same agreement among themselves as to their disputes.

In short, "our strongly federalistic government" has nothing to do with the case of outlawry.[67]

[67] Levinson to Joseph H. Himes, January 26, 1927. This shows Levinson's technique of dodging a question by answering another instead of the one propounded; however, there is no evidence that he consciously changed the question asked into another one that he could answer. It was when the inquirer refused to be diverted that outlawry developed; for, if he saw that he was not answering, he went to work to find an answer or changed his position. It is unfortunate that this one was not pushed harder, but it seemed the reply given always satisfied the inquirer, so we have no way of knowing what Levinson would have said had he been held to the point. He did not agree with my comment here and quoted J. S. Mill as his authority. The statement from Mill which he cited (see "Can War Be Outlawed") is: "The usual remedies between nations, war and diplomacy, being precluded by the Federal Union, it is necessary that a judicial remedy should supply their place. The Supreme Court of the federation dispenses international law, and is the first great example of what is now one of the most prominent wants of civilized society, a real international tribunal." But the whole chapter, "Federal Representative Governments," in which

The problem of the use of force in international relations was one to which Levinson gave much thought. He was not a pacifist, a believer in nonviolent resistance, like Jesus or Tolstoy. He said that all pacifists should support outlawry, but he did not want pacifists to claim that outlawry was their program, lest they should antagonize possible converts who were suspicious of pacifism. He, himself, believed in the use of force against individuals[68] but not in the possibility of its use against states, because "if war were declared a crime like murder and France started a war it is not possible to put France to death; it is not possible to imprison France; it is not possible to starve France.[69] What may be done

---

this statement appears is concerned with setting forth the conditions under which a federal political union can exist. And the next paragraph following the one quoted contains the following statement: "The powers of a federal government naturally extend not only to peace and war, and all questions which arise between the country and foreign governments, but to making any other arrangements which are, in the opinion of the states, necessary to their enjoyment of the full benefits of union. For example, it is a great advantage to them that their mutual commerce should be free, without the impediment of frontier duties and custom-houses. But this internal freedom cannot exist if each state has the power of fixing the duties on interchange of commodities between itself and foreign countries, since every foreign product let in by one state would be let into all the rest; and hence all custom duties and trade regulations in the United States are made or repealed by the federal government exclusively" (J. S. Mill, *Considerations on Representative Government* [New York: Henry Holt & Co., 1882], p. 328). Far from giving support to the contention for which Levinson was using the quotation, namely, that a court could operate against a background of political anarchy, it seems to me that the whole chapter supports the opposite position. For a better discussion of this point that a court is not alone sufficient see C. Howard Ellis, *The Origin, Structure, and Working of the League of Nations* (London: George Allen & Unwin, 1928), pp. 474 f.

[68] "The Sanctions of Peace."

[69] It seems that the small number of states in the international community is another argument against the use of force. Each state will have an occasional urge to gain some immediate advantage regardless of the effect on the growth of a legal order. The temptation to gain that advantage increases in proportion to the uncertainty of the long-run benefits resulting from a well-developed legal system. A small number of states accentuates the uncertainty of the long-run advantages because arrangements—log-rolling—looking to the satisfaction of immediate desires can more easily be accomplished among a few than among a large number. In the second place, once a state has been restrained by the collective system, it will not be likely soon to approve the condemnation of another which attempts a similar action, since that would discredit itself. Neither would a state which wished in the near future to make a similar move. Since the number of states is small, a few disaffections quickly

with an individual, who can be reached and punished whether for breaking a domestic law or a law of nations, cannot be done with a sovereign nation."[70]

He illustrated his belief in the impracticability of force in international relations[71] by a treaty between states A and B.

There are three relative positions of strength between Nations A and B, viz.:
1. A may be the exact equal of B;
2. A may be stronger than B;
3. B may be stronger than A;

In the first supposition manifestly neither can enforce the compact nor punish for a breach; in the second B cannot enforce or punish; and in the third A can not enforce or punish. Thus it is clear that sanctions are not feasible or possible in contractual treaties.[72]

He went on to explain that a military alliance could not be enforced, for, if the crisis came and—if it were a triple alliance—one of the three refused to respond to the call, "how are you going to enforce this alliance?"[73] His answer was "good faith," for "one nation," he said, "cannot compel another to fight for it."[74]

Starting with good faith, or "the plighted word," he worked

---

reduce the preponderance of power of the collective group so materially as to raise a serious question if the long-run gains from maintaining the legal order are worth the immediate sacrifices. Wright gives four reasons why it is more difficult to apply physical force to a state than to an individual ("Outlawry of War," p. 98, n. 101; also see J. L. Brierly, "Sanctions," *Transactions of the Grotius Society*, XVII [1932], 67).

[70] Levinson to Charles W. Eliot, January 28, 1925. Force against individuals is all right; force against groups is bad because it is war; a nation can resist the attack of another, that is all right because it is self-defense, not war (see above, pp. 195 ff.). I have never been able to find a substratum of reason on which these points could be reconciled with one another. The best that I can do is to say that he was using war in the popular sense as violence in the first instance and in the technical sense as a source of rights in the second.

[71] "How," he never tired of asking, "can you get rid of war by using war?"—that is, the use of force against nations.

[72] "Can Peace Be 'Enforced'?" When Professor Wright read this statement, his comment was: "This shows that self-defense may be useless, not that a collective sanction is" (see below, p. 208, n. 76).

[73] *Ibid.*

[74] Levinson, "The Prevention of War," *Yale Daily News*, April 21, 1925.

out a fivefold program for the "enforcement" of peace.[75] It is (1) good faith, (2) public opinion, (3) nonrecognition of changes made by the use of force, (4) the use of force by each state to punish individual war-fomenters among its nationals, and (5) the use of whatever means are necessary, including armed force, against a "mad-dog" state.

1. Since treaties rest ultimately on the good faith or the plighted word of their signatories, good faith should be relied upon. "This simply means that any arrangement, call it league, protocol, alliance or treaty, must in the last analysis rest upon the good faith of the parties involved."[76]

2. Public opinion was considered basic by him, perhaps more basic than reliance upon good faith. In the first place, the outlawry of war, by closing the gap between morality and law, would give a new significance to all the means of peace—diplomacy, arbitration, adjudication, etc.—thus freeing public opinion from the millstone of war. "Therefore the basic dependence must be upon public opinion—educated, alert, conscious of its power, and able to function."[77] As an aid to public opinion he would—after September, 1929—give the World Court "jurisdiction on the petition of an interested nation to investigate the charge of a breach of the Peace Pact. The court to have the power by the free consent of the nations to hear the case in a summary way, its doors open to the press and the public."[78] And he would also have the signatories of the Pact of Paris agree:

In case of the unfortunate action of any nation which amounts to an actual or immediately threatened breach of the Peace Pact . . . . to communicate with one another fully and frankly in order to acquire the fullest knowledge of the

[75] This program is of the period beginning September, 1929.

[76] "Can Peace Be 'Enforced'?" Levinson was doing a service in pointing out the basic importance of good faith or the "plighted word" in international life (see the Eastern Carelia Case, ser. B, No. 5, commented on by Lauterpacht, op. cit., pp. 2 ff.). But to use good faith as a substitute for sanctions would seem to be misapplying it, for that would mean placing reliance upon the "plighted word" of the state which had broken its pledge, for it is only against the state which has violated its agreement that there is any occasion for the application of sanctions. It would seem, therefore, to the extent to which good faith could be relied upon, sanctions would be effective against a violator of the "plighted word."

[77] "The Sanctions of Peace."   [78] Ibid.

situation, to consider the most efficient pacific measures to be taken jointly or separately to meet the exigencies of the particular situation and to tender friendly advice and offices to any or all the nations involved.[79]

3. The policy of nonrecognition as announced by Secretary Stimson January 7, 1932, was the application of Levinson's null-and-void idea which he had first published in December, 1921, and which has been discussed earlier in this chapter.

4. Since Levinson believed that force against individuals would be needed "until the millennial advent of the brotherhood of man," he advocated that each signatory of the Pact of Paris incorporate the following into its criminal code:

Any person, or persons, who shall advocate orally or in writing, or cause the publication of any printed matter which shall advocate the use of war between nations, in violation of the terms of the Pact of Paris, with the intent of causing war between or among nations, shall be guilty of a felony and upon conviction thereof shall be imprisoned not less than —— years.[80]

5. The last means of the "enforcement" of peace—the use of whatever measures might be necessary, including armed force, against a mad-dog nation—is one which Levinson would not include in any survey of his theory but which is in it, although one will find very little, if any, reference to it in his published writings. But there are frequent mentions of it in his letters around 1928, when his correspondents insisted on knowing what would happen if some state did wantonly breach the peace pact. His reasons for saying as little as possible about such a breach were that it was "inconceivable" that anything like that would actually happen, and that to keep talking about some "mythical" mad-dog state would stimulate the war psychology. But, nevertheless, he insisted that Europe could depend on the United States in such an

[79] *Ibid.*

[80] *Ibid.* About 1920 he favored having his proposed world court given the power to punish war-fomentors; but he dropped that project, after James Brown Scott asked him if he could imagine the United States as surrendering Woodrow Wilson to trial in a world tribunal. It is not quite just to raise the same question with regard to Germany's or Italy's punishing their own chief war-fomentors, since he did indicate that public opinion might be hampered in some places. "With the peoples in each country understanding the true meaning of the Peace Pact, the question of war and peace is in their hands, at least in those countries where there is sufficient liberty for public opinion to function" (*ibid.*).

eventuality, though the United States would not be bound in advance to take any action of any kind except to consult, nor would the United States permit anyone else to make any decisions which would in any way obligate it.

This statement that Levinson during the period of 1925–29 was willing to admit the use of force by nations in their relations to one another is so much at variance with what are ordinarily accepted as his principles that perhaps some quotations from his letters should be given as evidence that it is not based upon a slip of the tongue or taken out of the context. If France would join with the United States in outlawing war on a basis of the age-old tradition of mutual friendship, he wrote in 1925,

she would have an invisible alliance greater than any possible military alliance that could be conjectured or dreamed of. For, once the nations are in a compact to do away with war, if Germany (and I use this illustration merely as representing the quintessence of France's fear) should violate such a general treaty and at once break the laws of God and man, she would bring down upon herself not only the anathema of the world but all its resisting power.[81]

I haven't any doubt that if an honest Outlawry treaty is entered into and the existing mechanisms are adjusted and possibly new ones created to fit the situation, including a reasonable code, that the United States would be the first perhaps to resent an insolent breaking of the peace by a Mussolini. . . . .[82]

One of the strongest statements was made to Lieutenant Commander Kenworthy to the effect that Europe should assume that the United States would stand shoulder to shoulder with the states which kept the treaty in good faith, because he had no doubt what "we would do in a bold case of the violation of such a treaty."[83]

What we may do in the event of this bandit nation showing up and suddenly breaking the laws of God and man is a different proposition. To bind ourselves in advance is to adopt the whole theory of Article 16 of the Covenant and to finally succumb to the blandishments of sanctions so fostered in Europe and so . . . . struggled for by Shotwell.[84]

[81] Levinson to Brown, May 15, 1925.

[82] Levinson to Dewey, March 2, 1928.

[83] Levinson to Kenworthy, June 5, 1928. This letter is quoted more fully below, pp. 293-94.

[84] Levinson to Dewey, February 15, 1929.

Any kind of commitment as to what the United States will do in the event that a ghost of an aggressor will be found in the international closet is doomed to defeat. Not that our country might not actually participate in an outrageous situation. I am not that sort of a pacifist at all. But our hands must be free.[85]

There are some details of his theory which have either not been mentioned here or have received only passing attention under some other head. Such, for instance, are his insistence that there could be no withdrawal from the peace pact[86] and that the code should be ratified by vote of the people in all countries—a point which was dropped after Harrison Brown pointed out how a Cushendun would be glad of such an opportunity to play on popular passions to defeat the treaty;[87] his belief that there should be no attempt to provide a means of solving all disputes—some controversies could not be settled and they should be left unsettled without resort to arms; and his opposition to an "all-in" arbitration agreement. Such details, however, are foreign to the purpose of this chapter, some having played practically no role of importance, others having been introduced merely for tactical purposes. Hence their place is in other chapters in which the primary object is to follow the progress of outlawry in practice rather than to trace the development of its theory. After this survey we may now take up again the thread of the story.

[85] Levinson to McDonald, February 6, 1929.

[86] Alfred Zimmern says: ". . . . It is, practically speaking, irrevocable" (*The League of Nations and the Rule of Law, 1918–1935* [London: Macmillan & Co., Ltd., 1936], p. 392). And Miller agrees that so "long as grass grows and water runs" the states are bound "forever and forever" (*The Peace Pact of Paris* [New York: Putnam's Sons, 1928], pp. 146 ff.).

[87] The plan to have a great popular referendum in each state to vote war out once and for all became less important because of the inclusion of the people in Article I of the Pact. "The High Contracting Parties solemnly declare in the names of their respective peoples . . . ." (for passing comment see John Colombos, "The Paris Pact. . . . ," *Transactions of the Grotius Society*, XIV [1928], 87). This inclusion of the people was thought to be of importance by the Japanese government, for it declared that the phrase "in the names of their respective peoples" was inapplicable as far as Japan was concerned (*Treaty for the Renunciation of War* [Pub. No. 468 (Washington: Government Printing Office, 1933)], pp. 99 f.).

CHAPTER XIII

THE FRENCH MAKE AN OFFER

LEVINSON had been planning to go to Europe for three years. In 1925 some plans were discussed; in 1926 he even made reservations for May 15 but had to cancel them. And when, by the middle of the summer, all his arrangements were complete, even to letters of introduction from Borah to the American ambassadors to England and France, his affairs again kept him in the United States. He next planned to sail in April, 1927. This time he went.

His reasons for going were threefold. In the first place he was genuinely attracted to Harrison Brown and wished to discuss outlawry in full with him and perhaps employ him for service in Europe, as Harry Elmer Barnes had highly recommended him for such work. Secondly, as he wrote to Senator Borah, he was convinced that he could develop "some kind of momentum abroad" that might be of "worth-while value." He had done as much by letter as he thought it possible to do. And as usual he believed that he needed to talk with as many leading politicians, like Chamberlain and Briand, as he could reach; with editors like J. L. Garvin of the *London Observer*, Members of Parliament like Arthur Ponsonby, ministers of religion like F. W. Norwood and A. Maude Royden, and influential peace leaders like Gilbert Murray. He hoped to add to the momentum by persuading as many important people as possible to review Morrison's book, *The Outlawry of War*. He hoped, also, that the generated momentum would lead to the adoption of a resolution for the outlawry of war by the British Parliament, similar to that which Borah had introduced in the Senate. Although he had failed to achieve the results in the Senate which Ponsonby needed to enable him to sponsor such a resolution in the Commons, Levinson was hopeful that the way might be paved for action there, even if it preceded the adoption of the resolution on this side. He confided to David

[212]

Starr Jordan his high hopes of legislative progress. If Ponsonby's resolution could be put through Parliament and Borah's through the Senate, "we will be making," he wrote, "an Anglo-Saxon tender to the world of durable peace through the abolition of war and not by an Anglo-Saxon alliance for the maintenance of peace à-la-Hearst."[1] Finally, he was going to Europe for a rest. "After the press of the fall and winter's work both in law and outlaw," he wrote to his daughter, Helen, in London, "I am very tired."

Part of his preparation for departure was to write a large number of letters to various persons asking for an opportunity to talk with them. Walter Strong, the publisher of the *Chicago Daily News*, directed the representative of the *News* in London to help Levinson get interviews in Britain, especially one with H. G. Wells.

On April 6, Levinson, with Mrs. Levinson and John, their youngest son, left for New York, preparatory to sailing on the "Leviathan" on April 9. But, as the train neared Cleveland on the afternoon of April 6, the gods must have smiled as the newsboy boarded the train to bring "Captain Outlawry" the evening paper. It brought the news that Aristide Briand, foreign minister of France, was using the terms of outlawry.

M. Briand, who "read nothing but understood everything," had used the term originated by Levinson when he gave the famous statement to the Associated Press that day, thereby starting the wheels of diplomacy to grind out the Pact of Paris. Among other things the French foreign minister said:

If there were need for those two great democracies to give high testimony to their desire for peace and to furnish other peoples an example more solemn still, France would be willing to subscribe publicly with the United States to any mutual engagement tending "to outlaw war," to use an American expression, as between these two countries. The renunciation of war as an instrument of national policy is a conception already familiar to the signatories to the Covenant of the League of Nations and of the treaties of Locarno.[2]

[1] Levinson to David Starr Jordan, February 19, 1927.

[2] David Hunter Miller, *The Peace Pact of Paris* (New York: Putnam's Sons, 1928), Doc. I, p. 155. The whole original statement of M. Briand in the French and the English translation is printed here. The French translation of the term "to outlaw war" is "*mettre la guerre hors la loi.*" This is the term which Harrison Brown used

The occasion for this statement of French solidarity with the American people was the tenth anniversary of the entrance of the United States into World War I.

Aside from the balance of political forces both in France and in the rest of Europe, some interesting speculation arises as to the influences playing on Briand which led him to make this statement. David Hunter Miller is of the opinion that Professor Shotwell was instrumental in procuring it. He visited Briand on March 22.[3] There is some significant evidence on these points in the Levinson correspondence.

The general campaign for acquainting Europe with outlawry has been described in an earlier chapter. But, in particular, Harrison Brown had been sending outlawry printed matter to the French Foreign Office as early as 1925. And the outlawry number of the *Christian Century*[4] had been sent to Briand. According to Brown, "to outlaw war" had become a familiar phrase in France by the spring of 1927.

In addition to this, Briand was represented by his secretary, Léger, on various occasions as being anxious to try a new departure in dealing with the United States. Instead of the usual European style, he wanted a policy more nearly calculated to meet American wishes. Léger assured Levinson, according to a cablegram of the latter, that Briand was acting on a new policy, not according to the plan outlined by Shotwell.[5] And Harrison Brown reported later that Léger said: "Briand's idea in his offer was to depart from his European line and to find one more acceptable to American opinion."[6] That Briand was interested in

---

when he translated it into French and which M. Briand used and placed in quotation marks. Mr. Brown always lamented that he could not find a French translation which would be as "sloganesque" as the English original.

[3] *Ibid.*, p. 7 (see also Pearson and Brown, *The American Diplomatic Game* [New York: Doubleday, Doran & Co., 1935], pp. 16 f.; also Alfred Zimmern, *The League of Nations and the Rule of Law, 1918–1935* [London: Macmillan & Co., Ltd., 1936], p. 390).

[4] December 23, 1926.   [5] Levinson cable to Robins, May 24, 1927.

[6] Brown to Levinson, July 15, 1927. This rather important letter is quoted at greater length below, pp. 232 f. It must be added that the subject under discussion in the letter quoted was the specific offer of a draft treaty and not the statement to the press; but, in view of the evidence which appears in the letter from John Dewey

outlawry is shown by a letter of Dewey's reporting a conversation with Shotwell with regard to the latter's visit at the Quai d'Orsay. "Shotwell said in so many words that Briand asked him what the meaning of 'outlawry of war' was, and that he replied, 'La rénonciation de la guerre comme moyen de la politique.' "[7]

There is evidence to indicate that Shotwell would certainly not have encouraged Briand to use the term, "to outlaw war." Levinson had coined the term in the connotation in which it was being widely used; a neutral observer was of the opinion that Shotwell and Levinson disliked each other, and it is a matter of common knowledge that the two men were frequently at sword's points;[8] and, finally, the professor regarded the term as a misleading one when used in that connection.[9] On the other hand, it seems relatively certain that Levinson had nothing to do with the phrase, "the renunciation of war as an instrument of national policy," since, apparently, he did not use it in his correspondence before June, 1927; besides, he felt it lacked something, and there was Shotwell's connection with it. "The expression 'renunciation of war as an instrument of national policy,' " he said, "is intriguing and valuable but doesn't quite touch the heart of the matter."[10]

which is cited next, it seems probable that Briand had the same attitude when he made his first statement.

[7] Dewey to Levinson, March 5, 1928.

[8] Pearson and Brown, *op. cit.*, pp. 14 ff.

[9] J. T. Shotwell, *War as an Instrument of National Policy* (New York: Harcourt, Brace & Co., 1929), chap. x, "The Resolution of Senator Borah and the Outlawry of War." For comment on this point see above, p. 190, n. 17.

[10] Levinson to Fisher, March 31, 1928. There were occasions on which he referred to war as an "instrument" for the settlement of disputes, as, for example, in his draft treaty published in the *Christian Century* (below, p. 223). The sense in which he used the term "instrument," it would seem, was practically identical with that of his frequently employed term, "institution." It is likely that Levinson felt a distinction could be made between "instrument" or "institution "in the legal sense as a source of rights when applied to war and Shotwell's use of "instrument" when qualified by using it in connection with "national policy." Hence his statement that the professor's phrase did not "quite touch the heart of the matter." His own comment is that the phrase "war as an instrument of national policy" did not necessarily confine the idea to war between nations; it could mean war for internal policy as well. So he objected to the phrase because it lacked precision.

From April 15 to May 3, 1927, Levinson was in England, in a daily whirlwind of conferences with American and British newspapermen, Members of Parliament, editors, members of the government, and peace leaders. Conferences with the American ambassador, Mr. Houghton, and with the German ambassador, Dr. Sthamer, were among the many. There is no record of what he talked about with all these people, as there were no letters to report his conversations and his diary simply mentions the interviews without further comment. It is certain that his pride was jarred on one occasion. Harrison Brown tried to get an appointment for him at the British Foreign Office, only to be informed that "the outlawry of war is all buncombe."[11] But it is probable that Briand's statement played an important part in the conversations, along with the general discussion of the outlawry of war. Dr. Nicholas Murray Butler had loosed a flood of discussion in America with his letter to the *New York Times*, which pointed out the importance of the Briand statement.[12] Irving Fisher saw the Butler letter and telegraphed to Levinson suggesting that the peace forces unite on the Briand statement and asking Levinson to get the approval of Borah. The telegram was forwarded by cable to Levinson in London. Robins cabled that Borah was considering making a statement.

On Wednesday, May 4, Levinson arrived in Paris. The next day he was in conference with Paul Scott Mowrer, representative of the *Chicago Daily News*. Mowrer made arrangements for Levinson to see Briand's confidential secretary. This first visit, on May 6, to the Quai d'Orsay is reported in the diary as follows:

Conference with Leger at Quai D'Orsay, H. Brown accompanying. Talk lasted over an hour and was most satisfactory and reassuring. Immediately cabled Borah then called on Mowrer and reported conference with Leger. In afternoon called on Mr. Miller, Sec'y to Amb. Herrick. Went to Ambassador's residence with Brown and conferred an hour and a half. Later report[ed] to Mr. Mowrer and arranged to see Babcock of Carnegie Foundation here.

One of the first points which came up in this initial meeting was the distinction between aggressive and defensive war. Levinson

11 Levinson to Kenworthy, June 5, 1928.
12 April 25, 1927.

asked Léger if France did not think Germany was the aggressor in the World War, and Germany think Russia, and Russia Austria-Hungary, etc. On getting an affirmative reply to these questions, the Chicago lawyer emphasized his point about the difficulty of defining the aggressor and the institutional status of war. Léger appeared to be satisfied with this idea, and the basis was laid for their future relations. Briand later commented to Levinson on this interview: "I have never known my Leger to give his confidence to any man so quickly and so fully as he did to you."

On May 8 Levinson cabled Irving Fisher, Senator Borah, and Raymond Robins, "reporting confirmation by Leger of unconditional outlawry proposal." The cable to Borah was: "Direct official confirmation willingness for absolute compact stop immediate statement invaluable. Address Hotel Astoria Paris Levinson." The diary report for May 9 is: "Called on Miller at American Embassy, went over whole Outlawry scheme and explained result of my interview with Leger. Left Miller Outlawry papers and promised to get up statement as suggested by Amb. Herrick."

Either the efforts of Levinson and Robins were bearing fruit with Borah,[13] or he had become interested of his own accord in the Briand statement, for he wrote a letter to Harry Emerson Fosdick on May 6 commenting favorably on it,[14] and on May 9 he commended it again in a speech at Cleveland,[15] an account of which Robins cabled immediately to Paris. On the same day Senator Walsh of Montana made a speech in Paris also favorable to Briand's statement of April 6. The Paris papers carried reports of this senatorial approval of their foreign minister, and Levinson used such publicity to advantage.

He was able through Mowrer to get another appointment with Léger for the next day. Again the diary for May 11:

Kept appointment for the second interview with Leger at 37 Quai d'Orsay at end of which he asked me to prepare language covering my idea of the essence

[13] C. O. Johnson, *Borah* (New York: Longmans, Green & Co., 1936), p. 397. Borah appeared at first to view the Briand statement with coolness in a letter he wrote to Sherwood Eddy on April 29.

[14] *Ibid.*, p. 397.   [15] *Cleveland Press*, May 10, 1927.

of an Outlawry Treaty. Three hours later I returned with the paper which my daughter Helen took to him. He asked to see me and we had further conference. He was satisfied with the draft.

The next day, May 12, he had a long conversation with Stephen Lausanne, the editor of *Le Matin*. Again the report of the diary:

Went all over the French-American situation with Briand suggestion of April 6 and my conference with Leger and a general discussion. After satisfying him that our plan does not involve the relationship between a nation to its colonies, etc., he seemed to warm up to the general idea very well. He asked me to come to see him again on my return to Paris.

(Levinson was leaving for Geneva the next day.) Later the same day Mowrer was calling upon Léger, so Levinson drove with him to the Foreign Office. Again the diary:

Called on Mowrer in the afternoon and drove him over to Leger's office where he had a conference. He kindly took a note to Leger from me containing a clipping showing resolution of a large American peace group asking the President to respond to Briand's advances for an Outlawry Treaty.

Evidently American public opinion had begun to move, owing partly to the stimulus of the Butler letter to the *New York Times* of April 25. Levinson spent some time trying to get Ambassador Herrick persuaded that it would be well to give the Briand proposal a favorable mention in his Memorial Day address and at the Ambassador's request prepared a paper for him.

The next two days, May 13 and 14, were spent motoring to Geneva with Senator Walsh of Montana. During his stay in Geneva and the vicinity, he had conferences with Rappard, Christian Lange, Miss Doty, Norman Davis, Arthur Sweetser, and others. Before leaving he received a cable from Mowrer: "Briand refuses to act without Washington approval. Fears reaction French opinion against us if proposal made and officially ignored. Essential smoke out Coolidge."

The "smoking-out" process was started by cabling the following message to Colonel Robins in New York on either May 16 or May 17:

Definite Paris message says Briand satisfied [with] our publicity, but must have some direct approval [from] Washington fearing reaction French opinion if proposal made and officially ignored stop Walsh justifies Briand stand. Agrees you should see Executive [President] immediately. Show him opportunity [to be] unanimously backed stop if necessary enlist Dwight's [Morrow] aid stop official proposal absolutely insures passage our [Borah Outlawry] resolution. Walsh concurring stop cable plans then I would return Paris for pressure stop use discretion about friend [Borah]. Cause paramount.

Robins answered immediately: "Move suggested involves supporting incumbent [Coolidge for third term in White House] do you advise this [?] Dwight either [in] Geneva or Paris." Levinson rejoined:

Realize possible commitment. Procuring treaty worth all risks but escape if possible. Besides believe candidacy [of Coolidge for third term] will collapse or Friend [Borah will] never start stop consider suggestion incumbents informal favorable response in speech Decoration Day stop Mowrer aiding with Herrick stop trying locate Dwight.

But, before "Dwight" could be located and counseled with, Paul Scott Mowrer telegraphed that Morrow was sailing for home on May 16. And in the meantime Levinson went back to Paris, where he received a cable from Robins, who had gone to Washington, where he had seen "our friend," i.e., Borah. Levinson received this cable early on May 20. It read:

Comprehensive talk with friend. Incumbent disclosed hostile attitude toward statement [by Briand on April 6]. [In] recent conversation with friend, incumbent refused interview with Wellshot [Shotwell] on statement. He thinks Wellshot [Shotwell] originated statement which [if] true am inclined against interview [with President]. Friends position neutral.

The Levinson advisers in Paris wanted to keep the information in the last cable to themselves, but "Captain Outlawry" thought the best way to show Léger they were on the square with him was to show him the cables. The diary for May 20 gives the story of the next move.

Called on Mowrer with the cable answers relating both to Borah and the President. Mowrer then called up Leger who asked us to come over immediately. We had a long and intensely interesting conference as a result of which I then cabled Robins fully, urging him [Coolidge?] to act favorably on the Briand proposal or to indicate favorable attitude toward Briand's making a formal proposal for an Outlawry Treaty. Leger seemed inclined to consider making a treaty proposal anyway but vastly preferred to have some official encouragement from

Washington. Leger realized the importance of Briand following up his informal suggestion with a concrete proposal for a Treaty; otherwise it might be said as it is in fact being said that the suggestion of April 6 was a mere clever and diverting piece of strategy. It was my opinion which I had thought out between the lines of the cable that if the President showed opposition to Briand's wonderful proposal, it was because he, the President, feared that this revolutionary scheme for peace would play hob with his own ambitious hopes for the Disarmament Conference to be held in June at his initiative. I urged this on both Mowrer and Leger and stressed the danger for France because of the unfortunate position she had constantly been put into at the various preceding Disarmament Conferences. He asked me to collect all the clippings I could find indicating the tremendous trend of public opinion in the U.S. favorable to the Briand proposal. Mowrer and I also went over the political situation in America including the position of Butler and Borah both lending their powerful support to the Outlawry idea. I also gave Leger in some detail the talk I had with Senator Walsh enroute Geneva and there in which Walsh gave unstinted and enthusiastic approval for the Briand suggestion. I promised to return to Quai d'Orsay when I heard again from Robins and got the result of his hoped-for interview with the President.

The cable to Robins referred to was:

Delayed answer consulting inside people stop see incumbent sure. If he appears hostile, manage postponement five days for action here stop all believe motive is fear spoiling political capital [of] June [Naval Disarmament] conference where officials here again put in false position. Also possible rivalry friend [Borah] and Nicholas [Murray Butler] stop assured Wellshot [Shotwell] did not originate but idea new policy adopted stop if party willing alls well, if not and answer delayed, think can get proposal interim which if refused enables crusade on vital issue led by friend possibly also Nicholas stop dealing at source [Léger, French Foreign Office] who awaiting results your conference stop creating great sentiment for friend here, London, Berlin. When does he go west.

Robins, faithful to the orders from Paris, saw the "incumbent" and found that the reserved Mr. Coolidge evidently believed in the sanctity of dignity and the sacred prerogative of the diplomat to pursue the even tenor of his way undisturbed by the noisy clamor in the market place, for the cable was: "Had interview, found resentment against public appeal; matter must follow regular channels, declined commitment stop leaving for Florida tomorrow superintendent seriously ill." This cable was received in Paris close to midnight on May 20. The diary for May 21 continues:

I went to Mowrer with this answer, discussed it fully, we agreeing upon its illuminating character. I then went to 37 Quai d'Orsay but found M. Leger gone for the week end but that would be back Monday morning, May 23. I then went to Brentanos and got all available copies of New York Times showing editorials and letters indicating tremendous pressure from people of U.S. in favor of Briand proposal and urging action by the President etc. Meantime Harrison Brown returned to Paris and I went over the whole matter with him.

There are two reports about what happened on the next visit to Léger. The first is in the diary:

Got clippings from number of issues of New York Times consisting of editorials and letters regarding the Briand proposal. Took these to Mr. Mowrer and had preliminary conference with him but he was unable to go with me to M. Leger's because he was absorbed in writing up the Lindbergh Aviation trip across the Atlantic. Harrison Brown went with me and we talked with Leger about an hour. I gave him the clippings, etc., which he looked over and kept. He also asked me to keep the May 7th dispatch of Mowrer about myself in that number of Chicago Daily News. We went over the situation together. He told us he had spent two-day week end with M. Briand at the latter's country place and that M. Briand was in full accord with every thing we were doing in developing and offering to America an Outlawry Treaty by France. We discussed Decoration Day, the effect of the Lindbergh successful flight and the great enthusiasm he was accorded in Paris. He said the officials were planning to give Lindbergh a private lunch at the Quai d'Orsay at which M. Briand might take occasion to suggest the offering of the Outlawry Treaty to Ambassador Herrick. Leger thought after reading the two cablegrams I showed him that it would be best for Briand to make a concrete offer some time this week and before May 30th. He said he thought the offer should be made through the regular diplomatic channels and that it would be made public in the due course of time, he was not sure that it would be made public for several days after May 30th. He summed up by saying that he saw no reason why the concrete proposal for the Treaty could not be made within the next few days. I asked Leger whether he might arrange for me to meet M. Claudel, the French Ambassador to the U.S. and discovering that M. Claudel was then at Quay d'Orsay, Leger went out and brought M. Claudel after a few minutes and introduced him to Mr. Brown and myself. Leger then retired and promised to see me on my return from Berlin. Claudel, Brown and myself had quite a few minutes friendly talk in which Claudel said that he was in enthusiastic accord with the Briand proposal and would do everything in his power to bring it to fruition. He said he would not return to the U.S. until September and I promised to see him in Washington in the Fall.

The reference to Decoration Day is evidently to what Ambassador Herrick should say anent the peace move and perhaps is a report of the paper previously referred to that Levinson had prepared for the Ambassador.

The second account as to what happened at this conference was that which Brown himself gave me when I talked with him in Levinson's office in June, 1934. After talking with him for over an hour, I asked what incident in his relation with Levinson stood out most vividly in his memory. Here is the answer as I wrote it down a short time after the interview was over:

That romantic little incident in the Quai d'Orsay. I remember we decided we would go back to Léger and see what could be done; for forty-eight hours Sol had been talking to me without ceasing, going over the whole thing time and again. He is just the opposite of me, he thinks when he talks; I never will forget, we were in a little dingy office waiting for Léger to come in; and he was talking away just as hard as ever to me when all at once, he said, "Let's check this over." He took an envelope out of his pocket and wrote a couple of sentences on the back of it. Soon after Léger came in. After talking a bit, he said, "What definite things do you Americans have to offer?" Then Sol told him what he had written on the envelope. God! I should have snaffled that envelope.

I then asked Brown what happened to the paper, and he answered:

I think he gave it to Léger. But anyway that was the Kellogg Peace Pact. The two sentences he wrote on that envelope were the two articles of the Pact. They were never changed materially.

It is possible that the events which Brown related occurred on some other date than May 23. However, this seems the most probable time since, according to the diary, Brown did not accompany Levinson on his visits to M. Léger after May 8 until May 23. And, according to Brown, the interview in which Levinson gave him the two-sentence suggestion was not the first interview in the Foreign Office. There were subsequent visits to Léger, but it seems unlikely that the two-sentence suggestion was made then because, according to Léger, the proposal which Briand expected to make for a treaty was at the time of the later visits relatively well formed in his mind; therefore Léger would not be asking for suggestions.

There is another reference in the diary to a paper which Levinson prepared and which his daughter took in to Léger. This has been discussed above. However, Brown was not present at this time. Consequently, the only deduction is that there were two papers containing suggestions.

Exactly what these papers contained is of interest; but, since there are no copies of them available, all that one can do is to come at the contents in an indirect manner. Because Levinson had been talking for years about a treaty to which all the nations could adhere and which would outlaw war, it is possible to find in general what he had in mind.

The first indication is the draft treaty which he had prepared for the outlawry number of the *Christian Century*.[16]

DRAFT TREATY TO OUTLAW WAR

We the undersigned nations of the world hereby condemn and abandon forever the use of war as an instrument for the settlement of international disputes and for the enforcement of decisions and awards of international tribunals, and hereby outlaw the immemorial institution of war by making its use a public crime as the fundamental law of nations. Subtle and fatal distinctions between permissible and nonpermissible kinds of war are blotted out; the institution of war is thus outlawed, as the institution of duelling has been outlawed; but the question of genuine self-defense, with nations as with individuals, is not involved in or affected by this treaty. In order to provide a complete and pacific substitute for the arbitrament of war, we hereby agree to take immediate action for the equipment of an international court of justice with a code of the laws of peace, based upon equality and justice between all nations. With war outlawed and the code approved and ratified, the court shall be given jurisdiction over all purely international disputes as defined and enumerated in the code or arising under treaties, with power to summon in a defendant nation at the petition of a complaining nation and to hear and decide the matters in controversy. We hereby agree to abide by and in full good faith to carry out the decisions of such international tribunal. The judicial system thus established, being a complete substitute for the outworn and destructive war system, will enable the nations to adopt far-reaching and economically vital programs of disarmament.

[Signatures of the nations][17]

This draft treaty contains the original threefold plan of Levinson—outlaw, codify, and adjudicate. There is every reason to

---

[16] "The Draft Treaty To Outlaw War," *Christian Century*, December 23, 1926.

[17] *Ibid*. This draft treaty may also be found in Charles Clayton Morrison, *Outlawry of War* (Chicago: Willett, Clark & Colby, 1927), pp. 61 f.

believe that in his conversations with Léger he concentrated on the first—namely, the outlawry of war. It is probable, therefore, that the first sentence only of this draft treaty should be considered as throwing light on what he must have given Léger. Furthermore, he had long been urging that such a treaty be kept simple and short. This attitude is reflected in a letter to Professor Dewey which he wrote on his return to America. It becomes evident in this letter that the last part of the *Christian Century* draft treaty concerning codification and adjudication were not submitted to Léger. He wrote:

> Briand himself agreed with me that the proposal should be simple and utterly free from any inference that he was trying to inveigle the United States into European traps. . . . . I hope you will take occasion when the time is ripe, or at anytime, to write an article in the New Republic showing the necessity of keeping the Franco-American pact simple. For example: there is no need of setting up machinery of arbitration etc. We already have the old Hague Tribunal and the League Court is available to a non-member as well as to a member of the League.

There were repeated references in his diary to the necessity for a short treaty. From that record it seems that keeping the treaty short was one of the foremost burdens of his mind not only in his conferences at the Quai d'Orsay but with every other person of importance that he came into contact with, from Ambassador Herrick to H. G. Wells. Léger also in his talk with Levinson was strong for simplicity and conciseness.[18]

Another bit of evidence as to the contents of the papers which Levinson gave to Léger is the draft treaty which he prepared for Secretary Kellogg. He arrived in New York on the night of June 14 and went immediately to Washington for conferences with Raymond Robins and Senator Borah. The latter made an appointment for him with the Secretary of State for June 16. At the close of this interview, which lasted for three-quarters of an hour, "he asked me to prepare my idea of a draft treaty based upon my own experiences and my contact with the French Foreign Office." On June 20, after he had time to think the matter over, this was the draft he forwarded to Secretary Kellogg.

[18] See below, pp. 229 ff., for the quotations from the diary concerning this point.

THE FRENCH MAKE AN OFFER

DRAFT TREATY OF PERPETUAL PEACE AND AMITY BETWEEN THE UNITED STATES OF AMERICA AND THE REPUBLIC OF FRANCE

ARTICLE I

The United States of America and the Republic of France hereby agree to a perpetual treaty of peace and amity and mutually covenant that they will not resort to war or to the exercise of force in any form with respect to any dispute or question that may hereafter arise between them.

ARTICLE II

It is expressly agreed that nothing herein contained shall affect the rights of the United States in its traditional policy with reference to the American continents under the Monroe Doctrine.

ARTICLE III

The high contracting parties, in so far as relates to the two nations, hereby renounce, abolish and outlaw the institution of war as a method of settling international controversies.

ARTICLE IV

The high contracting parties further agree that while the right of legitimate self-defense against actual attack or invasion is recognized as inherent and ineradicable it is not involved in or affected by this treaty, and its exercise could only be necessary in the unthinkable case of either party hereto violating the convenants herein contained.

ARTICLE V

The high contracting parties further agree that neither of them will take possession of any territory or do any act that may be in derogation of, in resistance or prejudicial to the rights or claims of the other contracting party except by virtue of the terms of an award or decision of an arbitral or judicial tribunal in a controversy duly and voluntarily submitted to such a tribunal by the parties hereto.

ARTICLE VI

The high contracting parties further agree that the taking possession of any territory or the doing of any act by either of the parties hereto in derogation of, in resistance or prejudicial to the rights or claims of the contracting party, except as provided in Article V, shall constitute a violation of the spirit and essence of this treaty.

It is nearly certain that Article II covering the Monroe Doctrine was not included in the suggestions handed to Léger. When this point came up in a conversation he was having with Gilbert Murray, he urged, according to the diary, "that the Treaty itself should be kept very simple, direct and unconditional as desired by the French and that it would be for the President and the Secretary of State to make provisos regarding the Monroe Doctrine, etc., if desired."

A rough draft of an Article II was found written in pencil with interlineation and sections marked out. It also gives an indication of the type of treaty which he had in mind. It has been photostated in order to give an example of his method of preparing drafts of this type.[19] The last three or four lines of the photostat are suggestive of Article I of the Pact of Paris.

Another sample treaty, the one which best met his criterion of simplicity, had been suggested to Garvin. "All civilized nations hereby agree to abolish and prohibit the use of war as a method of settling international disputes."[20]

From these draft treaties we may gain some conception of what was in the papers which he prepared for the benefit of Léger. The use which Léger made of these will be indicated in a later paragraph.[21] But in the meantime the record of Levinson's conferences at the Quai d'Orsay and elsewhere is of interest.

On May 25 Levinson arrived in Berlin, where he had "long talks" with Dr. de Haas, Dr. Martius, both of the German Foreign Office; with F. A. Voigt, "the brilliant Berlin correspondent" of the *Manchester Guardian;*[22] and with Dr. Schurman, the American ambassador. His purpose was to join deletion of the war-guilt provision from the Treaty of Versailles with an outlawry-of-war treaty and a financial settlement which would provide an adjustment of reparations and a solution of the war-debt problems. He hoped that once a bilateral treaty was signed between the United States and France, other nations such as England and Germany could be persuaded to follow the example.

---

[19] See facing this page.   [20] Levinson to Garvin, December 28, 1925.

[21] Pp. 229–30.

[22] Voigt must have been deeply impressed with Levinson, for he dedicated his book, *Unto Caesar* (New York: G. P. Putnam's Sons [1938]), "To S. O. Levinson the father of 'Outlawry' with affectionate admiration." He also refers to Levinson's activity as a "prodigious" "one-man achievement" in persuading "his own country, England and France—the other Powers, 59 in all, following suit" to accept his "idea" (p. 281).

ARTICLE II

The high Contracting parties while realizing that war as an institution for the settlement by force of international controversies can only be outlawed by a change of international law through the common agreement of the civilized nations, expressed in treaties and by a Code of international law putting war outside the pale, and ~~setting up~~ providing for a Court with independent power, ~~with jurisdiction~~ to construe the law and to hear and decide all determinations disputes, as far as compatible with ~~human rights and the necessary free~~ human progress and the ~~largest~~ ~~development~~ free development of nations, — The high Contracting Parties do hereby, as an act effective between themselves and as an example for ~~the~~ other peoples, ~~condemn, renounce and~~ abandon the use of war as a method ~~of~~ ~~settling~~ international controversies.

During his two-day stay in Berlin he received an answer to the cable he had sent earlier to Borah urging the Senator to remain in Washington until after his return to the United States. Borah was evidently getting interested in European affairs at this point, for he indicated that he would probably cancel western speaking engagements so as to be in Washington to see Levinson on his return.

On May 28 Levinson was again in Paris calling on Léger at the Quai d'Orsay. The diary report of this meeting is as follows:

He told us that Briand had given a private lunch to Amb. Herrick and Lindbergh on the preceding Thursday at which Briand told Herrick that in the course of a very few days he would make a formal proposal through Mr. Herrick to the United States for a simple but thorough going treaty outlawing war between the two countries. . . . . Leger said he thought the paper would be handed Herrick by the following Tuesday and we all hoped Herrick might have sufficient authority by Monday May 30, to mention the matter in some form in his Decoration Day address in Paris. We told Leger Mr. Brown and I were leaving for London on Monday to return late Wednesday. He asked us to call at Quai d'Orsay Thursday.

Evidently President Coolidge's desire for the matter to come through the proper channels, as indicated by Raymond Robins' cablegram, was about to be fulfilled. In the diary for May 30 occurs Levinson's further comment on this visit to Léger:

I forgot to say that Leger had informed us that on their visit to England Briand and himself had visited with our Ambassador, Mr. Houghton, advising him of the Outlawry proposal and of their intention to follow it up provided they had reasonable encouragement from Washington and he further stated that Mr. Houghton said he was about to leave for the United States and he would probably report and push the idea of the Outlawry Treaty. This is all the more significant to me in view of the dinner conference I had with Mr. Houghton in London of which I have given a brief account earlier in this diary.

The statement by Léger that an offer would be made to the United States provided there was evidence of its being favorably received by Washington is perhaps the explanation for Levinson's relaying to him every bit of information he could gather by cable and from the press of what Washington was thinking. He makes frequent references in the diary to either sending or taking all this kind of information to the Quai d'Orsay.

The last days of May were spent in London in conferences with many people. There was a special meeting called for Levinson in the office of the Independent Labour Party. Attending this meeting were, among others, Arthur Ponsonby, Fenner Brockway, Runham Brown, and Walter Ayles. He also had long conversations with J. L. Garvin and Norman Angell. The burden of the discussion was the nature of the steps for England to take, when once the proposed Franco-American treaty was completed, to carry the plan forward.

Representatives of the *Chicago Daily News*, along with Harrison Brown, were Levinson's constant guides and counselors wherever he was. When he was in London, Constantine Brown was with him. In Paris it was Paul Scott Mowrer, and in Berlin it was Edgar Ansel Mowrer. Frequently he was in telephonic communication with Paul Mowrer in Paris. The explanation of his ability to get into touch so readily with anyone he wished lay not only in the fact that his name was so well known but also in the contact-making power of skilled pressmen, who were at his beck and call.

On June 1 he was back in Paris. The next days were spent in going carefully over the situation with the Mowrers. And then, failing to get in touch with Léger, he called upon Ambassador Herrick at noon on June 3.

I was fortunate in getting an immediate audience. I reported to him the general favorable reception of the Franco-American proposed treaty in England, in Geneva and in Germany. I told him of the enthusiasm of Dr. Schurman for the entire scheme of Outlawry and general adjustment. [The latter was the financial settlement he was working on.] Mr. Herrick twice assured me in his talk that the negotiations for the treaty were proceeding satisfactorily and that while the matter was now in the diplomatic channel and he could not tell me much, he knew I would be delighted at the outcome within a few days. He also told me that he had modified to some extent his Decoration Day address based on suggestions I had made two weeks before. (It did not strike me that there was much modification except that he added a good word about the Outlawry Proposal of Briand.) He gave me a message to Borah about his Russian speech.

Just what Mr. Herrick meant by saying the matter was in the diplomatic channel is not entirely clear. David Hunter Miller is of the opinion that, "M. Briand, impressed by the turn of events here, made some inquiry as to whether the Department of State did or did not want a treaty, with the suggestion that if it did, whether it was not for the two Governments concerned to draw up the paper rather than others."[23]

That the matter had been taken up with Herrick, as Léger said it would be, is substantiated by a press notice of the State Department of June 11, 1927:[24] "In response to an informal inquiry made on June second by M. Briand, Foreign Minister of France, through Herrick, the American Ambassador, the latter has been authorized to say that the United States will be pleased to engage in diplomatic conversation on the subject of a possible agreement along the lines indicated by M. Briand's statement to the press on April sixth last."[25] However, it would seem that by June 4 the matter had gone further than a mere informal inquiry, according to Léger's conversation with Levinson on that date. In this conversation he also indicated what use he had made of the written suggestions which the American lawyer had given him. This is the diary report of Levinson's visit to the Quai d'Orsay.

On Saturday the 4th of June, we met Leger at his office at 11 o'clock. He told us that he and Briand had been very much disturbed by the outside interference of Shotwell and others at Columbia University prematurely and without warrant offering a form of Outlawry Treaty burdened with many complicated

---

[23] Miller, *op. cit.*, p. 9.   [24] *Ibid.*

[25] Professor Shotwell says (*op. cit.*, p. 72) this reply of Secretary Kellogg's "in the language of diplomacy is a somewhat definite hint to let the matter drop. This hint was strengthened in the news item which followed that 'those whose views might be sought by the Administration expressed the opinion that no such treaty of peace was necessary between France and the United States and indeed, that it would not even be desirable.' . . . . The anonymous authority quoted in the Washington dispatches went so far as to suggest that the Bryan Treaty must have been overlooked by M. Briand for no new treaty would likely be any stronger in the provisions for preserving peace than those in the existing treaty." The rest of the evidence which Mr. Shotwell produces to show Washington hostility to the Briand proposal along with the above is certainly conclusive, especially if the unnamed authority was either inspired by Kellogg, which seems to be Shotwell's inference, or if he knew what he was talking about in mentioning the Bryan Treaty, for it was inoperative owing to the failure to keep in existence the Commission of Inquiry for which the treaty provided. Neither France nor the United States had appointed anyone to this office when the former members had died. Perhaps the unnamed authority, the person to whom the administration might turn for advice, did not know this.

promises, etc. Leger spoke with a great deal of feeling and quite at length. He said it was their desire to keep the proposal perfectly simple and thorough-going and not to give the U.S. the impression that Briand was trying to lure our government into European politics by another route; that they had taken the few lines that I had prepared for them at their request and had even left out a few of the words so as to be sure that no possible inference of conditions could be drawn and that if any conditions were to be inserted, they would be at the suggestion of the United States. He assured me that he and Briand had the same view as myself in this subject and that they were not employing the expression "Outlawing Aggressive War" or using any other language than that of perpetual peace and the unconditional outlawing of war between the two countries. I told him not to be too much exercised over this irritating interference as it could have no effect on our administration and would only be effective if the French paid any serious attention to it. He told us that an official, although informal proposal was in Mr. Herrick's hands, awaiting only word as to whether the U.S. would be glad to receive a proposal. This of course is a mere formality.

On the same day as this interview with Léger, Levinson sent further cables to Robins and Borah. They were substantially alike; that to Borah is quoted, as it emphasizes the diary.

Todays interview official said all annoyed Wellshots [Shotwell] public interference stop reassured proposal contains simple absolute wording free from any other commitment as promised stop arrive Washington morning fifteenth please get Raymond to meet with you and me there.

A description of the leavetaking, supplementing the diary account, may be of interest. Léger put his arm on Levinson's shoulder and said: "I don't know what we would have done without you in this critical situation. You have been of splendid service to us. I hope we will be able to continue our mutual relations." To which Levinson replied: "Certainly, but on one condition. If at any time for any reason you change your position, will you let me know directly, or indirectly through Harrison Brown?" Léger agreed to do that. In a later passage in Levinson's diary, dealing with other interviews which he had in Paris during the stay there from June 1 to June 4 inclusive, occurs the following interesting paragraph, in which there is an indication that the French may have been thinking of negotiating similar treaties with other states:

The interview with Leger on Saturday June 4 was my last with him. I omitted a very important thing he touched on. He said that while he and Briand wanted to keep the original Treaty simple and merely between the United States and France, they both realized that such a treaty being made would serve as a model for the other nations of the world which were willing to Outlaw War. He also expressed great appreciation of our work together and of our mutual confidences and hoped we would continue our confidential relations until we had succeeded in getting a mutually satisfactory treaty of outlawry formulated and ratified. He also said that he and Briand would be delighted if Senator Borah would come to France as they regarded him as not only one of the great statesmen of the world but a man of sincere conviction and honesty of purpose.

Léger's statement that they used Levinson's suggestion as a basis for the proposed treaty is interesting. Even if one discounts it somewhat, first, on account of the human tendency to give a person in face-to-face contact all the credit one can and, in the second place, on account of the likewise human tendency to remember all the complimentary words of a conversation of that type in their most complimentary form, still one is forced to concede significance to this statement of Léger's, because it seems to fit into the pattern of events in a way which lends weight to it. When in a body of evidence every detail that can be checked by evidence from other sources is thereby corroborated, we accept the rest with the greater confidence.

But, apart from Levinson's connection with the text of the French offer, there can be little doubt of his connection with the spirit of the French offer. It has been indicated earlier in this chapter that Professor Shotwell was probably the author of the phrase, "the renunciation of war as an instrument of national policy" and that he used it in an attempt to explain the outlawry of war. Consequently, when Briand used Shotwell's phrase and not Levinson's in the treaty which he submitted to the United States after his proposal to outlaw war between France and the United States, it would seem that Levinson's was the influence to which the proposal was due. There is another function which Professor Shotwell thought Levinson performed. There was need according to the professor,[26] for someone to interpret to the French the middle western outlawry-of-war philosophy, which was simply the Puritan tradition of morals and religion applied to international affairs.

[26] *Op. cit.*, p. 47.

Mr. Levinson arrived in Paris in the days immediately following M. Briand's declaration and quickly discerned the opportunity which it had opened up for interpreting to Europe the program of war outlawry. . . . . Any student of literature or morals knows how far removed from Continental ways of thinking is that portion of England or America which maintains the Puritan outlook, or even that much larger portion which cherishes it in retrospect. In politics the distance to be bridged is greater still, because politics reflects not only the content of divergent pasts but the variant interests of the present as well; the differences in political attitudes are due to geographical as well as to historical factors. Moreover, each body of opinion, the continental European and the continental American, is so sure of itself as to be largely indifferent to the other. Now, when Briand called the attention of Europe to the 'American expression to outlaw war,' the author of the expression was happily at hand to convince his European listeners that it represented a real political force in the United States.

On the other hand, from the evidence available it would seem, apart from whatever share Shotwell had in persuading Briand to make the statement to the press on April 6 and in interpreting outlawry to him, that he did not contribute materially to the form of the treaty or, indeed, to the spirit of the proposal. Early in May the professor had left a draft treaty of ten typewritten pages with the foreign minister, according to a report which Léger gave to Levinson.[27] As to the spirit of the proposal, Harrison Brown after a talk with Léger made this significant report on July 15:

He repeated that Briand wanted the simplest thing possible that would coincide with American ideas, had those ideas proved to be something in the style of the Shotwell affair they would have been accepted but at the same time they were mighty relieved to find that that was not so. The danger of the Shotwell proposal was that it really did resemble Briand's European arrangements, Leger said that had he himself read it when far away and not in touch he would have thought it had been inspired by Briand.

Therefore it was quite liable to take in American opinion.

He again said that Briand's idea in his offer was to depart from his European line and to find one more acceptable to American opinion. This of course is all

[27] A copy of this proposal may be found in *ibid.*, p. 271. A tendency on the part of the French Foreign Office to move in the Shotwell direction may be seen in the French notes of January 5 and January 21, 1928, in which the desire was stated to restrict the renunciation to aggressive war instead of war in an unqualified sense (*Treaty for the Renunciation of War* [Pub. No. 468 (Washington: Government Printing Office, 1933)], pp. 14 and 19).

in accord with Briand's reputation for elasticity of mind, his offer was in fact an attempt to extend his well-known flair for opinion to America, to feel warily for that opinion, make sure it really *was* American opinion and then play the cards they wanted in the way they wanted, knowing that fundamentally they both wanted the same thing—Peace. It was here that your advice was so invaluable.

I mentioned Butler and Leger said that Briand had not intended to see him but that he (Leger) had insisted. Butler was talking a lot of bunk about his mile long effusion. Briand had him up and changed his whole tone so that after the interview Butler was stressing the need for simplicity, and saying that only two articles were necessary! Briand seems to have said roughly "No doubt you mean well but you keep saying that I want this and that and the other but you have not seized the idea that I want the simplest thing possible which will outlaw war between us, your more complicated scheme may be all very well but we happen to be launched already in another boat and you are not being very helpful." Leger did not see Butler on purpose but he arranged for Briand to see him.[28]

The comment which Briand himself made as to the parental responsibility for the Pact of Paris is of interest. The European statesmen had met at The Hague in the summer of 1929 for the conference out of which the Young Plan came. Levinson went there and succeeded in convincing Stresemann to issue a statement on August 27 celebrating the anniversary of the Pact. Briand issued a similar statement and shortly sent for Levinson to come to his hotel. As they met, the French foreign minister said, "I am happy to meet the real father of the Pact of Paris." "But," replied Levinson, "the father would have died childless, M. Briand, had it not been for you."[29]

Levinson saw Léger last on June 4. Between that date and June 11, when he sailed, he was in England seeing more people, among whom were J. L. Garvin, Philip Kerr, Gilbert Murray, and H. G. Wells. However, this activity has little to do with the subject of the present chapter beyond the fact that by interview-

[28] Brown to Levinson, July 15, 1927. It might be of interest to add that Harrison Brown was of the firm opinion that Léger had himself written the Briand statement of April 6, 1927. He felt that Briand never did understand America very well but that, while Léger had been stationed in the Far East, he had studied the United States and seemed to understand the American viewpoint.

[29] As reported to the author by Levinson.

ing as many influential people as he could he was contributing in England, as he had contributed in France and Germany, to the popular movement which was sweeping the statesmen before it and forcing them to try to give direction to it before they were overwhelmed and compelled to accept something which would be even more objectionable.[30]

The French offer bears the date of June 20, 1927. It was handed to Herrick, and he transmitted it to the Department of State.[31]

[30] See Miller, *op. cit.*, pp. 8 f.; also James T. Shotwell "The Pact of Paris," *International Conciliation* (Bull. 243 [October, 1928]), pp. 11 ff.; also Pearson and Brown, *op. cit.*, chap. i; and a telegram from Briand to Claudel: "Recevant hier l'ambassadeur des Etats-Unis, je lui ai marqué toute mon appréciation de l'accueil que l'opinion américaine, sans distinction de partis, a réservé à l'idée d'un pacte d'amitié perpétuelle entre nos deux pays. Le sentiment public américain s'étant exprimé spontanément, et dans le sens le plus favorable, sur une suggestion faite aussi discrètement que possible pour ménager les convenances du Gouvernement fédéral, j'ai cru devoir prier M. Herrick de s'enquérir aujourd'hui de l'accueil que le Gouvernement américain serait prêt à réserver à une offre formelle de traité d'amitié perpétuelle emportant prescription absolue de la guerre entre la France et les Etats-Unis (le soin étant laissé au Gouvernement fédéral d'indiquer lui-même les modalitiés qui répondaient le mieux à ses vues pour la préparation de ce traité)" (*Pacte général de renonciation à la guerre* [Paris: Imprimerie des journaux officiels, 1928], p. 5). Also: "It seemed clear that no treaty of such world-wide importance, ... could be taken without the support not only of the statesmen but of the press and the people of the world themselves, and, as you know, the multilateral antiwar treaty was negotiated in the blazing light of full publicity" (Kellogg's Address to World Alliance for International Friendship, November 11, 1928, found in J. T. Gerould, *The Pact of Paris* [New York: Wilson Co., 1929], pp. 116 ff.).

[31] See Appen. C for the substantive articles of the proposed treaty.

CHAPTER XIV

THE LABORS OF LEVINSON

THE labors of Levinson, like those of Hercules, appeared to increase in difficulty in geometric ratio after he arrived in his native land. However, unlike Hercules, he had only three. He had to educate and convert the cautious Kellogg and the inert Coolidge; to convince his lieutenants that the Briand proposal was not venom; and to transmute their constitutional obstructionist attitude with regard to international matters into one of co-operation and support. The captain of the hosts of outlawry had to keep a watchful eye not only on the enemy but also on his own soldiers, each of whom carried a marshal's baton in his knapsack. And he had to prevent the Briand proposal from being changed by its friends or foes in such a way that any agreement arising out of it would be defeated in the Senate or be a violation of the principles of outlawry.

It is with these three labors that this chapter is concerned. However, since he was engaged in all three of them at the same time during the ensuing six months and because of their interrelationship, an attempt will be made to deal with them together chronologically.

On his arrival in New York, June 14, 1927, he went immediately to Washington. All three of his labors began in those Washington conferences, in which he demonstrated to his own satisfaction that a prophet is without honor in his own country.

He talked with Robins and with Kellogg and had two long conferences with Borah, who was convalescing from a tonsillectomy. Robins was then, and continued to be, enthusiastic for the Briand proposal. As to the Senator's attitude on June 15 and 16, there is no direct statement in Levinson's own letters to indicate that Borah was suspicious of entangling alliances; and one gets the impression from the letters to Holmes, Dewey, and others that

[235]

the Senator was pleased. However, a few days later in a letter which Robins wrote to Levinson there is evidence that the Lone Wolf was sniffing the air for a trap. Said the colonel:

> I hope you have seen our Senator and that he is more amenable than when we last saw him. For there is a real danger to his leadership of the peace forces in this, that should he be over-meticulous or oppose outright the terms of the French proposal, he will lose that leadership for good. It would be the last straw in what would seem to be a consistent course of proposing and then opposing as was charged by Lippmann in his attack.[1]

From Borah's later actions it is evident that the colonel had grounds for skepticism.

The best account of the conversation which Levinson had with the Secretary of State is found in his letter to Harrison Brown.

> [Borah] made an appointment for me to see Secretary of State Kellogg the next morning (June 16th) at ten o'clock. I had not had personal contact with Kellogg for a great many years. . . . . We had a splendid talk, although I found him quite unacquainted with the theory of outlawry and considerably in the dark as to what M. Briand really wanted. We spent three quarters of an hour together and I had an opportunity to expound the cause to him to some extent and particularly to give him the benefit of my contact with Quai d'Orsay and emphasize their sincerity of purpose. Among other things I said they had not mentioned the debt question to me at all and he answered he was convinced that the adjustment of the debt had nothing to do with Briand's proposal. (There had been some newspaper talk to the contrary.) At the close of the interview he asked me to prepare my idea of a draft treaty based upon my own experiences and my contact with the French Foreign Office. I told him how deeply I regretted the unwarranted interference of Shotwell, *et al.* and the harmful nature of their voluminous provisions which were distasteful alike to Briand and to me. He indicated the same state of mind, which has since been very much confirmed. He said he had not taken the matter up with Borah but would. I left him a copy of the London Observer interview with me May first and promised to send him some Outlawry pamphlets. He thanked me unusually for coming to see him.[2]

In accordance with the request of Kellogg, Levinson prepared a draft treaty and sent it to him with the following letter:

[1] Robins to Levinson, June 26, 1927. The reference to Lippmann could have been to the article, "Outlawry of War," *Atlantic Monthly*, August, 1923, or to the article, "Concerning Senator Borah," *Foreign Affairs*, January, 1926, pp. 211 ff.

[2] Levinson to Brown, June 28, 1927.

THE LABORS OF LEVINSON

My Dear Mr. Secretary:

Pursuant to your kindly suggestion I have prepared and enclose draft form of treaty between the United States and France.[3]

I respectfully submit the following comments:

1. The treaty should be kept perfectly simple. This will avoid the inference of European complications or subtle indirections; the common people will be able to understand it and furnish public support for it; and it will make for harmony between the Administration and the Senate. Besides, a short, simple treaty is exactly what M. Briand had in mind.

2. For similar reasons it would seem wise not to lug in arbitration provisions which necessarily involve European mechanisms and lead indirectly to the League; nor disarmament, although this type of treaty should lead inevitably to drastic disarmament in the near future. These can be covered independently at the proper time. The same applies to changes in and codification of international law.

3. It is most important not to qualify the outlawing of war between the two nations by such an expression as "outlawing *aggressive* war," which on analysis means nothing, as aggression is never admitted, is an act of war itself, and is the common charge made against its belligerent in every country.

4. Likewise, the exclusion of matters of "National Honor" and "vital interests" would greatly weaken, not to say emasculate, a treaty for the disavowal of war. Italy, for example, claimed that her "controversy" at Corfu was a matter of "national honor." It is redolent of the obsolete duelling system.

5. It has seemed to me vital to protect our Monroe Doctrine and also to prevent any ultra-pacifistic inference of the abandonment of the right of self-defense. These to my mind are the two protective safeguards that will satisfy the American people.

I submit, Mr. Secretary, that you have an opportunity for service on behalf of world peace in the making of this treaty that is rare in the annals of history. International war, once in operation, has gotten beyond human control. Its progressive destructiveness, with its colossal economic waste of life and property, makes the remedy of modern war worse than the disease.

If I can be of service under your leadership I consider it an honor to place myself at your command.

Allow me again to express my appreciation of your generous reception of me last week.

I am taking the liberty of mailing you, separately, a few pamphlets on the Outlawry of war. Of course, war can be fully outlawed only by the common consent of practically all the civilized nations. In the meantime, however, you can help build a foundation for the structure of durable peace by the model of the first treaty in human history for the abolition of war.

Sincerely yours,[4]

[3] This draft treaty is quoted above, p. 225.

[4] Levinson to Kellogg, June 24, 1927.

[237]

It is of particular interest to note that the paragraphs numbered 1–4, inclusive, contain suggestions which were very close to what was actually done in the negotiation of the Pact. That is, the treaty was kept short, if that can be said to be the same as "simple"; no provisions for arbitration were "lugged" in; Kellogg was insistent in the note to France as of January 11, 1928, that there should be no distinction drawn between aggressive and other kinds of wars; and there were no reservations relative to "national honor" and "vital interest" written into the treaty. With regard to his paragraph numbered 5, the matter of self-defense was taken care of in the preamble of the treaty, but no provision with regard to the Monroe Doctrine was included. The evidence in Levinson's diary indicates that he had encouraged the French to leave it out, because there would be time enough for it when the proposal reached Washington if the United States wanted it included. So it appears probable that Levinson decided to add this provision to his draft treaty after talking with Borah to make it acceptable to the Senate and also to Kellogg, who in the preceding six months had been acting with regard to Mexico and Nicaragua as if he thought the United States was in deadly peril and would therefore require all the safeguards and guaranties imaginable in any treaty she might make. It is also interesting to note that in the last paragraph of the letter the need for a world-wide agreement was suggested—an agreement which could be built on the proposed treaty with France.

The next report with regard to Kellogg, Borah made to Levinson when he went through Chicago on his way west.

Borah came to Chicago, arriving Sunday afternoon, June 26th. I spent two hours with him and also saw him the next morning before he left for Denver where he is billed for a great speech. We went over almost everything. Among other things he told me that Kellogg had sent for him and while he thought it was on another matter it was only to discuss the Briand proposal and an outlawry pact. This gave Borah the opportunity of expounding to Kellogg the gist of outlawry which of course Borah did in fine style. Kellogg told him that the Briand proposal in words would arrive here with Ambassador Herrick early this week and wanted to know whether Borah was favorable to it. The latter replied that it depended upon what it was; if it was on the line of the Shotwell agreement he would be in solid opposition. Here again was displayed an inimical attitude toward Shotwell and his fellows. Kellogg told Borah he expected to receive a draft treaty from me and that he would send Borah copy of the Briand proposal, etc.[5]

Apparently, neither Levinson nor Borah felt that Kellogg understood outlawry. On Monday morning after Borah had started on west, Levinson sent ten more outlawry pamphlets and another letter to Kellogg. Aside from listing the titles of the pamphlets, it contained two paragraphs:

I saw Senator Borah yesterday and I was delighted to know of your good interview and the prospects of harmonious action with reference to the Franco-American proposal. I took the liberty of giving him copy of the paper I sent you. On reading it he seemed to approve it highly. I discussed the matter at length with him and he is pretty generally in accord with the ideas expressed in my letter to you.

Aside from the humanitarian aspect of this matter, it has great political potentialities. After the frictional differences created by the contest over the League and the Court a simple clean-cut position against war would re-dedicate the great Republican Party as the party of abolition.[6]

Borah promised to send Levinson a copy of the Briand proposal and all other papers as soon as he received such matter from Kellogg. But Kellogg apparently forgot his promise, for months later Borah said he had heard nothing from him.

Levinson, at the time Borah left Chicago on June 27, was well satisfied with the state of affairs. "The net result is that the Franco-American Pact is now in the best possible hands and the skies are clear." The political situation was entirely satisfactory. "The relations between the President and Borah (including Kellogg) are better than they have been for two or more years."[7] He did not know whether Coolidge would run for renomination or not, but it could "go either way and still be vitally promotive of our cause."

With Borah "highly approving" the draft treaty which Levinson had drawn up for Kellogg, with the Secretary apparently interested, and with a promise of a copy of all papers, "Captain Outlawry" was ready to turn his attention to lining up his lieu-

[5] Levinson to Brown, June 28, 1927.
[6] Levinson to Kellogg, June 27, 1927.
[7] Levinson to Brown, June 28, 1927.

tenants in New York, Chicago, and elsewhere. Professor Dewey appeared to be lacking in enthusiasm for the Briand proposal. Some letters of patient explanation went to him. Holmes also needed some encouragement, which he received. Oggel expressed his doubts by asking: "Why not take in the rest of the nations and make it complete?"[8] These men were not kicking over the traces in a way to endanger the shafts or the persons around. In fact, they were soon convinced of the validity of the proposed treaty, but not so Morrison. He was in one of his best "against" moods.

The Briand statement of April 7 had failed to appeal to him at the time it was made, if a failure to comment on it in the *Christian Century* is any evidence of his reaction. He had met with an accident and been confined to bed for a month from the latter part of April; nevertheless, he wrote an editorial, "Briand Opens the Door," which appeared in the *Christian Century* for May 26, 1927. He maintained that the "so-called 'outlawry' " proposal was little more than an incident in M. Briand's thought and would have been dismissed as such by the public at large had not the keen eye of Dr. Nicholas Murray Butler, president of Columbia University, lighted on it. It was Dr. Butler's letter to the *New York Times*, published seventeen days after Mr. Briand's original "statement had been made and forgotten, that galvanized the proposal for a new treaty with France into life."[9]

An outlawry treaty just between France and the United States was "artificial" outlawry, and the treaty would be "impractical" and "futile," for "an agreement between two nations not to fight each other while each retains the right to fight any other nation is no more the outlawing of war than an agreement between two individuals not to steal from each other, while each maintained his right to steal from anybody else, would be outlawing theft. Such an agreement might be a sign of friendship or a counsel of prudence, but it could hardly be regarded as a highly virtuous moral act."[10] While, doubtless, Briand had found "gratification

[8] Oggel to Levinson, June 23, 1927.

[9] Morrison, "Briand Opens the Door," *Christian Century*, May 26, 1927, p. 646.

[10] *Ibid.*

in the response which the American public . . . . [had] made to his suggestion—since the American public found out with aid of Dr. Butler, that there was a suggestion to respond to . . . ." and while Dr. Butler must also have felt "the satisfaction that comes from a sense of service well performed," if either of them were earnest or sincere in wanting to rid the world of war, they should be in favor of widening the treaty to take in all the nations of the earth.

This editorial "infuriated" Levinson, "written as it was," he said, "while I was abroad without communicating with me."[11] Although he "scolded" Morrison about it, the scolding failed to produce a repentant and contrite heart in the editor of the *Christian Century*.

Morrison's book on outlawry had not yet been sent to the publishers, and he was planning to include an addendum chapter on the Briand proposal. In this he was also going to pay his respects to Shotwell. After his sneer at Butler in the editorial of May 26, referred to above, no particularly vivid imagination is needed to guess what sort of things he said of Shotwell in view of the latter's draft treaty and his greater activity. His remarks on the Briand proposal were still more elaborated and caustic than those in the editorial. Levinson was almost frantic; the chapter "was perfectly insulting to France";[12] and, since Borah had a high regard for the judgment of its author, he feared the argument would convince Borah that Briand's proposal moved on cloven hoofs. "The stuff he has, if he wins Borah over to him, will betray everything I have tried to do within the last two months."[13] When Morrison started one day to read the chapter to Levinson, the latter, according to his own confession, "exploded," whereupon Morrison "walked out," leaving Levinson sadly perplexed. "I don't know," he wrote to Robins, "what we are going to do about that chapter."[14] But a day or two later: "I apologized to him etc.,"[15] and the debate was on again—several

[11] Levinson to Robins, June 30, 1927.   [12] *Ibid.*   [13] *Ibid.*

[14] Levinson to Robins, June 27, 1927.

[15] Levinson to Robins, June 30, 1927.

sessions of it—all, however, to no avail. Ultimately the expert peacemakers found a basis for an armistice.

> He finally agreed this morning not to send it to Borah, or to send anything to Borah until you get here and we could have a three-cornered conference. I told him that if you were not in accord generally with my views, sad as I would be, I would abandon my position. The thing is so confoundedly simple that it is most discouraging to have to spend so much time in this 95° weather with one of your associates. It is hard enough in this world to cope with your opponents; it is so hard when you have to fight with your coadjutors.[16]

When the colonel arrived, he sided against the editor and in favor of the lawyer. It was decided that the addendum chapter, if it were used, should favor the Briand proposal for a Franco-American outlawry treaty. In the meantime Borah had seen a proof copy of the main manuscript; he had high praise for it, but advised against making any mention of "Briand's gesture." It would be better to wait to see just what that turned out to be, he thought. This threw new confusion into the outlawrist camp for they wanted a "ringing commendation from the Senator." However, it was finally decided to include the addendum chapter and to try to get Borah to write a commendatory review. In the addendum Shotwell was represented as a tyro in international affairs, wishing to encumber the proposed treaty with complicated provisions and not knowing the difference between the Locarno agreements with their sanctions for enforcement and the proposed Franco-American treaty, which was to depend entirely upon the good faith of the signers for the fulfilment of their obligations. The proposed treaty was of great significance, because it opened the way for many others like it, which would eventually result in all nations' having renounced war.[17]

Meanwhile Levinson had received no inkling of the terms of the note from Briand which Herrick was supposed to have delivered by then to Kellogg. Accordingly, he inquired of his Senator on July 8 as to the wording of the note. Then came the shock, which made Levinson "somewhat sick":

[16] *Ibid.*

[17] Charles Clayton Morrison, *The Outlawry of War* (Chicago: Willett, Clark & Colby, 1927), pp. 283 ff.

I have not heard anything from Kellogg in regard to the Briand proposal. In my opinion, we will never hear anything from Briand's proposal that amounts to anything. The more I study the Briand proposal, the more I think it is a piece of dynamite for outlawry.

I have just read Doctor Morrison's addendum to his book, and while I think he has written a magnificent book, I am wholly unable to agree with him on his addendum. My opinion is that a two-power treaty is not an aid to outlawry but a distinct hindrance and embarrassment.[18]

Levinson's reaction to this letter was unique. It was one of the few times, if not the only time, when his feelings were wounded and he admitted that there could be such a thing as defeat. For the moment he forgot his motto of turning liabilities into assets and going right ahead. He was more willing to criticize Borah than ever before.

First he says he has not heard from Kellogg and therefore has not the text of the proposal. He then says the more he studies the proposal the more he thinks it is a piece of dynamite for Outlawry. What kind of logic or sense is that? He hasn't read the paper and therefore the more he studies it the more he is convinced, etc. . . . .

While we can explode with one another on this situation, we have simply got to keep Borah in line and do whatever is necessary to that end. It is certainly not very flattering to me that my judgment, having been on the ground, seems to count for nothing, and that, too, in the absence of the text of the proposal itself.[19]

I am beginning to feel a sense of helplessness about him that may even include the European trip. If he carries with him any such views as contained in this letter—and he certainly ought to write me genuinely—this trip will do far more harm than good. Of course, [he added quickly], he won't carry on that way and then it is an outrage that he takes such a position with us.[20]

Pulling himself together, he went on to plan what could be done to calm the palpitating heart of the scared Borah. Colonel Robins was the man to do it. He should go to Boise and "attempt to draw out" the Senator and "argue out with him what he considers 'dynamite' or a 'distinct hindrance and embarrassment' in the Briand proposal. . . . . I think you can coax and persuade him to the correct point of view."[21]

[18] Borah to Levinson, July 12, 1927.
[19] Levinson to Morrison, July 15, 1927.
[20] Levinson to Robins, July 15, 1927.   [21] Ibid.

For six long days Levinson "pursued the golden path of silence" with the Senator because he didn't want to "cause any breach" and because he could not "very well be a hypocrite and say what . . . . [he didn't] mean." But by that time, July 21, the colonel had been through "a few mentally pugilistic rounds with the Senator." His telegraphic report showed the Senator still opposed to the French proposal and still considering Morrison's approval of it a betrayal of outlawry. "Captain Outlawry" then tried his hand at an appeal. The Briand proposal had given outlawry more publicity than could have been secured with five million dollars worth of advertising. The result was the creation of a favorable public opinion, so that, if the treaty could not be held to simple terms, "free from entanglements with European mechanism," then the Senator could offer his outlawry resolution first, and by reason of the treaty force consideration of his resolution. Besides, Borah was usually not suspicious, like Jim Reed, that "every advance to us by a foreign nation conceals a cloven hoof." Moreover, had not Briand's original proposal suggested an outlawry treaty between the United States and France, ". . . . TO FURNISH A SOLEMN EXAMPLE TO OTHER PEOPLES"?[22]

But this appeal from Borah obstructionist to Borah reasonable was in vain; it was only by constant references to the "goblins," Shotwell, *et al.*, that he could be enticed back into the outlawry ranks. Listen to his indictment of the Briand proposal.

I have your letter of July 21st.

I am perfectly satisfied that a two-power treaty is at war with the whole theory of outlawry. I thought so before I read Doctor Morrison's book and now it seems to me perfectly plain.

You cannot put an end of war as an institution for the settlement of international disputes until you offer a complete substitute for war in the settlement of international disputes.

That substitute must consist of a code of international law rejecting war as an institution for the settlement of international disputes, providing for a code of law and an independent judicial tribunal to construe the law. A two-power treaty agreeing not to go to war assumes that you can stop war without a substitute and leads the popular mind to believe that all there is to outlawry is an agreement not to go to war.

[22] Levinson to Borah, July 21, 1927; Levinson's capitalization.

An agreement not to go to war so long as war is recognized as a legitimate institution is a delusion and a snare.

I would not myself agree for my country not to go to war under any circumstances unless there was a substitute for war to settle controversies with other nations. M. Briand's proposal does not contemplate outlawry in any sense whatever, it is merely an agreement,—altho the pistols are at your feet and the code of honor requires you to use them under certain circumstances, nevertheless, you agree not to do so. But everyone knows the agreement is worthless when the exigency arises.

Levinson, it is a case similar to the proposition which confronted the fathers when they met to organize the government of the United States. There were those who felt that all they had to do was to make some additions to the old confederation. There were others who knew perfectly well that they were building upon a wholly different principle and that a compromise of that kind would be deadly.

The thing for M. Briand to do is not to propose a two-power treaty but to propose that France join with the United States in asking for an international conference to codify international law, in which code of laws war is to be denounced as an institution for the settlement of international disputes. M. Briand's proposal is the old system absolutely with simply another "fetching" title, which "fetching" title they have stolen.

I do not see how anyone who has read Doctor Morrison's book can compromise on this matter with a two-power treaty. It is at war with every principle laid down in the book. That is the reason I said what I did when I wrote you. It is as clear to me as the noon-day sun. And when you come to understand the genesis of M. Briand's proposal, it is perfectly clear that he hasn't in mind any such thing as outlawry. M. Briand regarded the League as outlawry of war. He regarded Locarno as outlawry of war. Both of which rest upon force with war as the ultimate arbiter.[23]

In the meantime Levinson, after the first disappointment and bitter feeling of helplessness at Borah's desertion, "snapped back to normal." "The old boy [Borah] could not be worse therefore he must get better. Anyway we vitally need his help. Though in future cause must always remain paramount. . . . ." he wired to Robins. His regular letter-writing, even to Borah, reverted to its

[23] Borah to Levinson. There was no date on this letter, but there is no chance of a mistake with regard to the general period when it was written, because of the evidence found in the letter itself. The reference to a former letter, "That is the reason I said what I did when I wrote you," is most likely to the letter quoted above, p. 243, dated July 12, 1927. Incidentally, this statement is, by implication, exceptionally devastating to Borah's own position with regard to the League and particularly with regard to his opposition to including a political settlement in the Washington disarmament arrangements of 1922.

usual tone. With the Senator the old pastime which the Senator loved so well, getting ready to run—or, rather, running privately but never publicly—for the presidential nomination, was resumed without interruption; and the "goblins"—Shotwell, Butler, Hughes, and whatever League champions happened to be in the public eye—were dangled constantly before the Senator's vision as a dire threat to "America first."

If . . . . our two dearest foes, Hughes and Butler, can work their will on the Briand Proposal, we are indeed in a dangerous situation. Of course, you know I believe, without any mental reservation, that you can stop this whole parade and get the correct wording in the bilateral Treaty.[24]

It is not quite accurate to say that the continual waving of this red flag at Borah sent him back into support of outlawry, for Levinson had amended his draft treaty slightly to meet objections raised by the Senator; yet, when the report came that he was coming back, the red flag was the chief thing in evidence, as appears from Robins' report of an interview with him.

This morning I was with Borah for more than an hour. I believe that he now sees the significance of the Hughes, Kellogg, Shotwell, Butler combination in shaping the Briand proposal. He gave me his promise that he would watch this item closely and that he would fight to prevent its being betrayed by that group. He also agreed—not very eagerly but I thought genuinely—that if it could be held to the simple declaration that force and war would no longer be used between France and America in the settlement of any question arising between these nations, and this properly safeguarded as in your final draft of this proposed treaty which I had and was able to discuss with him in a friendly fashion, it might be the beginning of the realization of the policy of outlawing the war system in international law.[25]

And, as will appear later, this threat—of changing a simple treaty into a complex one in which there would be definitions of different kinds of war—continued to be of use in holding Borah in line.

Kellogg had promised to give Borah a copy of the Briand proposal, but for some reason he failed to do this. As far as any public indication went, Kellogg had received nothing; and even the French Foreign Office had, apparently, not had so much as an

[24] Levinson to Borah, September 19, 1927.
[25] Robins to Levinson, October 3, 1927.

acknowledgment of the receipt of the Briand note. In the middle of July, Léger, according to Harrison Brown, began to wonder why no word came from Washington. Poincaré was always ready to overthrow Briand; and, unless something was forthcoming, Briand's gesture might be used against him. On July 25 Brown cabled that Léger was surprised there was no word from Kellogg. Levinson suggested reasons for delay. Kellogg and Herrick had both been ill; Coolidge was away from Washington and was hoping, he thought, for something at the Naval Disarmament Conference. Harrison Brown kept seeing persons connected with the Quai d'Orsay to inquire about the state of affairs; and, finally, during a League meeting at Geneva in the latter part of September, he buttonholed Briand when the latter went out to the lobby to smoke.

I could not get from him a definite answer as to an acknowledgment of the receipt of the Treaty having reached Paris, but he said that he hoped the matter would very shortly be taken up again under favorable conditions. I said, "so you are satisfied with the progress of events?" He replied that he was, that he hoped the atmosphere would be right for the renewal of conversations and here he twinkled at me, "Anyhow I intend to wake that affair up again very shortly now."[26]

About the middle of October some sort of a conference, in which Borah participated, was held in Washington. Most likely it was called on the initiative of the Secretary of State. Levinson heard of this and cabled Paul Scott Mowrer in Paris to see Léger and to suggest that the French ambassador to Washington, M. Claudel, should see Borah with regard to the wording of the treaty. Claudel did see Borah, but on whose initiative or what he said, no record is available. However, Raymond Robins saw the Senator and reported on October 26 that Borah "intends to declare for Outlawry and to say that the Briand suggestion should be made the basis for Outlawing War between the United States and five great nations."[27] As far as the Senator could observe, the State Department was making no move in regard to the matter, and he himself seemed to feel it was "rather remote and minor in

[26] Brown to Levinson, September 24, 1927.
[27] Robins to Levinson, October 26, 1927.

importance." Though he had been against a bilateral agreement, he now appeared favorable to a six-power treaty. But the lack of consistency between opposition to a bilateral pact because it would not change international law and support of a six-power pact which would not do so either, did not escape Levinson.

> After going through miniature hell . . . . with him, I now find that he has come around pretty much on the bilateral treaty issue. . . . . Confidentially, he is now considering utilizing the Briand proposal as the basis for a treaty among the five big powers outlawing war. . . . . Think of it! You know how he rebelled at the idea of trying to outlaw war by a two-power treaty because you couldn't change international law except by a general treaty. Now he proposes to outlaw war with five powers as if five of the sixty nations could change international law any more than two of them can. However, I ought to be grateful for this change of heart without caviling about it.[28]

Borah had planned to make his pronouncement for a multi-power outlawry pact at a speech he was to make in New York on November 10, 1927. However, he was prevented from keeping this engagement by Mrs. Borah's being taken ill. He asked Levinson to speak in his place, and at Levinson's request he sent a telegram to the Rev. Sydney Gulick, secretary of the Federal Council of the Churches of Christ in America, who appears to have been the chairman of the meeting. He closed his telegram with these words: "M. Briand has suggested the first step. Let us suggest the second and include Great Britain, Japan, Germany, and Italy. That would furnish a real foundation for Outlawing War sincerely."[29] But it appeared the Senator was willing to make a two-power pact if one of the other powers did not agree, and then, as Dr. John Haynes Holmes understood him, other bilateral pacts were to follow—probably the next one would be made with Japan.

Meanwhile, Levinson had kept up a steady fire of arguments for keeping the treaty simple; and at his insistence Harrison Brown did the same in France, and especially at the Quai d'Orsay. "I was assured that Briand's intentions on this matter had not changed and that the Quai d'Orsay fully realized the neces-

[28] Levinson to Holmes, October 28, 1927.

[29] Borah to Gulick, November 10, 1927.

sity of keeping to the original plan if the Pact was to be used as a new opening to larger issues."[30]

Suddenly the "Shotwell danger" appeared in another form. Senator Capper, according to the *New York Herald* for November 23, 1927, was preparing to introduce a resolution "along the lines [of], but widening, the Briand Proposal." Capper asked Levinson for advice as to the wording of the resolution—advice which was furnished. Levinson explained the objections to defining an aggressor and urged that the resolution be revised accordingly before Capper introduced it. He thought he had carried his point; but, when Robins called later at Capper's office, he learned that the resolution had come from Shotwell, that the Senator had been communicating with Butler, and, further, that Capper had decided to introduce the resolution in its original form. If necessary, he said, it could be amended in committee hearing in accordance with Levinson's suggested revision.[31] Thereupon Levinson, after failing to reach Capper on the telephone, went to Washington to see him in person. Though he arrived too late to prevent the use of the original resolution, he felt he had persuaded the Senator to accept changes later. He also, after a long talk, secured a promise from Hamilton Fish to introduce the revised Capper resolution verbatim.[32]

Another source of worry had been the attitude of Coolidge. He had not liked the way the Briand proposal had been made in the first place. There had been too much talk, he complained, in the market place, too much public attention called to it; it had not been handled in the regular way; and, if the United States were to pay any attention to it, it would have to come through the regular channels. Perhaps it was an antidote to all this publicity that Washington became so silent, no word being spoken on the subject for months. Then, during the last few days of November, the *Chicago Tribune* carried articles by Arthur Sears Henning

[30] Brown to Levinson, November 2, 1927.

[31] He introduced it, December 9 (*Congressional Record*, LXIX, 351; *Senate Joint Resolution 14* [70th Cong., 1st sess.]).

[32] *House Joint Resolution 94* (70th Cong., 1st sess.) was introduced December 13 (*Congressional Record*, LXIX, 623).

which indicated presidential opposition to the Briand proposal. Levinson talked to the President's secretary on the telephone but, receiving no assurance, he called a council of war with some of his lieutenants in Washington for two days later. Coolidge made good his opposition by raising the question of the constitutionality of an outlawry treaty in his message to Congress on December 6. But the tide of public opinion was running strong, and he was not the man to make a stand against it; before long he boarded the bandwagon by declaring against any attempt to define an aggressor. On December 23 the press carried a statement that Kellogg had had a conference with the Senate Committee on Foreign Relations.[33] Under date of December 28, 1927, the cautious Kellogg handed Ambassador Claudel a note which embodied the suggestion of Borah, that the great powers should be invited to join with France and the United States in renouncing war as an instrument of national policy. So the three labors of Levinson were now well in process of completion.

[33] See Pearson and Brown, *The American Diplomatic Game* (New York: Doubleday, Doran & Co., 1935), p. 27, for an entertaining and pungent description of the meeting.

CHAPTER XV

HARRISON BROWN PEDDLES OUTLAWRY AND FINANCIAL ADJUSTMENT

URING the last half of 1927, while Levinson was waiting for the hesitant Kellogg, toiling with the intractable Borah, and checking what appeared to him the officiousness of Shotwell, outlawry activity was going ahead under full steam. Harrison Brown had begun to give his full time on July 1, 1927, to evangelizing Europe. He sent long and frequent reports to his "Captain General," which were answered as lengthily with advice, inside news, explanation, and exhortation. By way of making outlawry more attractive to Europe, Levinson had developed means of linking it with reparations and war-debt settlement. His first plan on these lines was published in December, 1927, and Harrison Brown was commissioned to add financial readjustment to his stock of outlawry goods for exhibition and sale in Europe.

Harrison Brown had been initiated into the official methods of outlawry propaganda during Levinson's visit in April and May, 1927. The arrangement between him and Levinson was indefinite as to precisely what he was to do and the length of time he would continue in Levinson's employ, except that for a trial period he was to devote his entire time after July 1 to the interests of outlawry. Where he should go, whom he should see, and how much he could disclose of the information which Levinson was continually sending and which frequently was of a confidential nature was left largely to his own judgment.[1] In fact, it appeared that Levinson was almost an ideal employer, for he even seemed to leave it to Harrison Brown himself to decide what his own salary and expense account should be. For several years the evangelization of Europe cost the American Committee for the Out-

[1] Levinson to Brown, October 10, 1927.

lawry of War, alias S. O. Levinson, from ten to fifteen thousand dollars annually, even after the signing of the Pact of Paris.

The reason for qualifying "ideal" by "almost" was the Levinson habit of suggesting to his representative, as if they were mere routine, things for him to do, before which the exploits of Odysseus himself would have paled. Shortly, for instance, after Harrison Brown had begun to devote his full time to outlawry, his chief suggested that he should go to England and get the Tory government to offer the United States a treaty similar to the Briand proposal. "If you can succeed in getting into the open a proposal for an outlawing pact between Great Britain and the United States, it will be worthy of a solid month of your time," declared the lawyer from the city which was in a fever to "bust" George V in the "snoot."

Brown did go to London, where he saw a number of members of Parliament, spoke to a meeting of the Independent Labour Party in its rooms in the House of Commons, and tried to get outlawry on the agenda of the Labour Party for debate at its fall conference. By the end of the month he returned to Paris, where he talked to Léger at the Foreign Office. He saw D'Ormesson, "a hoary-headed blue blooded old reprobate who writes leaders in the semi-official Temps." This conservative in everything but war had claimed to have been converted and had promised to discuss outlawry in *Le Temps*. Others who appeared favorable to outlawry were Ernest Renauld, Prudhommeaux, Demartial, leaders in the Rightist movement, in the support of the League of Nations, and in a radical peace society, respectively. After a conversation with the editor of *La Volonté*, an article appeared under the title, "La Guerre hors la loi."

In Brussels he saw Senator La Fontaine, who had been lecturing "on the necessity for Outlawry (tho not your scheme) for many years both in Europe and America."[2] He also talked with some of the leading Belgian editors.

But he was constantly meeting with something very like a sneer. With what face could America advocate an international order having law as its basis when within its internal jurisdiction a

[2] Brown to Levinson, August 11, 1927.

couple of helpless aliens, Sacco and Vanzetti, were being dealt with in the worst antilegal style? This was the question which was in people's minds and too often on their lips. Levinson, on the other side of the Atlantic, just smiled it away, until he could report that Borah had offered his services in the defense of the luckless targets of New England patriotism. This was some help in freeing outlawry of the incubus of the Sacco-Vanzetti trial.

Brown made important contacts in Holland, where he became aware of "the nearest thing to civilization I have found." After a two and one-half hours' talk with "Professor Dr. D. Van Embden, economist, publicist, leader of the Radical Party," he received a promise that the professor would introduce and sponsor an outlawry resolution similar to the one which Borah had presented to the United States Senate. He also saw Dr. Luiburg, acting president of the Privy Council and member of the delegation at Geneva, and Mrs. Kluyver, secretary to the Geneva delegation and a permanent official in the Foreign Office. She not only became a convert to outlawry but also a missionary for it. He found the registrar of the Permanent Court of International Justice, Mr. Hammorskjold, "prodigiously well informed about Outlawry," though his interest was scientific only.

On the way to Geneva for the meeting of the Assembly in September, he visited Berlin and Lausanne; and, though his stay was brief at each place, he saw key people. At Geneva he made the acquaintance of Von DeWald of the *Frankfurter Zeitung*, who introduced him to several members of the German delegation. He talked with everyone he could meet. One day he reported having seen seventeen different persons. In addition to extolling the virtues of outlawry, he gathered interesting information. Norman Angell was curious as to what had happened at Paris during April and May; and, in return for what Brown could tell him, the author of *The Great Illusion* described some of the backstage negotiations leading up to the Geneva Protocol and explained how the pacifist MacDonald had been convinced of the necessity for the use of force in international affairs by his talk with Angell and Herriot and how Angell had worked back and forth between the two premiers.

Harrison Brown got a press card to the first gallery at Geneva, and then after meetings he would "bluff" his way into the lobby where all the foreign ministers and journalists were. He joined the International Club so that he would have a place to which to invite guests, and he made friends with everyone, especially secretaries, whom he found to be "wonderful" people, very useful not only as the source of information which could not be wormed out of their employers but also as a sort of barometer of the official atmosphere. A good secretary was frequently the chief's mind relaxed. Briand and Chamberlain were "two Gods nobody dares to button-hole." Briand particularly liked to jest at the expense of the newspapermen. One day in the lobby, coming upon a French journalist deep in a paper, he flicked it out of the astonished man's hand with his stick as he smiled: *"Ah, la Presse!"* Despite the Frenchman's cat attitude toward the mice of the press, Brown did accost him on one occasion to find out that Briand was satisfied with the state of affairs between the United States and France and that he intended keeping negotiations moving with regard to his proposal for a bilateral anti-war pact.

During the 1927 Assembly of the League the renunciation of war was in the air. Germany announced adherence to the optional clause of the World Court statute. Stresemann reiterated his agreement to "the idea of proclaiming once more in a solemn and decisive form the wish of states to abolish all recourse to violence." Poland had made a proposal of a similar type. Politis and Loudon used the term "outlawry of war." The latter favored the Assembly's making a declaration which would prohibit any recourse to war, even the "so-called legal wars in accordance with article 15, paragraph 7 of the Covenant. . . . ." He also thought "it would be desirable that the Assembly should recommend the conclusion as between two or several states of a treaty which would outlaw war, thus replying to the sound of the bell on the other side of the ocean which had found an echo on the European side, more particularly in France."[3] Brown learned later that, in addition to himself, Mrs. Kluyver of the Dutch dele-

[3] Brown to Levinson, September 21, 1927.

gation, one of his converts, had also been talking to Loudon and had got him to read some of the outlawry literature.

Brown continued to broadcast literature and to write letters calling attention to the printed matter he was sending out, as has been indicated in a former chapter; and he continued to do all he could to help individual peace workers and peace societies. However, now his most important activity was his personal interviews.

While he was in Geneva attending the Assembly of the League, he received Morrison's book, *The Outlawry of War*. His first reaction to it was extremely favorable. He could not express how "bucked" he was about the book. He gave a copy to every important person he met who would promise to read it. A copy was sent to Léger and another to Garvin and still another to Mrs. Swanwick of the British *Foreign Affairs*, though it was not easy to get from her a promise to read it. By this means the book achieved considerable currency among political leaders. A few months later, when he met Ramsay MacDonald, he learned that Arthur Ponsonby had left a copy with the Labour leader, who claimed to have read it, although Brown felt that, if he had, he had not understood it. Brown also arranged to have it reviewed in many magazines and discussed in newspapers in nearly every country in Europe and in England.

His later reactions to the book were not so favorable, although he continued to use it. He found that Morrison's writing, like his conversation, tended to outrage his opponents personally. Nearly all who read the book said it was "filled with 'Thank God we are not as other people.' " Gilbert Murray resented it, and G. Lowes Dickenson went to considerable pains to point out how Morrison, in destroying the World Court and disregarding the League of Nations was putting out the last spark of hope for Europe. Consequently, Brown started making suggestions for slight changes which would make later editions of the book more useful. One of his first observations was:

There is one thing which struck me and which appears to have struck others over here, a little thing and almost certainly unintentional but capable of arousing a quite disproportionate amount of irritation and antagonism, that is the spelling of the League without capitals. People say "you talk about War as an institution, can you not admit the League to be one?"[4]

Later he went through the book, marking words, phrases, paragraphs, and even one whole chapter for omission, and suggesting other changes to make it more of a plea for outlawry and less of an attack upon existing peace activity and machinery. But the editor of the *Christian Century* must have loved the wounds of battle, whether in the flesh of friend or foe, for in later editions the League of Nations was neither capitalized nor dealt with more gently.

Brown had insisted that in any outlawry treaty, if self-defense were reserved, a loophole was left for ruining the whole project with an excuse for perpetual armaments. The inclusion of self-defense, he contended, made the outlawry treaty similar in essence to the Shotwell proposal. In letter after letter he complained that America's insistence on self-defense, when the United States could not even imagine any power strong enough seriously to threaten her security, served to cast suspicion upon anything with an American stamp on it. Levinson's answer was: "You are too receptive, not to say too willing to listen to the objections to the right of self-defense. . . . ." He went on to argue that the right of self-defense did not leave a loophole:

We condemn a defensive war, as we do any other kind of war. But we say the right of self-defense is inherent, but is not war. . . . . Now, do you want me to wait for five or ten years before organizing and crystallizing American opinion on the subject? . . . . But there is no law, no treaty, no agreement that can take away the right of self-defense from any person, corporation, municipality or nation.[5]

Let those persons who wanted to talk about leaving out self-defense go to the world convention to be called for the formulation of a general outlawry treaty and argue the case, but, in the meantime, all should support outlawry with all their might. However, whether the European arguments against the admission of self-defense were sound or not, when Borah reintroduced his outlawry resolution in December, he made no reference to it.

[4] Brown to Levinson, October 13, 1927.
[5] Levinson to Brown, September 9, 1927.

There had been feeling in some quarters that Great Britain and the United States should enter into what was called an "all-inclusive" arbitration treaty which would provide that any dispute failing of settlement was to be submitted to an arbitration tribunal. After the Briand proposal had been made to the United States, there was an increased demand for such a treaty as a sort of a "me-too" reaction to the Briand gesture. Levinson was unalterably opposed to an "all-in" arbitration treaty with any country. "No nation, perhaps least of all ours, will submit or agree to submit, all controversies (outlawry or no outlawry) to a foreign tribunal."[6] Such matters as the Monroe Doctrine, immigration, tariff, prohibition, he protested, neither should, nor ever would, be "submitted to international arbitration or judicial control." It was an altogether different matter to agree not to go to war. In case two states found themselves unable to solve a dispute, they might well let it remain unsolved; they could, however, refrain from appealing to the court of war. After war had been ruled out, he favored arbitration for those disputes which the parties to them were willing to submit to an arbitral tribunal. The only way in which arbitration could really be made effective was to outlaw war; then, with "the restrictions and handicaps on the workings of arbitration" removed, it would be used constantly.

Harrison Brown was instructed to use this type of argument against an "all-in" arbitration treaty in England. He found division of opinion. J. L. Garvin and the Astors seemed to feel such a treaty was desirable and the time for it opportune, while those not so close to the government, like the Labour and liberal groups and Scott of the *Manchester Guardian*, favored some kind of an arrangement "à la Briand." Levinson's arguments against an "all-in" agreement were not well received. The answer Brown got, he said, when he used such arguments was: "Sure enough, the United States wants peace in Europe where it has so much money invested, but it will find some means of excepting every single question which will touch her interests";[7] so he advised caution

[6] Levinson to Borah, June 29, 1927.

[7] Brown to Levinson, January 3, 1928.

in making use of the statement that there were some questions on which the United States would not arbitrate. While Brown was commissioned to prevent the British from offering an "all-in" arbitration treaty to the United States, he was to persuade them to offer an outlawry treaty "à la Briand." Levinson had himself made a gallant effort in behalf of such a project when he had visited London in April and May, 1927. The plan agreed upon in a meeting with some of the Labour members of Parliament contemplated the signing of an Anglo-American outlawry treaty; Borah was to get his resolution passed by the United States Senate—". . . . this would in effect tender to all civilized nations a similar if not a general Outlawry Treaty"[8]—and a similar resolution was to be introduced in the House of Commons. But, as before stated, with the British Foreign Office he had absolutely no success.

After the meeting of the Assembly, Levinson wrote to Brown suggesting that he should go to England to persuade the Tory government through Garvin to make an outlawry proposal to the United States. If the Tories did that, it would be a "ten strike for the conservative government following its repudiation of Locarno [?] and other military alliances and guaranties."[9] Besides, if they did not, Labour would either force their hand or throw them out and do it themselves. If the British would do this, it would be a great help in this country; and "we can then proceed to Germany and the other countries. . . . . Indeed, I think so strongly of this that if I am needed there I would consider coming just for that purpose, either for Great Britain, or, if you can accomplish this, for a crusade in the other countries."[10]

Sentiment in Britain was forming for outlawry, according to the weekly *Manchester Guardian* for October 21, 1927, which after commenting on the outlawry of war quoted the following extract from a "manifesto" of the Liberals: "We hold that the complete suppression of war as a means of settling disputes between nations

[8] Levinson's diary of trip to Europe, 1927, at May 31.

[9] Levinson to Brown, October 10, 1927. He probably meant the Geneva Protocol.

[10] *Ibid.*

[258]

should be the dominant policy of every country." And the Labour party appeared to favor a bilateral outlawry treaty between the United States and Great Britain.

In November Harrison Brown began to report from London. In general he found Liberals and Labourites favoring more and more an outlawry treaty in preference to an "all-in" arbitration agreement, not so much, perhaps, because they preferred the one to the other in itself as because they thought that there was a better chance of getting the former. In addition to Kerr, Ponsonby, Kenworthy, and others, who had been conversant with outlawry for some time, Lloyd George, G. Lowes Dickinson, Arnold Forster—a close friend of Cecil's—and Harold Laski favored an Anglo-American outlawry treaty. Lord Robert Cecil thought that, if the United States offered such a treaty to Britain, public opinion would force the government to accept it. Harold Laski was talking with MacDonald almost constantly about outlawry, and he had planned to bring up a resolution on the question in the Union of Democratic Control in March. He was attempting to bring one of the Scotts of the *Manchester Guardian* into line, and he suggested to Brown that he should persuade one of the great newspapers to run a referendum on an Anglo-American outlawry treaty.

With the Conservatives the trend seemed more and more toward an "all-in" arbitration treaty. Garvin, who was thought to be very close to the government, felt that a mistake had been made at the beginning in not inviting Briand to consult with Britain. Thirty years before, an arbitration treaty had been offered to the United States; but it had not been approved by the Senate. Now, however, that the Irish question was out of the way, he could see no reason why it should fail. Lord Astor took the same view but stressed the point that no government would try anything with America unless it had an assurance of not being "frozen off." In government circles there seemed to be a confident feeling that the United States was not likely to sign any outlawry agreement. Wickham Steed had lunched with President Coolidge. Among other things the President had told him that in his opinion the Briand proposal would not pass the Senate, which was a "very curious body." Coolidge had expressed some appreciation of Borah, but he apparently supported his opinion with regard to the difficulty of getting a treaty through the Senate by saying that Borah did not "follow through."

Harrison Brown's real disillusionment with the Tories came when he talked with Lord Cushendun. His lordship thought an "all-in" arbitration treaty would not be possible because reservations would be made. And as for multilateral treaties, they were not practicable either, since what was suitable in one case would not be in another. As for giving up the right to fight, regardless of circumstances, he could easily think of situations in which the British Empire would want to fight, and "anyway, an engagement that we would not go to war in any event would weaken our diplomacy from the outset."[11] Besides, any nation, America included, would break such an engagement when its interest demanded; therefore, such an agreement was not worth the scrap of paper it was written on, said the man who in eight months was to sign the Pact for the Renunciation of War in behalf of His Majesty, the King of Great Britain, Ireland, and the British Dominions beyond the seas.[12]

This was too much for the ex-Tommy who had had to go to such extreme lengths to get into the British army in 1914. What more evidence, he asked, was needed of impending doom, when England was led by such "cretins as the Cushenduns, the Kelloggs, the Baldwins and the Chamberlains?" Anybody who saw them at close quarters and would afterward lift a finger to "defend his King and country" deserves to get blown to hell and "I hope he will!"

But before we take up the negotiations which were to end with Cushendun's solemnly fixing his signature to what he had been so certain would be only a scrap of paper, it is perhaps in place to notice the purpose to which Levinson thought war debts and reparations might be put in such negotiations.

While in Europe in 1927 he spent considerable time talking

[11] Brown to Levinson, January 8, 1928.

[12] *Treaty for the Renunciation of War* (Pub. No. 468 [Washington: Government Printing Office, 1933]), p. 2.

about reparations and debts and collecting information relevant to the problem. A settlement might be worked out, he was sure, which would take the whole problem from the political chessboard and which would be to the advantage of all the states concerned. It was his hope that, when he had produced the outlines of such a settlement, Borah could appropriate it as his own and use it as a bridge on which to cross from the Senate to the White House. "As I spent considerable time here and in Europe, collecting and assembling the materials . . . . intending it solely for you, it will be a great disappointment if it happens not to appeal to you,"[13] he confided to his Hamlet.

His professional experience led him to believe that any plan would first have to satisfy the creditor nation. Accordingly, as it took definite form in his mind, he was careful to get the opinions of Chicago bankers and persons free from the taint of "European mindedness." By shortly after the middle of November he reported that every "big banker" except Dawes, who was supposed to be still "pretty much married" to the Dawes plan, was from "unstintedly" to "almost wildly" enthusiastic over his "plan of readjustment."

This plan was published in the *New Republic* of December 7, 1927, and in the *Chicago Daily News* of December 2. The next day the *News* printed interviews with important financiers who approved it.

Briefly, the plan was this: (1) The United States was to receive the "present worth" in cash of all war debts owed to it. (2) The amount of the German reparations was to be fixed, and this amount was to be raised by the sale of bonds. (3) The proceeds from the sale of the bonds were to be used to retire all outstanding reparations and Allied and inter-Allied governmental debts. (4) All the nations involved were "to sign a treaty of peace, open to all other civilized nations, wherein there will be substituted for the sixty-two years of debt installment payments by our European debtors, a sixty-two-year experiment in world peace, by the renunciation for that period of the use of war for the settlement of international disputes. In other words, to get also from this ad-

[13] Levinson to Borah, September 19, 1927.

justment the ideal for which we fought in the War—the ending of war by international agreement."[14]

The usual methods of publicity were followed. The usual struggle to line up Borah began, and the hesitant Hamlet assumed, as usual, his constitutional attitude of opposition. At first, he appeared unwilling even to offer the plan for the *Congressional Record*. Senator Thomas J. Walsh of Montana, who approved it, was willing to do so in his stead, but, because of his own ill health and of the plan's international importance "thought the head of the Foreign Relations Committee by all means should handle it."[15] And Robins resumed the struggle with Borah. The Senator, after a little, promised to place the Levinson plan in the *Record* but claimed that he did not understand it and treated it "with amused indifference." "And yet we thought he might be a candidate for the Presidency! ! !"[16] gasped the exasperated colonel. However, the breathing space of the Christmas season and the prompt appearance of other more pressing matters postponed the issue.

The approval which the financial plan received was well-nigh unanimous. Some of the correspondents of the *Chicago Daily News* interviewed the financial and political luminaries in Washington and New York. Though none of these persons would permit themselves to be quoted publicly, they accepted the principle of such a debt settlement. The inference from the confidential report of the correspondents to their editor was that Coolidge, Kellogg, Castle, Mellon, and the Treasury foreign-loan expert, Redpath, were also in agreement with it.

Raymond Robins found Mr. Dwight Morrow more than passingly interested. He asked the colonel for a copy of the plan for the senior partner, J. P. Morgan. Shortly, Robins understood, the partners would have called Levinson in for a discussion of the details had it not been for his "aberration" on peace. It was all very well for an "uplifter" like Robins to gesticulate about soft-headed things like prohibition and peace, but that a hard-headed

14 *New Republic*, December 7, 1927, p. 61.

15 Levinson to Herbert Croly, December 3, 1927.

16 Robins to Levinson, December 5, 1927.

reorganization lawyer like Levinson should do so, it was conveyed to the colonel, was beyond the understanding of the Morgan partners.[17] But Levinson, while he was not in the habit of turning the other cheek, had plans of his own for J. Pierpont Morgan and Company.

The general idea in the country, Levinson believed, was that J. P. Morgan had made "five hundred million dollars or more net profit out of the war and the transactions since as a result of the war." If so, here was "a grand opportunity for them to take the load in handling a proposal of this kind in whatever final form it takes without compensation."[18] He wanted Robins to put this idea of the Morgan firm handling the loan without commission "into the mind of your great friend," Morrow. But if there had to be commissions, it was, anyway, the "logical firm to do it—the biggest and the best."

When the plan appeared, Levinson cabled Brown to get the foreign reactions. Brown found Europeans in places of responsibility more tight-lipped than Americans. In the first place, they had a feeling of ennui with private American plans for all the ills of the world. Brown was frank. "The truth is," he wrote, "that there is no proof that the Plan is anything more than a private scheme and everybody is fed up on private plans."[19] Responsible people wanted to be assured, first of all, that the plan had some chance of official consideration. In the second place, it seemed that they did not wish to appear overanxious to open the debts and reparations questions with the United States. However, he was able to report very favorably of such opinions as were expressed. Among those who approved were Gilbert Murray, Sir Thomas Barclay, Sir George Paish, who had been a financial adviser to the government, Jean Monnett, of whom, to quote Robins, Morrow had said that he was "one of the best financial minds on this planet," and Salter. Most of these men, however, objected to attaching the outlawry provision to financial adjust-

[17] But one of the partners had written an excellent book, Dwight W. Morrow, *The Society of Free States* (New York: Harper & Bros., 1919).

[18] Levinson to Robins, December 20, 1927.

[19] Brown to Levinson, December 15, 1927.

ment. Salter was of the opinion that such an arrangement would have a bad effect on both parties because of the suspicion of self-interest. Levinson countered with: "This is of great importance because, in my humble opinion, in view of our political complexities and our multifarious demagogisms, it would be difficult to get an economic plan ratified where it related purely to dollars."[20] Salter's additional reason for separating peace and debts was his feeling that nothing could be done that year in regard to debts; but, if the multilateral proposal which had already been made by Kellogg were pushed, something could be done a little later for peace.

Salter's view appeared to be confirmed when Briand capitulated to the cautious Kellogg on March 30, 1928; and, while Levinson was very much attached to the plan for international financial adjustment, he was by no means a "hot friend cooling" toward his first love, outlawry of war. Consequently, on April 4, 1928, he decided that the plan for general European "appeasement" must be sidetracked to clear the right of way for outlawry and cabled Harrison Brown: ". . . . Undesirable mentioning economic adjustment until after treaty conference called otherwise demagogues here would selfishly and [ruthlessly] misinterpret. . . . ."[21]

[20] Levinson to Sir Thomas Barclay, February 6, 1928.

[21] Levinson to Brown, April 4, 1928. It was impossible to be sure from the copy of the cable whether or not the word in brackets was "ruthlessly."

CHAPTER XVI

THE KELLOGG PROPOSAL TO WIDEN
THE BRIAND OFFER

JUST why Kellogg waited six months before replying to the Briand proposal of June 20, 1927, is beyond the province of this investigation.[1] However, there is some evidence available as to why he insisted on a multilateral pact's being substituted for the proposed bilateral pact. It is with this process of widening the Briand proposal that this chapter is concerned.

Briand himself suggested in his statement to the Associated Press on April 6, 1927, that in order to "furnish to other peoples an example more solemn still, France would be willing to subscribe publicly with the United States to any mutual engagement tending 'to outlaw war,' to use an American expression, as between these two countries."[2] In his address delivered at the signing of the Pact of Paris he said:

I never contemplated for one moment that the suggested engagement should only exist between France and the United States. I have always thought that, in one way or another, by multiplication or extension, the engagement proposed would in itself possess an expansive force, strong enough to reach rapidly all the nations whose moral adhesion was indispensable.[3]

However, the French notes of January 5,[4] and 21,[5] 1928, show that he preferred the treaty to be signed bilaterally first, whatever his intentions were with regard to drawing other states into that or other agreements. The suggestions that the proposed

[1] Some of the reasons suggested by various persons are collected in "Salmon O. Levinson and the Peace Pact," pp. 345 f. (typed), in the Libraries of the University of Chicago.

[2] David Hunter Miller, *The Peace Pact of Paris* (New York: Putnam's Sons, 1928), p. 155.

[3] *Treaty for the Renunciation of War* (Pub. No. 468 [Washington: Government Printing Office, 1933]), pp. 314 f. This agrees with the impression which Levinson recorded in his diary after his last visit in 1927 with Léger (see above, pp. 230 f.).

[4] Below, p. 268. [5] Below, p. 269.

agreement be made multilateral appears to have come first from Borah. He made a speech to a meeting of the Grange in Cleveland early in May, in which a statement to that effect was made.[6] This was followed by Dr. Morrison's editorial in the *Christian Century* for May 26, in which was proposed as a test of Briand's good faith his willingness to widen his offer to renounce war with all states.[7] Morrison later receded from this position under strong pressure from Levinson and Robins, but Borah insisted for several months during "his summer madness" that a bilateral treaty was 'poison to Outlawry." Finally, he too receded somewhat under the pressure and pleading of Levinson and Robins. While he would support a bilateral treaty, he much preferred that the United States should make it a six-power treaty. He came to this conclusion after the middle of October. On November 10 he sent a telegram[8] to Mr. Sydney Gulick of New York, in which this proposal was stated publicly. In a meeting of the Senate Committee on Foreign Relations, which Kellogg attended, he again is reported to have proposed a six-power treaty.[9] There were later visits by the Secretary to the Senator's home, where this matter was gone into, according to the reports which Borah gave to Levinson; and on December 23, 1927, Levinson cabled Harrison Brown: "Borah yesterday proposed an international Christmas gift absolute Outlawry agreement by extending Briand proposal to include England Germany Italy Japan."

It was with this attitude of the chairman of the Foreign Relations Committee of the Senate as a background that Kellogg handed a note to Claudel, the French ambassador to Washington, dated December 28, 1927. After reviewing the Briand proposal, he added that "in view of the traditional friendship between France and the United States" and

in view of the common desire of the two Nations never to resort to arms . . . . it has occurred to me that the two Governments, instead of contenting them-

---

[6] *Cleveland Press,* May 10, 1927.   [7] Above, pp. 240 ff.

[8] The telegram is quoted in part above, p. 248.

[9] Pearson and Brown, *The American Diplomatic Game* (New York: Doubleday, Doran & Co., 1935), pp. 27 f. This account makes it appear as if Borah were responsible for keeping the proposal alive.

selves with a bilateral declaration of the nature suggested by M. Briand, might make a more signal contribution to world peace by joining in an effort to obtain the adherence of all of the principal Powers of the world to a declaration renouncing war as an instrument of national policy. Such a declaration, if executed by the principal world Powers, could not but be an impressive example to all other Nations of the world, and might conceivably lead such Nations to subscribe in their turn to the same instrument, thus perfecting among all the Powers of the world an arrangement heretofore suggested only as between France and the United States.

The Government of the United States is prepared, therefore, to concert with the Government of France with a view to the conclusion of a treaty among the principal Powers of the world, open to signature by all Nations, condemning war and renouncing it as an instrument of national policy in favor of the pacific settlement of international disputes. If the Government of France is willing to join with the Government of the United States . . . . and the other principal Powers of the world into an appropriate multilateral treaty, I shall be happy to engage at once in conversations looking to the preparation of a draft treaty following the lines suggested by M. Briand for submission by France and the United States jointly to the other nations of the world.[10]

Levinson from the first regarded any attempt to extend the proposed Franco-American pact to other states as the wrong procedure. He wanted to concentrate every effort on rushing the bilateral treaty through to avoid any slips. Then it would be time to approach other states, in accordance with what he understood Briand's plan to be. Even after several notes had been exchanged between Washington and Paris, he still felt the two-power pact was better. He wrote to Harrison Brown:

Between you and me and the gatepost, I would have liked it better if the original bilateral treaty proposed by France had been worked out and signed. Then we would have rushed all over Europe and got tenders from the other nations to both France and the United States for the same kind of treaty.[11]

Another procedure that he advocated was the calling of a conference in which many political and economic adjustments could be made along with the negotiation of an outlawry treaty.

It would seem, therefore, that only Borah of the outlawrist group had any part in initiating the movement to make the pact

[10] *Treaty for the Renunciation of War*, Kellogg to Claudel, December 28, 1927, p. 11.

[11] Levinson to Brown, February 17, 1928.

multilateral, and as between him and Kellogg it would seem from the evidence available in the Levinson correspondence that he deserves the greater share of the credit.[12]

On December 28 Kellogg had given his note to Claudel proposing that other powers be invited to join France and the United States in renouncing war. Seven days later, January 5, 1928, Claudel transmitted the French answer proposing that the United States and France sign the agreement immediately which would provide for the renunciation of "all war of aggression," and then all other states should be invited to adhere. The relevant paragraph of the note follows.

I am authorized to inform you that the Government of the Republic is disposed to join with the Government of the United States in proposing for agreement by all nations a treaty to be signed at the present time by France and the United States and under the terms of which the high contracting parties shall renounce all war of aggression and shall declare that for the settlement of differences of whatever nature which may arise between them they will employ all pacific means. The high contracting parties will engage to bring this treaty to the attention of all states and invite them to adhere.[13]

Kellogg's rejoinder to this note was dated January 11. He was "deeply gratified" that both governments were so closely in accord as far as the multilateral feature of the proposed treaty was concerned. But the immediate signing of the treaty by the two governments and a later submission to the other states was open to the

objection that a treaty, even though acceptable to France and the United States, might for some reason be unacceptable to one of the other great Powers. In such event the treaty could not come into force and the present efforts of France and the United States would be rendered abortive. This unhappy result would not

---

[12] Levinson said this is an understatement, that Borah deserves "*all* the credit" for making the pact multilateral. One story from a most trustworthy source has it that Kellogg went one evening late in the fall to the Borah home and knocked persistently until the Senator, who was alone, finally opened the door. The Secretary related how he had mulled over what to do with the Briand proposal until the answer came to him in a flash in the middle of the night, "Why not make it a multilateral agreement?" The astonished Borah was shocked into silence that the Secretary should claim to him the authorship of an idea that Borah himself had been advocating for months.

[13] *Treaty for the Renunciation of War*, Claudel to Kellogg, January 5, 1928, p. 14.

[268]

necessarily follow a disagreement as to terminology arising prior to the definitive approval by any Government of a proposed form of treaty, since it is by no means unreasonable to suppose that the views of the Governments concerned could be accommodated through informal preliminary discussions and a text devised which would be acceptable to them all.[14]

And therefore he hoped the French government would be willing to join with the other governments for the "purpose of reaching a preliminary agreement as to the language to be used in the proposed treaty." But with regard to renouncing only "all war of aggression," as opposed to war without any qualification, he began to use the ideology and even the language of the outlawrists.[15] He noted that France, in the expression of a desire to join with the United States in proposing a multilateral treaty for the renunciation of war

apparently contemplates that the scope of such treaty should be limited to wars of aggression. The form of treaty which your Government submitted to me last June . . . . contained no such qualification or limitation. On the contrary it provided unequivocally for the renunciation by the High Contracting Parties of all war as an instrument of national policy in the following terms:[16]

Here followed the two articles of the proposed treaty which Briand had transmitted to him in June, 1927.[17] He hoped that the two governments could join in transmitting the original proposal to the other great powers.

On January 21 Claudel replied for his government. The original proposal, if confined to France and the United States, had appeared "both desirable and feasible by reason of the historical relations between the two Republics"; but, if this original plan were to be expanded, he "felt bound to point out that the new negotiation as proposed would be more complex and likely to

[14] *Ibid.*, Kellogg to Claudel, January 11, 1928, pp. 15–16.

[15] Here Kellogg was using the term "war" in what the outlawrists called the "institutional" sense, as opposed to the popular meaning of war as "violence between nations." He did not expect, as he later made clear, to renounce war as violence when necessary for self-defense. He was asking for a renunciation of war as a source of title, as an alternative to peaceful relations among nations, as "an institution," as Levinson would say. This is the nuclear idea of the outlawry concept.

[16] *Treaty for the Renunciation of War*, p. 16.

[17] The two articles are quoted in Appen. C.

[269]

meet with various difficulties."[18] As to the question of whether the United States and France should first sign the treaty and then invite others to adhere, as France had suggested, or invite others to sign along with them, as the United States had suggested, it was "essentially" a question "of procedure"; and, though France's suggestion had been made with a view to "more speedily and more surely" achieving the end mutually desired, France was "ready to concur in any method which may appear to be the most practicable." However, with regard to the distinction between "war" and "war of aggression" he was not ready to yield so easily. He thought "the American Government can not be unaware of the fact" that most of the powers of the world both great and small, "are already bound to one another by a Covenant placing them under reciprocal obligations, as well as by agreements such as those signed at Locarno in October, 1925, or by international conventions relative to guaranties of neutrality, all of which engagements impose upon them duties which they cannot contravene."[19] He also called attention to the fact that all the members of the League had adopted a resolution the preceding September. "In that resolution the powers were led to specify that the action to be condemned as an international crime is aggressive war and that all peaceful means must be employed for the settlement of differences, of any nature whatsoever, which might arise between the several states."[20] So long as France and the United States were drawing up a simple bilateral compact, it could be of the nature suggested originally by Briand "in the light of the century-old relations between France and the United States," but "when confronted by the initiative of the United States in proposing a multipartite covenant, [France] had to take into consideration the relations existing among the various powers which could be called upon to participate therein."[21] Therefore, a change in the proposal had been made by the French government in view of prior obligations; and the form which the suggestion had taken was inspired by the formula "which has al-

[18] *Treaty for the Renunciation of War*, Claudel to Kellogg, January 21, 1928, pp. 19–20.

[19] *Ibid.*, p. 20.   [20] *Ibid.*   [21] *Ibid.*, p. 21.

ready gained the unanimous adherence of all of the states members of the League of Nations, and which for that very reason might be accepted by them with regard to the United States, just as it has already been accepted among themselves."[22] The note ended with:

> Subject to these observations, the Government of the Republic would, moreover, very gladly welcome any suggestions offered by the American Government which would make it possible to reconcile an absolute condemnation of war with the engagements and obligations assumed by the several nations and the legitimate concern for their respective security.[23]

Within a period of twenty-seven days Kellogg had written two notes to the French, and both of these had been replied to. But the last French reply explaining why France could sign a bilateral treaty with the United States which would not be suitable as a multilateral agreement stopped the nervous Kellogg. He is reported to have gone to Borah wringing his hands and muttering to himself: "What'll I do now?" It seems that while Borah was not panicstricken, he did not have the crushing answer on the tip of his tongue. The negotiations were on the verge of breaking down; the moment had come for Levinson to intervene—the man whose life-motto was to turn liabilities into assets and proceed as before.

Levinson had gone to California in the latter part of the Christmas season to visit his sister, Daisy Harrison, and did not get back to Chicago until Sunday, January 22. During the next few days he wrote a large number of letters. Among others there was one to Coolidge praising the Kellogg proposal as "the greatest milestone in the history of world peace"; another went to Quincy Wright, commending him for his argument in the January 12 issue of *Foreign Notes* that it was constitutional to renounce war. He thought the last Kellogg note

> was a perfectly corking tender to France and the world. This is the nearest approach to an Outlawry treaty that has ever been officially proposed by any government. In my humble opinion, it will ripen, sooner or later, into a sound treaty and the rest will take care of itself.[24]

[22] *Ibid.*   [23] *Ibid.*
[24] Levinson to Oggel, January 24, 1928.

He admitted that he was somewhat disappointed at "not feeling the thrill of satisfaction that ought to come from daily publicity and discussion in governmental, political and press circles of the idea that has been dormant so long and has been so much abused and ridiculed."[25] The objections which the French had raised "are so easily answered and removed, and the position of our government is so sound, that results must come, sooner or later," he assured Coolidge.[26]

From January 23 to January 27 he was very busy working on the answer to the last French note. In several letters written during the stay in Chicago he mentioned that he was working on a paper, and on Saturday, the twenty-eighth, his secretary, Mrs. Kelly, wrote to Harrison Brown that he had been in a conference all morning, considering the "revision of the paper he is taking to Washington." That afternoon he and Robins went East.

After arriving in Washington, they telephoned Borah, who invited them to see him about eleven o'clock, Sunday morning, January 29. As they were going to the Borah home, Robins told Levinson to read to the Senator the paper they had been working on during the preceding days. Levinson replied that he was no schoolboy, that he didn't have to give a speech by rote, but that he would tell the Senator what the idea was. During the ensuing conversation Borah asked Levinson if he had by any chance reduced his ideas to writing. Whereupon the lawyer took the paper from his pocket and started to read. Borah took it out of his hand with some such remark as: "I want to use that in an article which I am preparing for next Sunday's *New York Times*." While the sources of the information as to what happened during the interview are oral reports—the first, from Dr. Morrison two years after the event, the second, from Levinson several years later—there is documentary evidence to substantiate the story even in most of the details.

The argument which Levinson put to Borah was that, if a multilateral agreement condemning and renouncing war could not be made because it would violate French obligation under the

[25] Levinson to Holmes, January 24, 1928.
[26] Levinson to Coolidge, January 24, 1928.

Covenants of the League and the Locarno agreements, then for the same reason the French could certainly not make a bilateral agreement with the United States. But, contrary to Briand's contention, a multilateral agreement would be the very way to remove the evils which he himself had feared in a bilateral treaty. If there were a bilateral treaty and Belgium and the United States became involved, the French would not be free to assist Belgium against the United States, whereas if the agreement were multilateral, a United States attack on Belgium would release France of all obligations not to give assistance to Belgium.

One cannot be sure that Borah would have failed to think of this line of reasoning; but, when Levinson and Robins called on him, all that he had in mind was an appeal to Europe. What he actually did was to take the Levinson memorandum, add some introductory and concluding paragraphs, and publish it in the *New York Times* the following Sunday, February 5.[27] Later, when Borah talked to Levinson, it was his habit to refer to this article as "our article." It will appear later how Kellogg made the central idea in the Borah article the basis of his reply to the French. Consequently, it would seem safe to say that the evidence available indicates that the chief credit goes to Levinson at this turning-point in the negotiations.

On February 6, when "Captain Outlawry" read the Borah article in the *Times*, he was much "set up" over the fine spirit the Senator had manifested to Europe. Said he to Colonel Robins:

The old boy has outdone himself. I hardly dared believe my eyes as I read along the beautiful conciliatory and persuasive way in which he set forth the matter. You were right in your immediate judgment of Borah's "case" on my little paper. It largely figures in the center of the article.[28]

Only to a few of his closest collaborators did he reveal that he had helped with the preparation of it, and to none of them—in letters at all events—nor to me, did he ever indicate the extent to which Borah had made almost verbatim use of his memorandum. He always referred to the article as "the Borah article."

[27] For convenience in comparing the Levinson memorandum and the Borah article, relevant parts have been placed in parallel columns (see Appen. B).

[28] Levinson to Robins, February 6, 1928.

Levinson's reports of his visits to Borah during the last days of January are important as giving his impression of the relation of the chairman of the Committee on Foreign Relations of the Senate to the secretary of state.[29] On his return to Chicago on February 4, Levinson sent a cablegram in code to Harrison Brown. When decoded, it read:

Just returned. Briand treaty situation perfect for Borah, Kellogg, and Coolidge all working in harmony. Borah publishing this Sunday *Times* comprehensive article destroying Briand's objections, mailing copies. Briand's answers fatally injuring Covenant in press and public opinion. Our party taking deadly advantage. . . . .[30]

He wrote to Oggel that Borah had largely managed the last Kellogg note, and to a Dr. Magnes he said: "Under the powerful stimulus of Senator Borah the administration has offered what practically amounts to a real outlawry of war treaty."[31] And to his son, Ronald, he reported: Borah "has had an immense amount to do with this entire thing."[32] "Kellogg," he found, "is feeling very much set up by his position . . . . and the European intentions through the reply" [i.e., the French note of January 21].[33] He understood from the Senator that Kellogg would answer the last French note "in about two weeks"—which would be about February 20—and on the lines, he thought, of the Borah article. But when there was no word by February 21, he went to Washington "to see that the point of view so splendidly stated by Borah in his *Times* Article is made the basis for a reply by the State Department." Who all the people were that he saw is not recorded, but it is clear that he was satisfied with the State Department, for he cabled Harrison Brown the day he returned: "Inside word early official reply on desired lines including Borah's position and will crystallize into political national plank

[29] The contents of the Borah article when compared to the Kellogg note of February 27 shed further light on this relation.

[30] Levinson to Brown, February 4, 1928.

[31] Levinson to Dr. J. L. Magnes, February 7, 1928.

[32] Levinson to Ronald Levinson, February 13, 1928.

[33] Levinson to Brown, February 4, 1928.

June. This is tremendous."[34] And when Kellogg did reply to the French, Levinson wrote to Borah:

> .... I must write my overwhelming word of congratulation and gratitude to you on your invaluable aid in getting the administration entirely behind Outlawry. I do not see how we could have done it better if we had been able to write it ourselves. At least you have gotten the institutional idea into the correspondence which is worth its weight in radium.
>
> It is difficult for me to convey to you the thrill of joy that came to me as I read at the breakfast table on Wednesday morning the reality of the reply message to France such as you had assured me would probably go forward. Reality sometimes altogether outweighs expectation where the issue is so vital.[35]

As Levinson had predicted, Kellogg's answer to the French note of January 21 was based on the same line of argument as that of the Borah article in the *Times*. The chief difference between the Kellogg note of February 27 and the Borah article of February 5 was that Kellogg used the idea contained in the article without elaborating or illustrating it. He did not refer to obligations of France other than those in the Covenant of the League, whereas Borah, on the contrary, had discussed others also. And he pointed out, in addition, that American nations, members of the League, at the recent Havana conference, had taken a position with regard to war similar to that he was asking all the nations to take. Relevant sections of his note follow.

> Without, of course, undertaking formally to construe the present treaty obligations of France, I desire to point out that if those obligations can be interpreted so as to permit France to conclude a treaty [for the unconditional renunciation of war] .... it is not unreasonable to suppose that they can be interpreted with equal justice so as to permit France to join with the United States in offering to conclude an equivalent multilateral treaty with the other principal Powers of the world. The difference between the bilateral and the multilateral form of treaty having for its object the unqualified renunciation of war as an instrument of national policy, seems to me to be one of degree and not of substance. A Government free to conclude such a bilateral treaty should be no less able to become a party to an identical multilateral treaty since it is hardly to be presumed that members of the League of Nations are in a position to do separately something they cannot do together..... If .... members of the League of Nations cannot, without violating the terms of the Covenant of the League,

[34] Levinson to Brown, February 24, 1928.
[35] Levinson to Borah, March 2, 1928.

agree among themselves and with the Government of the United States to renounce war as an instrument of their national policy, it seems idle to discuss either bilateral or multilateral treaties unreservedly renouncing war. I am reluctant to believe, however, that the provisions of the Covenant of the League of Nations really stand in the way of the cooperation of the United States and members of the League of Nations in a common effort to abolish the institution of war.[36]

Here followed a reference to the renunciation of war by seventeen American nations in the Sixth International Conference of American States at Havana. In a later paragraph, after "trust-[ing]" that such a proposed treaty would not be found inconsistent with the Covenant of the League, he said:

On the contrary, is it not entirely reasonable to conclude that a formal engagement of this character entered into by all of the principal Powers, and ultimately, I trust, by the entire family of Nations, would be a most effective instrument for promoting the great ideal of peace which the League itself has so closely at heart?[37]

It will be noted above that the Secretary used the term "effort to abolish the institution of war" and in a later paragraph he said: "The Government of the United States desires to see the institution of war abolished. . . . ."[38] There was no terminology more characteristic of the outlawrists. During the note-writing which resulted in the Pact of Paris, Levinson was disappointed that it could all go on without Kellogg's once using the specific word "outlaw" in connection with war. But, beyond mentioning this to his intimates like Professor Dewey, he did not complain. However, Kellogg did recognize publicly that the treaty was an outlawry treaty. In the speech which he made before the Council on Foreign Relations in New York, March 15, 1928, he said, after discussing the arbitration agreement which he had signed with France in February:

I know of but one other form of treaty which can be concluded for the purpose of preventing war and that is a treaty in which the parties specifically bind themselves not to resort to war. It is this kind of treaty which people have in mind when they discuss treaties for outlawing war, and it is a novel idea in modern international relations.[39]

[36] *Treaty for the Renunciation of War*, Kellogg to Claudel, February 27, 1928, pp. 22–23.

[37] *Ibid.*, p. 23.   [38] *Ibid.*   [39] *AJIL*, XXII (1928), 253.

He then went on to discuss the diplomatic correspondence with the French government relative to such a treaty.

However, Kellogg's unwillingness to use the terms "outlaw" and "outlawry" was in no wise shared by the press. According to Harrison Brown, from the time when Briand made his proposal to the United States, the European press in referring to the negotiations and the proposed treaty always used them. This was also largely true of the American press, so that in both Europe and America the "renunciation of war" proposed by the treaty was understood as being identical with outlawry.

Despite Levinson's disappointment that the term "outlaw" was not used by Kellogg so much as he would have liked, he supported the Secretary in every possible way. He wrote letters of praise and encouragement to him. It was in answer to one of these letters that Kellogg, after expressing his appreciation of Levinson's approval "of our position," said that he had handed a note to the French ambassador answering his of January 21, 1928. And he was sure Levinson would be interested in it. Levinson was indeed interested if one may judge from the telegram he sent to the Secretary as soon as he had seen the note. It was: "By your masterful reply to France the Kellogg proposal immortalizes itself. You have struck a mortal blow at the barbarous war system for which the gratitude of humanity and the Nobel Peace Prize should be yours."[40]

In addition to encouraging Kellogg directly, he attempted to uphold his hands, in the first place, by keeping the peace workers at peace with one another at least on the surface and, in the second, by starting a campaign to prevent his old friends, the isolationists, from curdling the milk of human kindness which might flow from the negotiations then under way as they had done with the Covenant of the League.

Keeping Professor Shotwell and Dr. Morrison from each other's throats was a matter which required tact, patience, and plain talk, though Levinson did give the professor a vicarious kick as a stimulus to the harmonious co-operative spirit. Lunching one day with Shotwell, Dewey found him "tired and discour-

[40] Levinson to Kellogg, February 29, 1928.

[277]

aged." According to Dewey's report, Shotwell had got Briand to go so far toward the outlawry idea that Nicholas Murray Butler had called him down. Yet Morrison persisted in misrepresenting him; and if it was not stopped, in spite of his desire not to start a dispute within the peace forces, he would in self-respect be forced to retort in kind. He wanted the pro-League forces to support the Briand proposal, but Morrison had so emphasized the juridical at the expense of the political means of settlement as to leave the impression that the outlawrists were opposed to the use of political means. Dewey urged Levinson to write an article explaining how political adjustments would have a place in international affairs. Levinson wrote the article, but he scoffed at the idea of Shotwell's having had any influence on Briand except, perhaps, to get the word "aggressive" added in the later diplomatic exchanges.

And besides this, I have the direct word of one of the biggest men at Quai d'Orsay that Briand did not act on Shotwell's suggestion. Shotwell boasted of this in New York while I was in Paris, I was advised by cable. I went directly to Quai d'Orsay and it was denied emphatically. They did admit that he had been there as twenty-five others had been there.[41]

He also doubted if Shotwell was genuinely interested in the negotiations except to include by one means or another the "aggressor idea" and "put the United States at the military beck and call of Europe. . . . ." Later when James G. McDonald insisted that Shotwell was sincerely supporting Kellogg and quoted his articles in the *New York Herald Tribune* to prove it, Levinson replied that he did not read Shotwell's articles as McDonald did, but:

So far as Shotwell is concerned, I shall be satisfied with one thing, and with one thing only. That is, that he write a letter to Secretary Kellogg, or, if he prefers, to Senator Borah, in which he warmly and unequivocally approves the Kellogg proposal and promises to lend his support to it with a view to the utter abolition of war as an instrument of national policy and as a method of settling international controversies. I would like a copy of that letter and then I think we can proceed in unity.

One other word. If the advocates of peace, both here and in Europe, fail to unite behind the Kellogg proposal, the hopes of peace will be shattered for many a long year to come.[42]

[41] Levinson to Dewey, March 2, 1928.
[42] Levinson to J. G. McDonald, April 7, 1928.

He did admit that Morrison ought to be more conciliatory and tried to keep the minister-editor from writing an article on the "aggressor business," which if done in the usual Morrison style would inevitably stir up a fuss. He thought Borah had broken the ground for sort of sidestepping at present this issue and allowing [the people who wanted to determine beforehand when the right of self-defense could be invoked] to preserve under our suggestions a modus for enabling the European nations to keep their war commitments in the event of a breach of the proposed plurilateral treaty.

Morrison was "almost heart-broken" when Levinson was not "crazy" about his article; but the "Captain General" wanted everyone to get behind Kellogg, and he insisted "very frankly" that Morrison use discretion to prevent a "recrudescence of his book-position."

Levinson's plan to prevent his old allies, the isolationists, from causing trouble called for the adoption of the Borah resolution by the Senate. He had been urging Borah to force the resolution to a vote before Kellogg suggested widening the Briand proposal, so that, when a bilateral pact was signed, the resolution could be used as evidence that the United States would sign a similar treaty with any other nation. But his reasons for wanting the resolution passed changed with the progress of the negotiations. Coolidge had only voiced the opinion of many when he doubted if that "curious body," the Senate, would approve such a treaty. Levinson thought the Senate's adoption of the resolution would prevent its scuttling the treaty. He had found that Senator Walsh of Montana would support the resolution, and he was certain that with administration support the resolution would pass easily. "Here is a chance for Kellogg to profit by the mistake, or at any rate the experience, of Wilson,"[43] he argued to Robins. ". . . . No Senator" he went on "—including Jim Reed himself— will dare take a public stand against the abolition of war at this stage of the political game—certainly no Senator that has the political bee in his bonnet, which represents them all, and certainly not a Senator that is a real candidate." As usual Borah made no move to push the resolution to a vote. Levinson got

[43] Levinson to Robins, March 14, 1928.

Justice Allen and Robins and Morrison and Dewey, each in his own way, to start wooing the hesitant Borah, but all in vain. However, in view of the fact that for once the Senator had adopted a constructive attitude, as was shown by his collaboration with Kellogg, Levinson appeared unwilling to run the risk of adopting cave-man tactics to win the backward Borah. Consequently, he let the matter drop when the Senator insisted, as he did to Morrison in a letter on April 9, that any attempt to bring the resolution to vote would look as if he were "breaking into the diplomatic interchanges of views." He added:

I am in constant touch with the State Department in regard to the matter and the State Department is doing everything in its power to promote the enterprise. I feel in the interest of the cause, I must work thoroughly with them.

I had a conference this afternoon and I think you will be pleased with what will go forward in a day or two.[44]

Levinson, too, may then have thought it best to let matters rest, because the Senator, in the midst of his labors with the State Department for a universal outlawry-of-war treaty, showed tangent tendencies by sponsoring a resolution to codify the law of sea warfare—a vagary which "Captain Outlawry" could not understand, since such action meant that the Senator either did not begin to comprehend the meaning of outlawry or he had no confidence in it and since he was on record as opposing all such "half-way measures"—a record which Levinson gently called to his attention. But when the Senator persisted, Levinson dropped that, too, after mentioning that the Shotwell "crowd" believed in such things and were supporting him. In the spring of 1928, Borah had also indulged in another flight of fancy; he wanted to purify the Republican party by giving back the tainted campaign contribution of Sinclair. Levinson not only sent a handsome check to cover or blot out one little spot but also raised some money from the La Salle Street neighborhood. Before long, however, Borah became so engrossed with electing the "Great Engineer" that he dropped the idea of purifying his party.

The reaction of Europe to the exchange of notes, as Harrison

[44] Borah to Morrison, April 9, 1928.

Brown understood it from his contacts and from the press, is of interest. Kellogg's first note of December 28, created much favorable interest as reflected in the press. The first reply of the French on January 5, agreeing to widen the treaty but limiting it to wars of aggression, "caused unfriendly reactions, ranging from abuse to sarcasm over a general background of witty cynicism." But this was changed by Kellogg's second note, dated January 11, in which he insisted that all war be renounced. Brown found in three hundred and fifty press clippings, first, surprise and indignation and then incredulity and virulent scorn, that a general pact should include all wars. The papers marveled at the patience of Briand in continuing to seek a compromise on such a point. There was only one exception to the "argument that France cannot in any circumstance go beyond the Outlawry of 'Aggressive' war because of her engagements under the Covenant. . . . ."[45] References to Monroe Doctrine reservations, to the Nicaraguan war, and the big navy program provided an easy basis for wit. Two quotations from the press are illustrative. The first is from the Paris *La Cité* of January 13.

> We must beware of these fine fellows, gorged with the wealth they have lifted from the Allies and who now are trying to drug us all, the better able to fish in our troubled waters. A little more, and since they have become pro-German, they will be looking on the Old World as just a common Lusitania which they can torpedo at their leisure.

The second is from the *Antwerp Matin* for January 16.

> Kellogg must mean war of aggression. Not to stipulate this would be to penalize self defense, which is absurd and would constitute an "invitation to every aggressor and to every Government of bad faith since they would know in advance that no other nation would go to the help of their victim."[46]

Harrison Brown's own summary of the general reaction was:

> This American idea of outlawing war is not only fantastically trustful and naïve to a degree which induces a suspicion of hypocrisy, but is also in direct conflict with the continental policy. It was bad taste enough on the part of America to want to extend the pact proposal to all, but since they do ask that,

[45] Brown to Levinson, January 23, 1928.

[46] Translations by Harrison Brown.

then obviously it can only refer to aggressive war, and aggression must be both mentioned and defined.[47]

At more than one juncture Brown predicted a breakdown in the negotiations. He was evidently underestimating the importance of one of the factors which he was reporting, namely, the determination of the French to get some kind of an agreement with the United States at whatever cost. Paul Scott Mowrer said that Léger had given him to understand that "anything with the United States was better than nothing," and Mowrer had concluded that "they hope sooner or later to get a declaration out of us that we won't interfere with possible eventual League sanctions against an aggressor."[48] As the negotiations progressed, the tone of Brown's letters changed; he, too, began to feel that France would not let the matter drop. It was pointed out in an article in *Le Temps* for February 21 that America must be ready to do something because of the new spurt of peace activity, evidences of which were the Capper and Burton resolutions with regard to arms for aggressor nations, the Gillett motion relating to the World Court, the Borah campaign for the outlawry of war, and "the inquiry made last summer in London and Paris by Mr. S. O. Levinson, the Chicago attorney and Borah's collaborator, into the welcome which the Governments of Western Europe would be likely to extend to Outlawry." The article went on: "If M. Aristide Briand and his collaborators had refused to pay attention to these new witnesses and had refused any collaboration with American diplomacy; if they had missed this chance or . . . . [rejected] the opportunity—their lack of foresight would have

[47] Brown to Levinson, January 23, 1928. This seeming incompatibility between the Kellogg and the European views was typical of the *impasse* which was always arising between the outlawrists and other peace workers. Both believed in violence for self-defense and neither in violence for offense, the confusion arising from the use of the term "war." The outlawrists used it in a technical and legal sense, meaning an institution which was the source of rights; the others used it in the popular sense of violence. The outlawrists either could not or would not make this distinction clear in the minds of the others or the latter either could not or would not understand the distinction. The confusion which existed between the Levinson group and the Shotwell group on this particular point was the basis for much of the bad feeling between the groups. For further comment on the uses of the word "war" see above, pp. 190 ff.

[48] Brown to Levinson, January 8, 1928.

been great and their responsibility heavy."[49] Brown thought this statement in *Le Temps*, which he considered a semiofficial journal, much more than "counter balance [d] [the] reams of the balderdash I have quoted previously from the ordinary gutter press," for the "French people don't believe the press or public men anyway."

After visiting the new states of Europe, he concluded that the note-writing should be continued despite anti-Kellogg reactions in the British Tory press and the comment of "Pertinax" in *L'Echo de Paris* after the Kellogg note of February 27. The latter comment was: "It only remains for us to play at being deaf too, and to re-edit in some form or another our note of the 20th of January." Brown suggested that if they persevered until the matter got before the Assembly of the League they would find allies both among some of the smaller states and in the Secretariat who would help them "to knock hell out of the British and the French governments."[50] Despite his distrust of the governments of all Europe, he found, as March progressed, more evidence that they were determined to get some kind of a commitment from the United States. From a talk with the private secretary of Austen Chamberlain, he gathered that the British foreign secretary "simply did not know what to do with regard to America" but that he was "guided chiefly by the anxiety to do nothing to offend"—an impression which appeared to be shared also by Wickham Steed. Litvinoff told Brown that his own—the Communist—disarmament project was the only practicable one but that if Gibson mentioned the Kellogg proposal he would offer Russian cooperation. Count Bernstorff was certain that German support of the Kellogg proposal could be counted upon. In Geneva the itinerant reporter found much support in the Secretariat, and Gilbert Murray assured him that he and Lord Robert Cecil were doing much behind the lines to assure English acceptance if the pact were opened to other signers. They worked quietly in order not to cripple it in America by making it appear as if it were connected with the League of Nations. And about March 20 Brown

[49] Translation by Brown in letter to Levinson, February 24, 1928.

[50] Brown to Levinson, March 2, 1928.

learned from Paul Scott Mowrer that the French reply to the Kellogg note of February 27 would be favorable.

This reply was dated March 30, 1928. As to the contention that France could enter into a treaty with the United States which it could not enter into multilaterally, Claudel simply brushed aside such argument as Borah had used in his *Times* article and Kellogg had cited in his last note by saying that the contemplated treaty was drafted to limit strictly the obligations "to those relations in law resulting from intercourse between two signatory states alone," and "furthermore, as regards two countries like France and the United States morally united as they are by ties of time-honored friendship, other contractual engagements concluded by one or the other power could never constitute in fact anything but purely theoretical obstacles."[51] As to making the treaty multi-lateral, as well as an unqualified renunciation of war, "if Your Excellency really believes that greater chances of success may be found in this formula . . . . the French Government would hesi-tate to discuss longer the question of its adherence to a plan which the American Government originated and for which it is respon-sible," and consequently it was, without "losing sight of its inter-national obligations, ... disposed . . . . to suggest immediately to the German, British, Italian, and Japanese Governments that they join in seeking, in the spirit and in the letter of the last Ameri-can note, any adjustments which in the last analysis may be forthcoming with respect to the possibility of reconciling previous obligations with the terms of the contemplated new treaty."[52]

There were "three fundamental points" which the French gov-ernment noted in its understanding of the attitude of the Ameri-can government. First, "all the other governments of the world" were to be admitted to "participation in that treaty." Second, ". . . . if one of the signatory states should fail to keep its word, the other signatories should be released from their engagement with respect to the offending state." Third, "my Government likewise gathers from the declarations which Your Excellency was good enough to make to me on the 1st of last March, the assur-

[51] *Treaty for the Renunciation of War*, Claudel to Kellogg, March 30, 1928, p. 29.
[52] *Ibid.*, pp. 29–30.

ance that the renunciation of war, thus proclaimed, would not deprive the signatories of the right of legitimate defense."[53] In addition, if it was already understood that the obligations of the new pact would not in any way prejudice previous obligations, "then the differences of opinion which have appeared in the course of previous phases of the negotiation have to do more with words than with the reality of the problem facing the two Governments to-day."[54]

He then proposed that the substance of the original Briand draft treaty be used in submitting the proposal to the four other powers plus a safeguard of self-defense, a provision as to when the treaty should go into effect, and a stipulation that in case of the treaty being contravened by one party to it all others would be released with respect to that state.[55]

Kellogg, according to Levinson, was flabbergasted by this reply.

My little visit with Kellogg was interesting and unsatisfactory. He seemed to be obsessed with the idea that France was unreasonable, making impossible conditions and that he was through writing notes, etc. He was very nervous, walked up and down in an agitated way and spoke almost with vehemence. I called his special attention to what I think is the greatest paragraph in the reply. Referring to the signatories, this paragraph reads: "They would specifically undertake, among themselves, to refrain from any attack or invasion, and never to seek the settlement of any difference or conflict, of whatsoever nature or origin, which might arise between them, save by pacific means."

I think to you and to me this is the gist of the whole matter. The troubles that seem to afflict the Secretary struck me as mere questions of phraseology, as the diplomatic triumph has been complete. . . . .

The only impression I got from the Kellogg interview is that, my dear Borah, you still have an enormous job on your hands taking care of the situation in the interest of world peace, for the political crisis that is fast developing, and to prevent the collapse of the project which the thinkers of the world have inextricably identified with you.[56]

---

[53] *Ibid.*, p. 30.   [54] *Ibid.*, p. 31.

[55] It is significant in the light of the collective system to notice that, when Claudel was repeating Briand's phrase in regard to the condemnation of war as an instrument of national policy, he appeared to give his interpretation of this phrase by adding this clause: "or in other words as a means of carrying out their own spontaneous, independent policy" (*ibid.*, p. 31).

[56] Levinson to Borah, April 7, 1928.

To Levinson the reply was wholly acceptable. The explanation of the note which he probably gave to Kellogg and Borah and certainly to Dewey, who showed signs of alarm, was:

The French were caught with bad logic and a bad reason for refusing to accept a multilateral treaty in the precise terms of its proposed two-power treaty. Being caught with a poor defense it was impossible to make a good defense and therefore Briand in effect says to Kellogg: "We have explained our position, we feel that we are right, you don't agree with us, but in as much as you are taking the lead and taking the responsibility, we do not care to argue the matter further, but will join under your leadership, etc." This is the way that any controversialist does that gets into a bad box by poor reasoning. He doesn't care to pursue the matter further, but he yields on different grounds.

He went on to suggest that perhaps he and Dewey should "get up, with great care, a brief but comprehensive form of treaty or proposal embodying the gist of the conclusions arising from the official correspondence and send it to Senator Borah, upon whom, after all, in my opinion, we have got largely to rely for vigor of action and for the virtue of accomplishment."[57]

Something evidently had happened in the relations between Borah and Kellogg—something of which Levinson became aware on his visit to Washington during the first week of April and which made him lose confidence in Kellogg and feel that the Secretary was claiming more than his rightful share of the credit for what had been going on. As to what this something was, I have been unable to find sufficient evidence in the correspondence to hazard more than a surmise. However, there are traces of this change of feeling in the letters quoted above, which were written on April 7, 1928. The second letter which he wrote to Borah on that date contains a clearer indication of it, in addition to throwing some interesting light on Borah's political methods and paying a tribute to his political services as sincere and heartfelt as anything Levinson ever wrote but which should surely have stirred sentiments of remorse in the recipient, if he retained any memory of his fierce opposition to the beginnings of the very project for which he was now being praised.[58]

[57] Levinson to Dewey, April 7, 1928.

[58] It must be recalled that the project had now come to have the form which Borah desired from very early in its development, and perhaps he was entitled to oppose at one time and take credit at a later time; yet it seems that the purpose of nego-

THE KELLOGG PROPOSAL

I have not adequately expressed to you my eternal appreciation of the manner in which you have served the cause of Outlawry both in the years past and more especially in your most skillful handling of the recent official correspondence. It seems almost unbelievable to me, a fanatic of ten years standing, dreaming of the day which might come after I had succumbed to old age, when our government would propose to the nations of the world to abolish and outlaw war. That situation, which is gloriously here, could not possibly have been created without your lion's share of participation. It is probably impossible for you to realize what this means to me and to my life.

But I wish especially to emphasize the great-hearted position you displayed the other day. Once before I had this experience with you, namely in the spring of 1923. Then we were struggling with the partially disclosed intolerable status of the Harding administration. You then were willing to yield to Sen. Johnson the leadership in the political fight if he thought the chances of success were adequate, but that if it were to be a losing race of protest against political corruption and the betrayal of representative democratic government then you would make the race on the theory of a willing, personal self sacrifice. The only condition you named was that the principles to which you were devoted should not be compromised.

Last Wednesday you again thrilled me by a recital of self-effacement before the majesty of a great cause. Here is a situation in which you are, on the merits, entitled to all of the political benefits and glories that flow from devotion to and development of the greatest of all humanitarian projects. Nevertheless, sensing the potential danger to the cause, you willingly subordinated yourself to the point of effacement in order that another, fortuitously in a position of practical accomplishment, may reap the rich rewards of his own ambition.

I do not mean to flatter, nor to indulge in unnecessary emphasis. You and I have worked together for a good many years and you have been a great source of mental and moral liberation to me in many public questions. I have perhaps had more ambition for you than you have had for yourself. This ambition has been prompted because of the tremendous gifts that you possess, the power of good you hold for our impaired democracy and because I believe you to be of the same mold as the great founders of our government.

It is therefore all the more wonderful that the spirit of generosity and self-effacement has characterized your consecration to worthy causes. I know of no public man that begins to approach you in terms of moral and intellectual power, nor one who would have the courage and the spiritual self abnegation that you have so marvellously displayed.

Please accept what I say as a deep seated personal tribute from one friend to another, a tribute that is the most richly deserved of any that I have ever attempted to pay.[59]

---

tiation is to change a proposal to meet the desires of the parties to it and that, if the negotiation is killed at its inception, it cannot develop to suit anyone.

[59] Levinson to Borah, April 7, 1928.

In due time Kellogg was able to compose himself sufficiently for a conference with regard to the last French note. A report of this was the letter Borah sent to Levinson which, incidentally, was the Senator's reply to the letter quoted above in full. It is:

DEAR LEVINSON:

I have your letter under date of April 7th. I greatly appreciate your letter. It is another illustration of your over-generous regard for myself.

I had a conference yesterday with the Secretary of State and Under-Secretary Olds. I think the next move will be a very important one. I am of the opinion that we are reaching the place where foreign powers will have to either accept or reject our proposition substantially as made.

Very respectfully,[60]

The conference referred to was held on April 9; two days before, Claudel and Kellogg had agreed to submit to Great Britain, Germany, Italy, and Japan for their consideration and comment the entire correspondence which had passed between the United States and France with regard to the proposed multilateral treaty.[61] And on April 13 Kellogg had delivered to the respective foreign offices the relevant correspondence and a draft treaty which was "practically identical" in Articles I and II[62]—there being only three articles, the last concerned with ratifications, etc.—with the original Briand proposal to the United States, together with a short note in which the correspondence between the United States and France was briefly reviewed. The other powers were asked to pass upon the question of whether they could join in an unqualified "renunciation of war" treaty. Such a treaty "would have tremendous moral effect and ultimately lead to the adherence of all the other governments of the world."[63]

[60] Borah to Levinson, April 10, 1928.

[61] State Department Press Release, April 7, 1928.

[62] For copy of this draft treaty see Appen. D.

[63] *Treaty for the Renunciation of War*, note of the government of the United States to the governments of Great Britain, Germany, Italy, and Japan, p. 32.

CHAPTER XVII

THE STATES ACCEPT THE MULTI-
LATERAL TREATY

FOLLOWING the action of the American government of April 13, 1928, the French government also submitted a draft treaty to Great Britain, Germany, Italy, Japan, and the United States on April 20, 1928.[1] This treaty contained six articles, the last being concerned, as was the American proposal, with provisions for ratification, deposit, etc. More specific than the American draft with regard to the renunciation of war as an instrument of national policy and the use of pacific means only as a means of settling disputes, the French draft (1) defined the meaning of the phrase "renunciation of war as an instrument of national policy"; (2) specifically excluded "legitimate self-defense" from the restrictions of the treaty; (3) provided for the automatic release of all powers violating it; (4) provided for the recognition of the validity of rights and obligations established in prior treaties; and (5) provided that the treaty should be offered for universal acceptance and should not come into force until such acceptance, unless otherwise provided for.

As Harrison Brown had predicted, German approval was immediate. On April 27 Stresemann on behalf of his government accepted the American draft, on condition that (1) the obligations of prior treaties would not be invalidated, (2) the right of self-defense would not be impaired, and (3) the treaty would be open for universal adherence.

The next day, April 28, Kellogg in an address to the American Society of International Law discussed in some detail the "six major considerations" which the French had added to the draft treaty that he had submitted to the powers on April 13. (1) His draft treaty, he maintained, in no way impaired the right of self-defense:

[1] For copy of this draft treaty see Appen. E.

That right is inherent in every sovereign state and is implicit in every treaty. Every nation is free at all times and regardless of treaty provisions to defend its territory from attack or invasion and it alone is competent to decide whether circumstances require recourse to war in self-defense. If it has a good case, the world will applaud and not condemn its action.[2]

(2, 3, and 4) With regard to the prior obligations in the Covenant of the League, the Locarno agreements, and the treaties of neutrality, he could not see that the Covenant of the League imposed any obligation to go to war or that, if the proposed treaty were made universal, it would conflict with the Locarno or neutrality treaties, since, as long as the commitment of the proposed treaty remained inviolate, the war commitments under the prior agreements would remain in suspension. Only with the violation of the proposed treaty would the other obligations come into force. (5) As to the relation of the signatories to a treaty-breaking state, there could "be no question as a matter of law that violation of a multilateral anti-war treaty through resort to war by one party thereto would automatically release the other parties from their obligations to the treaty-breaking state. Any express recognition of this principle of law [was] wholly unnecessary."[3] (6) The desirability of making the treaty universal was also apparent. He reiterated that his plan of opening the treaty first to the signature of the six leading powers would provide the most practicable means of bringing it quickly into effect and of agreeing

[2] *Treaty for the Renunciation of War* (Pub. No. 468 [Washington: Government Printing Office, 1933]), note of Kellogg to France, Great Britain, Italy, Japan, Germany, Belgium, Czechoslovakia, Poland, and Irish Free State of June 23, 1928, p. 57.

This argument, including its very phrases, with regard to the right of self-defense being an inherent right was one which Levinson had been using in season and out for several years. However, the statement is not all good outlawry doctrine. Levinson recognized that a nation as well as an individual would not be a good judge in its own case; he was therefore favorable to giving a court jurisdiction to decide when the pact had been violated. And, according to Levinson, using whatever means necessary to stop an invader was no more "war" than resisting a personal assailant was dueling.

[3] *Ibid.*, p. 58. In points 2, 3, 4, and 5 Kellogg was following most closely the line of argument in the Borah article in the *New York Times*, February 5, 1928 (see above, pp. 272 f., and Appen. B).

easily on the wording of a treaty which the rest of the states would be most likely to approve.

The Kellogg move of April 13, in sending an invitation to four other powers to join with the United States and France in renouncing war, struck a responsive chord in Britain. Harrison Brown reported all but unanimous approval, alike in the press and in the private talk of responsible officials. Tyrrell at the Foreign Office, whom Brown expected to be the next British ambassador to France, was making rather extravagant statements about the really great initiatives for peace, like the "Wilson League," the Washington and London conferences, and the Dawes plan, having all come from the United States. The only sour note from the European sounding board was a twang in the French press, an echo, Brown thought, from official circles. Tyrrell admitted that England was placed in a delicate position with regard to France. If the French government refused to co-operate, then, of course, he doubted if England could do anything either. Madariaga had visited the Quai d'Orsay and "tried his darndest to get a simple acceptance" of the American proposal. At one time the French decided to accept the American note of February 27 unconditionally; but the Quai d'Orsay was divided, and the favorable reply was torn up, the note of March 30 being substituted for it. The "people in control," according to Brown, "are out for sabotage." There was talk of a conference of legal experts to find the meaning of the terms in the Kellogg draft treaty. Chamberlain appeared willing to accept this suggestion, but Stresemann killed it by refusing to send his representative, Gaus, to any such conference.

Brown began to disparage the French. He cabled that they were trying to "wreck" the whole scheme, whereupon Levinson lectured him about being so cynical with France. "For years we tried to get some government in some way to make a proposal to outlaw war but without success, even in our own country. In some way Briand and even Leger got hold of the word 'outlawry' and used it,"[4] and all outlawrists, he warned, ought to be grateful to them regardless of their intentions. Goethe had said: "If you

---

[4] Levinson to Brown, May 8, 1928.

take a man to be better than he is, you make him better than he is." Léger and Briand were not as bad as Brown thought, and his attacks would make them worse. They were to be informed of Levinson's faith in France, of his high personal regard for Léger, of how he had been defending France against all attacks in this country, and how he wanted "to see France arm in arm with the United States and not dragged in by her hair."

Brown retorted in kind. He had seen Léger, and the French interpreted the whole affair as an attempt to wreck the League. The only Frenchman who seemed the least bit favorable was Léon Blum. They were going to insist at all hazards on a provision releasing signatories to any pact which might be signed from their obligations to a violator of the pact; the pact would have to be signed simultaneously, and prior alliances would have to be safeguarded above everything else. And as for taking men for better "than they are," it was his duty to report things as they were, there being no gain in writing only "what would please you." "You must remember," he insisted, "Leger is only a mouth-piece of a policy," and it was necessary "to realize the distinction one is bound to make between officials and their personal qualities." Neither the French public nor Léger, who was as "charming personally as ever" and "wanted to be remembered to you," understood outlawry. But he ended more optimistically by predicting that, although Great Britain would probably send a note pleasing to France, yet eventually, if Kellogg remained steadfast, Britain would side with the United States in forcing the French to "climb down." However, it would help a great deal if the Secretary of State would give some hint as to future co-operation with Europe.

In the United States peace opinion was pretty generally solidified in support of Kellogg. No longer was the indefatigable Chicago lawyer "considered something of an Ishmaelite" in League quarters; rather, as this movement grew, he found himself "as welcome as spring sunshine." Even Shotwell, Dewey wrote, "is entirely favorable," although the reflex reaction of Levinson was "But I don't believe it."[5] He reported to Kellogg: "All the peace

[5] Levinson to Brown, April 27, 1928.

groups in Chicago, especially including all the major League advocates, have been thoroughly converted to your treaty. . . . ."[6] And in Washington "my inside information is that everybody, from the President on, is 18K fine on Outlawry. Oh, the miracle of it!"[7] On Memorial Day Coolidge had some nice words to say for the current peace proposals in general and for the French in particular for originating them. After noting that this was already having a good effect, Levinson mused: "Isn't it interesting to remember back a year ago when I tried, oh so hard, to get the President to make the same kind of a speech on Decoration Day, 1927?"[8] And when things appeared to move a little slowly, he impatiently inquired: "With the President, Secretary Kellogg and Senator Borah all now in harmony, why don't they strike while the iron is hot?"[9] Apparently remembering his own difficulties with that trio, he felt that surely the rest of the world should move quickly when they all three started pulling in the same direction at the same time. And then an argument occurred to him to goad the European peace workers to greater effort. "One thing is sure—League sentiment is bankrupt in this country if the European nations defeat the Kellogg proposal."[10] It would mean "victory for the isolationists" for an "indefinite" period and "utter withdrawal" of "America from Europe for ten years."

He had some advice for those Europeans, like the French who, according to Brown, felt they were living beside a tiger which they had been prevented from destroying at Versailles—advice which had a strange sound coming from a man who had worked so closely with men like Borah and Reed and Hearst.

I still wonder whether you [i.e., the reader of the letter, Kenworthy, M.P.] thoroughly realize the opportunity that is afforded Europe and especially Britain to enlist the cooperation probably for all time of this great country against war. I am no maudlin super-patriot but I have every confidence that my country will answer the call of moral responsibility the same as she would a legal duty. We will not now nor in the future make military alliances in a time of

---

[6] Levinson to Kellogg, April 24, 1928.

[7] Levinson to Brown, April 27, 1928.

[8] Levinson to Brown, June 5, 1928.

[9] Levinson to Brown, June 1, 1928.

[10] Levinson to Brown, April 27, 1928.

peace. We will not make commitments in advance in unknown contingencies for the use of force. We will not permit an exotic body to tell us on which side to fight—pretentious as that may sound. But we would like a simple treaty with clear and unmistakable commitments to peace so that he who runs may read. I have no doubt of what we would do in a bald case of the violation of such a treaty. But international public opinion would beat us to it.[11]

The first state to reply to Kellogg's invitation of April 13 to sign an anti-war treaty was Germany, as has been noted earlier in the chapter. Mussolini gave a noncommittal reply for Italy on May 4. The only definite thing in his note was:

Your Excellency is aware of the fact that there is under consideration the proposal for a preliminary meeting of the legal experts of the powers whose direct interest in the proposed treaty has been enlisted. The Royal Government has adhered to this procedure, but has clearly pointed out that, in its opinion, such a meeting can only be effective if the participation of a legal expert of the Government of the United States is assured.[12]

Reiterated in the closing paragraph was "the lively desire of the Royal Government that the participation of the United States in the preliminary meeting mentioned above be not lacking."

Austen Chamberlain replied for Great Britain on May 19. He had compared the French and American draft treaties; and in the light of Kellogg's address to the American Society of International Law (which has been cited above) there appeared to be no serious divergence. The American draft contemplated no deprivation of the right of self-defense! The signatories would, of course, be released from their obligations as against a violator of the pact, though the inference was that some definite provision to this effect was desirable. The position of the British government in regard to prior obligations was "identical with that of the German Government as indicated in their note of the 27th April." But, though Kellogg had made his agreement with this attitude clear, His Majesty's government would prefer an inclusion of a specific mention of these previous obligations, as the French had suggested in their draft treaty. Then came the part of the note which set Levinson tearing his hair.

[11] Levinson to Kenworthy, June 5, 1928.

[12] *Treaty for the Renunciation of War*, Italy to the United States, May 4, 1928, p. 43.

The language of article 1, as to the renunciation of war as an instrument of national policy, renders it desirable that I should remind your Excellency that there are certain regions of the world the welfare and integrity of which constitute a special and vital interest for our peace and safety. His Majesty's Government have been at pains to make it clear in the past that interference with these regions cannot be suffered. Their protection against attack is to the British Empire a measure of self-defence. It must be clearly understood that His Majesty's Government in Great Britain accept the new treaty upon distinct understanding that it does not prejudice their freedom of action in this respect.[13]

As to the treaty's being as nearly universal as practicable there was agreement; however, "it would be embarrassing if certain States in Europe with whom the proposed participants are already in close treaty relations were not included among the parties." The proposed Pact was one which concerned the Dominions and India as well as His Majesty's government in Great Britain; they would no doubt accept an invitation to adhere. Consequently, His Majesty's government "will gladly co-operate in the conclusion of such a pact as is proposed and are ready to engage with the interested Governments in the negotiations which are necessary for the purpose."

The hint to invite the Dominions to sign was acted upon within three days. On May 22 notes for this purpose were given to ministers in Canada and the Irish Free State, and to Austen Chamberlain for transmission to Australia, New Zealand, the Union of South Africa, and India.

The Japanese reply of May 26 included a reference to self-defense, the obligations under the Covenant of the League, and the Locarno treaties. The imperial government "would be happy to collaborate with cordial good will in the discussions with the purpose of securing what they are persuaded is the common desire of all the peoples of the world—namely, the cessation of wars and the definite establishment among the nations of an era of permanent and universal peace."

It will be instructive to see Levinson's reactions to some features of the replies of the powers to Kellogg's invitation to adhere to the outlawry treaty. He spent several hours with Borah before Kel-

[13] *Ibid.*, British note to the United States, May 19, 1928, p. 45.

logg's subsequent note went out—a note for the preparation of which the Senator had been called to Washington.

All four of the powers had implied that they wanted a conference of some kind to draw up the treaty. This was the very thing for which Levinson had been working for three-quarters of a year. He had written to Dewey early in April:

> I have struggled, as you know, and am still struggling, to get an international conference at which all of these burning questions, reparations, debts, revision of the treaty of Versailles, world peace, will be considered together.
>
> One of the great subjects I have had in mind is to use the various leverages of economic adjustment for the purpose of securing at least that minimum of concessions from the hard provisions of the Paris treaty so necessary to permanent good will among the late belligerents. And yet, we cannot and dare not halt the acceptance of the great Outlawry proposal which the people have the opportunity to compel.[14]

He wanted such a conference held in Washington, for it would "suit the American people if they can see what is being done instead of feeling that our representatives have been buncoed in Europe." However, as indicated in his letter to Dewey, he was beginning to cool toward the idea of a conference. There were two reasons. In the first place, there was talk of the need for the experts to define terms, and he was against any definitions. Let the parties sign first and define to their hearts' content later was his order to Brown. "Ultimately we must have a code and the code can contain all the distinctions and niceties of legal protection that human ingenuity and expert voluminousness can command." In the second place, he did not want anything to divert public attention from the simple outlawry treaty, which was bound to go through if it could be kept in the center of the stage with all eyes focused on it. A conference before the 1928 election would most certainly, he thought, stimulate demagoguery and divert attention.

With regard to self-defense, Levinson did not believe any mention need be made of it in the treaty, since he had been contending for years that it was an inherent and inalienable right. On similar grounds he maintained that any breach of an outlawry

[14] Levinson to Dewey, April 7, 1928.

treaty would necessarily release the other signatories from their obligations as against the power committing the breach. He held this to be a principle of law which was as valid in international law as it had always been in municipal, and the statement of this view in "the Borah article" of February 5, 1928, was of his contribution. Viscount Grey had agreed that neither self-defense nor release as against an aggressor needed specific mention in a treaty but that, if the powers so desired, both points could be safeguarded by an exchange of notes. Levinson thought this suggestion "the best thing yet," and he began to urge it with Borah. "All that is necessary to safe-guard self-defense," he advised the Senator, "is an exchange of notes"—notes that should call the attention of the world to the fact that, according to the legal principles of every civilized country, "a breach of the Outlawry treaty would release the other signatories from their obligations as to the treaty-breaking signatories."[15] But he also agreed with a statement attributed to Briand, which appeared in the *New York Times* of May 6, that the release provision might be included in the preamble to the treaty. After spending a week end in Washington and seeing a good deal of Borah, who had come to Chicago on another week end, to speak on the future of the Republican party, he predicted to Harrison Brown: "It looks more and more as if the explanatory safe-guards will be put in the preamble of the Kellogg treaty."[16] As to making the treaty universal, he was, by May, 1928, 100 per cent plus in favor of it. He was glad to see the British Dominions invited to sign; he thought it would be wise if other countries were also invited to adhere among the original signers to avoid any appearance of Anglo-Saxon favoritism.

It was, however, the British reference "to certain regions of the world" which "constitute[d] a special and vital interest" for the welfare of the Empire that caught his attention above all else in the four replies and set him on the trail of the unspeakable Tories. The British note bore the date of May 19. Under date of May 21 a letter to Borah contained this paragraph:

[15] Levinson to Borah, May 23, 1928.
[16] Levinson to Brown, May 31, 1928.

Let me add a word about the paper I left with you yesterday. I fully agree that the obscure and indefinite British condition should be rejected, but if Britain insists upon conditions then I think this paper will be a good antidote. In other words, if conditions are to be added, clauses, reservations, or what not, then Great Britain will get what you think she doesn't want. She may then prefer to do what her people will make her do anyway—accept the proposal unconditionally.[17]

The right of self-defense covered the British regions of "vital interest," but he feared this was an opening for a reservation. If that was what the British government had in mind, he warned Harrison Brown that they were playing with dynamite in American public opinion. If they added any reservations at all, "God help [the treaty] when it gets to the Senate." And then he may have given some inkling as to what was in the paper he left with Borah when he added: "If Great Britain is smart she will not start anything because we will attach reservations that will make Chamberlain and his ilk squirm and writhe."[18] However, while he urged Brown and every other person who had any influence in England to stop any movement toward reservations, he became disturbed over the effect of such reservations on his former bedfellows. "A simple treaty" would "go right through for a touchdown," but "once make an opening for reservations," he admonished Brown, "and the old guns of isolationism, of distrust, of foreign suspicion and revived partisanism will make havoc of the treaty itself."[19]

But in the latter part of May and the early part of June, 1928, his real wrath was diverted from the Tories and concentrated on the first man whose nomination for the presidency was due, it was being asserted, to successful "publicity bally-hoo," Herbert Hoover. It would be time enough to turn his attention to the Tories again after they had written another note and after he had attended the convention in Kansas City where he thought a man "too close to knowledge of Teapot Dome"[20] was being "steam rollered through by the worst methods including those of 1912."[21]

[17] Levinson to Borah, May 21, 1928.

[18] Levinson to Brown, May 28, 1928.   [20] Levinson to Borah, June 27, 1928.

[19] *Ibid.*   [21] Levinson to Glenn, June 8, 1928.

While the fact may be of interest that his estimate of Mr. Hoover—afterward so greatly changed—until about July 1, 1928, was as low as that of the American majority in 1932, for the purpose of this study his close contact with Borah during this period and especially his trip from Kansas City to Chicago with the Senator is more relevant.

Levinson's own summary of his visit to Borah appeared in a letter to Brown:

. . . . I saw a lot of him and he and I came back to Chicago on the same train and in the same drawing room. We had a wonderful time together and he is as enthusiastic about Outlawry as you or I, which is saying much. He told me in confidence that he was called back to Washington by Secretary Kellogg to frame the reply and jokingly said "as you want it." I hope this is so because, as I told Borah, we ought to adopt Briand's suggestion if it is humanly possible to do it and give France the victory, and especially because it is exactly what I want and it is in strict accord with the idea that you know I originated because I sent you an advance copy before it was incorporated into Borah's article of February 5 in the New York *Times*. It is wonderful how that simple idea has carried all through. The release of other signatories on a breach by one is strictly analogous to familiar legal doctrine in almost every civilized country. Besides it both aligns itself with common sense and will be an inevitable result anyway. Thus is swallowed up this whole mixed problem of the right of self-defense. That is a grand side-stepping and solution. . . . .

In deep confidence, Howard [Sir Esme] gave his assurance of an unconditional acceptance.[22]

It is difficult to know just how much Borah was influenced by Levinson or, indeed, how much the Senator influenced Kellogg. As to the Levinson influence, there is no doubt that his ideas on the negotiations were poured into the ear of the Senator during their more than usual number of meetings during May and early June, and many of the ideas which Levinson held appeared later in official form. If one were to make a generalization, perhaps the Chicago lawyer's influence over the chairman of the Senate Foreign Relations Committee resembled the pull of the sun in determining the slant of a leaf rather than the act of the florist in changing the position of a plant. For the most part, with the exception of the *New York Times* article of February 5, 1928, the

[22] Levinson to Brown, June 18, 1928.

Senator took from the father of outlawry as the bee takes from the flower, transforming the borrowed juices into something of its own, rather than as the ant takes the grain of wheat, storing it up as wheat. On the other hand, it seems probable that the Secretary of State more nearly resembled the ant in his relation with the Senator.

Borah, according to Levinson, would oppose any distinctions, additions, or reservations to the treaty. He might be willing for some explanatory matter to be put into the preamble, but that was the extreme limit to which the Senator could be budged. Kellogg would probably take the same line as Borah, but it was not certain. When the Senator was called back to Washington to help with the note of June 23, the fears as to Kellogg's sticking qualities were justified, for, according to Raymond Robins, who was with the Senator immediately after the conference with the Secretary: "He [Borah] had a real battle to preserve the integrity of the Kellogg proposal. But he thinks he has won that battle for keeps now. More details when we meet."[23] Borah's statement of the same date as that of the note with regard to this conference corroborates the second part of Robin's report.

I believe it [the treaty] will go through practically as proposed. Indeed, I am sure there will be no change in the treaty itself. There may be an expression in the preamble to satisfy the situation in regard to one particular matter. But the treaty as a treaty will stand in my opinion and will be accepted.[24]

On June 23 Kellogg's rejoinder was delivered at the respective Foreign Offices of Belgium, Czechoslovakia, France, Germany, Great Britain, Irish Free State, Italy, Japan, and Poland. With regard to self-defense, the obligations imposed by prior treaties, the relations with a treaty-breaking state, and universality of the treaty, he simply quoted relevant parts of his address to the American Society of International Law. As to the signers of the Locarno treaties, he was inviting each of them to be among the original signatories of the proposed treaty. Provision was made in the preamble for this. He was also willing for all the parties to the neutrality treaties to be original signers. However, he thought they could be invited to adhere later, thus expediting matters.

[23] Robins to Levinson, June 24, 1928.   [24] Borah to Levinson, June 23, 1928.

He proposed to change the preamble so as to recognize the principle "that if a state resorts to war in violation of the treaty, the other contracting parties are released from their obligations under the treaty to that state." The clause as amended was: "Convinced that all changes in their relations with one another should be sought only by pacific means and be the result of a peaceful and orderly process, and that any signatory Power which shall hereafter seek to promote its national interest by resort to war should be denied the benefits furnished by this treaty. . . . ."[25] In view of his explanations and the changes proposed, the objections, he felt, were cleared away. He closed by stating that his government was then ready to sign this treaty and by expressing the "fervent hope" that the other governments to which the note was addressed would be willing immediately to sign also. It will be noted that the one thing which all four of the powers had mentioned, namely, the meeting of experts to agree on the exact wording of the treaty was sidestepped entirely.

Poland and Germany were the first to accept the draft treaty.[26] France, the Irish Free State, Italy, Canada, Belgium, Great Britain, Czechoslovakia, and Japan followed in the order named, the last notes being dated July 20.

In these notes of acceptance, there are five matters deserving of special comment. (1) Most of the states expressed their understanding that the new treaty in no way deprived them of the right of self-defense or changed their obligations under the Locarno agreements or the Covenant of the League and that all signatories would be released as against a state breaking the Pact. Those not making any specific reference to these points were Germany, Canada, India, New Zealand, and Japan. (2) Frequent reference with approval was made to the fact that the treaty was

[25] *Treaty for the Renunciation of War*, note of the government of the United States to the governments of Belgium, Czechoslovakia, France, Germany, Great Britain, Irish Free State, Italy, Japan, and Poland, delivered at the respective Foreign Offices, June 23, 1928, p. 56, and at p. 60.

[26] The note of Poland was dated July 8, 1928, but it was not presented to the American minister until July 17, whereas the German acceptance was put in the hands of the American ambassador on July 11, so that actually Germany was the first to reply (*ibid.*, pp. 63 and 65).

originally open to all parties to the Locarno agreements and that it was to be subsequently open to universal adherence. (3) France and Czechoslovakia appeared to underline the word "national" in the phrase "renunciation of war as an instrument of national policy." Observe the emphasis in the French note:

> First of all it follows from the new preamble that the proposed treaty indeed aims at the perpetuation of the pacific and friendly relations under the contractual conditions in which they are to-day established between the interested nations; that it is essentially a question for the signatory powers of renouncing war "as an instrument of their national policy," and also that the signatory power which hereafter might seek to promote its own national interests by itself resorting to war, should be denied the benefits of the treaty.[27]

In the note from Czechoslovakia this statement appeared: "By their signature, the contracting parties will renounce war as an instrument of their national policy aimed to satisfy their selfish interests."[28] (4) The Germans used the phrase "Aechtung des Krieges" as descriptive of the proposed Pact. The official English translation of this phrase for the note of April 27, 1928, was "outlawry of war."[29] But the translation for the note of July 11 was "renunciation of war."[30] According to common German usage and all the German dictionaries that I have been able to consult, "to outlaw" is the proper translation of the word *aechten*. It is probable that the translation, "renunciation of war," was used for the second note because it was the phrase which was most often employed officially to describe the new treaty. (5) Austen Chamberlain again emphasized the "vital interest" of Great Britain in certain regions and the conditions this imposed on her acceptance of the treaty. He said:

> As regards the passage in my note of the 19th May relating to certain regions of which the welfare and integrity constitute a special and vital interest for our peace and safety, I need only repeat that His Majesty's Government in Great Britain accept the new treaty upon the understanding that it does not prejudice their freedom of action in this respect.[31]

27 *Ibid.*, French note to the United States, July 14, 1928, p. 68.
28 *Ibid.*, Czechoslovakian note to the United States, July 20, 1928, p. 79.
29 *Ibid.*, German note to the United States, April 27, 1928, pp. 38 ff.
30 *Ibid.*, German note to the United States, July 11, 1928, pp. 65 f.
31 *Ibid.*, British note to the United States, July 18, 1928, p. 73.

Immediately on seeing the British note, Levinson telegraphed Kellogg:

Amazed at Britain's pseudo and indefinite Monroe Doctrine reservation which is not supported even by her own dominions. This destroys simplicity and openness of your fundamental proposal and if retained will certainly either block its passage through the Senate or stimulate that body to weight your Treaty down with emasculating reservations. Am confident that continued refusal by you to barter away international salvation for a box of Pandora will quickly bring withdrawal or political revolution in England. That the fatal blow should come from Britain cannot be the final result. Your handling of negotiations has been a series of beneficent triumphs which must not be nullified now.[32]

A similar telegram was also sent to Borah. The Senator reassured him in a telegram as follows:

I had thorough understanding with Secretary before leaving Washington about this matter. Feel sure there is no danger of his modifying his position. Had a message from him today which indicates that fact. Am keeping in touch with the situation.[33]

To which Levinson telegraphed this sigh of relief: "Deeply relieved and grateful. Hold the fort."[34] Kellogg replied to Levinson's telegram with his interpretation of the British note:

I note your telegram about the so-called indefinite Monroe Doctrine reservations proposed by British. I have not been asked by them to make any reservations in the treaty and am not going to make any reservations in the treaty at all and the British notes are only unilateral declarations.

I am enclosing you a copy of the correspondence down to and including my note of June twenty-third. You will see on page 25, sub-division 10 of the original British note that Great Britain claims that there are certain regions which constitute especial and vital interests of the British Empire, the protection of which is necessary to her self-defense and in the last note she refers to this one and uses substantially the same language. Great Britain does not ask us to change the treaty or to make any specific declaration to her note asking that the United States agrees to this principle. Like the Monroe Doctrine, it is simply a matter of self-defense. If the United States has any special interests, such as we have in Panama, of course we have a right to defend them. In any event, the Monroe Doctrine has been from its inception a matter of self-defense in this country, and

[32] Levinson to Kellogg, July 21, 1928.
[33] Borah to Levinson, July 21, 1928.
[34] Levinson to Borah, July 23, 1928.

I do not think it is necessary for us to pay any attention to this discussion or any of the other discussions which appear in the various notes since they call for no change in the simplicity of the treaty itself.[35]

But Levinson refused to be comforted so easily by these reassurances from Borah and Kellogg. In the meantime, Brown had learned from Gaus, the German government's legal expert, that the British and French had been planning to send some kind of separate document along with their notes of acceptance, which he thought would have sabotaged the Pact completely. Their legal experts, however, Hurst and Fromageot, had had a conference with Gaus, who understood outlawry better, thanks to his contacts with Levinson in May, 1927, and Gaus had persuaded them to give up the separate protocol idea. This information convinced Levinson that the British were preparing the way for reservations. His fear was increased when Brown cabled him from Stockholm:

Notes are contrary to all expectations [as] Europe understands Austen retains war instrument [for] imperialism since defense covers other interpretations stop essential we obtain your press criticism then universal revolt against Tory manoeuvers practically certain stop reservations are further criticized as making Pact weaken Covenant.[36]

In Levinson's book of strategy the best defense was always offense. The way to keep the British from actually going further in regard to a reservation was to bring every possible pressure to get them to withdraw the statement with respect to "vital interests" in unspecified regions. He telegraphed the Brown cable to Borah and wrote a letter to Kellogg pointing out how Chamberlain was "slipping one over on" him by reviving the "dangerous and subtle phrase 'of national honor and vital interest,' " which the Secretary had been able to eliminate from the "renewed Root arbitration treaties"; he then went on to frighten the nervous Secretary by telling him the *Chicago Tribune* was "fiendishly looking for your scalp," and, unless "you will be able to prevail upon the British authorities to withdraw this condition," difficulties could be expected in the Senate, where Swanson was already

[35] Kellogg to Levinson, July 23, 1928.
[36] Brown to Levinson, July 26, 1928.

threatening trouble and a "Jim Reed" could be expected to deliver a philippic on a "British Monroe Doctrine."[37] On the same day that he wrote to Kellogg he sent cablegrams to Brown and Philip Kerr. Brown was urged to go to England at once to try to get the "vital interest" condition either removed entirely or some other phrase substituted, so that there could be no doubt that the right of self-defense covered the whole matter. This was emphasized to Kerr, and both were warned that the British were subjecting the treaty to great risk in the United States Senate, either in the way of reservation or in the way of outright defeat. This done, he soliloquized to Borah, "I presume I ought not to get so worked up in summer on this proposition," but the negotiations had been handled so superbly from the American end "that it particularly pained me to have the damned old Tories dictating to us in any way."[38]

While Borah was not so visibly perturbed, yet, knowing the Senate as he did, he recognized that the treaty might be in for heavy seas when that body began to consider giving its "advice and consent." Consequently, he took two steps to hold his colleagues in check. He asked Raymond Robins to be thinking

how we can best get [the treaty] into the campaign in those states where Senators are to be elected. I think it ought to be accentuated.

It is very clear to my mind that the opposition to this treaty is not because they are afraid it is not effective but because they are afraid it will be effective. The opposition is coming from the militarists, from those who scoff at the idea that we can get along in this world without the institution of war. We can afford to meet them on the issue as they have presented it. But it ought to be met as much as possible before the people in the coming election.[39]

The other step was to take away the chief objection which he surmised the enemies of the treaty could urge against it. He wrote to Secretary Kellogg:

If I understand correctly the opposition in certain quarters, it would be based upon a desire to fully protect the Monroe Doctrine. My own opinion is that the Monroe Doctrine is in no wise embarrassed by the Treaty. But it seems

[37] Levinson to Kellogg, July 28, 1928.
[38] Levinson to Borah, July 30, 1928.
[39] Borah to Robins, July 25, 1928.

to me if the South American Countries . . . . should adhere to the treaty, the basic objections, even according to the viewpoint of the objectors relative to the Monroe Doctrine, would be removed. I have no doubt the South American Countries would be glad to adhere. And if after the signing of the treaty at Paris a move were made to bring these countries in, in my opinion, it would practically remove all possible objection. I submit this for your consideration. I am anxious to speed the ratification and it is in the interest of time that the suggestion is made.[40]

However, the Senator could not share Levinson's fear of the effect of the British "vital interest" statement on the treaty. His interpretation of the legal effect of that statement as well as of what he called the other "side remarks" which were being made is contained in a letter to Levinson of August 2, 1928.

Levinson, I may be extremely obtuse, but I am unable to understand how talks and suggestions on the side can have the slightest effect upon the terms of the treaty as it will be signed. The treaty speaks in plain terms for itself. And if some official passing over the stage at a particular hour makes a comment as to what he understands it to mean, especially if that comment is made for home consumption, I do not understand it has any effect whatever upon the plain terms of the treaty. The only way the treaty could be affected would be by an exchange of notes made at the same time or by an additional or contemporaneous agreement. . . . .

I had a letter yesterday from Professor Borchard in which he seemed to think that these statements made by the British Government and by France would have the same effect upon the treaty as if they were reservations to the treaty. If there is any such doctrine or principle as that, the treaty would not be worth a damn. Any Government could change it by stating how it understood it to be. There will be no reservations attached and there will be no construction of theirs accepted. The only thing involved in this is the standing of these governments with their own people.

For myself, I do not propose to proceed in the debate upon this subject upon the proposition that this treaty is in the slightest affected by these side remarks.[41]

Philip Kerr agreed that the "vital interest" statement in the British notes was unfortunate, and he tried to get Lloyd George to clear it up in so far as a member of "His Majesty's opposition" could clear up a matter of that kind, "for if it gets off on a wrong start it may produce endless trouble." The relevant parts of this letter dealing with the "vital interest" statement, Kellogg's use of

[40] Borah to Kellogg, July 28 1928.

[41] Borah to Levinson, August 2, 1928.

the term, "self-defense," and the effect of the Pact on the Covenant of the League are as follows:

I am not sure, however, that the situation is as serious as you think it is, if you study carefully the text both of Sir Austen Chamberlain's and Mr. Kellogg's remarks. . . . . To my mind the essential thing is to fasten on the words "interference" and "attack" [in Chamberlain's statement] and to pin the British Government down to them. If by this reservation Chamberlain means that he wants to make it clear that, if any other power tries to interfere with the Suez Canal or any of the other territories for whose good government we are still responsible or attacks them, the British Government has the right to use force to repel such interference or attack, there is no particular harm in the interpretation, because such interpretation is implicit in the Pact itself. If, on the other hand, he means that the British Government reserves the right to use war as an instrument of its national policy in order to promote or expand or to defend its special interests in these regions, then the Kellogg Pact is completely nullified. I have talked the matter over fully with some members of the Cabinet though not with Chamberlain, and in my view Chamberlain's meaning is the first and innocuous meaning, though it requires to be made clear. . . . .

If the essential interpretation of . . . . [his remarks on self-defense] is based upon the words "to defend its territories from attack or invasion" Kellogg's remarks are harmless. If, on the other hand, Mr. Kellogg means what all nations in the past have meant by self-defense, namely, the right to take forcible action against your neighbour because you are frightened that he is going to take action which will damage your vital interests, then Mr. Kellogg's remarks nullify Mr. Kellogg's Pact. Personally, I believe that Mr. Kellogg's interpretation like Sir Austen Chamberlain's is the first. But that also requires to be cleared up.

Harrison Brown has probably already told you that the League of Nations crowd are much upset because they think that Mr. Kellogg's interpretation, echoed by Sir Austen Chamberlain, has weakened the Covenant of the League, because it appears to restore to the nations the right to use force in self-defense, which they have promised under the Covenant not to do without first allowing nine months' delay for the mediatory and pacific offices of the League, World Court or arbitral procedure.

My own view is that the proper procedure to-day is not to make too great a row about these interpretative remarks made by Briand, Austen Chamberlain and Kellogg, provided they are not embodied in the text of the treaty. . . . .[42]

Brown had reported that in some respects the new treaty did weaken the Covenant. His emphasis was different, however, from Kerr's, who saw the states slipping out of the obligation to wait nine months before taking up arms. Brown said the Cove-

[42] Kerr to Levinson, July 30, 1928.

nant did "at least make an effort to prevent nations using their own 'judgment' as to when a war of 'self-defense' shall be proclaimed, and of course there is nothing at all in the Covenant which could be interpreted as a cover for British imperialism."[43]

As Brown made his rounds in London, trying to impress persons of influence that something should be done about the "vital interest" statement in the first British note, he found an "oasis of brilliance in a desert of imbecility." Ambassador Houghton and Mr. Atherton at the American embassy really seemed interested. Once they appeared on the verge of making a little progress with Chamberlain; but something happened; he thought another American was getting tips from Washington and going over Houghton's head.

When he returned to London for the last days of July, he was joined by Charles Clayton Morrison in the attack on the "vital interest" statement. Morrison went to the British Foreign Office to see Chamberlain. But the foreign secretary was ill and unable to see him, so the editor drew up a memorandum which, according to his cablegram to Levinson, reached the Premier on August 2. In it the dangers to the new treaty in the way of emasculating reservations in the American Senate were emphasized unless the "vital interest" conditions were made to fit under the self-defense umbrella. But when he and Brown began to apply pressure on "vital interest," they were met everywhere with the argument that Kellogg had reserved the Monroe Doctrine. This they vehemently denied. They sent pages of cablegrams to Levinson pleading for some official denial of any Monroe Doctrine reservation. But Levinson wanted neither Borah nor Kellogg to make any such statement. "Why," he cabled, "should Britain risk forcing inclusion of doctrine when she now has advantage of omission." The whole tenor of his page-long cable was, Why can't the unspeakable Tories be reasonable and make concessions to suit the fancy of the unreasonable Senate and the irrational *Chicago Tribune?*

Harrison Brown found a smaller but, by reason of contrast, a more brilliant "oasis" in the person of Sir Arthur Willert in the

[43] Brown to Levinson, July 27, 1928.

British Foreign Office. Sir Arthur was "very sympathetic." The "British course was one of extreme honesty"; however, he was impressed with Borah's fear that the Senate might get out of hand. He was a close friend of the Senator's, and Brown suggested that he might get into direct contact with him to get his mind put at rest with regard to the Monroe Doctrine reservation. He doubted the propriety of this but would pass on "all I said to the American Department." He was impressed with the information Brown had picked up in his recent European journey to the effect that Chamberlain would probably be in for some criticism at Geneva at the hands of the small nations. He indicated that a speech by someone might be feasible if it really became necessary, but the moment was not ripe yet. A few days later Brown saw Sir Arthur again, who said that perhaps some satisfaction could be given with regard to bringing the "vital interest" condition within the self-defense interpretation. However, no developments became visible, and Brown grew bitter in his letters as he told of his interviews at the British Foreign Office. Willert had gone away, presumably for a vacation, and the man Norton, whom he saw in Willert's place, said the "vital interest" statement was not a reservation but a caveat. It was an explanation; it would be too bad, he opined, if the Senate killed the treaty, but then the blame would be all on the Senate; the only cure for the caveat was universal signature of the treaty. It made no difference to him, the enraged Brown fulminated, if America did change her course as a result and became a world menace. "In the long run both the American people and the European peoples would be the bled victims of these damned old men—more fools they for not being more enlightened and more clamorously anti-war!"

That the text of the treaty alone would be signed was the only ray of hope coming from the gloomy inkpot of Harrison Brown in answer to Levinson's insistent cables that the "vital interest" statement be watered down—cables which kept going forward until within a few days of the actual signing of the pact. Brown had an "important conference with Gaus," who agreed that this was true; however, he "deplored the reservations" and "was appalled when I told him that Borah was really concerned about the Senate prospects and begged us to do all possible to avoid such a catastrophe as non-ratification would be." The important thing to watch, according to the German legal expert, was

the protocol signature, that is the verbal display which habitually accompanies the actual text of treaties setting forth the objects.

If there is no mention of the reservations therein there will be no juridical or other serious grounds for the Senate to take the reservations into consideration. I immediately cabled Morrison in Paris suggesting that he should try to see the Washington functionary who is arranging the details with the French expert Fromageot and do his utmost to warn him about this point.[44]

There were two other matters upon which Harrison Brown had a good deal to say in his reports as a result of his contacts with persons at the British Foreign Office and elsewhere just before the signing of the treaty.

The first was in regard to getting an invitation sent to Russia to adhere to the new treaty. He had raised this question as early as April, when he inquired of Levinson if the enthusiasm for the Kellogg proposal on the part of the Tories might not be due to the omission of an invitation to the Soviets to be among the original signers. But in August he first wrote, and then cabled, with great urgency. If Russia would sign, it was a "monstrous stupidity" to withhold the invitation. It was dangerous to treat that state as one of the minor ones, for such action might arouse the "prestige" issue. Edgar Mowrer felt that the Soviets were already a little "sore" that they were not in on the "ground floor." It would be well for a Russian observer to be invited to be present at the signing ceremony in Paris where he could receive verbal explanations. Finally, Levinson was stirred to action, and he began to send telegrams to Borah. Unfortunately, all but the last two of these telegrams appear to be missing from the files. However, those which were found tell their own story. This counsel to make haste slowly came from the Senator on August 13: "Rome was not built in a day. Continue to pray incessantly." Whereupon the up-and-doing lawyer retorted immediately: "But

[44] Brown to Levinson, August 23, 1928.

Rome was burned in one day while Nero fiddled. However, I adopt your hint of patience."[45]

The second issue which Harrison Brown raised was the matter of next steps. What did Levinson and the United States propose to do after the treaty was signed? It has been indicated above that Levinson felt that if the Pact were signed universally in good faith, United States' action against a mad-dog nation could be counted on. However, he did not want it talked about publicly, nor did he want the United States to be legally bound in advance to take any such course. Brown wanted Kellogg to make some public statement as to what he intended to do. Although Levinson was "planning all sorts of things to be done after the treaty" was signed, he thought "it would be a mistake to have Kellogg or anyone else make a pronouncement about what is going to be done afterwards or what instrumentalities are going to be used. That is along the Shotwell line," which meant that the League and the "European instruments and treaties and pet methods" were to be preserved. "The way to preserve them is to say nothing about them now."[46]

Briefly, Levinson contemplated three next steps. (1) August 27 "should by common consent become the great holiday of the world, celebrated in common by all peoples as a festival of Peace —the day of deliverance from the slavery of war. Thus shall peace become the power of the governed, as hitherto war has been traditionally the power of the governors."[47] (2) The League of Nations "should by resolution announce to the listening world its acceptance and adoption of the Treaty renouncing and outlawing war. . . . ."[48] "The day a strong, unconditional outlawry resolution is adopted by the Assembly will mark the apotheosis of the League."[49] (3) International law should be codified.

[45] On August 27 a note was transmitted through the French ambassador at Moscow to Litvinoff. Litvinoff's answer on August 31, accepting the invitation to adhere for his government, is a classic of searing sarcasm couched in diplomatic language (*Treaty for the Renunciation of War*, pp. 259 ff.).

[46] Levinson to Brown, June 18, 1928.

[47] Levinson to Mrs. R. R. Stephens, executive secretary, Chicago Council on Foreign Relations, August 24, 1928.

[48] *Ibid.*   [49] Levinson to Eichelberger, August 8, 1928.

With war ruled out, the making of a code becomes greatly simplified. Almost every reasonable question, doubt, difficulty that has been raised could be covered and safeguarded by the code. And of course the international courts must be equipped with affirmative jurisdiction in their own sphere of action, so that they are not dependent as now on securing consent of the disputants for its exercise.[50]

As the time came near for the signing of the treaty, Levinson began to receive recognition from many quarters. Although no man is a hero to his valet, he was to his secretary, Mrs. F. B. Kelly. She wrote this tribute to him on the signing of the Pact of Paris.

It seems almost unbelievable that your dream of long-ago yesterday has been realized. I was afraid to hope, in spite of the speed with which things have been moving since your visit to Europe, lest something would happen to shatter the dream and dim the hope. It has been a privilege to have been associated in even a lowly capacity with the brilliant "father of outlawry." . . . . The only fly in the ointment is that you, who have given so much of yourself, your time and energy to the cause, should not receive proper recognition. Of course I know how you feel about it yourself—rather to be unnoticed than to have Outlawry lost. . . . .

I know Mrs. Levinson must be gloriously proud. It brings a lump to one's throat to contemplate what it all means.

My unstinted admiration to a really great man—one of God's noblemen.[51]

Benjamin V. Becker, his partner for more than thirty years, joined in the praise; Mr. Becker quietly started the drive to get the Nobel Peace Prize for him—quietly, because he expected Levinson to object to public activity for fear of injuring the treaty before it was signed. Business friends like Mr. August Gatzert and Mr. Marshal Solberg began to bring his activities to the attention of the Prize committee, the former by getting letters written to the committee, the latter by seeing the members in person while on a visit in Norway. Ambassador Claudel telegraphed him: "I know what great part you had in the working out of the idea of outlawry of war and it is just that you share the honor as well as the joy of the present success."[52] Borah wrote, "You will take your place yet along the side of the Hebrew prophets."[53]

[50] Levinson to Mrs. Stephens.
[51] Mrs. F. B. Kelly to Levinson, August 28, 1928.
[52] Claudel to Levinson, June 20, 1928.   [53] Borah to Levinson, July 19, 1928.

THE STATES AND THE MULTILATERAL TREATY

On August 27, 1928, the representatives of fifteen governments gathered in Paris to sign the Treaty for the Renunciation of War, which action, according to Levinson, would probably mark that day as a holiday that "not even Christmas, unrecognized by hundreds of millions, [could] compete with in universality of appeal and application," for this treaty would most likely "divide history into two parts—the reign of war, and the reign of peace." These words of the "prophet Levinson" as well as the spirit of his gospel, the combination of legality and morality, were echoed by Aristide Briand as he welcomed the assembled plenipotentiaries. He said:

To-day's event marks a new date in the history of mankind. . . . . war is at last legally stripped of what constituted its most serious danger: its legitimacy. Henceforth branded with illegality, it is by common accord actually outlawed [*mise hors la loi*], so that the guilty nation would incur the certain repudiation and the probable enmity of all its cosignatories. It is the institution itself of war which is thus directly attacked in its very essence. It is no longer merely a question of defensive organization against the scourge but of attacking the evil at its very root.

Thus the legitimacy of recourse to warfare, as an arbitrary and selfish means of action, shall cease to exert its latent menace against the economic, political, and social life of the peoples and to make all real independence for small nations in international discussions illusory. Freed from such bondage, the nations that have signed the new contract will gradually abandon the habit of associating the idea of national prestige and national interest with the idea of force. And this single psychological fact will not be the smallest gain in the evolution that is needed to lead to a real stabilization of peace.

It may be objected that this pact is not practicable; that it lacks sanctions. But does true practicability consist in excluding from the realm of facts the moral forces, amongst which is that of public opinion?[54]

[54] *Treaty for the Renunciation of War*, pp. 313–14. For the treaty complete, see Appen. F. Dr. Charles Clayton Morrison, who witnessed the ceremony of signature, sent the following cablegram, according to Mrs. Levinson, to her husband: "With my own eyes, I have today seen your dream come true."

CHAPTER XVIII

THE RATIFICATION OF THE PACT AND AFTER

I T WAS not long after Mr. Hoover had been "steam rollered" through the convention at Kansas City before Levinson recanted his first, hasty opinion and recognized him as a great "progressive and humanitarian statesman" who, he was sure, would in his desire to "abolish poverty" produce "some great propositions" with regard to "unemployment and depressions." On the other hand, the pronouncement in Smith's speech of acceptance on international affairs he described as "the worst I have ever seen. I hope he didn't write it himself, for if so, he is hopelessly confused." Taking the speech as the occasion, he had exclaimed in a letter to Irving Fisher: "It is almost incredible that the hope of world peace is now in the hands of the republicans."[1] The first object in the battle for the ratification of the Pact of Paris was, therefore, to secure the election of the great engineer.

In addition to the fact that he was himself a staunch Republican, Levinson had two main reasons for wanting Hoover elected. First, in spite of Hoover's having failed to give what he considered a satisfactory indorsement of the Pact of Paris, he felt it would fare better with him as president because it had been negotiated and signed under Republican auspices. The Republican platform contained an indorsement of the outlawry of war, the first indorsement in any platform which had been satisfactory to Levinson. Borah had given Mrs. Levinson his official convention badge in honor of this event. With Smith as president, Levinson feared the natural Democratic revenge for Republican defeat of the League of Nations. He thought there was evidence in Smith's speeches of lack of enthusiasm for the treaty, though it must be added that from the same speeches Professor Dewey had come to the opposite conclusion. However, Dewey did agree that the

[1] Levinson to Fisher, September 10, 1928.

[314]

Democrats might have a retaliatory spirit as a result of the sort of campaign the Republicans were carrying on. Other evidence of Democratic opposition was a letter which Mrs. Quincy Wright had received from Mr. Henry Morgenthau, in which the former ambassador had stated that he was postponing his speechmaking tour against the Pact of Paris until after the election. The reason for the postponement, however, was a request of the Democratic National Committee. In addition to all this, Levinson had

> very great misgivings when I consider that the greatest influence on Smith and his closest associates comes from the people who have an extreme complex against Great Britain, to wit, the Irish Catholics. I have many friends among these people, but I remember from the old League fight how they felt then and I know how they feel now.[2]

They would be a brake on the Senate when it came to approving a treaty which outlawed war with Great Britain.

The second reason for favoring Hoover was Borah's enthusiasm for him. Robins had found Borah much pleased with the Republican nominee and well satisfied with his own position in the campaign plans. The Senator regarded the unconditional ratification of the treaty as dependent on Hoover's election. He was somewhat taken aback that the indorsement of the Pact and the outlawry idea was so feeble in the acceptance speech, but he was able to think of extenuating circumstances. However, one gathers the impression from the correspondence during the campaign that the Senator's love for Hoover arose from his greater abhorrence of Smith, whose acceptance speech in particular he regarded as "fraudulent and crassly partisan."

Levinson's feeling for Hoover became so strong that it led him into verbal clashes with some of his best friends. He simply could not understand how the Rev. Mr. Oggel—a good Presbyterian and a "dry," a man who placed the peace of the world above every other mundane thing—could think of voting for Smith, a "wet," and jeopardize the hopes of mankind for peace. With Professor Dewey it seemed advisable to tread more softly, for, even though Robins had referred to the philosopher as mourning over the death of his wife like a "stricken giant of the intellect," he

[2] Levinson to Brown, October 10, 1928.

[315]

was still able to deal crushing blows in an argument over the respective merits of Smith and Hoover. Consequently, Levinson, without making any great attempt at proselyting or showing any keen sense of personal injury, dismissed the matter toward the last of October with "you can just make up your mind that if Smith is elected you will have to shoulder lots of responsibility about the progress of Outlawry because my influence will be on a very low level."[3]

But with John Haynes Holmes and Oswald Garrison Villard it was different. Holmes, in a sermon, had referred to both the major parties as "rotten to the core," as looting the Treasury when either got in control of the government; and, as for himself, "I would cut off my hands," he declared, "before I'd vote for either of them." Levinson wrote him an injured and disappointed letter, telling of his own embarrassment because of his close connection with the magazine, *Unity*, of which Holmes was the editor, and inquiring if the paragraph which he quoted from an account of the sermon were authentic.

You know that in Hoover, Borah, and Robins, as well as my own partner, Glenn, prospective Republican Senator, I have tied up all my hopes of public service, particularly the international. I must confess that this extreme statement of yours gave me a kind of sickening feeling in the midst of otherwise radiant hopes.[4]

Dr. Holmes sent a propitiatory reply. The paragraph quoted, he explained, was out of its context. He was sorry to hurt Levinson, but "you want me to be myself and not anybody else not even yourself!"[5]

The following excerpts from a letter written by Levinson to his friend, Mr. Oswald Garrison Villard, need no explanation.

On my return from Maine I was shocked to find in the October 3rd number of the Nation your editorial on Senator Borah. I was shocked—I was pained, hurt, and would have written you immediately but waited for my impulsive indignation to subside to conviction. In my years of friendly contact and at least moderate cooperation with you and The Nation, have I misunderstood you entirely? I have acted upon the assumption that The Nation stood for individual

[3] Levinson to Dewey, October 30, 1929.

[4] Levinson to Holmes, October 25, 1928.

[5] Holmes to Levinson, October 29, 1928.

liberty within the law, the right of every man to have his own views and convictions in religion, in politics and in public affairs, and a correlative right to express those views. Is it possible that it is you alone who enjoy this right and that you retain the prerogative of vituperation and insult towards any man whose views do not coincide with yours? . . . . I emphasize this because otherwise you ought to be delighted to see the Republican party getting in a substantial way into the hands of some of our leading progressive and humanitarian statesmen; men who are above the breath of suspicion and who are devoted to their standards and ideals of government and the rights of the people. Senator Borah had most to do with the framing of what is the best platform of the Republican party in the last forty years. He also had much to do with the selection of the candidates who stand squarely on this platform and who will carry all the important planks into execution. We will hear no more of the "old guard" or of the "invisible interests" if Hoover is elected and continues, as he will, to have the magnificent support of Borah.

. . . . I should think your grandfather would turn over in his grave when you grossly and inexcusably insult the greatest man representing the greatest causes of the present day.[6]

Villard's rejoinder, Levinson's next onslaught, and Villard's later blasts are hardly relevant to this inquiry.

As the election drew near, Levinson's feeling about Mr. Hoover could have been well summed up in words borrowed from Longfellow's "Building of the Ship":

> Humanity with all its fears,
> With all the hopes of future years,
> Is hanging breathless on thy fate!

As has been noted in the preceding chapter, Borah wanted to inject the Pact into the senatorial campaign of 1928. Raymond Robins was much opposed to this, particularly on account of Senator Johnson, whom Borah had wished specifically to put on record as favoring the treaty. The colonel feared such a course in California, where Johnson's election was as "well assured as anything in the future politically could be." An "attempt to put him on record, might easily be the means of getting a fiery denunciation of these peace organizations and the Pact, and then he would have to live up to his thoughtless diatribe." His conclusion

[6] Levinson to Villard, October 9, 1928. The reference to co-operation with the *Nation* was most likely occasioned by Levinson's contribution of $1,500 to the support of the magazine. It is presumed the grandfather referred to was that other editor, William Lloyd Garrison.

in general was: "Most of the States present conditions of assurance of election one way or the other. In the south this is specially true. It might be worth while to have the question put up to candidates where the contest is close."[7] Levinson was very anxious for the issue to be used in the presidential campaign. He had criticized the Republicans for failing to make political capital out of the Pact of Paris in the pre-convention campaign, and he wanted Hoover and Borah to make a strong appeal to the peace sentiment, using the Pact as a basis.

However, Kellogg evidently remembered a former campaign in which one party took a definite stand for a peace treaty, while the other stood on both sides until after the election, and then a few of its spokesmen interpreted the verdict as a popular repudiation of the treaty. At any rate, he wanted the Pact left entirely out of the campaign, apparently to avoid forcing anyone to oppose its ratification. His wishes on the whole were respected by the chief Republicans, as neither Hoover nor Borah used the treaty as Levinson had hoped.[8] Kellogg also had made an effort to safeguard the treaty from Democratic opposition, as Levinson learned when he saw the secretary in Chicago on October 20. The gist of this effort is described as follows:

Frank L. Polk, former under-Secretary of State under Wilson, and now a leading New York lawyer, gave assurances in writing that at an appropriate time Smith (or some one for him) would do the needful and announce for unconditional ratification. Of course this would make it really non-partisan and take it altogether out as a campaign issue.[9]

Although Polk had made this promise in September, no satisfactory statement had been made by Smith himself or authoritatively in his behalf; and Levinson began to bring all the pressure he could muster on persons who had influence in high Democratic circles to induce Smith or someone like John W. Davis or Franklin Roosevelt to make the statement desired. However, the only statement made was one written by Mrs. Franklin Roose-

[7] Robins to Levinson, September 2, 1928.

[8] See Pearson and Brown, *The American Diplomatic Game* (New York: Doubleday, Doran & Co., 1935), pp. 40 ff., for an interesting account of how Kellogg appeared to stumble onto the idea of the nonpartisan handling of the treaty.

[9] Levinson to Dewey, October 22, 1928.

velt to Mrs. Quincy Wright favoring the treaty. He therefore, on October 26, began to urge Borah to bring the treaty into the campaign.

My suggestion is that unless a clean cut statement is forthcoming before your speech in New York, you go into this matter in your own way. For example, you have been prevented, by reason of Kellogg's desire and the promise made, from stating to the people your tremendous interest in this campaign because of the Outlawry treaty, the endorsement of which you had written into the platform and for which you are splendidly responsible. Here is a great Republican asset which we are trading off for a mess of pottage and don't even get the mess of pottage.[10]

While Levinson was assisting with his right hand in the election of Mr. Hoover, he kept his left hand busy trying to force the Tories to recant the "vital interest" condition to their acceptance of the Pact of Paris.[11] His method was twofold. First, he insisted that, since the "vital interest" condition was not formally incorporated into the treaty, it had no binding effect and should therefore be recalled as useless verbiage. There were several arguments which he urged in support of this contention. Some of his points were: (a) The "vital interest" condition was of no effect since the statement was merely the expression of an opinion of a minister, while signing the treaty was an act of a sovereign government; (b) the condition was of no effect by reason of vagueness, "certain regions" being so indefinite that the parties to the treaty could not know what the obligation was; (c) there was no recognition of the "vital interest" condition by other states in the exchange of notes; and (d) two states—Russia and Egypt—expressly stated that they were adhering to the text of the treaty only.[12] Second, he kept urging Harrison Brown and men like Garvin and Kerr to persuade some responsible British minister to disavow the "vital interest" condition. The easiest and most satisfactory way, in his opinion, would be for Kerr or Lloyd George

[10] Levinson to Borah, October 26, 1928.

[11] See above, pp. 295, 297 f., and 302 ff.

[12] He might have also added Afghanistan, Persia, and Turkey. Each in its note of adherence made some exception indicating expressly that only the treaty exclusive of other documents was being signed (for each note see *Treaty for the Renunciation of War* [Pub. No. 468 (Washington: Government Printing Office, 1933)], pp. 118, 239, and 297).

or MacDonald to ask one of the ministers during question time in Parliament if the condition was not covered by self-defense. Or perhaps it could be disavowed in the debate on the Pact.

Brown tried to do something. Kerr gave him an introduction to the chief of the American Department of the British Foreign Office, Mr. R. L. Craigie. Craigie listened attentively to the Levinson attack on the Tories from the mouth of Brown, how they were responsible for the difficulty in the United States Senate, how the "sleeping dogs of isolationism" were likely to be aroused, and how the responsibility for a Monroe Doctrine reservation, the fanning of the flames of anti-British feeling, perhaps even the complete failure of the treaty lay entirely with them. He asked Brown to prepare a memorandum covering these matters for Austen Chamberlain's benefit. Craigie also said that the British had made no reservation. What had been done was to provide a safeguard against Britain's being made a technical aggressor in case the Empire was threatened. Nothing came of the memorandum; and all the comfort which Brown could give his increasingly agitated employer, as the autumn temperatures dropped toward winter, was his own guaranty that, once the British people were given the opportunity to vote, the Tories would be turned out and Labor given a chance. The king had become very ill, and Levinson thought the American public's solicitude for His Majesty's health might be a means of warming the frigid Tories. Whether or not, faithful to the suggestions pouring in on him by letter and cable, Brown did or did not make an appeal on the basis of America's "affectionate sympathy" for the king, as shown by "millions of our people listen[ing] nightly over the radio to get a midnight bulletin" of his condition, he did react to Levinson in typical Brown fashion. In keeping with the tender sentiments of the Christmas season, he wrote on December 25, "I hope the old mutt gets better," because the Tories would "go back with a bang if he died."

Levinson had a partially sympathetic listener in Philip Kerr, who cabled him in response to one of his pleas that the conference of the Labour party in October had passed a resolution deploring the action of the government "in weakening significance [of] Pact by reserving right of self-defence and defence of unspecified regions."[13] However, Kerr advised that the less noise made about reservations the better, since he thought the British conditions were all covered by self-defense, whereas, if the issue were forced, the government would be jockeyed into the position of having to take a stand which might very easily be much worse. It was of immediate importance to get public opinion committed to the broad principle that the nations were renouncing war and were giving a pledge to use only peaceful means. Later "it will become more and more clear that it will be necessary to define the distinction between war and the use of force for self-defence or the maintenance of reasonable order."[14] After receiving five or six letters and cables in December, Kerr replied early in January that something might be done when Parliament opened on January 22, but he doubted if the Tories would move, "simply on the ground that they have been warned from every quarter that the only thing for them to do at present is to hold their tongues altogether, because whatever they say will be used in evidence against them by somebody."[15] He hoped something might be done after the Pact was ratified. He, too, was expecting the Conservative government to be turned out at the next election.

But J. L. Garvin was a different man from either Brown or Kerr. He apparently understood perfectly the Levinson method of attack as a means of defense. In September he wrote:

Mr. Kellogg's conspicuous avoidance of this country by comparison with France and Ireland was so queer and so conspicuous an accompaniment of the Pact, that it compelled a profound and continued silence on our part. Self-respect demanded that much.[16]

But the big question was: Would the United States join the "fire brigade" promptly if a conflagration broke out, "or only look on until the flames . . . . have made renewed war a raging fact?" What he wanted was an agreement that a conference should be held in the event of a threat to peace and the states "refusing con-

[13] Kerr to Levinson, December 11, 1928.

[14] *Ibid.*   [15] Kerr to Levinson, January 2, 1929.

[16] Garvin to Levinson, September 13, 1928.

ference and delay," "put to the ban." The "ban economic would suffice if America joined in applying it."

"If America will take no practical responsibility whatever, not even in this limited and even minimum sense, for safeguarding the observance of peace, then, sooner or later, the imminent peril of war will be the fact of facts in spite of the pact of pacts."[17]

To Levinson it was perfectly obvious why Kellogg had not gone to London. It was that miserable " 'vital interest' condition unfortunately labelled by Chamberlain himself in Parliament and elsewhere 'British Monroe Doctrine.' " Why, "even Mussolini . . . . accepted the Pact without raising new questions," yet "we had the most disconcerting situation of the nation we ought to work best with and which ought to have given us the most cordial response in fact making the most trouble." Calling the condition in the note of acceptance the " 'British Monroe Doctrine' has been widely interpreted here as an attempt of the Tories to goad the United States Senate into a real resolution on the Monroe Doctrine and thereby shift the responsibility for defeat of the Pact from themselves to the Senate."[18] And then he must have raised his voice in a tone of injured dignity as he dictated: "Now I ask in all fairness, how could Mr. Kellogg go to London and be entertained by the Tory Government in these circumstances without further jeopardizing the ratification of the treaty and without putting himself into a false position?"[19] After two narrow-margined, single-spaced, typewritten pages of this sort of argument, he went on in six more of the same kind to show why a reservation by the Senate might be fatal to the treaty, why the United States did not need to reserve the Monroe Doctrine, how Mr. Garvin was all mixed up about the antiquated aggressor business, etc.

Garvin promptly answered, saying a long correspondence was not satisfactory; a fifteen-minute conversation would be much better. He did not want America to be involved in a

[17] *Ibid.*

[18] Levinson to Garvin, November 9, 1928.   [19] *Ibid.*

technical obligation against an "aggressor," whom it may be impossible to de-fine . . . . but I do desire with all my soul that on America's initiative, there shall be a binding agreement that no signatory shall resort to arms against an-other signatory without previous conference and an appointed term of delay.[20]

About the middle of December Levinson renewed the argu-ment by cable for Tory repentance. Four cables and a letter went forth in less than a month, going over the ground each time as to why the Tories should recant. In the last one he reported that he had seen the British ambassador to the United States who had "agreed and half promised action." On January 9 Garvin re-plied, "there are things I can do and things I cannot do"; but at the moment and perhaps for some time to come he preferred to remain "an independent critic only—separated from official pro-ceedings."

I thoroughly understand the American situation—at least I spare no pains to understand it, but whatever it may be, the situation on this side is far more delicate and complex. For the British Empire, with its commitments all over the world, is a real thing, and in my opinion, a beneficent thing, as, if anything ever goes seriously wrong with it, the rest of the world will find out too late.

No man has ever been a stauncher friend to another country these many years than I have been to America. Whether the British reservations ought to have been formulated as they were and whether they might not have been formulated otherwise, is a matter about which one has one's own opinion. But to advocate now the withdrawal of the reservations would be absolutely im-possible for any purpose of repute on this side. Of course the Monroe Doctrine is reserved to the fullest extent and not only so, but America, and America alone, is free to give that Doctrine any interpretation wide or narrow, general or specific, that she thinks well. By comparison, the British reservations themselves are entirely reasonable in principle, apart from any controversy about the meth-od of formulation, and are entirely in accordance with the spirit of the Pact.[21]

This was the end of this phase of the correspondence between Garvin and Levinson, though out of respect for Levinson's irre-pressibility one should observe that the approval of the treaty by the United States Senate on January 15 rather than this letter of Garvin was the probable reason.

It should be added that events were occurring as if made to Levinson's order, though he gave no sign of being aware of them.

[20] Garvin to Levinson, November 23, 1928.
[21] Garvin to Levinson, January 9, 1929.

The Tories were being pommeled daily in Parliament by the op-position on account of the "vital interest" condition. Ramsay MacDonald on November 6 in the amendment to the king's ad-dress started the attack by quoting Charles Clayton Morrison to the effect that the Tories by adding their reservation had opened the door to the destruction of the treaty by the Senate.[22] And it seems that the very disavowal which Levinson had been demand-ing was made, for in the Senate debates Borah quoted a respon-sible British minister as saying that the "vital interest" condition was covered by self-defense.[23]

While Levinson was throwing stones at the British government and while it may have appeared to such a person as Garvin that he was trying to shift responsibility from the Senate, his real at-tention and energy were concentrated on that body. As soon as the election was over, he began an intensive campaign for uncon-ditional ratification of the Pact of Paris. This campaign led him into the closest co-operation with his old enemies and directly into conflict with many of his old friends.

Since his visit to Europe in April, 1927, he had paid less atten-tion to the publicity methods for popular indoctrination de-scribed in some detail in an earlier chapter.[24] His efforts had been directed more largely toward getting into personal touch with people in official positions or people of influence with such. But with the signing of the treaty on August 27, 1928, he again turned part of his attention to building up popular support for the treaty. Up to the election his conception of the best popular agitation had been to support Hoover; afterwards the agitation was directly for the treaty. He departed from his habit and did some public speaking. One address was given before the Chicago Council on Foreign Relations when a "lot of out-of-town big bugs" were there. Another was given in Cleveland. Persons who expressed an interest in the treaty by writing an article were congratulated on their having time to study the matter so deeply; all kinds of queries were answered; letters to stimulate interest were written; the passing of resolutions to be sent to senators, to Kellogg, and

[22] *Parliamentary Debates, Commons* (5th ser.), CCXXII, 19.

[23] *Congressional Record*, LXX, 1727.   [24] Chap. v.

Coolidge, and the writing of individual letters to these officials were encouraged; and the other techniques described above were revived as rapidly as possible.

The peace organizations and sentiment in the United States continued to support the treaty practically unanimously. Former animosities were largely forgotten. "What is pleasing to me, and astounding too, is the way most of these old League people are treating me,"[25] he wrote to Brown after attending a meeting in which supporters and opponents of the League and World Court partisans had all vied with one another in praise of the Pact. As the fights over the League and the Court receded into the past, the bitterness lingering about the halls of memory tended to lose its sting in the comradeship of the new cause. "After all," he philosophized to his clerical friend, Dr. Holmes, whom he had been castigating six weeks before for his aspersions against the Republican party, perhaps partly as retraction of that very castigation,

as we get a little older and the years that bring the philosophic mind have come, we find that we are all of us fallible and not quite so bad as other people think us. . . . . Take for example the way I have been treated by the peace groups. I am rather ashamed of the extreme distemper I felt for a long period and the rough way in which I handled so many. As I see them now, most of them genuinely friendly and appreciative, eager to confess their ineptitude with reference to our cause and extending the hand of fellowship and cooperation, I am tremendously stirred. I still reserve out two or three characters that I can't swallow, showing still that I have some of these bad qualities and am therefore utterly disqualified to lecture anybody on that subject.[26]

The last lingering crisis among the peace workers occurred at Geneva during the Assembly of the League in 1928. Dr. Morrison had gone to Europe that summer and, after being present at the signature of the Pact in Paris on August 27, had attended the meeting of the Assembly in Geneva. One of the peace groups was planning to humiliate him; but, according to Harrison Brown, a fight was avoided by Arthur Sweetser and Clark Eichelberger, who changed the tone of the meeting. At a later meeting Morrison spoke, and Brown felt that the hatchet among the American

[25] Levinson to Brown, November 17, 1928.
[26] Levinson to Holmes, December 13, 1928.

peace groups had been buried. But a little later Brown was somewhat concerned about a letter of Morrison's to the *Manchester Guardian*. If there were many more such letters, he said, the movement for reservations to the treaty would be greatly strengthened. The editor of the *Christian Century*, however, avoided trouble during his stay in England, as far as the record indicates. He did some speaking, and he must have made a good impression since, as previously mentioned, Ramsay MacDonald quoted him in the amendment to the king's speech to Parliament.[27]

Levinson was concentrating all his energies upon the unconditional ratification of the Pact. His motto with regard to reservations was: "They shall not pass." A single reservation, he feared, might undo the whole treaty. "Do you know," he inquired of Mr. Horace J. Bridges, "that a single reservation put on by our Senate . . . . would mean that a new treaty was made, that all previous steps would be legally blotted out and that the treaty as reserved would have to be resubmitted to all the nations?"[28] Each of the powers, he predicted to Coolidge, then would like to inflict a wound to match the one made by the Senate, so that when it returned to the United States "it would be nothing but bandages." Besides, "the proposition that the United States is such a feeble, timid nation that it can't sign a simple, straightforward agreement not to go to war without plastering it over with ifs and ands is a humiliation to our people and will cause us moral degradation throughout the world."[29]

Every other peace project he thought should be dropped, for fear of stirring up animosities, until the treaty had been ratified. He wrote several letters to Irving Fisher and former Governor Baxter, of Maine, pleading with them to persuade Miss Esther Everett Lape and Mr. Frederick Libby to spend all their energies working for the Pact of Paris and let all mention of United States adherence to the World Court rest for the time being. The project always near to the heart of Borah and still nearer to that of

[27] See above, p. 324.

[28] Levinson to Bridges, November 17, 1928.

[29] Levinson to Coolidge, December 17, 1928.

Robins—the recognition of Russia—could wait, as also could the project which was fast coming to be his own great ambition—the settlement of the war debts and reparations. The peace organizations were mobilizing all their forces to defeat a cruiser bill which was being considered by Congress. "I am convinced that nothing will start serious opposition to the pact as much as a fight against the sixteen-cruiser bill."[30] "The thing is to let this bill pass as a victory for peace left over from last spring" when the peace group had beaten the number of cruisers down to sixteen. Coolidge had, in Brown's opinion, exhibited his "New England backwoodsman" outlook by giving an Armistice Day address which Walter Lippmann thought was "the worst speech delivered since the Armistice itself, except two or three by Mussolini."[31] And the peace people in Europe and America were criticizing him severely. But Levinson was quick to spring to the defense of the wizened Mr. Coolidge, even though Brown did throw up his hands in almost speechless amazement that his chief should be defending armaments when war was on the verge of being outlawed. But, countered Levinson, "I . . . . told [them] the critics of Coolidge that they had better direct their fight against the British Tories that had irritated and insulted the President and thwarted all his moves for limitation of naval armaments, rather than fight the man who was our greatest power in securing the consummation of the peace treaty."[32] "We ought to thank God," he warned Irving Fisher, "that we have got President Coolidge, Secretary Kellogg, and Senator Borah unalterably for absolute ratification of the pact—not to be looking for ways to criticize and irritate them."[33]

It seemed as if there were something about the atmosphere of the Senate which affected men strangely. Levinson's own junior partner, Otis Glenn, who, he was sure, was sound on the treaty, began to cause him worry within a month after his taking the oath of office. However, telegrams to both Borah and Glenn ap-

[30] Levinson to Fisher, November 19, 1928.

[31] Lippmann to Levinson, December 4, 1928.

[32] Levinson to Brown, November 17, 1928.

[33] Levinson to Fisher, November 19, 1928.

parently neutralized the environment. He admitted to Holmes that Borah's own past was rising up to hamper him in his leadership for the treaty.

> Very few people realize the extreme difficulty of his position. Here, as chairman, he is the leader for ratification and has to keep in line an incongruous miscellany of senators. He has to fight what are left of his old fellow irreconcilables; he has to placate his former antagonists, the League and Court people, and especially the Wilson democrats; he has to expound the problems relating to Monroe Doctrine, self-defense, no moral commitment, etc., in order to avoid any sort of condition or resolution or quasi-reservation being tacked on.[34]

In order to help corral this "incongruous miscellany of senators" Levinson carried on a personal canvass of his old friends, the isolationist senators. Senators Moses, Blaine, La Follette, James A. Reed, and Shipstead were all approached in whatever way he thought most likely to sterilize the antiforeign animus of each; a reasoned argument was made to La Follette, while to Shipstead he suggested that the germ of the treaty was found in the convention of 1787, and then he added: "I have been hoping that my irreconcilable friends in the senate will prove to the world that they have been fighting for peace and not for war."[35] He even tried to moderate the fright of the Hearst press at the calamitous dangers in the treaty.

It is, perhaps, in place to notice in general the consideration which the Senate gave the treaty, although on the whole it appears that the debate reflected rather seriously on the ability of the Senate to make any penetrating analysis of such a document. Some of the discussions bordered on the infantile, if not the imbecile. As, for example, when Senator Robinson of Indiana quoted an extreme statement of Dean Inge about the European feeling for the United States, the Hoosier alarmist concluded with:

> It may be confidently assumed, I take it, that in this statement he is giving voice to the popular English view. [This without any basis for his confident assumption, except his own *ipse dixit*.]
> Are we safe, then, in leaving in the hands of a hostile world the interpretation, so far as it refers to us, of a treaty that has such far reaching possibilities?[36]

[34] Levinson to Holmes, January 7, 1929.

[35] Levinson to Shipstead, December 17, 1928.

[36] *Congressional Record*, LXX (January 8, 1929), 1343.

This, too, in spite of the fact that Borah had made it absolutely clear that each nation was to interpret for itself its obligations under the treaty. However, at times the debate was more worthy of the occasion; and the speeches of Borah and of Walsh, of Montana, in support of ratification and of Reed, of Missouri, in opposition to it were of a relatively high order. But at no time during the debate did anyone, even Borah, appear to have grasped the distinction between war as an institution for the solution of disputes or as a source of rights and war as violence used in self-defense—the essence of the philosophy which Levinson had been pouring into some of their ears for nearly a decade. Neither did Borah appear to realize the significance of his own *New York Times* article of February 5, 1928, as an answer to most of the objections which were raised. Though it must be added that he did exhibit astuteness and agility in confusing shrewd opposition, even if this very astuteness and agility were at the expense of the treaty he was defending.[37]

The President submitted the treaty to the Senate on December 4, 1928, and it was reported back to the Senate from the Committee on Foreign Relations on December 19, 1928.[38] Borah opened the debate with regard to it on January 3, 1929.[39] His argument in the support of the treaty was of a negative character, that is, he maintained the treaty should be approved because it would not injure the United States; only incidentally did he claim benefits flowing from it.

His address was built on two main points with a corollary to the first. The first was:

[37] Levinson dissented from the part of this paragraph which raised a doubt about Senator Borah's understanding of outlawry. He admitted, however, that the Senator did not use the term "institutional" in quite the same sense as he himself used it. None of his collaborators did that at all times. He was sure that if the Senator had been allowed to make a full explanation without interruptions for questions a much more reasoned defense of the Pact as well as of outlawry would have been the result. Levinson was in the Senate during the debate on the Pact. When Borah finished his speech, Levinson asked why he hadn't mentioned a certain point. The Senator replied: "Shucks, I forgot all about that when they began to question me." Levinson took his material and went to see Walsh, of Montana, who made more nearly the kind of speech that he wanted (see below, p. 334, n. 53).

[38] *Congressional Record*, LXX, 851.   [39] *Ibid.*, p. 1062.

The question which may be considered first not only in point of time but in some respects in importance is that of the right of self-defense under the treaty. It is conceded upon the part of all now that the right of self-defense is in no wise curtailed or embarrassed by the treaty, the governments promptly acceding to it, that the right of self-defense is an inherent right, implicit, in every treaty; that it is a right which can not be bartered away, abrogated, or surrendered; and that each nation may under the treaty determine for itself when the right of self-defense arises and the extent to which it may go in defending its rights.[40]

He admitted that this might be considered a weakness, but it was a "weakness inherent in human nature and inherent in the conditions which obtain" and that no one would agree to a treaty which attempted to remove the right of a nation to determine for itself when it was in danger.[41] There was nothing added to the treaty by diplomatic exchanges.

The corollary to this first point was with regard to the Monroe Doctrine. He considered the Monroe Doctrine as "constituting an element of self-defense" and therefore no mention needed to be made of it for it was implicit in the treaty.[42]

When he was questioned as to whether the United States could have fought the Spanish American War if the treaty had been in existence, his answer was: "In my judgment it could, upon the theory which we professed to fight it. Our ships had been attacked, our people had been murdered, and we had a perfect right to defend ourselves against these attacks."[43] Even when it was urged on him that, after the "Maine" was blown up and the Spanish government had "made almost every conceivable effort to avoid war by peaceful means," if the treaty had been in effect then the United States would have been bound to have used peaceful means in seeking a solution, he still insisted:

[40] *Ibid.*, p. 1063.

[41] See below, p. 331, n. 44, which contains a critical comment on this point.

[42] It was later pointed out in a colloquy between Senators Walsh, of Montana, and Sackett that the Monroe Doctrine did not need reserving for another reason, as when it was breached by some power from another hemisphere the Pact of Paris would also be breached, thus relieving the United States from any obligation under the treaty as against the offending power. This is an illustration of a case in which it appeared that Borah did not realize the significance of the conclusion of his *New York Times* article of February 5, 1928 (*Congressional Record*, LXX, 1718).

[43] *Ibid.*, p. 1069.

We would not be bound under this treaty, in my opinion in any different way than in which we were bound at that time, for this reason: we either acted in good faith or in bad faith with reference to the reason why we fought the Spanish-American War. We could doubtless assign a bad reason and a hypocritical reason under this treaty. We were under obligations to settle with Spain at that time through peaceful means, according to the principles which we had announced for a hundred years, if we believed that Spain was acting in good faith, and that we could protect our rights through peaceful means.

But after the incident as it occurred, after our property had been destroyed and American lives destroyed, it was for the Government of the United States to determine what constituted a real defense of our rights; and when this treaty is ratified it will be for the Government of the United States to determine, upon any particular state of facts or any set of conditions, as to what constitutes a defense of its rights.[44]

[44] *Ibid.*, p. 1069. Senator Borah's words here are capable of being interpreted as utterly destroying the treaty he was defending. However, since the report (below, p. 336) which was adopted by the Committee on Foreign Relations and which was drawn up by the Senator himself does not go to such extreme lengths, it would seem that perhaps the Senator's words, spoken as they were in debate, lacked precision. He had, in fact, on another occasion taken a much more moderate position; he had said: "If we construe the treaty in the way that we construe to be self-defense, we have got then to make our defense before the world as to whether or not it was self-defense" (*Hearings before the Committee on Foreign Relations, United States Senate, on General Pact, etc., December 7 and 11* [70th Cong., 2d sess., 1928]). Authorities agree that a state may decide for itself the occasion for the exercise of self-defense when confronted by some imminent threat of irreparable damage, as may an individual; but, as with an individual, there may be a subsequent review of the action. This was the position taken by Kellogg in negotiations for the treaty. "Every nation is free at all times . . . . to defend its territory. . . . . And if it has a good case, the world will applaud and not condemn its action" (*Treaty for the Renunciation of War*, p. 57). Later, November 11, 1928, he said: "If it has a good case, the world will applaud it and not condemn it, but a nation must answer to the tribunal of public opinion as to whether its claim of the right of self-defense is an adequate justification for it to go to war." And later in the same address he said: ". . . . A nation claiming to act in self-defense must justify itself before the bar of world opinion as well as before the signatories of the treaty" (this address is printed in full in J. T. Gerould, *The Pact of Paris* [New York: H. W. Wilson Co., 1929], p. 116). For specific comment on Kellogg's stand see Q. Wright, "The Meaning of the Peace Pact," *AJIL*, XXVII (1933), 39 ff. For other comment supporting the position here suggested see Q. Wright, "Collective Rights and Duties for the Enforcement of Treaty Obligations," *Proceedings of the American Society of International Law*, XXVI (1932), 101; H. Lauterpacht, *The Function of Law in the International Community* (Oxford: Clarendon Press, 1933), pp. 177 ff.; J. L. Brierly, *The Law of Nations* (2d ed.; Oxford: Clarendon Press, 1936), pp. 257 f.; also J. M. Spaight, "Self-defense and International Air Power," *Journal of Comparative Legislation and International Law*, XIV (3d ser., 1932), 20 ff.

His "second proposition of importance" in his address was "the question of sanctions." "What argument," he inquired,

express or implied, do the signatories to the treaty make with reference to enforcing the treaty? Is force or punitive measures, expressed or implied, anywhere provided for in the treaty? If a nation violates the treaty are we under any obligations, express or implied, to apply coercive or punitive measures? I answer emphatically, No![45]

He then supported this point by reviewing the notes written by the governments and the statements of their responsible officials to show that there was no hint in them that the United States would be obligated to join with others or take any action by itself against a violator of the treaty.[46]

The debate on the treaty never got very far from these two points raised and discussed by Borah—the right of self-defense and whether or not it covered the Monroe Doctrine and the obligation of the United States against a violator of the Pact. Borah himself could hardly be deemed to have said more than a very few words as to the benefits of the treaty beyond his observation that he regarded the second article of the treaty as more important than the first and his hope that confidence might be built up by it which would lead to disarmament, until just a few minutes before the final vote, when he reiterated his belief that force had no place in international affairs, that all treaties, even military alliances, rested on the good faith of governments, and that, therefore, this treaty was of the greatest significance.[47]

The objections to the treaty were of two kinds. In the first place, many of those who favored it regarded it as a mere impotent gesture. Senator Bruce said he was voting for it because it would hasten entry into the League and World Court.[48] Others regarded it as worthless but supported it because its failure would be misunderstood. Senator Glass in announcing his vote for it said: "I am not willing that anybody in Virginia shall think that I am simple enough to suppose that it is worth a postage stamp in

[45] *Congressional Record*, LXX, 1065.

[46] See above, p. 329, n. 37, for Mr. Levinson's comment on Borah's speech.

[47] *Congressional Record*, LXX, 1728.   [48] *Ibid.*, p. 681.

the direction of accomplishing permanent international peace."[49]
Likewise, Senator Johnson, convinced of its complete nothing-
ness, rededicated to the Treaty these lines of Villon:

> To Messire Noël, named the neat
> By those who love him, I bequeath
> A helmless ship, a houseless street,
> A wordless book, a swordless sheath,
> An hourless clock, a leafless wreath,
> A bed sans sheet, a board sans meat,
> A bell sans tongue, a saw sans teeth,
> To make his nothingness complete.

A second group objected to the treaty because of its alleged
dangers. Senator Blaine offered a resolution disavowing the
British "vital interest" condition.[50] Later he changed his resolution to the effect that the Senate in approving the treaty did so
with the understanding that no "condition or reservation contained in the diplomatic notes exchanged during negotiations for
the treaty shall . . . . imply any admission of any reserve made in
connection therewith and not a part of the text of the treaty."[51]
This resolution was rejected without a roll call. Senators Moses
and Reed, of Missouri, sponsored a resolution which provided
that the Senate in approving the treaty did so with the understanding that (1) the United States was not obligated to use coercive measures against an offending nation, (2) no limitations
were imposed on the Monroe Doctrine, (3) the right of the United States to defend its territory, possessions, trade, or interests
was not impaired, and (4) the United States was not obligated by
the conditions of any treaty to which it was not a party.

Some of the friends of the treaty were hopeful in their praise of
it. For example, Senator Ransdell said: "The Briand-Kellogg
pact, declaring the outlawry of war . . . . is the most remarkable
step toward peace ever undertaken."[52] And Senator Walsh, of
Montana, began one of the most judicious and carefully prepared
addresses given in regard to the treaty with these words:

It is, in my estimation, a revolutionary pronouncement reversing the position
that war has hitherto occupied in the domain of international law. Heretofore

[49] *Ibid.*, p. 1728.
[50] *Ibid.*, p. 1045.
[51] *Ibid.*, p. 1727.
[52] *Ibid.*, p. 1480.

war has been regarded in international law as a perfectly legitimate means by which a nation might advance its interests or its policies. Whatever might be thought of the nation that precipitated hostilities and however unprovoked might be its attack on another country, it violated no law. It acted entirely within its sovereign right in doing so. It offended against no nation except the one assailed. If the treaty should be in force, it would be an outlaw in pursuing such a course. It would offend against every nation signatory to the treaty comprising, as it is expected, practically every civilized nation. It would become a law breaker and guilty of an international crime.[53]

Several times during the course of the debate Levinson and outlawry were mentioned. The general consensus was that he was connected with the treaty. However, there was a difference of opinion as to whether it represented what he wanted. For instance, Bruce held that the outlawry idea was too vigorous and virile to be represented by anything so backboneless as the treaty. Others seemed to feel that it was the essence of outlawry.

When men with the viewpoint of Moses and Reed, of Missouri, had heard Borah's explanation and defense of the treaty, they said they were in favor of it, if they could always depend upon its being construed in that way. Several of them then proceeded to interpret it in some of the many different ways in which it had been interpreted by various publicists, whom they quoted. Attention was also called to the fact that when the Supreme Court was interpreting a law, it would give no weight to a remark of a senator made in discussion of the bill, whereas it would lend some attention to a report of a committee. These men claimed that all they wanted was some assurance of the Borah interpretation. They could get such an assurance by a reservation, by a Senate resolution, or by having the Borah construction put into a report of the Committee on Foreign Relations and filed. They agreed that the first two means would not be wise because of the risk of affecting the treaty adversely with foreign governments. This,

[53] *Ibid.*, p. 1713. This is the speech for which Levinson collected a great deal of material (above, p. 329, n. 37). The point which Borah forgot and which Walsh used was Levinson's distinction between outlawry and arbitration. Under outlawry there were to be no exceptions. War was to be used in no case, whereas no state ought to agree to arbitrate all disputes. Matters internal in nature ought not to be submitted to arbitration, though a state promises never to use war with respect to such matters. Levinson thought so well of Walsh's speech that he had it reprinted and distributed widely.

James A. Reed agreed, would be very undesirable in view of the fact that Kellogg had taken the initiative in securing the adherence of nearly all the states of the world to the treaty.[54] At first Borah was willing to file a report; in fact he had drawn up one with the intention of filing it;[55] but, in view of the protracted debate, he had come to feel that perhaps even the filing of a report might be as unwise as a reservation, for the same reason. A petition had been circulated which called for the filing of such a report, and Reed claimed that about thirty senators had signed it. That was on January 14. Kellogg was opposed to this move according to the following telegram he sent to Levinson on the same day, January 14, 1929:

> Your telegram received. The last scheme of the men desiring to defeat the treaty is very ingenious is to get the Foreign Relations Committee to make a report interpreting the treaty. They are not particular what interpretation is put on it so that foreign countries will know that some interpretation has been placed upon it. They know of course that under the decisions of our courts while individual senator's remarks will not be considered in interpreting a treaty a report of a committee will. I think they have many signatures to their round robin which they would not have obtained had they known the effect. It is impossible for me to see everybody. Treat this as strictly confidential.

At this point Levinson became agitated. He thought the friends of the Pact were being maneuvered into a position similar to Wilson's in 1919–20 with regard to reservations to the Covenant of the League. He talked with Coolidge and with Vice-President-Elect Curtis, who was ill and in bed. Curtis, an expert on senatorial sensitiveness, was alarmed at the situation. Tactics were agreed on and Curtis left his bed to help smooth out the relations between incongruous personalities, relations which seemed to Levinson on the verge of becoming clothed in the porcupine skin of principle. Levinson went to individual senators, explaining to the irreconcilables that Borah was not deserting them and to the friends of the Pact how the anti's were drawing a herring across the trail. A little flexibility on the part of the friends of the Pact would leave the enemies stranded.

The next day Borah had evidently changed his mind about filing a report, for he simply stated: "Mr. President, your Com-

[54] *Congressional Record*, LXX, 1658.   [55] *Ibid.*, p. 1659.

mittee on Foreign Relations has unanimously agreed upon a report. . . . ."[56] The pertinent sections of this report are as follows:

The committee reports the . . . . treaty with the understanding that the right of self-defense is in no way curtailed or impaired by the terms or conditions of the treaty. Each nation is free at all times and regardless of the treaty provisions to defend itself, and is the sole judge of what constitutes the right of self-defense and the necessity and extent of the same.

The United States regards the Monroe doctrine as a part of its national security and defense. Under the right of self-defense allowed by the treaty must necessarily be included the right to maintain the Monroe doctrine which is a part of our system of national defense.

The committee further understands that the treaty does not provide sanctions, express or implied. Should any signatory to the treaty or any nation adhering to the treaty violate the terms of the same, there is no obligation or commitment, express or implied, upon the part of any of the other signers of the treaty to engage in punitive or coercive measures as against the nation violating the treaty. The effect of the violation of the treaty is to relieve the other signers of the treaty from any obligation under it with the nation thus violating the same.

This treaty in no respect changes or qualifies our present position or relation to any pact or treaty existing between other nations or governments.

This report is made solely for the purpose of putting upon record what your committee understands to be the true interpretation of the treaty, and not in any sense for the purpose or with the design of modifying or changing the treaty in any way or effectuating a reservation or reservations to the same.[57]

[56] *Ibid.*, p. 1727.

[57] *Ibid.*, p. 1730. Borah himself was of the opinion that this report as drafted and filed would have no effect on the interpretation of the treaty, as is shown by his letter to Levinson (quoted above, p. 306). However, he was there referring to notes exchanged between the governments preliminary to the signature of the Pact. In the debate also he denied that these notes changed the treaty. Kellogg agreed: "There is absolutely nothing in the notes of the various governments which would change this treaty, if the treaty had been laid on the table and signed as it is, without any discussion" (*Hearings before the Committee on Foreign Relations*). "There is nothing in any of these notes, or in my speeches sent to the signatory powers during the negotiations, which is inconsistent with, or changes the meaning of, the treaty as finally signed" ("Address to World Alliance for International Friendship," November 11, 1929, found in Gerould, *op. cit.*, p. 124). In agreement is Q. Wright, "The Interpretation of Multilateral Treaties," *AJIL*, XXIII (1929), 94. Borah thought well enough of this article to read part of it into the *Congressional Record* (LXX [February 2, 1929], 2671). Fachiri takes a more pronounced stand. After an examination of Permanent Court of International Justice cases he says: "I think it is incontestable

Shortly after this report was filed, the first and only roll-call vote on the treaty was taken. It should be added that, when Borah was asked if the State Department had any objection to the filing of the report, his reply was: "I am proceeding on my own responsibility." To a second inquiry he gave the same answer; and when the inquirer, Harrison, said he wanted to follow Borah and the State Department, too, the Senator replied: "If the Senator from Mississippi will follow me, he will be all right."[58] This was the entire discussion between the filing of the report and the vote on the treaty. There were eighty-six senators in the Chamber and eighty-five voted "Yea." Senator Blaine, of Wisconsin, cast the single negative vote.[59] Eight of the senators not present had themselves put on record as in favor of it and declaring that they would have voted "Yea" had they been present. So there were ninety-four senators in favor of the treaty, one against it; and one, Senator Goff, unaccounted for.

"Yea, Bo, What a shot . . . . ," was the telegram which Father Outlawry received the next day from his fourteen-year-old son, John, whose youthful ambition was to win triumphs in the world of golf as his father had just done in the Senate.

With the ratification of the multilateral treaty condemning war, one of the fondest dreams of Levinson was realized; but, like John Paul Jones, he had not yet begun to fight. Whereas he had been working for a threefold program—the outlawry of war, the codification of law, and the creation of a court—he now had a many-fold program. It included his fight for the World Court,

---

that the court has adopted the principle that international agreements must be interpreted by reference to their actual terms, without having regard to the negotiations or other *travaux préparatoires*. The only qualification is that the text must be 'sufficiently clear' to enable this to be done. If this condition is present the Court will reach a conclusion upon the text . . . . even if the *travaux préparatoires* contained matter inconsistent with the final text . . . ." ("Interpretation of Treaties," *op. cit.*, p. 745).

[58] *Congressional Record*, LXX, 1730.

[59] *Ibid.*, p. 1731. The Wisconsin legislature adopted a resolution censuring the Senator for this vote. It is interesting to note that all the rest of the senators who had been objecting in one way or another to the treaty voted for it. One explained his vote by saying that he did not want to be burned in effigy in his own state.

his trip to see the European experts to get the Root formula changed, and the long fight for American adherence to the Court; his efforts to promote a cash settlement of the war debts; his working-out of the nonrecognition doctrine during a visit to Paris and its adoption by the United States and the League of Nations with regard to the Manchurian incident; his championing the cause of disarmament; his efforts to close the so-called gap between the League Covenant and the Pact of Paris; his final trip to London to use the occasion of the king's coronation to plead for a general European adjustment, in a desperate effort to persuade the British to avert the impending holocaust; his ceaseless attempts to transmute Borah's inherent obstructionism into a positive leadership for some of these causes; and his fruitless shivering of a lance against Hitler to save a downtrodden people. But these campaigns are beyond the limits of this study.

In conclusion, it remains only to give a brief notice of the recognition accorded to Levinson and his work alike by his friends and fellow-workers and by the world at large as a result of the coming-into-effect of the Pact of Paris.

Borah's estimation of Levinson may be indicated by the following excerpts from two letters and from a speech delivered at the University of Idaho at the inauguration of the Foundation for Outlawry of War. The first letter is to Levinson; the second, to a third party.

I know how happy you must feel these days over the grand procession of the nations. There is one thing that gives me more pleasure than I find language to express and that is that your great work in this movement is being acknowledged and recorded. It has been a remarkable achievement. Nothing like it that I know of in the history of politics or international affairs. I want you to know how thoroughly it pleases me that more and more just credit is being given to you.[60]

The greatest credit for this entire movement belongs to Mr. Levinson. He really, so far as I can ascertain, was the author of the idea, and ceaselessly, persistently, uncompromisingly, urged it. Robins and some of the rest of us assisted. But I think the credit must go to Levinson. I am sure it should not go to Colcord. Plenty of evidence to that effect if it were necessary to be presented.[61]

[60] Borah to Levinson, September 5, 1928.

[61] Borah to Charles H. Strong, publisher of the *Chicago Daily News*. Samuel Col-

A lawyer by profession, engaged in active practice, daily advising in large business affairs, he yet found time for the great cause which was nearest his heart. The time and study he gave to the subject were extraordinary. His enthusiasm drove him past all obstacles and his restless and well-trained mind seemed to find inspiration rather than discouragement in the many questions which the problem presented. He was the first within my knowledge to reach the daring conclusion that war, as an institution, could, and should, be outlawed, placed beyond the pale or recognition of international law. His conception of peace was to condemn and renounce the use of force in international relations. A peculiar and exceptional glory attaches to his name by reason of this fact. In this view he long stood alone. But he labored untiringly. He built argument after argument around his theme. He has lived to see the great principle for which he contended recognized throughout the world. I regard the Peace Pact as the embodiment of the principle for which he has so earnestly contended. It may be that this principle is in advance of the times. Time alone can tell. But permanent peace must rest at last upon this great foundation principle. I pay sincere tribute to his ability, his vision, his great moral courage. . . . .[62]

The Foundation referred to above was Levinson's gift to the University of Idaho of fifty-five thousand dollars "to be held and administered in perpetuity as an endowment fund in honor of my friend, Senator William Edgar Borah, and to be known as the William Edgar Borah Outlawry of War Foundation."[63] Five thousand dollars "or such portion thereof as may be necessary shall be used for a portrait or bust of William Edgar Borah" and the income from the rest "shall be used to maintain a lectureship or other means for the promotion of the purposes of the Foundation at the discretion of the University of Idaho."[64]

A special meeting was held on the evening of Easter Sunday, 1929, in his honor. Rabbi Mann was one of the prime movers for this "big-blow-out," as Levinson himself described it. Borah was scheduled to pay the main tribute, but for some reason—possibly the feud with Hoover, hints of which had begun to develop in the

---

cord, a man living in New York, had been active in writing letters to Washington officials relative to "outlawing aggressive war." He had become interested in the matter about 1924, according to my information.

[62] C. O. Johnson, *Borah of Idaho* (New York: Longmans, Green & Co., 1936), p. 406. The speech was given September 23, 1931.

[63] Levinson to the University of Idaho, March 20, 1929.

[64] *Ibid.*

preceding November—he did not appear. However, the praise was overwhelming, as is evidenced by the following excerpt from the letter which Levinson wrote to Rabbi Mann, thanking him for the meeting. It is particularly characteristic of the writer.

> I was so thrilled and overcome by the tremendous weight and quality of praise that it has been difficult for me to find my normal bearings. Profoundly as I appreciate the spirit and the words it is impossible for me to apply their truth to myself. Praise is a strange thing; we all crave it and yet we know not what to do when it comes. In trying to be modest I fear most of us become hypocritical.[65]

In Geneva, Harrison Brown reported that Levinson's name was on the lips of many during the gathering there in September, 1928. In one meeting of the peace groups Madariaga gave him the full credit for the Pact of Paris. However, Brown reported that most of this was done *sotto voce*. Everyone seemed afraid to show any enthusiasm for the Pact of Paris or Levinson or even notice what had been going on for fear the Senate would interpret such things as conclusive evidence of some clever scheme to trick the United States and refuse to approve the treaty.

Both immediate friends and casual acquaintances of Levinson joined in a drive to get the Nobel Peace Prize for him. Harrison Brown, acting on his own initiative, wrote to numbers of distinguished and influential people in Europe and America, urging them to write to the committee of award in his behalf; and not a few of them did so. Editorials appeared in such journals as the *Manchester Guardian*,[66] calling on the committee to give Levinson the prize. However, Brown heard in England that Kellogg was very anxious for it and was getting a lot of important people to write in his behalf. Consequently, Brown said, the committee could hardly pass over an official connected with the actual negotiations of a treaty to give the prize to a private individual for the same treaty. But still "if you are not to be included I hope

---

[65] Levinson to Dr. Mann, April 5, 1929.

[66] Ten years later the foreign editor said: "If the Nobel Committee were as discriminating in their political as they are in their scientific or literary judgment, Mr. Levinson would be a holder of the Nobel Peace Prize . . . ." (F. A. Voigt, *Unto Caesar* [New York: G. P. Putnam's Sons, 1938], p. 281; also see above, p. 226, n. 22).

they keep the old faggot [Kellogg] waiting." This was probably what happened, since the prize was omitted in 1929 and given to Briand and Kellogg jointly the next year.

Levinson's attitude toward having the prize is interesting. At first he objected to his friends' working for it; later he did not object, although he had early nominated Kellogg for it; later he would have been glad for it but did not want it to cause a coolness between himself and Kellogg; and, later still, when Kellogg had not treated him fairly in an article on the "Outlawry of War" for the *Encyclopaedia Britannica*, he was rather anxious that, at any rate, Kellogg should not have it. Part of a paragraph of a letter in which he gives his attitude is revealing:

> I am appreciative of his and your, as well as others, efforts to secure for me the Nobel Peace Prize. First of all, I would consider it a betrayal of my own convictions and independent peace of mind if I did anything to obtain it or even if I nurtured an ambition for it. I have never taken anything in any form for any public service I have ever tried to render and I hope I will not begin at this late date. You recall that famous line of Milton: "Ambition, that last infirmity of noble minds." Of course in quoting this I probably am assuming that I have a "noble" mind, but that isn't the gist of the thing. I am grateful and happy in the almost inconceivably rapid development of the Outlawry movement and its concrete crystallizations. As Wordsworth in his "Intimations of Immortality" speaks of "thoughts that lie too deep for tears" so I feel that the realization of the first concrete foundation of Outlawry in the Pact of Paris creates thoughts that lie too deep for exultation or jubilation and that rather call forth those of thanksgiving and humility.[67]

When the man whom he and Irving Fisher referred to in their letters as "Stimmy," a fellow-member of the Yale class of 1888, became secretary of state in President Hoover's cabinet on March 4, 1929, Levinson was treated with much more cordiality and respect in the Department of State than had been his lot when Kellogg had been the occupant of that office. It was in keeping with this respect and disposition to give him credit that Secretary Stimson sent him a personal invitation on behalf of the President and himself to be present as the only invited guest at the procla-

[67] Levinson to Harrison Brown, October 10, 1928.

mation of the Pact of Paris on July 24, 1929, in the White House. William Hard said of this occasion:

> It was a graceful gesture of recognition that the secretary of state and the president extended the other day at an otherwise wholly official affair to a private citizen.
>
> Alone among diplomats and other high official dignitaries in the east room of the White House and at the luncheon afterward, on the occasion of the celebration of the coming into force of the Kellogg-Briand pact, was this private personage, S. O. Levinson of Chicago.[68]

Institutions of higher learning vied with one another in conferring honorary degrees upon him in recognition of his services. Grinnell College and DePauw University were among the first so to honor him. Despite the fact that his early ideas with regard to the League of Nations were opposed vigorously by members of the faculty of the University of Chicago, he has been given due credit by them for the Pact of Paris. Professor Paul H. Douglas, in a protest to the editor of the *Survey* against an article which gave Professor Shotwell credit for the Pact, declared that

> . . . . the real originator of the whole proposal is of course not Professor James T. Shotwell of New York, but Mr. Salmon O. Levinson of Chicago. . . . . It is possible that Professor Shotwell suggested to Briand that he propose the outlawry of war between France and the United States, although even here Professor Shotwell could only have been a retailer of the idea originated and promoted by Mr. Levinson.

> Although I have in the past believed that Mr. Levinson like all enthusiasts, has somewhat exaggerated the importance of outlawry as a sole instrument for peace, nevertheless no one can deny that his work for outlawry has been one of the most moving and effective individual crusades of which this country has record. I know of nothing which equals it save the crusade by that other American Knight-errant, David Lubin, for the creation of the International Institute of Agriculture.[69]

And it was through the efforts of one of those having the most faith in the League of Nations, Professor Quincy Wright, that the Father of Outlawry was granted the Rosenberger Medal by the University of Chicago, "in recognition of his important contribu-

[68] *Milwaukee Journal*, July 28, 1929.

[69] Douglas to the editor of the *Survey*, November 22, 1928.

tion to the improvement of international political relations in instituting and promoting the movement for the Outlawry of War."[70]

In 1934 he was made a chevalier of the French Legion of Honor in recognition of "his efforts in laying the ground work for the Briand-Kellogg pact of Paris outlawing war, and for his other efforts in behalf of amity among nations."[71]

[70] *Chicago Daily News*, June 16, 1931.

[71] *Ibid.*, March 11, 1935.

APPENDIX A

RESOLUTION FOR OUTLAWRY OF WAR FIRST PRESENTED TO SENATE BY WILLIAM E. BORAH, FEBRUARY 13, 1923[1]

WHEREAS war is the greatest existing menace to society, and has become so expensive and destructive that it not only causes the stupendous burdens of taxation now afflicting our people, but threatens to engulf and destroy civilization; and

WHEREAS civilization has been marked in its upward trend out of barbarism into its present condition by the development of law and courts to supplant methods of violence and force; and

WHEREAS the genius of civilization has discovered but two methods of compelling the settlement of human disputes, namely, law and war, and therefore, in any plan for the compulsory settlement of international controversies, we must choose between war on the one hand and the process of law on the other; and

WHEREAS war between nations has always been and still is a lawful institution, so that any nation may, with or without cause, declare war against any other nation and be strictly within its legal rights; and

WHEREAS revolutionary war or wars of liberation are illegal and criminal, to wit: high treason, whereas, under existing international law, wars of aggression between nations are perfectly lawful; and

WHEREAS the overwhelming moral sentiment of civilized people everywhere is against the cruel and destructive institution of war; and

WHEREAS all alliances, leagues, or plans which rely upon force as the ultimate power for the enforcement of peace carry the seeds either of their own destruction or of military dominancy to the utter subversion of liberty and justice; and

WHEREAS we must recognize the fact that resolutions or treaties outlawing certain methods of killing will not be effective so long as war itself remains lawful; and that in international relations we must have, not rules and regulations of war but organic laws against war; and

WHEREAS in our Constitutional Convention of 1787 it was successfully contended by Madison and Hamilton that the use of force when applied to people collectively, that is, to states or nations was unsound in principle and would be tantamount to a declaration of war; and

WHEREAS we have in our Federal Supreme Court a practical and effective

[1] Senate Res. 441 (67th Cong., 4th Sess.).

[345]

model for a real international court, as it has specific jurisdiction to hear and decide controversies between our sovereign States; and

WHEREAS our Supreme Court has exercised this jurisdiction, without resort to force, for one hundred and thirty-five years, during which time scores of controversies have been judicially and peaceably settled that might otherwise have led to war between the States, and thus furnishes a practical exemplar for the compulsory and pacific settlement of international controversies, and

WHEREAS an international arrangement of such judicial character would not shackle the independence or impair the sovereignty of any nation: Now, therefore, be it

Resolved, That it is the view of the Senate of the United States that war between nations should be outlawed as an institution or means for the settlement of international controversies by making it a public crime under the law of nations and that every nation should be encouraged by solemn agreement or treaty to bind itself to indict and punish its own international war breeders or instigators and war profiteers under powers similar to those conferred upon our Congress under Article I, section 8, of our Federal Constitution which clothes the Congress with the power "to define and punish offenses against the law of nations": And be it

Resolved further, That a code of international law of peace based upon equality and justice between nations, amplified and expanded and adapted and brought down to date should be created and adopted;

Second. That a judicial substitute for war should be created (or, if existing in part, adapted and adjusted) in the form or nature of an international court, modeled on our Federal Supreme Court in its jurisdiction over controversies between our sovereign States, such court to possess affirmative jurisdiction to hear and decide all purely international controversies, as defined by the code, or arising under treaties, and to have the same power for the enforcement of its decrees as our Federal Supreme Court, namely, the respect of all enlightened nations for judgments resting upon open and fair investigations and impartial decisions and the compelling power of enlightened public opinion.

APPENDIX B

THE LEVINSON MEMORANDUM AND EXCERPTS FROM THE BORAH ARTICLE OF FEBRUARY 5, 1928

The Levinson paper is from a memorandum in the files marked "Draft of January 28, 1928." All of it is here reproduced except the first and last paragraphs. The Borah article is taken from the reprint which Levinson had made of the Borah article in the *New York Times* of February 5, 1928, as it was offered to the *Congressional Record*, February 6, 1928. Only the part that is similar to Levinson's, a little less than a third of the whole, is here reproduced.

THE LEVINSON PAPER

Now the plain fact is that the bilateral treaty proposed by M. Briand is identical in principle, as to war commitments, with the multilateral treaty offered by Mr. Kellogg.

By agreeing in a bilateral compact never to go to war with the United States, France could not carry out her obligations to go to war under articles 10 and 16 of the Covenant if war took place between the United States and any member of the League.

Suppose, for example, that war should occur between Japan and the United States, Japan being a member of the League.

Suppose, further, that Japan successfully invoked assistance from the League under articles 10 and 16 of the Covenant.

France would be unable to render any military assistance to Japan pursuant

THE BORAH ARTICLE

The plain fact is that the bilateral treaty proposed by M. Briand is identical in principle as to war commitments with the multilateral treaty offered by our Secretary of State, Mr. Kellogg.

By agreeing in a bilateral treaty never to war with the United States, France could not carry out her obligations to go to war under Articles X and XVI of the covenant if war took place between the United States and any member of the league.

Suppose, in the way of illustration, that war should occur between Japan and the United States, and, of course, I select Japan merely in the way of an illustration.

Japan is a member of the league.

Suppose further that Japan successfully invoked assistance from the league under Articles X and XVI of the covenant.

France would be unable to render any military assistance to Japan pursuant

[347]

to the Covenant because she had agreed in a bilateral treaty never to go to war with the United States.

The extension of the treaty from a bilateral to a multilateral arrangement only increases the occasions for this so-called breach of war commitments; it does not change the principle one iota.

If France intends to live up to the strict letter of her obligations under article 10 of the covenant "to respect and preserve the territorial integrity and political independence" of all the members of the League she could not possibly do it in case the United States got into war with *any* member of the League.

M. Briand has as logical a mind as there is in Europe and will see that the difference in that respect between a bilateral treaty and a multilateral treaty is nil.

It will not do to say that a bilateral pact does not violate the League commitments because forsooth there is no chance of France and the United States ever going to war.

Such a construction would be lackadaisical.

Moreover, if there is no shadow of danger of war between these two republics what is the need of making any treaty whatever renouncing war between them?

And as M. Briand made his original offer "as an example to other nations" how can it be such "example" if no other nation can sign the compact?

---

to the covenant because she had agreed in a bilateral treaty never to go to war with the United States.

The principle underlying a bilateral treaty is identical with the principle involved in a multilateral treaty. On the other hand, a multilateral treaty, binding all the nations, binding all the leading powers, makes war less likely than a treaty between two nations.

If France intends to live up to the strict letter of her obligations under Article X of the covenant, "to respect and preserve the territorial integrity and political independence" of all the members of the league, she could not possibly do so in case the United States got into war with any member of the league.

It will not do to say that a bilateral compact does not violate the league commitments, because, forsooth, there is no chance of France and the United States going to war.

To make such a statement as that would be to stamp the original proposition with insincerity.

If there is no shadow of danger of war between these two Republics, what is the need of making any treaty whatever renouncing war between them?

And as M. Briand made his original offer "as an example to other nations," how can it be an "example" if no other nation can sign the compact or if the United States and France are

Was the two power pact intended to be not only a "closed corporation" but a closed incident?

Now as to France's other compacts or alliances.

These are all supposed to be in harmony with the principles and provisions of the covenant and to be filed with the League.

But, let us assume, for example, in the case of Belgium which has been raised by the French, that France is absolutely obligated under her alliance to come to the relief of Belgium in case of attack.

This commitment can be easily protected.

All that is necessary is for the multilateral pact to be signed by Belgium, in which event all the signatories agree not to use war or force in any dispute or matter relating to Belgium.

Now if an attack nevertheless is made on Belgium by one of the signatories it would constitute a breach of the multilateral treaty and would thereby ipso facto release France and enable her to fulfill her military engagements with Belgium.

In other words, France's commitments to Belgium would merely be in suspense so long as the signatories kept their multilateral compact; there would be no violation thereof.[1]

Now Secretary Kellogg very wisely put into his counter proposal not only that there should be a multilateral treaty, comprising the big powers, but that it should be "open to the signatures of all nations."

unwilling to join with them in bringing about such a general compact? Was the two-power compact intended to be not only a close corporation but a closed incident?

As to France's other compacts or alliances, these are all supposed to be in harmony with the principles and provisions of the covenant and to be filed with the league.

Let us assume, for example, in the case of Belgium, which has been raised by the French, that France is absolutely obligated under her alliance to come to the relief of Belgium in case of attack.

This commitment can be easily protected.

All that is necessary is for the multilateral pact to be signed by Belgium, in which event all the signatories agree not to use war or force in any dispute or matter relating to Belgium.

If an attack, nevertheless, is made on Belgium by one of the signatories, it would constitute a breach of the multilateral treaty and would thereby, ipso facto, release France and enable her to fulfill her military engagements with Belgium.

In other words, France's commitment to Belgium would merely be in suspense so long as the signatories kept their multilateral compact; there would be no violation thereof.

Secretary Kellogg very wisely put into his counterproposal not only that there should be a multilateral treaty comprising the big powers, but that it should be "open to the signatures of all nations."

[1] This statement is significant because of the later use of the argument in the diplomatic exchanges and its incorporation in the preamble of the Pact of Paris.

The logical development of this idea would lead to the great result desired by Secretary Kellogg, namely, the general renunciation and outlawing of war as a method of settling disputes by *all* the nations.

Such a universal treaty would put an end to any question as to war commitments under the League covenant or other alliances because the occasion for their exercise could only arise in case of a flagrant breach of the treaty by one or more signatories, and as stated the legal effect of such a breach would be to free France from her alleged restraints.

And was this not Mr. Briand's purpose in proposing the pact "as an example to other nations"?

The logical development of this idea would lead to the great result desired by Secretary Kellogg, namely, the general renunciation and outlawing of war as a method of settling disputes by all the nations.

Would not such a treaty augment and strengthen beyond any words to describe not only every peace plan in the world, but the peace sentiment and the peace public opinion, which are just as essential in the cause of peace as treaties?

Such a universal treaty would put an end to any questions of war commitments under the league covenants or other alliances, because the occasion for their exercise could only arise in case of a flagrant breach of the treaty by one or more signatories and, as stated, the legal effects of such a breach would be to free France from alleged restraints.

And was this not M. Briand's purpose in proposing the pact "as an example to other nations"?

APPENDIX C

SUBSTANTIVE ARTICLES OF THE DRAFT TREATY BETWEEN FRANCE AND THE UNITED STATES PROPOSED BY M. BRIAND, JUNE 20, 1927

ARTICLE 1

The high contracting parties solemnly declare, in the name of the French people and the people of the United States of America, that they condemn recourse to war and renounce it respectively as an instrument of their national policy toward each other.

ARTICLE 2

The settlement or the solution of all disputes or conflicts, of whatever nature or of whatever origin they may be, which may arise between France and the United States of America, shall never be sought by either side except by pacific means.

APPENDIX D

SUBSTANTIVE ARTICLES OF THE DRAFT TREATY AMONG THE SIX GREAT POWERS PROPOSED BY SECRETARY KELLOGG ON APRIL 13, 1928

ARTICLE I

The High Contracting Parties solemnly declare in the names of their respective peoples that they condemn recourse to war for the solution of international controversies, and renounce it as an instrument of national policy in their relations with one another.

ARTICLE II

The High Contracting Parties agree that the settlement or solution of all disputes or conflicts of whatever nature or of whatever origin they may be, which may arise among them, shall never be sought except by pacific means.

APPENDIX E

SUBSTANTIVE ARTICLES OF THE DRAFT TREATY AMONG THE SIX GREAT POWERS PROPOSED BY THE FRENCH GOVERNMENT ON APRIL 20, 1928

ARTICLE 1

The high contracting parties without any intention to infringe upon the exercise of their rights of legitimate self-defense within the framework of existing treaties, particularly when the violation of certain of the provisions of such treaties constitutes a hostile act, solemnly declare that they condemn recourse to war and renounce it as an instrument of national policy; that is to say, as an instrument of individual, spontaneous and independent political action taken on their own initiative and not action in respect to which they might become involved through the obligation of a treaty such as the Covenant of the League of Nations or any other treaty registered with the League of Nations. They undertake on these conditions not to attack or invade one another.

ARTICLE 2

The settlement or solution of all disputes or conflicts, of whatever nature or origin, which might arise among the high contractlng parties or between any two of them, shall never be sought on either side except by pacific methods.

ARTICLE 3

In case one of the high contracting parties should contravene this treaty, the other contracting powers would *ipso facto* be released with respect to that party from their obligations under this treaty.

ARTICLE 4

The provisions of this treaty in no wise affect the rights and obligations of the contracting parties resulting from prior international agreements to which they are parties.

ARTICLE 5

The present treaty will be offered for the accession of all powers and will have no binding force until it has been generally accepted unless the signatory powers in accord with those that may accede hereto shall agree to decide that it shall come into effect regardless of certain abstentions.

APPENDIX F

THE PACT OF PARIS: THE TREATY FOR THE RENUNCIATION OF WAR OF AUGUST 27, 1928

The President of the United States of America, the President of the French Republic, His Majesty the King of the Belgians, the President of the Czechoslovak Republic, His Majesty the King of Great Britain, Ireland and the British Dominions beyond the Seas, Emperor of India, the President of the German Reich, His Majesty the King of Italy, His Majesty the Emperor of Japan, the President of the Republic of Poland,

Deeply sensible of their solemn duty to promote the welfare of mankind;

Persuaded that the time has come when a frank renunciation of war as an instrument of national policy should be made to the end that the peaceful and friendly relations now existing between their peoples may be perpetuated;

Convinced that all changes in their relations with one another should be sought only by pacific means and be the result of a peaceful and orderly process, and that any signatory Power which shall hereafter seek to promote its national interests by resort to war should be denied the benefits furnished by this Treaty;

Hopeful that, encouraged by their example, all the other nations of the world will join in this humane endeavor and by adhering to the present Treaty as soon as it comes into force bring their peoples within the scope of its beneficent provisions, thus uniting the civilized nations of the world in a common renunciation of war as an instrument of their national policy;

Have decided to conclude a Treaty and for that purpose have appointed as their respective Plenipotentiaries:

The President of the United States of America:......................

The President of the French Republic:..............................

His Majesty the King of the Belgians:...............................

The President of the Czechoslovak Republic:........................

His Majesty the King of Great Britain, Ireland and the British Dominions beyond the Seas, Emperor of India:

For Great Britain and Northern Ireland and all parts of the British Empire which are not separate Members of the League of Nations:..........

For the Dominion of Canada:....................................

For the Commonwealth of Australia:..............................

For the Dominion of New Zealand:...............................

For the Union of South Africa:..................................

[354]

APPENDIX

For the Irish Free State:...

For India:...

The President of the German Reich:................................

His Majesty the King of Italy:.....................................

His Majesty the Emperor of Japan:.................................

The President of the Republic of Poland:...........................

who, having communicated to one another their full powers found in good and due form have agreed upon the following articles:

ARTICLE I

The High Contracting Parties solemnly declare in the names of their respective peoples that they condemn recourse to war for the solution of international controversies, and renounce it as an instrument of national policy in their relations with one another.

ARTICLE II

The High Contracting Parties agree that the settlement or solution of all disputes or conflicts of whatever nature or of whatever origin they may be, which may arise among them, shall never be sought except by pacific means.

ARTICLE III

The present Treaty shall be ratified by the High Contracting Parties named in the Preamble in accordance with their respective constitutional requirements, and shall take effect as between them as soon as all their several instruments of ratification shall have been deposited at Washington.

This Treaty shall, when it has come into effect as prescribed in the preceding paragraph, remain open as long as may be necessary for adherence by all the other Powers of the world. Every instrument evidencing the adherence of a Power shall be deposited at Washington and the Treaty shall immediately upon such deposit become effective as between the Power thus adhering and the other Powers parties hereto.

It shall be the duty of the Government of the United States to furnish each Government named in the Preamble and every Government subsequently adhering to this Treaty with a certified copy of the Treaty and of every instrument of ratification or adherence. It shall also be the duty of the Government of the United States telegraphically to notify such Governments immediately upon the deposit with it of each instrument of ratification or adherence.

IN FAITH WHEREOF the respective Plenipotentiaries have signed this Treaty in the French and English languages, both texts having equal force, and hereunto affix their seals.

DONE at Paris, the twenty-seventh day of August in the year one thousand nine hundred and twenty-eight.

INDEX

Abraham Lincoln Center of Chicago, 9, 39 f.

Addams, Jane, 38 f., 43, 60 n.

Allen, Florence E., 109; Borah, to use influence with, 94, 280; codification of international law, 187; Europe, visit to, 166 f.; Harmony Plan, connection with, 144, 146 f.; techniques of influence, agreement with Levinson on, 103
—outlawry: early attitude on, 75; summarized, 75 n., 187
—World Court: Cecil's inquiry on changes in, 99, 112; jurisdiction of, 187; name used for, 152

Alvarez, A., 200 n.

American Committee for Outlawry of War, founding of, 69 f.

Angell, Norman, 228, 253

Anson, Pop, 4

Arbitration, Levinson's views on, 211, 257 f., 334

Arbitration Treaty, Great Britain and United States, 257

Artman, J. M., 69

Astor, Lady and Lord, 166, 257, 259

Atkinson, Henry A., 180

Austin, John, 199

Ayles, Walter, 228

Babcock, E. B., 216

Bache, J. S., 21 f.

Baldwin, Stanley, 169, 178, 260

Balfour, Lord, 64

Barclay, Sir Thomas, 263

Barnes, Harry Elmer, 212

Baxter, Percival, 326

Becker, A. G., and Mrs., 69 f.

Becker, Benjamin V., 7, 14 f., 158, 162, 312

Behren, von, 63

Bell, Sir Hugh, 166

Bernstorff, Count von, 283

Berolzheimer, Emil, 54 n.

Bingham, Hiram, 143

Blaine, John J., 328, 333, 337

Bliven, Bruce, 146

Blum, Léon, 292

Bodin, J., 185

Bok, Edward, 114

Bok Peace Award, 114, 127

Bondfield, M. G. (Miss), 166

Borah, William E., 57–59, 77, 81, 103, 113, 146, 173; Bok Peace Award, 114; Briand's statement, views on, 219; cabinet post for, 57; campaign of 1924, 134–37; Cecil, counseled about, 111; Coolidge, 124 f., 129, 132 f., 137, 175, 219, 239, 260; co-operation with other senators, 98, 106; Daugherty, dislike for, 129 f.; disarmament, 59 f., 66; disarmament conference, 61 n., 62; Garvin, opinion of, 171; good faith of nations, 160; "Hamlet," 127; Harding's offset for resolution, 99; Harmony Plan, 146–49; Hoover, 280, 298, 315 f., 339 f.; Johnson, relation with, 122 f.; League, outlawry as substitute for, 53; Moses' reservation to World Court, 161; peace forces reconciliation, 138, 140–42; political ambitions, 164; presidential candidate, 82,120 f., 124–26, 128, 163 f.; research for, 156; Sacco and Vanzetti, offer to defend, 253; sanctions, 85, 89, 91, 93, 158, 160, 197, 204, 332; Teapot Dome, 129–31, 280; third party, 121, 128; vice-presidential candidacy, 132 f.; "vital interest" and other reservations, 303–5, 308, 324; voted against what he talked for, 142, 146; war debts, 154, 261 f.
—Europe: interested in, 227; visit to, 98
—Kellogg: relations with, 286; uses his argument, 274 f.; see Kellogg
—Levinson: criticisms of, 243; compared him to Demosthenes, 161; first meeting with, 81; impatient with, 176; influence on, 299 f.; memorandum on treaties used by, 273; methods of handling, 82–84, 86, 94 f., 105 f., 117, 127 f., 142, 152, 161 f., 176, 178; praised, 312, 338; tribute to, 286 f.
—Morrison: faith in, 117; views on outlawry book, 241–43, 245
—outlawry: approval of, 55; foundation, 339; pamphlet, 71, 73, 75, 81,

[357]

INDEX

short treaty, 248; similar treaty with Britain, 252, 258 f.

Brown, Runham, 228

Bruce, W. C., 332, 334

Bryan, W. J., 134

Bush, Francis X., 70

Butler, N. M.: attacks on, 241, 246; Borah affected by, 246; Briand interview with, 233; Briand proposal, effect on, 246; Capper, relation to, 249; Shotwell's approval of outlawry, 278

—*New York Times* letter: effect on French outlawry proposal, 216, 240; effect on public opinion, 241

Butler, William M., 134 f., 151, 157

Buxton, C. R., 166

Callahan, Patrick H., 180

Capacity to pay, 153 f.; *see* War debts

Capper, Arthur: Borah relation to, 98; Levinson's relations with, 75

—outlawry: material published by, 106; plan mailed out, 73; resolution of, 249

Carnegie Corporation, 108

Casenave, M., 64–66

Castle, W. R., 262

Cecil, Lord Robert, 84; Levinson, contacts with, 101, 111 f.; Pact of Paris, support for, 259, 283; World Court, changes in, 99, 101, 103

—outlawry: comment on in England, 112; explained to, 165 f.; understanding of, 112; use of, in Pact for Mutual Assistance, 112

Chamberlain, Austen: America, solicitude for opinion of, 283; Geneva behavior, 254; Tory, example of, 169, 260; "vital interest" reservation, Kerr's remarks on, 307

—Pact of Paris: British notes on, 294 f.; legal meaning of, 291; "vital interest" reservation to, 212, 295, 298, 302, 304, 308 f., 320, 322

Charities, 9

Chess, 3 f.

Christian Century, outlawry issue, 179 f.

Churches, outlawry, adoption of, 119

Clark, J. Reuben, 105, 109, 151, 153 n.

Clark, S. H., 81

Clarke, John H.: Bok Peace Award, 114; foreword for outlawry pamphlet, 71; Harmony Plan, 144–47; League of Nations, support of, 38 f., 44; peace leader, 138

Claudel, H.: Borah, talk with, 250; Levinson talked with about French outlawry treaty, 221; Levinson's work, acknowledged by, 312; Pact of Paris negotiations, part in, 234, 247, 266, 268–71, 284 f., 288

Codification, 27, 199–202

Cohalan, D., 163

Colcord, Samuel, 338 f.

Collier, Mary, 113 n.

Colombos, John, 211 n.

Come-out-of-the-Court campaign, World Court, 162 f.

Coolidge, Calvin: French outlawry proposal, position on, 220 f.; Harmony Plan, in reference to, 147 n.; jingoistic address, 327; Robins, relations with, 77 f., 127 f., 135; Russian recognition, 125 f., 128; Senate, on treaties in, 259, 279; Shotwell, fails to see, 219; Teapot Dome, 128 f.; third term, 219, 239; war debts, 155, 262; weakness of, 123, 128 f., 132; World Court, attitude on, 125, 127, 152, 157, 181

—Borah: failure to support, 136 f.; feeling toward, 129 f., 132; on opinion of, 260; on ticket with, 132 f.

—Levinson: feeling about Coolidge, 126, 140; idea of functions of president, 130; supports Coolidge, 327, 335

—Pact of Paris, 218–20, 235, 247, 249 f., 259, 271 f., 274, 279, 293, 335; acceptance of, 250; attitude toward, 249; pressure to support, 324–26; resented popular appeal, 220, 227

—outlawry: added strength to, 128–30; attitude on, 124 f., 128, 134 f., 137; partial indorsement of, 134; understanding of, 134

Couzens, James, 97 f.

Cox, James M., 55, 57

Craigie, R. L., 320

Croly, Herbert, 25 f., 30, 50, 146

Cummings, Edward, 46, 79

Curtis, Charles, 335

Cushendun, Lord, 260

Daugherty, Harry, 129 f.; Harding, means of influencing for outlawry, 61, 63, 67 f.; ousting of, 129, 131

Davis, John W., 135, 137, 318

Davis, Norman, 218

Dawes, Charles G., 136, 160, 261

Day, Luther, 104

INDEX

INDEX

Pact of Paris, early reaction to, 235; politics, 1924, 121–26, 128 f., 131, 133–35; politics, 1928, 315–17; Russian recognition, 125, 128, 327; speaker for outlawry, 76–78, 92, 94, 118 f., 135, 147

—Borah: work with, 87 f., 90–93, 95, 120 f., 127–30, 135, 137, 147 f., 163 f., 174, 176–78; work with on Pact of Paris, 236, 241, 243, 245 f., 247, 266, 272 f., 280, 300, 305, 315; work with on war debts, 262 f.

Robinson, Joseph T., 328

Roosevelt, Franklin D., 318

Roosevelt, Franklin D. (Mrs.), 318 f.

Roosevelt, T. R., 42

Root, Elihu, 99, 105, 199, 200 n.

Rosenwald, Julius, 8

Royden, A. Maude, 166, 180, 212

Rubin, Cora, 57, 162, 176

Ruopp, Professor, 104

Russia: Pact of Paris, views on, 283; recognition of, 125 f., 128, 327

Sacco, 252 f.

Sackett, Frederic, 330

Salter, Sir Arthur, 263 f.

Sanctions, 27 f., 142, 185, 189–91, 206 n., 208 n.; Borah's corncern over, 89; enforcement of, 207–9; Pact of Paris, 332; use of, 160; see Borah; Levinson, sanctions

Schiff, Jacob, 13–15, 17–20, 23 f., 30, 96

Schurman, Jacob G., 226, 228

Schurz, Carl, 1

Scott, James B., 85, 89, 105, 108, 209 n.

Seiberling, F. A., 173, 180

Self-defense, 93 f., 307; Borah, 330; Kellogg on, 289 f.; necessity for, 197; outlawry, 195 f.; see Levinson, self-defense

Shannon, F. F., 180

Shipstead, Henrik, 104, 158, 328

Shotwell, James T., 117, 141, 185, 203, 219, 229 n., 231, 234, 236, 238 f., 241 f., 244, 246, 249, 251, 277, 292, 342; Briand, influence over, 215, 278; Geneva Protocol, outlawry in, 113; Kellogg, support of, by, 278; Levinson, disagreement on outlawry, 249; Morrison, conflict with, 277 f.; outlawrists, reconciliation with, 140 f., 144–50; outlawry explained to Briand, 215, 278; outlawry, meaning of, 190 n.;

outlawry and the Pact of Paris, 190 n.; Pact of Paris, contribution to, 232, 278; Pact of Paris, Levinson's part in, 231 f.

Sinclair, Harry, 280

Slemp, C. Bascom, 129–33

Smith, Alfred E., 314–16, 318

Snowden, Phillip, 108

Solberg, Marshal, 312

Spencer, Anna Garlin, 138

Speyer, James, 19

Sports, Levinson in, 4 f.

Sprague, A. A., 131

Stagg, A. A., 6

Stearns, F., 130

Steed, Wickham, 259, 283

Stern, Harry, 69

Sthamer, 216

Stimson, Henry, 6, 194 n., 341 f.; outlawry as nonrecognition, 192

Story, Moorfield, 31 f.

Strachey, J. St. Loe, 166

Straight, Willard (Mrs.), 109

Strauss, Henry X., 69

Strawn, Silas, 132

Stresemann, G., 233, 254, 289, 291

Strong, Walter, 38, 213

Sumner, Charles, 29–35

Swanson, Claude A., 304 f.

Swanwick, Helena (Mrs.), 255

Sweetser, Arthur, 218, 325

Taft, W. H., 49 f., 57 f.

Teapot Dome, 126, 128–31

Techniques of influence; see Levinson, techniques

Templin, Olin, 109

Thomas, Norman, 145 f.

Tinkham, George H., 174

Tittle, Ernest F., 180

Trevelyan, Sir Charles, 166

Tyrrell, Sir William, 291

Tyson, Russell (Mrs.), 69

Upham, Fred, 42

Vanzetti, 252 f.

Villard, Oswald Garrison, 34 f., 106, 114, 155; Hoover, 316 f.; World Court, 158 f., 161

[367]

PRINTED IN U·S·A·